Building Your Own Conscience

(Batteries not included.)

William J. O'Malley, S.J.

This we know: the earth does not belong to us; we
belong to the earth. All things are connected like
the blood that unites us all. We did not weave the
web of life, we are merely strands in it. Whatever we
do to the web, we do to ourselves.

—Chief Seattle (adapted)

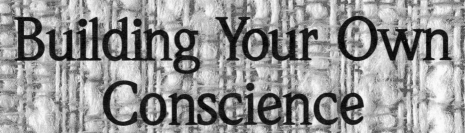
TABOR
PUBLISHING

111 ST. MARY STREET
TORONTO, ONTARIO, CANADA
M4Y 2R5

NIHIL OBSTAT

Rev. Glenn D. Gardner, J.C.D.
Censor Liborum

IMPRIMATUR

† Most Rev. Charles V. Grahmann
Bishop of Dallas

April 13, 1992

The *Nihil Obstat* and *Imprimatur* are official declarations that the work contains nothing contrary to Faith and Morals. It is not implied thereby that those granting the *Nihil Obstat* and *Imprimatur* agree with the contents, statements, or opinions expressed.

ACKNOWLEDGMENTS

Scripture quotations are taken from or adapted from the Good News Bible text, Today's English Version. Copyright © American Bible Society 1966, 1971, 1976.

Excerpts from *The Documents of Vatican II* edited by Walter M. Abbott, S.J. Copyright © 1966 by The America Press.

Excerpt from *Who's Afraid of Virginia Woolf?* by Edward Albee. Copyright © 1962 by Edward Albee. Used by permission of Macmillan Publishing Company, a division of Macmillan, Inc.

Excerpts from *A Man for All Seasons* by Robert Bolt. Copyright © 1960, 1962 by Robert Bolt. Reprinted by permission of Random House, Inc.

"The Road Not Taken" by Robert Frost. Reprinted from *Robert Frost, Complete Poems.* © 1969 by Holt, Rinehart & Winston.

Reprinted by permission of The Putnam Publishing Company from *LORD OF THE FLIES* by William Golding. Copyright © 1954 by William Golding.

Excerpt from *Ordinary People* by Judith Guest. Copyright © 1976 by Judith Guest. Used by permission of Viking Penguin, a division of Penguin Books USA Inc.

I AM WHAT I AM from "La Cage Aux Folles"
Music and Lyric by Jerry Herman
© 1983 by JERRY HERMAN
All Rights Controlled by JERRYCO MUSIC CO.
Exclusive Agent: EDWIN MORRIS & COMPANY, A Division of MPL Communications, Inc.
All Rights Reserved. Used By Permission.

Excerpt from *Making Sense Out of Suffering* by Peter Kreeft. Copyright © 1986 by Peter Kreeft. Published by Servant Publications, Box 8617, Ann Arbor, Michigan, 48107. Used with permission.

Excerpt from "A, B, and C" in *Literary Lapses* by Stephen Leacock. Books for Libraries Press, Freeport, New York, 1970.

Excerpt from *To Kill a Mockingbird* by Harper Lee. Copyright © 1960 by Harper Lee, copyright © renewed 1988 by Harper Lee. Reprinted by permission HarperCollins Publishers Inc.

Excerpt from *The Great Divorce* by C. S. Lewis. Copyright © 1946 by Macmillan Publishing Company, a division of Macmillan, Inc. Used by permission HarperCollins Publishers, London.

Excerpt from *Making Friends with Yourself* by Leo P. Rock, S.J. Copyright © 1990 by Leo P. Rock, S.J. Used by permission of Paulist Press.

Excerpt from *Fiddler on the Roof:* book by Joseph Stein, music and lyrics by Sheldon Harnick. Copyright © 1964 by Joseph Stein.

Excerpt from *Rabbit, Run* by John Updike. Copyright © 1960 by John Updike. Reprinted by permission of Alfred A. Knopf, Inc.

Excerpts from *Sharing the Light of Faith.* Copyright © 1979 by the United States Catholic Conference, Department of Education.

Reprinted by permission of The Putnam Publishing Group from *The Once and Future King* by T. H. White. Copyright © 1939, 1940, & 1958 by T. H. White. © renewed 1986 by Lloyd's Bank, Channel Islands, Ltd.

Excerpt from *Our Town* by Thorton Wilder. Copyright © 1938, 1957 by Thorton Wilder.

Excerpt from "The Skin of Our Teeth" from THREE PLAYS by Thorton Wilder. Copyright © 1957 by Thorton Wilder. Reprinted by permission of HarperCollins Publishers.

Excerpt from *The Velveteen Rabbit* by Margery Williams. Holt, Rinehart & Winston, 1983.

PHOTOGRAPHY

Full Photographics, Inc. 48, 154, 204, 274, 290
Jean Claude Lejeune 10, 23, 36, 58, 74, 86, 102, 114, 126, 140, 170, 188, 222, 238, 252, 309
Dale Sloat/The Stock Market cover

ILLUSTRATIONS

Mike Artell

CALLIGRAPHY

Bob Niles

Send all inquiries to:
Tabor Publishing
One DLM Park
Allen, Texas 75002

Printed in the United States of America

ISBN 0-7829-0112-3 (Student Text)
ISBN 0-7829-0113-1 (Resource Manual)

1 2 3 4 5   96 95 94 93 92

This book is for
Jerry McMahon,
Larry Madden,
Ed Nagle,
and
Bill Poorten,
sine quibus, Cuckoo Land.

CONTENTS

Introduction:

THE MORAL ECOLOGY

All but recent arrivals from Mars are aware—at times painfully—that we share a very fragile biological ecology, a web of interrelationships between ourselves and nature that we can freely violate by discharging untreated sewage, littering, oil spills, slaughtering endangered species, air pollution, and atomic waste. But we can't get away with it forever. No need for God to wreak vengeance on us for our self-indulgent ways. God programmed the vengeance right into the natures of things. We'll wreak the havoc on ourselves.

That real web of relationships between humans and our environment is paralleled in a real web of relationships between humans and humans. It's called objective morality: the moral (human) ecology.

Just as the biological web is invisible yet real, so is the moral web. It is objective fact, not merely subjective opinion. As with the biological ecology, you can prove the moral ecology simply by ignoring it long enough. It will rise up and take its inexorable revenge. Not eternal punishment; right here. Ignore the relationship between the liver and alcohol long enough, and you'll discover we don't tell things and people what they are and how they can be legitimately used; *they* tell *us.* Exploit human beings long enough, and they will rise up and take their revenge. Look at China. Eastern Europe. Africa. Our own streets.

Ignore the human ecology; deny it exists; impose your own ideas on people and legislate the ways to use them. But not for long. The house always wins. Nor are there any victimless immoralities: "It's okay as long as you don't hurt anybody."

Smoking grass, for instance, may not "hurt anybody" that you can see, but many people are in fact getting hurt. The only place you get grass is ultimately from the Mob. Every dollar profit they make off you, they can invest in picking up young girls at the bus station in New York, making them addicts and prostitutes. "Thank you very much for your support." What's more, I've never known illegal drugs to make the user more joyful, more open, or more sharing. Quite the contrary, they become secretive, cranky, and dull. Then the users themselves are human victims of their own self-absorption. And they impoverish those human beings who love them.

The ruthless world-beater who makes his or her way to the top by stomping on all the little people, the weak people, the people who still have consciences, does not need a thunderbolt to wreak stern judgment. The judgment has already been rendered, the punishment inflicted. Ruthless world-beaters are already serving out their sentences: to *be* mean-spirited swine—and everybody knows it but themselves.

If morality means what one must do in order to act humanly, every relationship—no matter how profound or trivial—is a moral relationship, because at least one member of the relationship is human.

We are not talking religion here. Religions may go beyond basic morality—being human—and specify further what their particular vision of God wants humans to do in order to fulfill their purposes in life. Muslims are far stricter on stealing and drinking and the role of women than Christians, for instance, but are far more lenient on the question of marriage. Even within particular world religions, the adherents almost always range from the fanatically puritan, through the more liberal, to the scarcely committed. Yet all of them—no matter what the religion or the shading of their beliefs—are human beings. Even irreligious people and atheists are human. And we all share the same fragile human ecology—and responsibility for it.

We may not like it. We may not acknowledge it. We may act contrary to it. But it's the truth. And the house always wins.

Self-possession is another of those happily-on-the-target expressions that has volumes to tell us if we pay close enough attention to it. Each of us begins life with a clear, God-given title to the self that is to emerge from within us. It belongs to us; we are given exclusive ownership rights and responsibilities. But long before the self has even had the chance to stand on its own two wobbly feet, all kinds of liens against the property, shares in the property bought and paid for, rights-of-way through the property have been established by others. The question of who owns what and who is responsible for what becomes the subject of most of the disputes that strew our path toward independence and the beginning of adulthood— and beyond. Perhaps as good a way as any of describing human growth toward wholeness is this: it is the process of clearing title to one's self. An adult, then, is one who exercises exclusive ownership rights and responsibilities for oneself. The self may be freely shared, but there is no question of either ownership or responsibility: adults own and take responsibility for themselves. In a word, an adult is self-possessed. For most of us the process of clearing the title takes a lifetime.

Making Friends with Yourself, by Leo P. Rock, S.J.

Morality in General

1. WHOSE TRUTH?

SURVEY

This survey is not an exercise for a grade, but a means to stir up interest, get an idea of varying opinions in your group, and focus on the topic. Circle the number on the rating scale under each statement that best reflects your opinion about that statement. On the scale

   +2 = strongly agree,
   +1 = agree,
     0 = can't make up my mind,
   −1 = disagree,
   −2 = strongly disagree.

Then share the reasons for your opinion.

1. Morality changes from culture to culture and from age to age.

   +2 +1 0 −1 −2

2. My opinion is as good as anybody else's.

   +2 +1 0 −1 −2

3. What I feel about another person is more important than what he or she is.

   +2 +1 0 −1 −2

4. True-for-me is not necessarily true.

   +2 +1 0 −1 −2

5. Laws and commandments make an act moral or immoral.

   +2 +1 0 −1 −2

6. Morality is usually decided by the majority of society.

   +2 +1 0 −1 −2

7. If there is no *objective* right or wrong—that is, independently of conflicting ideas of right and wrong—then there is no such thing as right or wrong.

   +2 +1 0 −1 −2

8. The question of the humanity of black people was settled by the Civil War.

   +2 +1 0 −1 −2

9. We merely had a difference of opinion with the Nazis over whether Jews are human.

   +2 +1 0 −1 −2

10. The humanity of Jews and blacks is debatable.

   +2 +1 0 −1 −2

A FABLE

TRACKING THE TRUTH

Once upon a time there was this duck named Bernie. But he didn't know his name or even that he was a duck for that matter, owing to the fact that heartless hunters had shot Bernie's old Mum and carried her off about two minutes after she'd laid his egg. What's more, Bernie's mental capacity was somewhat impaired from having to crack his shell all by himself, resulting in a mild concussion. This was only the first of many such cracks on the cranium because Bernie had no old Mum to show him how to get around and he kept bumping into things.

Now Bernie was anxious to get on with the business of living; but he had no idea at all what he was for nor what was safe to eat, and his belly was starting to rumble like a tiny cement mixer.

Just then a perky little bird settled on the bank of the pond and began to poke a spiky thing at the front of its face into the mud.

"Ahem," said Bernie.

The bird cocked a skeptical eye at him. "Yes?"

"Excuse me, but could you tell me who you are and what you're doing?"

"I'm a starling, you silly. I'm digging worms for lunch."

"Uh . . . and . . . uh . . . who am I, and what am I for?"

The starling squinted at him up and down. "Hmm. You look like an ostrich to me. Got long necks and big broad beams and funny flatfeet like yours. They're up over that hill. In the sand. Can't miss 'em."

"Oh. Of course," Bernie blushed. "I knew that."

So he waddled his way across the mud, up the weedy bank, and over the hill to a long stretch of empty sand. All over the place were what looked like headless, three-legged creatures covered with grey plumes. It wasn't till he was very close that he realized they were only two-legged things with their heads in the sand. Most likely they, like the starling, were poking their noses into the ground for food.

So Bernie took a deep breath and shoved his bill and his head into the sand. It was pretty dark in there, not to mention stuffy. He waited a long time for some food to show up, but pretty soon he panicked and pulled his snout out of the sand, coughing and gasping. "Whew!" he wheezed. "So much for that."

Bernie waddled over and pecked at the skinny leg of the nearest ostrich. No response. So he began to peck pretty insistently, until the ostrich pulled her head out of the sand just a bit and scowled at him with her big liquid eyes. "Go away," she muttered, her voice muffled by the sand. "We don't like intruders."

5

"I'll go away," Bernie quacked, "if you tell me who I am and what I'm for."

The ostrich, like an uncoiling snake, elongated her enormous neck, then brought her bald head down and peered directly at him with those enormous egg-shaped eyes. Her breath was pretty ripe.

"Hmm," she gargled along the length of her great throat. "Fluffy. Like an owl. In the woods. Drop out of trees. Eat field mice and rabbits and. . . ." She plunged her head back into the sand.

"Oh. Of course," Bernie shrugged. "I knew that."

So he waddled wearily across the scorching sand into the cool woods and looked up at the tall trees stretching up practically into forever. He wrapped his tiny wings around the rough bark of a relatively small tree and tried to climb, but his rubbery footpads just slipped away every time. He sat down and pondered, "I can't jump up there; so how. . . ?" But just then a furry little creature poked his head out of the weeds; and Bernie, whose reasoning was somewhat improving with exercise, stood up, rightly deduced this must be a field mouse, and set off in hot pursuit.

Not for long. That little rascal was greased lightning and out of sight in an instant. So Bernie flopped down, panting, beginning to despair in the fading light of his first-ever day.

"Whooo?" a chesty voice said somewhere overhead.

"Exactly my question," Bernie quacked and backed up, peering up into the gathering darkness. On a branch above him perched a squat bundle of feathers with flaring yellow eyes. "Excuse me, sir, but could you tell me who I am and what I'm for? I feel terribly lost. They told me I'm an owl. But that can't be true."

"I," rumbled the feather bundle, "am an owl, you presumptuous little twit. Just look at that ridiculous flat thing below your eyes. Look at those lily-pad feet. You are a duck. More precisely, a drake. A male duck. Any simpleton could see that. You're meant to pad around the pond, dive for fish, find a mate, and raise a family. Now good day. Better clear off. My sight's improving. You are beginning to look appetizing."

So in the last light of day, Bernie waddled hopefully back to the pond and stepped into the water. It was heavenly cool on his hot, weary webbed feet, and as he pushed out he found that the water held him up. Round and round he paddled, exulting. What was holding him up? So he poked his head down into the water, as the starling and the ostrich had done in the ground, and right before his eyes was a school of minnows. Quick as a wink, he sucked in a few. Delicious, and his little tummy stopped its yowling.

Bernie Drake was home.

▷ Questions

How do we find out what things really are and what they're for? Most often, other people tell us. But how do *they* find out? Again, probably from other people—parents and teachers and such. But if you were an alien from Alpha Centauri who did not know English, how would you find out what things really are and what they're for? Hint: How did people discover the world wasn't flat, tomatoes weren't poisonous, and bread mold could cure infections?

A READING

"What is REAL?" asked the Rabbit one day, when they were lying side by side near the nursery fender, before Nana came to tidy the room. "Does it mean having things that buzz inside you and a stick-out handle?"

"Real isn't how you are made," said the Skin Horse. "It's a thing that happens to you. When a child loves you for a long, long time, not just to play with, but REALLY loves you, then you become Real."

"Does it hurt?" asked the Rabbit.

"Sometimes," said the Skin Horse, for he was always truthful. "When you become Real you don't mind being hurt."

"Does it happen all at once, like being wound up," he asked, "or bit by bit?"

"It doesn't happen all at once," said the Skin Horse. "You become. It takes a long time. That's why it doesn't often happen to people who break easily, or have sharp edges, or who have to be carefully kept. Generally, by the time you are Real, most of your hair has been loved off, and your eyes drop out and you get loose in the joints and very shabby. But these things don't matter at all, because once you are Real you can't be ugly, except to people who don't understand."

From *The Velveteen Rabbit,* by Margery Williams

▷ *Questions*

Is what the Skin Horse says really true? Do we become real only when other people love us? If we aren't real or valuable *before* other people value us, how could they even *find* us—much less find us valuable? Does who we are come from outside of us? And does the author really mean "real," or is it possible she might have meant something else and used the wrong word?

THEME

EPISTEMOLOGY

The first step toward wisdom is to call a thing by its right name.

One day I was walking along a school corridor and saw a boy sitting on a bench reading *Of Mice and Men.* I stopped and said, "That's a terrific book."

"It's garbage."

Hmm. "Well, the author *did* win a Nobel prize."

"It's still garbage."

"How much have you read?"

"Ten pages."

That lad was saying more about himself than about the book or John Steinbeck or the Nobel Foundation. He was saying, in effect, "I'm an arrogant boob." He was claiming that his un-informed opinion was as good as anybody else's. Sorry. It's not. An opinion is only as good as the evidence that backs it up. And ten pages isn't much evidence at all. That boy was badly in need of a course in epistemology.

Surely you've been in an English class where someone said to the teacher, "Do you want what we really think, or do you want *your* interpretation?" The wise teacher answers that any interpretation is acceptable as long as the evidence in the poem or story backs up the opinion.

Very often, inexperienced readers believe an interpretation is no more than "what it makes me think about," or they take a couple of words and spin out their own poem. That's reading *into, not reading out of.* A poem or story is not a Rorschach test, a set of ink blots to unearth a patient's inner feelings. Authors write with a purpose, to say what *they* believe.

You're free to write your own poems, but you're not free to rewrite someone else's.

That's like covering a Rembrandt with your own imaginative graffiti. The poem itself tells you what you can legitimately say about it. If the evidence isn't there, your opinion is swamp gas; and you too are a prime candidate for a course in epistemology.

Epistemology comes from two Greek words. The first word, *episteme,* means "knowledge" and comes out of a further Greek root, *pistis,* meaning "trust." The second word, *logia,* means "study of," as in *biology,* which studies *bios,* "life." Epistemology investigates the origin, nature, methods, and limits of human knowledge.

How do we know that what we say about things, like what Bernie is, *is* the truth—and not just a figment of our imagination? How are we sure our opinions are solidly true and don't make us sound laughable, like the boy's opinion about *Of Mice and Men?* How can we trust that our ship won't fall off the edge of the earth or tomatoes won't kill us or bread mold can cure infections?

The answer is simple to describe but very, very hard to do: We take sightings; we experiment; we probe with our minds. And where do we find the evidence? Not inside our minds—at least not to begin with. We find the evidence *outside* our minds in the objective natures of things.

There is a crucial difference between "objective truth" and "subjective truth." Objective truth—primary truth—is outside the mind; it remains true whether *you* agree with it, or like it, or are even aware that it is the truth: Fire burns, dropped objects fall, too much tension gives you a headache. If there are intelligent beings on other planets, they're there even if we've never experienced them. If a tree falls in the forest and there's no one around to hear it, there's still a noise.

Subjective truth—secondary truth—is inside the mind; it has value *only* if it conforms as closely as possible to what is, in fact, outside the mind. Objective truth validates your opinion's claim

to be true. If you say, "There's a unicorn in the garden, and it just ate a lily," I want a bit more evidence than what you *suppose* you saw. For all I know, it could have been a horse with an arrow in its forehead.

There is a crucial difference, then, between objective *fact* and my subjective awareness of the fact—my opinions. A lot of folks were of the opinion the earth was flat, but their subjective opinion didn't change the objective shape of the earth. That boy's opinion did not make *Of Mice and Men* "garbage." Had he been humbler, he would have said only what he really knew: "I haven't read enough of it to have a decent opinion, but what I've read so far doesn't appeal to me."

That may seem awfully finicky at first. But it's not. People can be hurt by others slapping the wrong subjective label on them with little or no evidence: "nerd," "moron," "cow." People can even get killed because of wrong labels, as when the Nazis labeled Jews and Slavs *Untermenschen,* "less than human." The first step toward wisdom is to call a thing by its right name. Then you'll handle it as it deserves.

"You *know* what I *mean!*" No, I only know what you *say,* and if what you say isn't what you mean, don't blame me for getting you wrong. It's your job to figure out and give evidence for your opinion, not mine.

The North and South did not merely have a difference of opinion over the less-than-human status of black people. The abolitionists were right, and the slavers were wrong. How do I know that? Because the humanity of black people is *not* debatable. It's a matter of objective *fact.* Perhaps it was an honor for Inca girls to be chosen Virgin of the Year and flung from the crags to placate the gods, but—no matter what the Incas thought—that action was immoral. Why? Because killing a human being for any purpose is premeditated homicide—not in my opinion, but objectively; it's a fact.

DILEMMA

Mrs. Esposito sat on the pink curve of plastic under the picture of some colorless flowers, her hooded brown eyes rimmed with tears, staring straight ahead. The sodden paper tissue moved from one cracked set of fingers to the other, as if by itself. From somewhere in the ceiling a soft voice purred, "Dr. Enderby, room 112, please. Dr. Enderby?" Mrs. Esposito was unaware of the voice.

"Why?" she whispered.

The haggard surgical resident sitting awkwardly next to her pushed his eyeglasses back up his nose, cleared his throat again, and sighed, "As I told you, Mrs. Esposito, as far as we can tell, the fall seems to have twisted the boy's spine. But that wasn't what caused his . . . his demise. It was a blood clot that formed and . . . and perhaps while he was being brought from the playground to the hospital, the clot traveled to the brain, and. . . ."

The voice of the doctor was as meaningless as the cool distant voice on the public address system.

"He was only twelve years old." The woman's voice was as dry as paper. "Why?"

As the young doctor tried still a third time to tell Mrs. Esposito the perfectly obvious factors that caused her son to suffer a massive stroke, at 4:18 P.M., two days after his twelfth birthday, traveling along 36th Street to All Saints Hospital, the lady whispered once again, "But why?"

▷ Questions

The young doctor has a dilemma. He can't seem to give Mrs. Esposito a satisfactory answer and yet he has been as coldly objective as he is able, clearly seeing and stating the best medical response anyone could have expected and giving all the causes of her little boy's death. Why does Mrs. Esposito persist in asking her question?

FAITH REFLECTION

My brothers and sisters, fill your minds with those things that are good and that deserve praise: things that are true, noble, right, pure, lovely and honorable. Put into practice what you learned and received from me, both from my words and from my actions. And the God who gives us peace will be with you.

Philippians 4:8-9 (adapted)

Saint Paul gives us incredible leeway in what we find of interest to our minds. Does the Gospel place any limit on what we can search for? Is it possible that anything that is objectively, genuinely true could in any way threaten genuine religion? The church has many times gone back to reassess what it firmly believed was true: circumcision, the Jewish dietary laws, the almost immediate Second Coming of Christ, Galileo, slavery. This doesn't mean the Gospel was wrong, but only that our subjective understanding of the Gospel was wrong.

Vatican Council II taught something similar about the purpose of the human mind:

Truth is to be sought in a manner proper to the dignity of the human person and our social nature. The inquiry is to be free, carried on with the aid of teaching . . . and dialogue. In the course of these, we explain to one another the truth we have discovered, or think we have discovered, in order thus to assist one another in the quest for truth.

Declaration on Religious Freedom, 3

We need one another to find the truth, to check out our opinions and see that we haven't made any mistakes or left out something essential. That's why truth is easier to find in community than alone.

The church serves as a corrective, but we also have the obligation at least to speak up when we think the church is making a mistake. Only in that way can we help the church to grow; only in that way can the church lovingly show us where we ourselves may be wrong.

When you feel—rightly or wrongly—that the church is not doing something the way Jesus would do it, do you speak up—tactfully—or do you just sit, silent and resentful?

📖 FURTHER BIBLE READINGS

Skim these Scripture passages. Pick one that appeals to you and (1) summarize its main point, (2) tell how it relates to the chapter, and (3) list one or two thoughts that entered your mind when you read it:

◆ The Wealth of Wisdom   Proverbs 8:1-10
◆ Nature and God's Will   Job 38:1-7
◆ Solomon   I Kings 3:6-14
◆ Balaam   Numbers 22:22-35
◆ God's Will Everywhere   Acts 17:22-28

_____

_____

_____

_____

_____

_____

✏ JOURNAL

Most likely you've been in an argument with your parents—or with somebody—when suddenly it all became clear: They're right!

But you keep on arguing. When that happens, you're not honestly looking for the truth. What are you looking for? Why?

Understanding Epistemology

REVIEW

1. Why were the starling's and the ostrich's opinions about Bernie objectively wrong?

2. Why is gold objectively more valuable than dirt?

3. We routinely raise animals for food, but we find it repellent to raise humans for food. Why? What is the objective difference between a human and an animal?

4. Most civilized people find it at least "unfitting" to pour gas over a dog and set it on fire. Why? What is the objective difference between a dog and, say, coal or wood?

5. Teachers get pretty upset at cafeteria food wars. Why? It's not just the mess and the disturbance. What is the objective difference between throwing apples and oranges and throwing snowballs?

6. The chapter says that the "less than human" status of Jews, blacks, or slaves is not debatable; their humanity is an objective fact. How can we prove that?

7. In wars, soldiers consistently call the enemy insulting names: "palefaces and redskins," "damn yankees and dirty reb," "gooks and roundeyes." Why? In effect, what does calling others degrading names attempt to do to fellow human beings?

8. In school corridors, we hear "nerd," "wimp," "jerk." Why is that objectively wrong?

9. What is the objective value of a completely uninformed opinion? What is the only thing that establishes the truth or falsehood of any statement?

DISCUSS

1. You are faced with this difficult dilemma: On pain of death, you must choose one of three items that will be thrown into a fire: a little girl, a $50 bill, or the little girl's stuffed rabbit. Which do you choose? There are three very real but very different meanings to the word *value* in this case. What are they?

   The above dilemma is not just a silly example. For five years in the early 1940s men and women were faced with just such a dilemma: Process children in incinerators like so much garbage or go to the Russian front. What gives us the right to call people "less than human"?

2. Neurologists tell us that the two lobes of the human brain have two quite different but equally valuable purposes. The left brain analyzes; it takes objects apart to understand their inner workings; it is logical and painstaking; it underlies the scientific method. The right brain intuits; it has hunches that are not strictly logical but are still rational.

   A lie detector is a pretty reliable left-brain test of a person's truthfulness, but the person's mother's right brain would be a pretty reliable test too! Which lobe of the brain would have to be used in making each of the following difficult choices:

   a. Choosing which stock is the best prospect
   b. Choosing a college to go to
   c. Choosing which college is best for you
   d. Choosing the best career for you to pursue

   If you answered *just* the left brain or *just* the right brain, you're acting half-wittedly. Why? Can you make any of those choices with evidence so clear and distinct that you have no reason whatever to doubt your choice?

3. Contemporary schools are very heavily overbalanced in favor of educating the left brain: mathematics, science, declensions; even poems are not used primarily to "move the heart" (the right brain) but as items for left-brain analysis. What is the value of courses in art and music? They are not exactly marketable skills except for the enormously talented. Then again, what is the value of taking physical education?

4. When asked what is the first question he would put to a candidate for medical school, the physician in charge of admissions at a prestigious medical school answered immediately, "What was the last novel you read?" Why?

ACTIVITIES

1. Bring to class some object whose purpose you are betting no one else in the class can guess. Whoever in the class stumps everybody else, including the teacher, wins a prize.

2. What do you say to a friend who comes and says:

   Look, I've got to talk to somebody, and you're . . . at least I always thought you were . . . my best friend. I think I'm gonna give it all up. A friend of mine's got some pills. Why not! No lousy college will look twice at me. Combined 950 SATs? And my parents want me to be a lawyer, like them. Right. They are out so much, or away so much, I don't think I could even pick them out of a lineup. And when they're home it's nag, nag, nag. I tried to work. Honest t'God I did. But I'm so far behind. There's always this whine in my head that goes, "Just wait till tomorrow, baby! It gets worse!" And it does! So who needs it? Why keep playin' a game that's already lost?

2. WHAT BEING HUMAN MEANS

SURVEY

Circle the number on the rating scale under each statement that best reflects your opinion about that statement. On the scale

 +2 = strongly agree,
 +1 = agree,
  0 = can't make up my mind,
 −1 = disagree,
 −2 = strongly disagree.

Then share the reasons for your opinion.

1. Humans are no more than higher-level animals.

   +2 +1 0 −1 −2

2. Thinking can be reduced to the interaction of chemicals and electricity.

   +2 +1 0 −1 −2

3. Loving can be reduced to the interaction of chemicals and electricity.

   +2 +1 0 −1 −2

4. All nonhuman species—animal, vegetable, and mineral—are programmed to perform only within strict limits.

   +2 +1 0 −1 −2

5. No lion can refuse to act leonine, but human beings can refuse to act human.

   +2 +1 0 −1 −2

6. Objective morality changes from age to age and from culture to culture.

   +2 +1 0 −1 −2

7. As far as we can tell, tigers and sharks do not suffer pangs of conscience.

   +2 +1 0 −1 −2

8. The theory of evolution shows conclusively that the species eased gradually and uninterruptedly upward from one to another.

   +2 +1 0 −1 −2

9. No effect can be greater than the sum of its causes.

   +2 +1 0 −1 −2

10. All the questions above are strictly a matter of subjective opinion.

   +2 +1 0 −1 −2

A FABLE

Ruby Petunia Fawn

Once upon a time there was this girl named Ruby Petunia Fawn, but her mother just called her Petunia because she was so cute and perky. Even after her mother died, when Petunia was about ten, she remained a very sweet-tempered young thing. This took some doing since her father (with unseemly haste) brought home a new wife named Cloaca who (of course) brought along her two warty and waspishly demanding young daughters who never called their new stepsister either Ruby or Petunia or Fawn, but usually just "Girl!" From that day, poor Petunia hardly had a moment's rest from dawn to well past sunset, hauling trash, scrubbing johns, and laundering her stepsisters' clothing.

One evening as Petunia sat weeping silently in the hayloft where she slept, too tired even to wash her face in the bucket of water, there was a sudden WHOOSH! of light. Before her stood a little old man with a starry dunce cap on a froth of white hair and a pair of round spectacles perched precariously on a long nose, which had developed a bit of a drip at the tip.

14

"Oh, mercy me!" the old man said, swirling his black and silver cloak as he looked around. "What happened? I got a call from Cleveland. You aren't Cleveland, are you?"

Petunia scrubbed her eyes with her fists and sniffed. "No, sir. I'm Ruby Petunia Fawn. May I help you, sir?"

The little man peered the length of his nose through his spectacles. "Ruby . . . Petunia . . . Fawn. But you seem to be a girl. Why, yes you are indeedy. But why are you crying, my dear?"

"Oh, it's nothing," she said, trying to smile. "Just wishing I were somewhere else. Someone else."

"Hmm," the old man said and cocked a tufty brow. "Your wish seems to have yanked me off course. Well, now. Can't resist a wish. Magicians' Oath, you know. So . . . what'll it be?"

"Pardon?"

"I'll change you into someone else, somewhere else. But we must hurry. Have to be in Cleveland. Something about a boy and a puppy, if I remember correctly. So?"

"I'd . . . I'd like to be a person, sir."

The magician opened his mouth in surprise and was about to speak; but clamped it shut, and gazed at the girl fondly as if there were more important things than stating the obvious.

"All right, then. Stand back a bit. Don't want to get caught up in this m'self. That's it." And he raised his arms high, drowning in his great silver and black cloak. "Anthraconite! Peridot! Sardonyx!"

There was a whirl of smoke where Petunia had been; and when it cleared, there was nothing on the straw but a ruby as big as your fist. The old magician stroked his chin, tapped his foot, pulled out his huge pocket watch, and tapped his foot some more.

"Hmm. That oughta do it," he whispered, and he snapped his fingers once, and in a puff, there was Petunia again, her eyes gaping as round and bright as bike reflectors.

"Tch-tch," the old man said. "Sorry about that, child. Wrong spell. Lost my concentration a bit, I suspect. But, uh, just out of curiosity, what was it like in there?"

"Beau-*tiful*," Petunia sighed, her pupils not quite dilated back to normal. "There were all kinds of fiery little pellets exploding into big waves of light, and then folding back into pellets again. And humming, like . . . like a dance of stars!"

The old man nodded. "Electrons, I suspect. Muons. Gluons. Quarks. That sort of thing. Were you frightened?"

"No," Petunia said. "Well, not exactly. It was really very beautiful and exciting but . . . but I wouldn't want to live there."

"Course not," he said. "Because you don't belong there. All right. Let's get serious about this." And his brow knitted with heroic intensity. "Groundsel! Portulaca! Periwinkle!"

Another whoosh of smoke, and when it melted into the air, there was a curly pink petunia poking out of the hay. The magician eyed his watch again, took several deep breaths, and snapped his fingers. Whoosh! There was Petunia again, swaying and smiling like someone just off a rollercoaster.

"Drat! Time-warp lag. Wrong spell again." The magician scowled, but he cocked an inquiring eye at the girl under the white tufts. "But, uh, tell me. What was it like in there?"

"Lovely," Petunia sighed. "It was so sweet-smelling. And so . . . so *alive*! So different from being a stone. Even a jewel. I could feel juices flowing through me and out into my arms; and I caught the light in my face, and it seemed to . . . to *purify* everything inside. Make it shimmer. But. . . ."

"Yes?"

"But it was so lonely. Like inside the ruby."

"Quite right. Because you don't belong in there. Hmm. Gotta get it right sooner or later." The old man's face twisted tighter than a fist, his arms flew out, and he shouted, "Markhor! Margay! Mazama!"

Ffft! And on the straw where Petunia had been was a fawn, looking around with big onyx eyes, yawning, and twitching its nose. It poked around in the straw, sniffing, and then began to caper around in glee. The magician eyed it with a sly grin, and the fawn looked up at him and seemed to grin back. The old man looked at his watch awhile, then snapped his fingers; and there was Petunia back again, somewhat dazed.

"Whoops!" he said, blushing slightly. "I really have to get this thing right. There's that puppy thing in Cleveland. But, uh, what was it like in there?"

"Ah," Petunia sighed, "it was so nice to move around, explore, smell the summer still in the straw. And to kick up my legs and prance. But. . . ."

"Lonely, eh?"

"Yes, and . . . well, I could see you. But. . . ."

"You couldn't talk to me, is that it?"

"Yes," she beamed. "That's it!"

"And that's why you're so sad here, child. You don't belong here either because you've got nobody to communicate with. And you are a person. But those dreadful people treat you no better than a stepping stone or a cabbage or beast of burden. A slave!" He shook his head in disgust. "Well, we'll take care of that. Here," he said and drew a big bathtowel from the depths of his robe.

"Let's forget magic. Even if I could get it right," he winked. "Now, wash your face in that bucket there." Petunia obediently washed her face and dried it, then turned to the old wise man.

"My, my," he grinned. "You are quite a pretty young miss, aren't you? Now here," he said and pulled out a business card. "You go see this gentleman in the capital. His name's Dowser. He's a lodge brother of mine and most trustworthy. And *well* connected. Comb your hair, put on your best dress, and go see that gentleman. You hear?"

"Yes, sir," Petunia said, bewildered.

"My, my!" the old man huffed. "Cleveland!" And off he went in a puff of smoke.

So Petunia combed her hair and put on her best dress, which was patched but clean, and she hit the road to the capital where Sir Dowser introduced her round, changed her name to Belle, and made her the top fashion model in the history of the kingdom. She was invited to balls where she stole the heart of the new young king, married him, and was crowned Queen Ruby Petunia Fawn Belle. And she completely forgot to invite Cloaca and her daughters to the wedding or the coronation.

They were livid.

▷ Questions

Jot down the things that Petunia and the ruby have in common. Then jot down the things that girl-Petunia and flower-petunia have in common, but the ruby does *not* have. Then respond to the following:

◆ What do Petunia and the fawn have in common but the ruby and flower don't?

◆ What qualities and abilities does Petunia have that *none* of the other things in the story have, not even the fawn?

A READING

In this selection from The Once and Future King *by T. H. White, Merlin has transformed young Wart (who will one day become King Arthur) into a fish, a hawk, an ant, and a goose so young Wart can discover, from observing other societies, the kinds of things a good king would do and not do to and for his subjects. In this final transformation, Merlin has made Wart (Arthur) into a badger who is sitting in a wise old badger's den, listening to him.*

"When God had manufactured all the eggs out of which the fishes and the serpents and the birds and the mammals and even the duck-billed platypus would eventually emerge, he called the embryos before Him, and saw that they were good.

"Perhaps I ought to explain," added the badger, lowering his papers nervously and looking at the Wart over the top of them, "*that all embryos look very much the same. . . .* whether you are going to be a tadpole or a peacock or a cameleopard or a man, . . .

"The embryos stood in front of God, with their feeble hands clasped politely over their stomachs and their heavy heads hanging down respectfully, and God addressed them.

"He said: 'Now, you embryos, here you are, all looking exactly the same, and We are going to give you the choice of what you want to be. . . . You may alter any parts of yourselves into anything which you think would be useful to you in later life. For instance, at the moment you cannot dig. Anybody who would like to turn his hands into a pair of spades or garden forks is allowed to do so. Or, to put it another way, at present you can only use your mouths for eating. Anybody who would like to use his mouth as an offensive weapon, can change it by asking, and be a corkindrill or a sabre-toothed tiger. Now then, step up and choose your tools, but remember that what you choose you will grow into, and will have to stick to.'

"All the embryos thought the matter over politely, and then, one by one, they stepped up before the eternal throne. They were allowed two or three specializations, so that some chose to use their arms as flying machines and their mouths as weapons, or crackers, or drillers, or spoons while others selected to use their bodies as boats and their hands as oars. . . .

"Just before it was time to knock off for Sunday, they had got through all the little embryos except one. This embryo was Man.

" 'Well, Our little man,' said God. 'You have waited till the last, . . . What can We do for you?'

" 'Please, God,' said the embryo, 'I think that You made me in the shape which I now have for reasons best known to Yourselves, and that it would be rude to change. . . . I will stay a defenceless embryo all my life, doing my best to make myself a few feeble implements out of the wood, iron and the other materials which You have seen fit to put before me. . . .'

" 'Well done,' exclaimed the Creator in delighted tones. . . . all the others will be embryos before your might. Eternally undeveloped, you will always remain potential in Our image, able to see some of Our sorrows and to feel some of Our joys. We are partly sorry for you, Man, but partly hopeful. Run along then, and do your best.'. . ."

▷ *Questions*

When the badger says *"that all embryos look very much the same,"* he talks in italics. Why? What point is he trying to make?

"You will always remain potential." Humankind is the only species not limited by its programming. What are the advantages of that situation? The disadvantages?

THEME
WHAT ARE HUMANS FOR?

One of the ways you can answer those questions is by asking what are human beings *not* for? Eliminate the wrong answers before you try to narrow down the possibilities to the "least wrong." All the cultures I've ever read about would find something *objectively* unfitting about raising human babies for food—something humanly repulsive. Enemy warriors, maybe, but not babies. Also I'm sure there is something *objectively* repellent in torturing a dog, as if it had no more feelings than a cabbage. Some people can go out on a Saturday, shoot Bambi—not even eat it—or torture a bull with knives in its spine to the cheers of the crowd. But something *humane* in us at least wonders if the pleasure of that show of skill balances the torment one can only guess a deer or a bull can feel and a vegetable cannot. Also, at least for those with the courage to think, there is something *objectively* unfitting about lobbing food that could feed a family around a cafeteria, as if food had no more inherent value than snowballs.

That may change from age to age, depending on the sensitivities of the audiences (subjective knowledge). But one has to believe that, even five thousand years ago, children were more valuable (not just more *valued*) than pigs; family dogs meant more than the family flower garden; the family meal meant more than stones.

Broadly speaking, earthly entities form four quite different groups: mineral, vegetable, animal, and human. We know that rocks can't take in food and grow or reproduce little pebbles. Not opinion; fact. We know cabbages don't scream when you plunge a knife into them, as cats do; cabbages don't feel. Not opinion; fact. We know that animals know, but we have no evidence they fear the not-yet-existent, like death. Animals can communicate over vast distances, sense changes in weather that no human can sense, and even sacrifice their lives for their own babies. But humans can sacrifice their lives even for the babies of enemies. Figure that one.

Simplified studies of evolution, like the ones you've been able to understand so far, make our knowledge of the evolutionary process seem far more certain than it really is. We've all seen pictures that show the slow, almost inevitable changes from an apelike creature walking on its knuckles to a fine specimen striding along with intelligent anticipation on his or her face. But we don't know that much about the big spaces in between. When we find a specimen that scholars believe to be humanoid, most often we have a bit of femur, a bit of jawbone, maybe a pelvis, and something that seems to be a tool that required an understanding of cause and effect. Experts take those pieces and—from what we know about muscles and bones—construct an *educated guess* of what that being might have looked like.

Similarly, no human has ever seen a live dinosaur. Dinosaurs were all long dead before "we" arrived. All we have is a bunch of bones and again—from what we know about musculature and bones—we have reconstructed educated guesses of what dinosaurs might have looked like. For instance, until quite recently, we thought dinosaurs dragged their tails behind them; now scientists believe they carried them in the air, as tightrope walkers hold out their arms, to balance themselves.

Vision...
It reaches beyond
the thing that is,
into the conception
of what can be.
Robert Collier

We have only a rudimentary idea of how things *got* the way they are, but it is evident to anyone with eyes to see that the four species are quite, quite different.

Rocks are inert. They have mass, weight, electrical charge, a carbon-datable age. But petunias are a *quantum* leap upward from rocks—even rubies. Unlike rocks, plants can take in food, grow, and reproduce. Fawns have all the qualities of the rock and petunia: mass, weight, electrical charge, ability to take in food, grow, and reproduce. But they can also *feel,* roam, run from danger, seek. That's one *big* leap! Humans not only have all the qualities and potential of the rock, the petunia, and the fawn, but far, far more—incredibly more, if we were not so used to it.

Animals know, but humans have at least the potential to *understand,* to see connections. The puppy whacked for wetting the rug doesn't feel (as far as we can see) real guilt; it can feel hurt, angry, and bewildered. But only humans have at least the *capacity* to put two and two together and understand that the carpet has a greater value than a piece of newspaper spread in the cellar.

Animals also can "love"; at least they can bring themselves to sacrifice for their young. But humans are the only species we know that can say, "I'd rather have you happy, even if it means that I'll be unhappy." That ability, in a sense, is what separates humans from animals—or from humans who have never evolved from more than "animals with human potential."

Animals can also grow. But they cannot grow "more animal"—more leonine or more fawn-like. Animals are prisoners of their DNA and environment. Humans are not. And that is one *super*-leap upward. Nature did not endow us with wings, but we have the wits to make wings out of cloth or wood or metal. If there is a new ice age, we do not have to crawl as far away as we can and die, like animals; we can make fire and survive. We are one *totally* different level of being and value.

Oh, we are animals, all right; and we have all their urges. But the human animal can *suppress* those urges for *reasons* no animal—or insufficiently evolved human—can comprehend. Put a raw steak in front of a hungry tiger; the tiger has no choice. Put a good meal in front of a human in exchange for betraying his or her friend, and he or she can refuse. No animal in heat can suppress the urge to couple; humans can. That separates human sexuality from animal sexuality. People governed *only* by their sexual needs, like animals, are still only potentially human.

What specifies our species—what makes it different from any other species we as yet know—is that we can understand as opposed to merely know; we can love unselfishly as opposed to merely feel affection; and we can grow *more human* as opposed to being slaves of our natural programming.

I AM THE MASTER OF MY FATE; I AM THE CAPTIAN OF MY SOUL.
WILLIAM ERNEST HENLEY

We are born human, but not fully human, only *potentially* human. There is the same difference between a human baby and an animal cub as there is between an acorn and a marble.

Baby : cub = acorn : marble

Plant an acorn and a marble. The marble's just going to lie there. But the acorn has at least the *potential* to become an oak. It may be buried in dead soil or among thorns or on rocks, or it may land in ground so sodden it will rot. The same is true of a child. A child may land in a ghetto, twenty to a room, with no father at home, treading water in third-generation despair. That child still has a chance; he or she is still free. But the child's chances are slim and the obstacles many. Even a rich child can grow up spoiled, unchallenged, without the heartbreak that makes hearts human; she or he can grow up in soil too rich and corruptive, and become whining, spineless, and suicidal. That child still has a chance; she or he is still free. But that child's chances are slim and the obstacles many, too.

Therefore, whatever makes us grow as knowers and lovers—more inquisitive, more caring, more open—is *good* because it fulfills our specific nature. Whatever makes us shrivel as knowers and lovers—more inward, more self-absorbed, more snarling—is *evil* because it is against our specific nature and makes us regress and degrades us to beasts or vegetables or lumps. No need for commandments and laws. It's rooted right in the objective *fact* of human nature. Commandments and laws were written for people who can't figure that out for themselves.

Only human nature is an invitation, not a command. Of all the four species, only we are free *not* to be human. No lion can refuse to be leonine, but the daily papers are filled with evidence that human beings refuse to act human. We are free *not* to know, *not* to love, *not* to grow more human. And we are free to treat our fellow humans *as if* they were nothing more than sheep or vegetables

or stepping stones. As far as we know, no tiger goes into a village, steals a lamb, and eats it; then mopes around, drowning in remorse, "Oh, my! I did it *again!*" But humans have at least that *capacity* for guilt. In fact, though many people moan about guilt trips, guilt is one of the qualities that separate us from beasts. What you get without guilt is Auschwitz and napalm and rape.

Human beings have the *potential* to be far more than mere higher-level animals. It is in our nature—and only in ours, as far as we know—to *go beyond* the animal in us. But that is not a command; it's an invitation. That's not an opinion; it's a fact. One only has to look at the spectrum of humanity, stretching from the nonaddicted pusher through the regular law-abiding citizen, to such men and women as Martin Luther King, Jr., and Mother Teresa, and the ordinary men and women who risk their lives to leap into freezing rivers to rescue drowning humans.

You are free to be human—moral—or to act like a beast or vegetate or be a lump. The choice is yours. And you only have one time around.

Unless you *choose* the effort of knowing and loving and growing, unless you choose the sacrifices and denials that morality entails, you automatically choose to be less than human.

No man is free who is not master of himself.

EPICTETUS

22

DILEMMA

Joe Carbone owns a small fruit and vegetable store in the Bedford-Stuyvesant section of Brooklyn, New York. He is sixty-eight years old and weary of shelling out hard-earned cash for more steel gates, for protection from the local teenage gangs, and for skyrocketing insurance costs. What had once been a lower-middle-class Italian neighborhood where everybody knew everybody had now become a black and Haitian neighborhood, with a sprinkling of Hispanics and, more and more, an influx of Asian refugees. Joe's kids are all married and are living on Long Island and in New Jersey; his wife died three years ago of cancer. Joe is ready to sell out and take what little money he has and move to Florida.

There is only one major problem. The only people who have shown an interest in buying Joe's place—with the money to pay for it—are the Nguyen family, a network of uncles, aunts, and cousins who escaped from Vietnam in the final days of the war and who worked at all kinds of menial jobs in order to make a living and establish a secure base so that their children could get an education and live better than they had.

Already there has been racial tension simmering in the neighborhood. Two oriental teenagers were jumped and beaten in the local high school; several Korean groceries have been bombed out or boycotted; graffiti have blossomed on factory walls warning the "slopes" to "Back off our jobs!" Three Vietnam veterans—two white and one black—visited Joe and told him, forcefully, that they didn't lose their best friends so that "the VC could invade our own damn neighborhood!"

▷ *Questions*

What is the basic "reasoning" behind the local resentments? Where are the flaws in that reasoning? Does Joe have any alternatives? What would you advise him to do?

FAITH REFLECTION

The psalmist described the dignity of humans this way:

> *O Lord,*
> *   your greatness is seen in all the world.*
> *O Lord,*
> *When I look at the sky, which you have made,*
> *   at the moon and the stars,*
> *   which you set in their places—*
> *what is man, that you think of him;*
> *   mere man, that you care for him?*
> *Yet you made him inferior only to yourself;*
> *   you crowned him with glory and honor.*
> *You appointed him ruler over everything*
> *   you made;*
> *   you placed him over all creation:*
> *   sheep and cattle, and the wild animals too;*
> *   the birds and the fish*
> *   and the creatures of the sea.*
> *O Lord, our Lord,*
> *   your greatness is seen in all the world!*
>
> Psalm 8:1, 3–9

Pope John Paul II echoed that human dignity when he addressed the United Nations in 1979. He said:

> *It is a question of the highest importance that in internal social life, as well as in international life, all human beings in every nation and country should be able to enjoy effectively their full rights under any political regime or system.*

If reason alone (as the chapter shows) and both Scripture and the church attest to the dignity of *every* human being, what effect does that have on arguments about abortion, war, capital punishment, and euthanasia?

📖 FURTHER BIBLE READINGS

Skim the passages. Pick one that appeals to you and (1) summarize its main point, (2) tell how it relates to the chapter, and (3) list one or two thoughts that entered your mind when you read it.

- ◆ The Good Samaritan — Luke 10:30–37
- ◆ "Come Higher!" — Luke 14:15–24
- ◆ Different Gifts — Genesis 49:1–28
- ◆ The Giving Soul — Hebrews 5:11–14
- ◆ Degrading — Isaiah 1:2–6

_____

_____

_____

_____

_____

✏ JOURNAL

No human is merely a higher-level animal. Each human has the *potential*—which no animal has—to be far, far more.

- ◆ What is the difference between *being* human and *acting* human?
- ◆ What test is there that you can apply to an entity to see if it is human—and not something less?
- ◆ When does a baby start being a human entity?
- ◆ When does a person in a coma stop being human?
- ◆ People in mental hospitals, children who murder without any remorse, Mob hit men—are all less than *fully* human, but are they less than human?

Understanding Humanity

REVIEW

1. Ruby Petunia Fawn *felt* less than human, even though objectively she surely *was.* What is the difference between "feel" and "be"?

2. Explain these statements:

   a. All other natures on earth are commands; only human nature is an invitation.

   b. Guilt is one of the many qualities that separate humans from beasts.

   c. Baby : cub = acorn : marble.

   d. Whatever makes us grow as knowers and lovers is good; whatever makes us shrivel as knowers and lovers is evil.

   e. Unless you *choose* to know and love, you automatically choose to be less than human.

3. Why is guilt often a very good thing?

4. What objective norm would tell you whether guilt is appropriate or inappropriate?

5. In a sentence or two, sum up what makes humans specifically different from all the other species.

DISCUSS

1. Nonaddicted pushers are undeniably human beings, and yet they have never activated their potential to grow as human beings. As such, they are little more than unevolved animals. True or false? Why?

2. Without naming any names, list all the *types* of people in your school who are consistently treated by others as less than human—and don't forget the adults too, like the people who have to clean up after the students.

3. Divide into pairs, probably best with someone you feel comfortable with. Without revealing anything no one else has the right to know, tell your partner about one painful occasion when you felt unjustly—inhumanly—treated. Go into detail, especially about the pain such treatment caused you.

4. The previous item spoke of things "no one else has the right to know." Why is that true? Does the public have "the right to know" about the private lives of notable figures? Is there a limit to that?

5. *Lord of the Flies* embodies the thesis: Human beings are evil at the core, and the only things keeping humans from open savagery are control by civilized society and its law enforcement agencies. *Catcher in the Rye* embodies precisely the opposite thesis: We are all born innocent and are corrupted—or even driven mad—by the wickedness of the society we are thrust into. Which thesis is true? Why? Or are they both true? Why?

ACTIVITIES

1. Read aloud—or even memorize—Shylock's response to Salanio and Salarino in *The Merchant of Venice,* Act III, Scene 1, that begins "To bait fish withal. . . ." What is Shylock trying to justify? What arguments does he use to justify it? Debate the points for and against Shylock's argument.

2. Sergeant Larry Kenny left his squad of men with their rifles aimed uselessly at Vietnamese old people and children, and climbed up the small hill toward the huts. He was only 20, but his haunted eyes and gaunt face held a weight of pain and loss one sees rarely even in homes for the aged.

   "That's all of 'em, sir," he said to the hard-eyed young lieutenant. "Nothin' but old folks too weak to run, and babies."

   "Waste 'em," the lieutenant said quietly.

   Kenny's weary eyes quickened, and he shot a look up at the man standing above him. "What?" he asked, his brow knotted in disbelief. "Sir, they're not the enemy. Not a single one of 'em's got the strength . . ."

   "Kenny, you heard me. We got our orders: 'Kill anything that moves.' They move. Waste 'em."

   "But, Lieutenant . . ."

   The lieutenant unholstered his pistol. "They're only gooks, Kenny. Gooks. Slopes. Waste 'em. Or else."

   Role-play Sergeant Kenny's court martial for not carrying out the lieutenant's order. Include the following characters: Sergeant Kenny, an army chaplain, a hard-nosed career colonel who is the lieutenant's superior, a lawyer from the judge advocate's office.

3. Find someone who was your age when President John Kennedy was assassinated—probably someone about 45-plus. Ask him or her whether there seems to be more or less evil in the world today than there was at the time they were your age. Then, the more important question: Why?

In matters of conscience, the law of the majority has no place.

MOHONDAS GANDHI

3. CONSCIENCE

SURVEY

Circle the number on the rating scale under each statement that best reflects your opinion about that statement. On the scale

+2 = strongly agree,
+1 = agree,
0 = can't make up my mind,
−1 = disagree,
−2 = strongly disagree.

Then share the reasons for your opinion.

1. All human beings are equal before the law and should be treated equally.

   +2 +1 0 −1 −2

2. Some humans, because of their special needs, deserve better treatment than others.

   +2 +1 0 −1 −2

3. Even people without religion need some consistent, personal ethical code.

   +2 +1 0 −1 −2

4. A society's ethical code can be objectively wrong, at least in some areas.

   +2 +1 0 −1 −2

5. Breaking any law of a legitimately constituted democratic society is immoral.

   +2 +1 0 −1 −2

6. Even childless people have ethical obligations to this generation's grandchildren.

   +2 +1 0 −1 −2

7. A personal ethical code is no different from what today is called "life-style."

   +2 +1 0 −1 −2

8. Genuine conscience comes from socialization: from parents, peers, media, and society.

   +2 +1 0 −1 −2

9. Having a too strict conscience is as dangerous as having no conscience.

   +2 +1 0 −1 −2

10. Someone without self-discipline is like a society without a police force.

    +2 +1 0 −1 −2

A FABLE

THE DUMB SHALL INHERIT THE EARTH

Once upon a time there was this boy named Paris, son of Priam and Hecuba, King and Queen of Troy. Paris was breathtakingly handsome and strong, but not too muscular in the IQ department, a fact even he thought was a fair trade-off. Some prophet predicted Paris would be the downfall of Troy, so his parents—reluctantly but with enlightened self-interest—tossed him out on a mountain to die when he was just a baby. Enlightened, not too smart. When prophecies are involved, some good-hearted shepherd invariably shows up and rescues the baby. When the gods make up their minds, you've got a snowball's chance to beat the odds.

Anyway, Paris grew up thinking he was no more than a son of poor clods and cursed to live a life of poverty, even though he had a face to open prestigious doors and have influential people eating out of his hands—not to mention sending wealthy damsels into swoons, rather than just peasant girls tumbling into wells when they turned around to stare adoringly at him.

Ah, but the gods keep their fingers in everybody's pies, tinkering, to relieve the boredom of perfection.

One day Zeus threw a party when the goddess Eris (whose middle name was Discord) was away so that the Olympians could have a bit of fun without discord. But old Eris got wind of it, and was she sizzling! So she made this gold apple inscribed "To the fairest"; and she sneaked invisibly into the soiree and rolled that apple right up to where Hera, Athena, and Aphrodite were buzzing the reputations of their dearest friends to shreds. The goddesses picked up the apple, looked at the inscription, and each one smiled knowingly at the other two, certain the apple was intended for her.

Now Hera was the wife of Zeus and mother of quite a few gods, but by no means all since Zeus was given to tomcatting up and down the Grecian peninsula and bringing home children he'd fathered in somewhat questionable circumstances. Hera was not at all amused and wanted a bit more attention from her unfaithful spouse. Awarding her the apple would do the trick. Athena was very beautiful, if a touch leathery owing to her keenness for mixing it up in battle, and she wanted to re-establish a reputation for looks as well as musculature. Aphrodite was the goddess of love, and she believed she had just about cornered the market where beauty was concerned.

Now none of the Olympian family was overly given to clear thinking, owing to quite scandalous inbreeding; they were more given to admiring themselves in the mirror and plotting against one another. But they were, to a god, smart enough to refuse any invitation to arbitrate a dispute between three hellcats like that. So Zeus decided they'd ask the handsomest man on earth since *he'd certainly have had experience choosing among gorgeous damsels. Guess who?*

Well, Paris didn't have to be asked twice. At last he had a chance to mingle with the people his fabulous phizz had made it practically his birthright to hobnob with. But when he arrived at Mt. Olympus, each of the three aggrieved goddesses crept into his quarters separately, and each made him an offer he couldn't refuse. Hera offered more power than all the kings who had ever lived. Athena, aware of his lamentably low brain wattage, offered greater wit and cleverness than even the wily Odysseus. But Aphrodite, an expert, sized up this guy and offered him the most gorgeous woman in the world, Helen. Nor was Aphrodite the slightest restrained by the fact Helen was already married to King Menelaus. Nor was Paris. So on the day of the contest Paris dutifully awarded the golden Apple of Discord to Aphrodite, sped down to Sparta to pick up his prize, and whisked Helen off to Troy.

Someone said wicked people don't cause all the trouble in the world; it's dumb people. Truer words were never spoken. As one might imagine, Menelaus wasn't too tickled to have his gorgeous wife given away at the whim of a goddess, so he packed every male in Greece into a thousand ships and sailed off to Troy to get her back. It took ten long years—and lots of very young corpses who could have been put to better use. The biggest dope since Pandora, Paris got the capital of France named after him, at least indirectly. And, if it hadn't been for his colossal screwup, we would never have had The Iliad *or* The Odyssey *or Aeschylus'* Oresteia *plays. You figure.*

▷ Questions

There are basically two motives for making a moral choice rather than an immoral choice: the *utilitarian* (whatever works) and the *altruistic* (whatever is honorable). The utilitarian's motive is enlightened self-interest. At bottom, utilitarians want to minimize pain and/or maximize profit. When utilitarians say "It wouldn't be right," they don't mean "It would be objectively wrong," but "We couldn't get away with it" or "Sooner or later it'll explode in our faces" or "We could make more by being honest." The altruist's motive is unselfishness based on principle and the welfare of others; when altruists say "It wouldn't be right," they mean "It would be *objectively* wrong, no matter how much I personally profit or lose" and "If I did that, I couldn't live with myself."

Say you've had a dog named Rags since you and she were just pups. She waits for you every day after school, follows you around, sleeps at the foot of your bed. What would you do if one of our three goddesses showed up tonight and offered you one *million* bucks to toss Rags off a cliff? What would be your motive?

Don't be too emotional or hasty. One million smackers is mucho cash. You'd have no more worries about college. You'd be set for the rest of your life and your children's lives. And Rags is getting pretty old.

RATHER FAIL WITH HONOR THAN SUCCEED BY FRAUD.

SOPHOCLES

A READING

In this scene from A Man for All Seasons, *by Robert Bolt, Sir Thomas More is trying to get home down the Thames River after an intimidating night interview with Cromwell, secretary to King Henry VIII. The king, whom More deeply reveres, desperately wants More's support in his divorce from Queen Katherine, but More cannot in conscience give it. On the way, More meets his lifelong friend, the Duke of Norfolk.*

NORFOLK: So listen to what I have to say: You're behaving like a fool. You're behaving like a crank. You're not behaving like a gentleman— All right, that means nothing to you; but what about your friends?

MORE: What about them?

NORFOLK: Goddammit, you're dangerous to know!

MORE: Then don't know me. . . .

NORFOLK: You might as well advise a man to change the color of his hair! I'm fond of you, and there it is!

MORE: What's to be done then?

NORFOLK: Give in.

MORE: I can't give in, Howard—You might as well advise a man to change the color of his eyes. I can't. Our friendship's more mutable than *that.*

NORFOLK: Oh, that's immutable is it? The one fixed point in the world of changing friendships is that Thomas More will not give in!

MORE: To me it *has* to be, for that's myself! Affection goes as deep in me as you think, but only God is love right through, Howard; and *that's* my *self.*

NORFOLK: And who are you? Goddammit, man, it's disproportionate! *We're* supposed to be the arrogant ones . . . and we've all given in! Why must you stand out? You'll break my heart.

MORE: We'll do it now, Howard: part, as friends, and meet as strangers.

NORFOLK: Daft, Thomas! Why d'you want to take your friendship from me? For friendship's sake! You say we'll meet as strangers and every word you've said confirms our friendship!

MORE: Oh, that can be remedied. Norfolk, you're a fool.

NORFOLK: *You* can't place a quarrel; you haven't the style.

MORE: Hear me out. You and your class have "given in"—as you rightly call it—because the religion of this country means nothing to you one way or the other.

NORFOLK: Well, that's a foolish saying for a start; the nobility of England has always been—

MORE: The nobility of England, my lord, would have snored through the Sermon on the Mount. But you'll labor like Thomas Aquinas over a rat-dog's pedigree. Now what's the name of those distorted creatures you're all breeding at the moment? . . .

A man's action is only a picture book of his creed.

Ralph Waldo Emerson

32

NORFOLK: Water spaniels!

MORE: And what would you do with a water spaniel that was afraid of water? You'd hang it! Well, as a spaniel is to water, so is a man to his own self. I will not give in because I oppose it—I do—not my pride, not my spleen, nor any other of my appetites but *I* do—*I!* Is there no single sinew in the midst of all this that serves no appetite of Norfolk's but is just Norfolk? There is! Give *that* some exercise, my lord! . . .

NORFOLK: *(Breathing hard)* Thomas.

MORE: Because as you stand, you'll go before your Maker in very ill condition!

NORFOLK: Now steady, Thomas. . . .

MORE: And he'll have to think that somewhere back along your pedigree—a bitch got over the wall!

(NORFOLK *lashes out at him; he ducks and winces. Exit* NORFOLK.)

▷ *Questions*

Norfolk is obviously a good, loving, loyal man. But what does More have that Norfolk does not? What is the "quarrel"—or at least the great difference—More claims has been between him and Norfolk all along? To help answer that question, think about what Norfolk means when he says "You're not behaving like a gentleman" and how it drastically differs from what More says in the final long speech that begins, "And what would you do . . . "?

Refer back to survey question 7 about the identity or difference between a personal ethical code, conscience, and life-style. What does Thomas More mean when he says, *that's* my *self?* What *is* his "self"?

THEME
CONSCIENCE

> *Conscience = self = Ego = soul = character = Who-I-Am*

Conscience is a set of guidelines for making moral choices. Faced with a demand for a quick decision, you can't go back to the beginning each time and reinvent the wheel. You have to have some basic *internalized* principles, or else you face your bewildering options with nothing but a "gut feeling" of which choice is right (moral, human) and which choice is evil (immoral, inhuman). And quite often selfish yearnings overbalance the evidence in favor of what is objectively the less moral choice. For instance, if you can save only one person out of three from a fire—a detestable bully or brilliant young physician (either of whom has a good chance to survive) or your brother (who has very little if any chance to survive)—whom do you choose? If your best friend asks you to lie for her, if you know your sister is hanging around with druggies, if some guy you've really wanted to become friends with asks to copy your math homework—what do you do? Tough dilemmas, but very real, everyday.

During battles, medics have precisely that kind of choice to make: Whom do I help first? The officers? The people I know? Start from the left and work my way to the right? To simplify (if that's the right word) those choices for medics caught up in the terror of combat, often blinded by fatigue and despair, doctors have devised a system called triage. *Triage* means "dividing victims into three groups," despite rank or relationship to the medics: first, those certain to survive; second, those who have at least a remote chance; and finally, those who have no chance at all. The only rational—if seemingly heartless—choice for the medics is to work on those who have a chance to survive, and not expend precious time, medicine, and skill on the almost surely dying or the sure survivors, no matter what their momentary pain. With that guideline, the objective truth can hold one's own personal preferences in check.

Conscience is just such a set of moral guidelines. It is surely not inborn; otherwise, you wouldn't have such a difficult time making ticklish decisions—and we would never have had people like Hitler. Conscience is either inherited or constructed for oneself—at no small effort. Either you take your conscience "off the rack," letting your moral choices be governed by what you're told by parents, peers, media, and society; or you fabricate a set of principles for yourself: You gather all the evidence you can about a moral question, sift it to find what is sound, and draw a logical conclusion about what *you* believe is the right and wrong choice in each particular moral situation.

We are all born healthy little animals, what Sigmund Freud called the *Id* (Thing): eating, sleeping, excreting, and exploring, unconditionally loved by our mothers. Mommy's more than happy to clean up after us because she knows we are just "doin' what comes natcherly."

But when a child reaches the age of about two, he or she has teethed and gotten control of his or her muscles. For her child's own good, the mother has to start distancing her child from herself, weaned the child, and probably has potty trained the child. Otherwise, the child will never be invited to parties! Also, during the "terrible twos," a child begins to "get into things." The mother has to teach a tiny person, not yet capable of logical thought or knowledge of cause and effect, that it's okay to bite the breadstick but not okay to bite the cat's tail or the electric cord. After all those months of unconditional love, the child begins to hear two words, *good* and *bad,* he or she has never heard before—and he or she will be hearing those words in some form forever after.

What Mommy is doing is taping onto the child's mind something Freud called the *Superego:* a kind of temporary conscience and survival manual till the child is old enough to form his or her own conscience. The child finds that when he or she throws the ball to Daddy, Mommy and Daddy smile and clap; but when he or she throws the spaghetti to Daddy, they frown and say "No-no!" The child is as incapable of seeing any logical connection between the two as the puppy who wets the rug and gets whacked for it; the commands are just arbitrary, but it's the parents' game so the child goes along. Enlightened self-interest; for the moment, the parents *are* the yardstick of the child's self-esteem.

All those do's and don't's are "taped" on the child's Superego, which is incapable of critiquing the do's and don'ts even when they are contradictory or when the child sees the parents doing exactly what they've forbidden him or her to do: "Okay for them, not for me." What's more, commands are taped with exactly the same force and resultant fear that a two-foot person feels looking up at a six-foot person. (That's why the meanies in folktales are giants. Folktales are told from the *child's* point of view.)

Later those commands *can* be critiqued. If the young person finds the commands don't agree with reality, he or she can ignore them. But, by far, the majority of people never do critique them—or are incapable of it—so they spend the rest of their lives governing choices by the same motives their parents had, even when those motives are wrong. If you ask teenagers their thoughts about welfare, nine times out of ten you're not talking to them but to their parents.

We also have to remember that in our age new factors Freud never could have dreamed of have, like television, entered the picture. While a child today is still in diapers on the living room rug, the tube is telling the child what's important, what's right and wrong, and very often the message is exactly the opposite of what not-so-cunning Mommy and Daddy are saying. Every ten minutes, no matter what the product, a voice on the TV is saying, "The more things you have, the happier you'll be.

We don't want to be like poor children. They have no Barbie dolls or Super Mario Brothers."

Over and over, for about 100,000 hours. Nifty brainwashing. And unerasable; saying, in effect, "Greed is a virtue."

What's more, many young people from a very early age seem fused to the stereo and the Walkman. When the TV isn't selling them the virtue of greed, pop music is selling them the virtue of lust (which TV does a pretty good job at, too). It begins to look close to unarguable that if a young person really likes somebody, having sex with him or her is as natural for humans as for hamsters. Young people *may* critique those messages, but it's difficult even to entertain the possibility that greed and lust may *not* be virtues, when you've heard they are, almost every waking moment since before you could think. With painful irony, it becomes easier to believe your own parents are wrong than that the media are wrong. The media become the Superego of the whole society.

Adolescence (= *becoming* adult) is the time when the ability to reason logically "kicks on." That is the time young people *can* begin to form what Freud called the *Ego:* a *personally validated* conscience—self/soul/character/Who-I-Am—independent of parents and media. Forming a personally validated conscience involves two difficult jobs: first, controlling one's own animal Id; and second, critiquing all the taped commands on the inherited Superego to see which agree with *objective* facts and which don't. "Fights don't settle problems" checks out. "Don't talk to people with dark skin" does not. Psychologists agree that those two jobs are precisely the task of adolescence: evolving an adult Ego.

First, fuzzy thinking confuses morality (humanity) with religion; and second, many schools are blinded by the "all-important" SATs. Therefore, most teenagers have to stumble around in the confusion of contradictory voices and slap together a "self"—a conscience—catch-as-catch-can.

Each of us has a "personality," an outward face and a basic posture in dealing with people. Usually this "outward face" is a result of one's reactions to parents and siblings. If, for instance, a pair of parents believe "spare the rod and spoil the child," one of their children could react defensively, feeling guilty, believing that "If I don't succeed, if I do bad, Mommy won't love me anymore." He or she will carry that defensive personality into school, into jobs, into marriage. A second child, coming into the same family situation, could see the older sibling victimized and resolve "that will never happen to me!" Such a child develops an aggressive personality. And—unless both are pulled up short and forced to reassess—they will continue that way the rest of their lives.

People who do pull up short and reassess have a chance to evolve a self: *character,* not just an external show but a deep leaden keel that helps them negotiate rough waters. People with only surface *personalities* merely rock and roll with the winds. That's what this book is for: To help you evolve a unique self so you won't be merely jerked around by your own Id and the false messages taped on your Superego.

Return to the root and you will find the meaning...
Sengstan

35

DILEMMA

The war that ended the world had been over for a week. In a subway station in Arlington, Virginia, Dr. Myra Ross tried to calm herself. Since the bombs there had been no communication. She couldn't remember anything about atomic half-life. There were only a dozen people left on the platform; the rest were stacked in the tunnel.

The water was untrustworthy. They had used a fire ax to open coin machines for food and soft drinks, but they were nearly gone. Fortunately, Myra had been on a call before she'd met her husband and her disabled daughter, Joy, for dinner, and her medical bag had been stocked. No one could guess how long they'd be there.

One of Myra's charges was the secretary of state, whose chauffeur had gotten him, his wife, and their daughter into the subway at the sound of the first sirens. Another was Dr. Chiarello, the last ever Nobelist for physics. He was cheerful, despite the braces on his legs.

The others included a black mechanic named Jesse, who had taken his six-year-old son and pregnant wife to the Vietnam Memorial to see the names of men he'd known. Mrs. Appleton at sixty was healthy but complained every waking moment. Marty Reiser, second-string Redskins' quarterback, had had his legs smashed and was delirious. Myra was sure Marty's date was a "pickup," but Cyndi had been of great help tending the wounded. Finally, Myra's husband, Art, a recovering alcoholic, showed signs of strain.

Because Myra was the only one with any real power left, the group had elected her to choose who would get the food to eat and who should be limited to the drinks.

▷ *Questions*

List the survivors in the order you would give them preferential treatment. What were your motives for each choice?

FAITH REFLECTION

Saint Paul wrote that the difference between what we will know in heaven is as great as the difference between what we know now and what we knew when we were little children:

> *When I was a child, my speech, feelings, and thinking were all those of a child; now that I am a man, I have no more use for childish ways. What we see now is like a dim image in a mirror; then we shall see face-to-face. What I know now is only partial; then it will be complete—as complete as God's knowledge of me.*
>
> *Meanwhile these three remain: faith, hope, and love; and the greatest of these is love.*
> 1 Corinthians 13: 11–13

As a child gradually emerges into adulthood during the period of adolescence, more and more opportunities arise to form—and test—a personally validated self. Deep within our human consciousness, God has implanted a hunger for the truth, for goodness, for love—all of which are at holy war with the unevolved beast in us, the Id. Human dignity lies in conquering that beast and in discovering God's law, written right into the way God made things and people.

All creatures deserve proper treatment simply because of the way our Creator made them. According to Vatican Council II:

> *By conscience, in a wonderful way, the law is made known which is fulfilled in the love of God and of one's neighbor. Through loyalty to conscience, Christians are joined to other [persons] in the search for truth and for the right solution to so many moral problems which arise both in the life of individuals and from social relationships. Hence the more a correct conscience prevails, the more do persons and groups turn aside from blind choice and try to be guided by the objective standards of moral conduct.*
> The Church in the Modern World, 16

What guides you in making important choices, such as the way you deal with your family, friends, strangers? With animals, food, the environment? Do you treat each *consistently* or haphazardly: as the mood strikes you or by what you can gain or lose? Are you, honestly, an altruist or a utilitarian?

📖 FURTHER BIBLE READINGS

Skim the passages. Pick one that appeals to you and (1) summarize its main point, (2) tell how it relates to the chapter, and (3) list one or two thoughts that entered your mind when you read it.

- ◆ Confidence   2 Corinthians 1:12–14
- ◆ A Clear Heart   Matthew 5:21–24
- ◆ Law and Conscience   Acts 15:1–21
- ◆ Law in the Heart   Romans 2:12–16
- ◆ Compromise   1 Corinthians 10:27–33

_____

_____

_____

_____

✏️ JOURNAL

This journal entry will take effort, but it is an effort to focus—for yourself—an ego-conscience. If that's not worth the effort, you will always have a personality, but it's unlikely you will ever develop a character.

Draw a line vertically down the center of a piece of paper. On one side of the line, list the do's and don't's your parents, teachers, and media have taped on your Superego that you have already checked against reality and find are now *wrong*— or at least far too simplified. On the other side, write the elements of your Superego that you now see for yourself are *valid*.

Understanding Conscience

REVIEW

1. Identify the terms *conscience, triage, Id, Superego, Ego, personality, character, utilitarian, altruist.*

2. What does the chapter mean when it speaks of taking your conscience "off the rack"?

3. If you don't evolve your own Ego (conscience), what in effect becomes your "conscience"?

4. Why does the chapter say that, when teachers talk to high school students about welfare, they are usually really talking to the students' parents?

5. Explain the statements:

    a. In great part, the media have *become* the Superego of our society.

    b. The most effective brainwashing is the brainwashing you don't know you're getting.

6. What are the two major jobs involved in finding a personal identity—a self?

7. What vice does television try in great part to convince us is a virtue? What vice does much of pop music try to convince us is a virtue? What effect do television and pop music have on the moral character of society?

DISCUSS

1. Roughly how many of your peers do you guess cheat routinely on homework, quizzes, and tests? What are the reasons most would give for doing that? Why is "Well, everybody *does* it" not a legitimate excuse? If trust and honesty are the glue that holds together the web of our human ecology, what is the effect of widespread cheating on the web of society?

2. When schools discover that a great deal of cheating is going on, the administration frequently will encourage teachers and exam proctors to have greater vigilance and require strong punishment when someone is caught cheating. Similarly, with the increase of crime in our cities, the almost automatic response is to call for an increase in the number of police. What would be a better way to attack the problems of cheating and crime at their roots?

3. Draw a line down the middle of a sheet of paper or on the chalkboard. On one side, brainstorm the values your parents and teachers have insisted that you develop since you were a little kid. On the other side, brainstorm the values that the media (TV programs, commercials, rock lyrics, magazine ads, movies, and so on) have insisted are important to any fulfilled person. How are the two sets of values alike? Different? Which source of information have you most listened to? Which source has the least to gain by trying to influence your choices? Which source do you trust most?

ACTIVITIES

1. The chapter has claimed that a great deal of pop music makes a virtue out of the vice of lust. Gather as many rock, heavy metal, and rap magazines that you can and comb through the lyrics printed in them. Try to prove that the chapter is wrong. But play fair. Don't just point out the lyrics that are either positive or neutral; there certainly are many of those. Are there any songs for which the magazines cannot legally print the lyrics? Why?

2. Your best friend, Jimmy Oteiza, came to you last Saturday in a real turmoil. His girlfriend, Carmen, had told him Friday night she was pregnant. The two of them had talked well into the morning about their choices: abortion, adoption, marriage. Jimmy was frantic, afraid of what his parents would say and do, afraid Carmen might have an abortion, and afraid that she might not.

Today, Monday, Jimmy comes to you again. This time he is not only in turmoil but furious. Carmen had told him on Sunday that she wasn't pregnant, that—in some confused way—she was "testing" him to see how much he really loved her. She thought that he recently had been showing too much attention to other girls. But (she says) she truly, deeply loves him and now she knows that he really loves her too.

Jimmy is one confused young man. He talks about all the genuine happiness he and Carmen have had together, about what they both thought was "the real thing" that would last a lifetime. But now he's not so sure. She's called Jimmy three times since yesterday and wants to be sure that they are still "together."

Why would Carmen pull something so cruel on someone she said she loved?

4. RELATIONSHIPS

SURVEY

Circle the number on the rating scale under each statement that best reflects your opinion about that statement. On the scale

  +2 = strongly agree,
  +1 = agree,
   0 = can't make up my mind,
  −1 = disagree,
  −2 = strongly disagree.

Then share the reasons for your opinion.

1. Your sister has a greater claim on your time and concern than a stranger does.

   +2 +1 0 −1 −2

2. If my brother were dealing drugs, I would protect him rather than his victims.

   +2 +1 0 −1 −2

3. The public deserves to know that the spouse of a film star has a drinking problem.

   +2 +1 0 −1 −2

4. It is unfair that U. S. workers get $25 an hour for the same work Mexican workers do for $2 an hour.

   +2 +1 0 −1 −2

5. No one on a public bus has the right to tell someone else to turn a radio down.

   +2 +1 0 −1 −2

6. A physically disabled person taking part in a race at a camp should be given a head start.

   +2 +1 0 −1 −2

7. I am not responsible for minorities being in low-paying jobs, but I am responsible for doing something to change that.

   +2 +1 0 −1 −2

8. All humans are created equal, but some were created "more equal" than others.

   +2 +1 0 −1 −2

9. People whose parents have worked hard have a right to more of this world's goods than people whose parents have not.

   +2 +1 0 −1 −2

10. Every human *deserves* a right to a chance, even if the rules have to change.

   +2 +1 0 −1 −2

A FABLE

ON THE FACE OF IT

Once upon a time there was this king named Grimwig who had only one daughter, Princess Hortense. Truth to tell, even in the opinion of the certified saints of the kingdom, Hortense was less than a knockout. Others who had seen the princess face-to-face turned pale at the memory and refused to discuss it. All the princess's servant women wore heavy veils and never looked at her above the neck.

Now King Grimwig wasn't getting any younger, and it was time to get to the business of insuring a smooth transition of power in the event of his heart-rending death. But Hortense's, well, unattractiveness posed a problem. So he consulted with his sister, the royal witch, Princess Peacock.

"We-e-e-ll," Peacock yawned, "the usual method is a trial, isn't it? A contest? A quest? Men simply can't resist competing. And the prize will be Hortense. Sight unseen, of course."

So the king began a series of tests, but so many fifth sons of impoverished kings showed up—hardy, skillful, and eager—that the tests multiplied geometrically in order to weed them out. Finally, Prince Blintz of Linz, scarcely recognizable under his scars from previous tests, was the only one to return with the egg of the Orc of Orkney, and he was declared the winner. But when the fortunate prince took one look at his royal intended, he fled straight into a monastery. As he left the royal hall, a single tear rolled down Princess Hortense's unlovely cheek, and from that moment she sat as immobile as an anvil, refusing to speak or bathe or take nourishment. So Princess Peacock proposed still another contest to marry off Hortense to whatever nobleman could bring her out of this unnerving walking coma.

Signs appeared all over the realm:

"WHICHEVER NOBLE MAN RELEASES PRINCESS HORTENSE FROM THIS WICKED SPELL SHALL HAVE HER TO WIFE AND INHERIT THE THRONE. CONTEST TODAY! 2:30 P.M."

Meanwhile, in the royal kennels, there worked a young man named Gryph. He was gentle of heart and beloved by his dogs and his mother—though not by too many others, owing to the fact that he was pretty ripe from mucking out kennels all day and because he had a head like a warthog. Without the tusks, of course. On the day of the royal decree, Gryph was walking through the streets of the town, tears coursing down his lumpy cheeks because in his pocket he carried a little puppy—the runt of her litter and born blind—that the heartless kennel master had sent Gryph to drown in the river that ran through the center of the town.

"Poor puppy," Gryph moaned and hauled the little thing from his pocket and held her to his cheek, where the puppy wagged her tail delightedly and licked his tears away. But at that moment Gryph spied the royal decree and stopped to read it.

41

"'Noble man,'" he read. "My mother always says," Gryph told the puppy, "nobility isn't in your parentage but in your heart." The puppy merely went on licking Gryph's whiskery cheek. "I'd like to help this poor princess." So Gryph put the pup back into his pocket and headed toward the palace to get on line and try to bring Princess Hortense out of her trance.

But when Gryph reached the palace square, it was completely deserted except for the guard at the gate. Gryph went up to him and said, "Excuse me, sir. Isn't this the day we try to save the princess?"

The guard scowled from under his tall fur hat. "Listen," he side-mouthed without looking, "word's gotten round. Even princes in debt up to their coronets said it isn't worth it. They say she's . . ." Then he shot a look at Gryph and gagged.

Undeterred, Gryph climbed the steps and walked along the echoing corridors to the great hall and peeked in. Around the huge, silent room, courtiers half-dozed against the marble columns. On the high throne, King Grimwig snored audibly; Princess Peacock idly scratched the back of her raven hair with the starry tip of her magic wand; and Princess Hortense sat staring, sightless as a statue in a cemetery.

"Ahem," Gryph cleared his throat, and Princess Peacock slowly turned a scornful eye at him.

"What do you want?" she snapped.

"I've come about the sign. To help the princess."

"What!" Peacock shouted, at which the king jerked out of his snooze. "The decree said 'nobleman,' you great horrid ox."

"It said 'noble man,'" Gryph said, knees beginning to quiver. "Nobleman is one word, but the sign. . . ."

"A technicality," Peacock hissed. "The royal sign painters are illiterates."

"My mother always says nobility is in the heart," Gryph said. "If there's a chance I can help the princess, I deserve that chance, don't I?"

"Deserve," Peacock said from a great height. "Deserve? Not . . . a . . . chance. You are . . . common. And besides that, you look like a warthog. We cannot have a warthog as king. I . . . we . . . the people simply wouldn't stand for it. We need a noble!"

"Are you being noble?" Gryph choked at her.

"He's got a point," the old king said. "All right, young man. Try."

Trembling, Gryph climbed the red-carpeted steps to the dais and looked sadly at the homely princess. He took the blind puppy from his pocket and laid it on her lap. The puppy licked the princess's freckled wrist with her little velcro tongue, and the princess's eyes flickered open. She looked at the puppy, and, slowly, a smile warped up the ends of her mouth and tears dribbled down her unlovely cheeks. Her eyes raised to Gryph and flinched a moment. Then she smiled again. "Thank you," she said. "You are a kind man."

The king and Peacock exchanged astonished looks. Then Peacock's face began to sag with the realization that even witches have a thing or two to learn.

▷ Questions

What do you deserve? List what you can legitimately expect, not just from your family and friends but from perfect strangers on the street, in the school hallways, at a game, or a dance? Now, what can others legitimately expect from you?

A READING

In the following selection, from Our Town, *by Thornton Wilder, Rebecca Gibbs is looking out at the stars with her older brother, George, on a clear summer evening.*

REBECCA: I never told you about that letter Jane Crofut got from her minister when she was sick. He wrote Jane a letter and on the envelope the address was like this: It said: Jane Crofut; The Crofut Farm; Grover's Corners; Sutton County; New Hampshire; United States of America.

GEORGE: What's funny about that?

REBECCA: But listen, it's not finished: the United States of America; Continent of North America; Western Hemisphere; the Earth; the Solar System; the Universe; the Mind of God—that's what it said on the envelope.

GEORGE: What do you know!

REBECCA: And the postman brought it just the same.

▷ *Questions*

Rebecca sees a series of concentric circles radiating out from Grover's Corners, from a single individual named Jane Crofut on a particular farm in a particular town to a radius that goes beyond time and space. At what point in that radiating series of circles have you personally allowed your interests to go and then stop? Is it possible that you are limiting the extent of the one life you have to live? Are you impoverishing yourself?

We know what we are but know not what we may be.
William Shakespeare

THEME

RELATIONSHIPS

We have been pursuing two questions throughout this book:

Who am I?
Where do I fit in?

Both questions are vitally important; without answers to both, we merely stumble around, *re*acting rather than acting, as victims of whoever is yanking our chains at the moment. Probably, most people in the world are too caught up in "more pressing" decisions or are too incapable of reasoning to answer either question. Most people are too busy making a living to find out what living is for. Thus, they merely tread water awhile, fight off the unexpected sharks awhile, and then die. Too bad, to live the only life one has and never know why.

Unfortunately, most people also answer the second question, "Where do I fit in?" *first,* and thus tailor who-they-are—not "I am who I *am*" but "I am what other people think of me"—to other people's expectations. Again, too bad, to expend the one life one has just being like all the other sheep, dancing to whatever tune the media choose to play.

Finding a unique self—an ego, conscience, ethic—is precisely what education is all about: building, painstakingly, a personal philosophy, brick by brick. But that takes a great deal of effort—not to mention making a great many choices that are often not "acceptable" to the other sheep.

Still (except for the very rare hermits), whether we decide to evolve a personally validated adult self or whether we refuse to think it out and automatically settle for doing what "everybody else" does, we have to live together. Solitary confinement is often a greater threat than death itself. But in exchange for the benefit of not having to go it alone, we have to make certain concessions, compromises—freely accept limitations on our personal freedoms. If you love someone, you automatically give him or her a "call" on your freedom, and you write blank checks that say "Let me know if you need help, even if it's inconvenient for me." Good parents do it all the time.

Even in Rebecca Gibb's larger circles, you have to yield some of your freedom. You are surely free to swing your arm; but that freedom ends at the tip of my nose, even if we've never met before. All you have to do to see how those freedoms are routinely violated is to visit or live in any big city. People who get on subways with boom boxes playing at eardrum-melting levels are "saying" something: "This space is *my* space!" The radius of their awareness is no larger than the confines of their own skins—and perhaps a few tested friends. People who spit in drinking fountains, who litter because it's "too far" to the trash barrel, who profiteer from pornography and manipulative advertising and drugs, are narrowing the scope of morality only to themselves. They live on one-way streets. Look up the word *autism.*

> *There is a sufficiency in the world for man's need but not for man's greed.*
>
> Mohandas Gandhi

OUR BIOLOGICAL ECOLOGY

Extraterrestrial explorers would pass a great many enormous planets on their long journey through the empty cold of space—some of them angry red, some glacial, some pocked and arid deserts of dust. Imagine the explorers' speechless awe as they shoulder past our moon, and see this enormous blue jewel, wreathed in scarves of clouds, sparkling in the sunlight! As they soar over the "amber waves of grain . . . the purple mountain majesties above the fruited plain," they do not believe their eyes. Surely this must be heaven!

But when they land and begin exploring with their close-up lenses, they would see what the inadequately evolved inhabitants had done with such a gift: birds smothered in oil, whole oxygenating forests hewn down to create wastepaper, rivers filmed with chemical scum and white-bellied fish, the "fruited plain" covered with asphalt and clotted with trash.

What opinion would these extraterrestrial explorers form of the shortsighted fools they were about to encounter? "Are they blind? Have they no concept of the future that they foul their own nest this way? What could possibly have motivated them to destroy something so precious? When they completely exhaust this paradise, where will they go?"

We have a very rich but very fragile relationship with our biological environment. It sustains us; supplies us with food, clothing, and shelter; opens itself for us to enjoy its nearly infinite variety. Until only recently in human history, there has always been plenty—more than enough for everyone—because there were so few of us. When the game or land in one area gave out, we could always move on. And so we plundered the earth, like Vikings who had another home to go to.

But it is only within the last forty years, since Rachel Carson opened our eyes, that we have begun to realize that the earth and time are running out. It took 300,000 years for the earth to contain two billion people; now two billion people are added every thirty years. Since you were born, we have produced a billion more hungry mouths.

But rather than ration what we have left so that all can have a fair share, the few gobble up all they can.

Gold and diamonds are precious because they are so rare. Now, at least, a few of us are beginning to realize that oil and timberland and wildlife are becoming precious too, because they are also becoming rarer every day. If one segment of the biological ecology profits unduly, some other area of the web has to "give." If I dump my waste into the water or the air (because it is too expensive to purify it first), everyone along the chain must pay for my self-service. If companies in the United States let off toxic chemicals into the air, the citizens of Canada are going to reap the acid rain. If collectors want elephant tusks for decorations, we will know of elephants only as we know of dinosaurs.

What is—objectively—more important: profits or people? Don't answer that too quickly. A great deal of the life-style of people in developed countries depends on raping the land. Although the population of the United States makes up only 4 percent of the world's people, we consume 40 percent of its fuel. To save the earth, are you personally willing to carpool? Cut down on random driving? Write Congress to promote more public transport? Eventually, by the natures of things, *all* parts of the web will have to pay. Even ours.

Two things fill the mind with ever new and increasing wonder... the starry heavens above me, and the moral law within me.
IMMANUEL KANT

OUR MORAL ECOLOGY

Just as you share an objective biological ecology— air, water, natural resources—you also share an objective *moral* ecology. You may not like that; you may not want that to be true; you may ignore it. But it remains as objectively true as the fact that dropped objects fall and fire burns. Violate the natures of things—like our human society—and sooner or later they will rise up and take revenge.

Our biological ecology of earth, air, water, and people is a web of interdependent physical relationships in which excessive strain in one area of the web results in the distortion of several other areas. Similarly, our moral ecology is a web of interdependent *human* (= moral) relationships; and if we let one area of the web swell out of control, other areas have to pay the price. We are free, for instance, to batter children, but the children will pay. We are free to embezzle, cheat the phone company, steal from the job, but the customers will pay higher rates while we profit. We are free to buy a shirt for only a few dollars, but that means some old lady in Taiwan has to work for two cents a sleeve. Who cares, right? She's in Taiwan; I'm here—and where *I* am is where it's *really* real. That's living in teflon cocoons.

Television is an enormous opportunity, not only for people who can't figure out anything better to do with their time, but also for advertisers who have a hypnotized audience that keeps the economy growing. But as a result of advertisers' profits, we risk having a nation of children who are passive, without imagination, and in lifelong service to infantile greed. The United States can consume an inordinately disproportionate share of the world's goods, but the natives—by their very nature—are getting restless. Teflon cocoons.

Why should sex be complicated with reverence? Not merely because Puritan religions and societies have condemned any human action that is pleasurable, but because sexual relations are ipso facto moral relations because they involve two human beings, not just two healthy animals. Sex involves fairness as much as a business deal or a football game. The human sexual act at least *ought* to be a *human* interaction since it involves two human beings, not just two animals. There at least ought to be not only a physical vulnerability to each other but a *psychological* vulnerability as well. A human at least ought not share what is objectively a most intimate encounter and then treat the other person as a stranger or someone he or she has merely gone to the movies with. If they haven't bared their souls, then their action has been merely animal—not human, not moral. Teflon cocoons.

Whoever argues against that is arguing against the way things are: Humans are not merely animals. Whoever argues against that is as great a fool as one who claims that we can dump industrial waste without worry, that we can exploit simple native populations, that media commercials are a blessing to the economy, and that the humanity of Jews and blacks is debatable.

It is not a matter of subjective opinion but objective fact: Gin has a stinger in it, sharks bite, rape victims suffer.

The other people on the subway are just as human as you are, and they have the same rights. Street people are human; retarded people are human; people in comas are human; people with strange accents are human; people in China, South Africa, and Lebanon are human. Even people you detest are human.

The Golden Rule, "Do unto others as you would have them do unto you," is not the private possession of any religion. It is a matter of human survival.

OUR humANITY
WERE A POOR THING
WERE IT NOT
FOR THE DIVINITY
WHICH STIRS WITHIN US.
FRANCIS BACON

DILEMMA

"My name is Pat Heffernan. My husband, Al, is a very successful lawyer, and I've given up my job as a teacher to help with his campaign for District Attorney. We have two daughters, Megan and Monica.

"Megan's a parent's dream: beautiful, athletic, polite, studious, much sought after by the boys. She was captain of the soccer team and had a part in the school musical. One painful, serious problem: She won't talk to either to us. Just polite nods and smiles and sentences with as few words as possible. It's as if she . . . resents us.

"Monica, our younger girl, is totally different, although just as noncommunicative. In her own way she's as pretty as Megan, but she refuses to do anything about her appearance, preferring to look like some biker groupie. She shouts a lot. Raw rage. Tests show that she's even brighter than

Megan, but she'll probably fail again. She hangs around with a surly bunch of boys and girls. The assistant principal tried to tell me they're doing drugs, but I just can't believe that.

"Each of the girls has her own room, with her own 'stuff,' and we never go in unless we knock or are asked. But they don't seem even to communicate with each other.

"Even though the campaign keeps us away a great many evenings, we have a live-in cook who has been with us since the girls were babies and who loves them almost as much as we do. We've tried to give them everything. We've tried to show interest in what they care about. I brought these two girls into the world. And now they're like strangers. Like . . . aliens. What did we do wrong? What do we do now?"

FAITH REFLECTION

Prejudice is like litter. The more "everybody does it," the more miserable life becomes for all of us. In the Letter from James we read:

> As believers in our Lord Jesus Christ, the Lord of Glory, you must never treat people in different ways according to their outward appearance. Suppose a rich man wearing a gold ring and fine clothes comes to your meeting, and a poor man in ragged clothes also comes. If you show more respect to the well-dressed man and say to him, "Have this best seat here," but say to the poor man, "Stand over there, or sit here on the floor by my feet," then you are guilty of creating distinctions among yourselves and of making judgments based on evil motives.
>
> James 2:1–4

We have a relationship with every other human being, simply as a result of our common humanity. But Christians have an even stronger relationship because at confirmation we freely ratified our baptism: We entered the Family of the Trinity. Our relationships with other people are not just those that bind the Human Family; the web that binds us is sanctified by the blood of Christ. If it is wicked for any human to humiliate another, it is twice-wicked for Christians.

Our concept of covenant comes to us from the Old Testament, in which Yahweh forms a covenant— a marriage relationship—with Israel. Even though Israel constantly deserted Yahweh and ran off to the gods of fertility cults, Yahweh remained faithful to Israel. At the Last Supper, Jesus said, "This cup is God's new covenant, sealed with my blood" thus joining us to God and to one another as brothers and sisters.

How do you make, seal, or break a covenant with your family? with your friends? with strangers? What covenant do you have with teachers—is it a *two*-way street? More important, how do you heal a broken covenant?

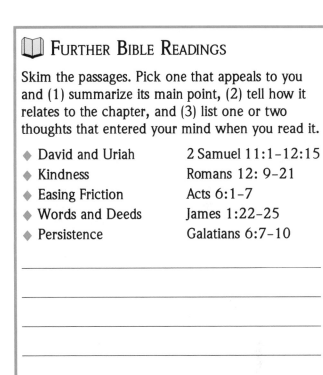

FURTHER BIBLE READINGS

Skim the passages. Pick one that appeals to you and (1) summarize its main point, (2) tell how it relates to the chapter, and (3) list one or two thoughts that entered your mind when you read it.

◆ David and Uriah	2 Samuel 11:1–12:15
◆ Kindness	Romans 12: 9–21
◆ Easing Friction	Acts 6:1–7
◆ Words and Deeds	James 1:22–25
◆ Persistence	Galatians 6:7–10

_____

_____

_____

_____

_____

JOURNAL

Nearly every day we see appeals for funds for people who can't help themselves: the homeless, AIDS victims, starving children, runaways. Your funds are limited. How do you deal with the faint quaver of guilt you feel every time those despairing eyes stare out at you from a magazine ad? You can't help them all. What *can* you do? No need to impoverish ourselves for others, but we can't stand idly by when there is something we *can* do. There is no such thing as an "innocent bystander."

(Note: Beware of writing "Well, you could. . . ." This isn't a homily to someone else; it's an honest assessment, for yourself, of ways in which you can contribute to the moral ecology in a more adult way.)

Understanding Relationships

REVIEW

1. What two questions does the chapter say form the basis of this whole book? Why does it criticize those who answer the second question first?

2. Did you look up *autism?* What does it mean?

3. Brainstorm everything that comes to us on television and list all the different kinds of programs, commercials, and so on. It is widely believed that, because children in a family "control the knob" in the evening (so they won't be left out), programmers gear their offerings to an eight-year-old mind. Is that true? Give your reasons.

4. What are the effects of television on the psychology of members of our society? Granted that anyone who finds those effects debilitating need not watch television, but the airways are public property, not the private property of the programmers and marketers. Do you believe the government should regulate television more than it does? What evidence backs up your opinion?

5. The chapter says that sex has an objective connection with fairness, in every case. What evidence does it offer to back up that claim?

3. Of the ten top grossing corporations in the U.S., all except IBM and AT&T are directly connected to selling vehicles and petroleum products. They gross $481 billion a year. Do you suspect that fact might have something to do with why our government has done so little to promote mass transportation? Is there some connection?

4. Does altruism have any place in business relationships, or must business relationships, by definition, be sheerly utilitarian?

5. Obviously, we cannot be expected to care for strangers living halfway around the world with the same concern we have for members of our own family. But, realistically, what responsibility do we have for people down the block? Street people in our large cities? Starving people in Ethiopia and Cambodia?

6. All humans—not merely Americans—have the right to life, liberty, and the pursuit of happiness (the pursuit, not the achievement). What's more, we are morally bound by the reality of our human ecology, by a responsibility not to stand by passively while those rights are violated. Do you, in practice, intervene when two older students embarrass a younger student?

DISCUSS

1. If the United States were a Monopoly board, the top 20 percent of our citizens would own 41 percent of the property and money, from Boardwalk to "In Jail"; the middle 60 percent of our citizens would own 54 percent of the properties and money, from "In Jail" to halfway through Mediterranean Avenue; the bottom 20 percent, 50 million people, would own only half of Mediterranean Avenue. At one time, Native Americans owned the whole board. Now they don't. What is just and what is unjust about that? What could reasonably be done to rectify the injustices?

2. What is the "hidden agenda" beneath each of the following statements? Is there any objective evidence to challenge them?

   a. "Now wait a minute, my grandparents came here without learning the language too. Nobody made any exceptions for them!"

   b. "I worked hard and long to get where I am. Those deadbeats on welfare got no right to live off my hard-earned money."

   c. " 'Those people' wouldn't be in such a lousy place if they didn't drop out of school and get pregnant and do drugs."

ACTIVITIES

1. On a photocopy of a map of the United States check off all the states you have personally visited. How "real" to you are the states you have never visited? Does travel *automatically* broaden one's perspective?

2. Set up a Monopoly board. Eight players arbitrarily chosen—tallest, shortest, oldest, youngest, and so on—receive an envelope containing tokens, money, and properties that have been unequally divided. Have them play awhile. After a few rounds, how do the players who received "less" feel about the game? How do the players who received "more" feel about the game? How do the players who didn't even get a chance to play feel about the game?

   Now, how would those three groups of players go about telling someone on third-generation welfare to make something of himself or herself?

3. You are both an engineer and an antique car buff, returning with your family from a weekend car auction. As you are traveling along a deserted two-lane country road, you see a car on the shoulder of the road with its hood up. Two men are standing by the side of the car; one of them is waving his arms at you. What do you do? Role-play your family making up their minds.

5. LEGAL/MORAL

SURVEY

Circle the number on the rating scale under each statement that best reflects your opinion about that statement. On the scale

+2 = strongly agree,
+1 = agree,
  0 = can't make up my mind,
 –1 = disagree,
 –2 = strongly disagree.

Then share the reasons for your opinion.

1. Every illegal action is automatically an immoral action.

+2 +1   0   –1   –2

2. Murder was evil long before there were laws and commandments.

+2 +1   0   –1   –2

3. Other people—even strangers—have legitimate claims on us.

+2 +1   0   –1   –2

4. Unlike other species, only humans are free to go against their nature.

+2 +1   0   –1   –2

5. Winning is not the most important thing; it's the only thing.

+2 +1   0   –1   –2

6. One either expends the effort to evolve a personally validated ethic or becomes a life-long victim.

+2 +1   0   –1   –2

7. There are some values even more important than one's life.

+2 +1   0   –1   –2

8. Better a live slave than a dead hero.

+2 +1   0   –1   –2

9. Healthy individuals can be free of any outside influences whatsoever.

+2 +1   0   –1   –2

10. Loyalty—to my family, my school, my team, my country—is more important than truth.

+2 +1   0   –1   –2

A FABLE
NOBILITY AND COMMON SENSE

*Once upon a time in a kingdom called Thebes there was this
princess named Antigone, the daughter of Queen Jocaste and
King Oedipus—who was not only her father but also, well, her
half brother. Oedipus and Jocaste, you see, had each gone to great
lengths to outwit a prophecy that Oedipus would marry his mother
and Jocaste would marry her son. And, of course, the two ran right
into one another, got married, and had four children. When they
discovered the truth, Jocaste hanged herself, and Oedipus put out
his eyes to punish himself for having been so blind all along.*

*The elders of Thebes chose Jocaste's brother Creon to be
king, rather than one of Oedipus' half brother/sons, which they*

thought a bit . . . indelicate. One son, Eteocles, was content with that and remained loyal to King Creon, but the other son, Polynices, got really lathered up and stormed out of town, looking for an army to take back what he thought was rightfully his. And he did. But with an insight rare in a head of state, Creon decided that rather than waste a whole generation of healthy young Theban boys, the two brothers would fight it out in single combat, winner take all.

As it turned out, it was one of those rare occasions when a battle actually did settle something. The two young men both won and lost, because each killed his opponent and, of course, was killed by his opponent. In other words, they both died, which more or less resolved the problem of who would be king.

Except that Creon was as unusually stubborn as he was occasionally shrewd. Since Polynices had been a traitor to the state, he would not be allowed the final human right: the rite of burial, which was forbidden to enemies and traitors. As a result, Greeks believed, Polynices's soul would have to wander forever and never find peace. War seldom has anything whatever to do with either nobility or common sense.

Now Antigone, who was the kind of girl the word noble was invented for, was not about to sit still for that. She was going to slip past the guards and bury her brother. Even though she knew, if she were caught, she'd be stoned to death. Noble people are seldom also gifted with common sense.

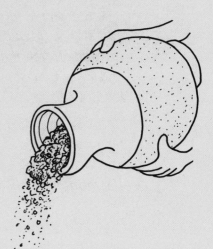

She asked her sister, Ismene, to help her. Now Ismene was very much gifted with common sense, not to mention good citizenship, much less respect for the healthy condition of her limbs and lovely skin. "Not on your life!" Ismene snapped. So Antigone went off alone and heaped earth all over her brother's corpse. And she got caught. Not too surprising, since she sat right down next to the grave and waited, calm as a clam. As I said, nobility and common sense don't often enjoy each other's company.

It also seems to be something of a constant that a crown often has an adverse effect on the wits it sits on. Since becoming king, Creon had really begun to think that his power to make things happen made each of those things not only automatically right but also unchallengeable. Antigone challenged him; so Antigone was going to die. Common sense.

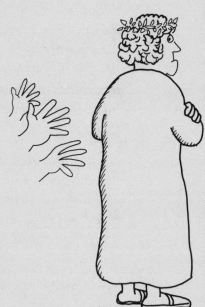

Well, half the town pleaded with Creon to be merciful, but a king is not to be lectured by a bunch of toothless old commoners. His son, Haemon, who was in love with Antigone, tried to show Creon that he was being unjust, but a king is not about to be lectured by a boy either. Even the guards who had brought Antigone in admired her spunk and asked Creon's mercy, but if a king gives in, every ninny in the kingdom is going to think the king's a wimp, right? Still, after all that badgering, Creon was beginning to hesitate.

So as an act of mercy, instead of stoning her, Creon had Antigone walled up in a desert place with enough food to keep her alive a week or two. Not much of an easement, but if the gods came and rescued her, Creon would change his mind. Common sense.

But an old blind prophet named Teiresias came to him and slowly, brick by brick, dismantled all Creon's arrogance and certitude (often the same thing), till finally the king relented and went himself to supervise the tearing open of Antigone's living tomb.

Too late. At the far end of the tomb, Antigone was hanging by the neck in a linen noose. And clinging to her, too late to save her, was Creon's son, Haemon. And as the king entered the tomb, Haemon drew his sword and killed himself.

▷ Questions

This little story has not been as upbeat as the others you have read so far, but it does raise an interesting question: Which is better: to die like Antigone or to go on living like Creon?

A READING

In this selection from Lord of the Flies, *by William Golding, a group of British schoolboys has been marooned on an island during a world war. There are no adults, and the boys have no idea what to do. So Ralph blows a large pink conch shell to bring them together.*

"Yes. There are pigs on this island."

All three of them tried to convey the sense of the pink live thing struggling in the creepers.

"We saw—"

"Squealing—"

"It broke away—"

"Before I could kill it—but—next time!"

Jack slammed his knife into a trunk and looked around challengingly. . . .

"We can't have everbody talking at once. We'll have to have 'Hands up' like at school."

"Then I'll give him the conch. . . ."

"He can hold it while he's speaking.". . .

The older boys first noticed the child when he resisted. There was a group of little boys urging him forward and he did not want to go. He was a shrimp of a boy, about six years old, and one side of his face was blotted out by a mulberry-colored birthmark. . . .

The small boy held out his hands for the conch and the assembly shouted with laughter; at once he snatched back his hands and started to cry.

"Let him have the conch!" shouted Piggy. "Let him have it!"

At last Ralph induced him to hold the shell but by then the blow of laughter had taken away the child's voice. Piggy knelt by him, one hand on the great shell, listening and interpreting to the assembly.

"He wants to know what you're going to do about the snake-thing."

Ralph laughed and the other boys laughed with him. The small boy twisted further into himself. . . .

"Now he says it was a beastie."

"Beastie?"

"A snake-thing. Ever so big. He saw it. In the woods."

"You couldn't have a beastie, a snake-thing, on an island this size," Ralph said kindly. . . .

Jack seized the conch.

"Ralph's right, of course. There isn't a snake-thing. But if there was a snake we'd hunt it and kill it. We're going to hunt pigs to get meat for everybody. And we'll look for the snake too—". . . .

Ralph was annoyed and, for the moment, defeated. He felt himself facing something ungraspable. The eyes that looked intently at him were without humor.

"But there isn't a beast!"

Something he had not known was there rose in him and compelled him to make the point loudly and again.

"But I tell you there isn't a beast!"

The assembly was silent.

▷ Questions

There are two antagonistic forces at work here: one symbolized in the organizing and civilizing power in the conch (the Superego); the other symbolized in the dark animal power in the pigs, Jack's knife, and the "beastie" seen by the boy with the mulberry mark (the Id). Make two columns and list all the other details in the passage that show those two antagonistic forces. Ralph insists there are no such things as "beasts." But there are. What are they?

THEME
LEGAL/MORAL

Laws are written for people who don't want the trouble of thinking for themselves. It should be pretty obvious from what we've seen so far that objective morality is not in our heads but in the natures of things and that even though it may not be our subjective opinion, it is also a fact that human beings have more objective value than cabbages or koala bears or curbstones; and therefore, it is immoral, inhuman, to treat human beings as less than they are.

There really shouldn't have to be laws against spitting in the subway or letting your dog do his business on the public sidewalk, much less against holding people in slavery like cattle or beating your own children to death. But people do it. So laws are written for people who want reality to yield to their desires and whims rather than their yielding to the unchangeable natures of things.

Some people believe in Satan, a disembodied evil spirit who goes about trying to seduce other- wise upright folks to dehumanize themselves and others and who is the source of all the evil in the world. Perhaps there is a devil, but I doubt Satan's really necessary. There are two factors in the human makeup that make Satan's existence and work unnecessary: narcissism and inertia.

Narcissism is self-absorption—the inner need to feel that we are OK, all-right-with-the-world. Narcissism makes us feel very, very reluctant to admit that we have genuinely made a stupid mistake and that, at least for the moment, we have no *right* to feel OK, until we set things right again. Inertia is just plain laziness, another reluctance built right into the way we are made. Inertia resists, first, the effort to think at all, and second, the effort to go back to the first wrong turn and start over again.

Narcissism = self-absorption

Inertia = laziness

Some people also believe in original sin. Now whether a literal Adam and Eve once ate a piece of fruit at the behest of a snake is somewhat doubtful. Even Aesop didn't expect his readers to believe there really was a time when animals literally talked to people. But whether people believe that a literal Fall ever occurred or not, there's no denying the results: we definitely are selfish—narcissistic and unwilling to confess mis- takes, and subject to inertia and unwilling to change. That's an objective fact that has nothing to do with any religion. All you have to do is scan any daily paper to prove it.

Part of the reason for human narcissism and inertia is that we are born not fully human but only "humanizable;" our nature is the only nature that is an invitation, not a command. Our human potential is *real*, but many are reluctant to make the effort to *actualize* that potential. We are free *not* to be human, to act *in*humanly and refuse to treat ourselves, our neighbors, and our physical and moral ecologies as they legitimately deserve.

The beast in us—the Id—can outshout both the temporary conscience taped on our Superego by the authorities of our childhood or even a personally validated Ego-conscience. We are free to operate against our *objective* best interests. It is far better all round that we don't sulk and hold grudges, that we tell the truth rather than defend ourselves with self-deceiving lies, that we keep our mitts out of one another's cash registers. But (1) that is humbling and (2) that takes effort—both of which are completely against our deep-rooted, stubborn, and *subjective* self-interests: narcissism and inertia.

Therefore, if we are to live together, somebody has to ride herd on the Ids of those who refuse to ride herd on their own. That's where the law comes in. In theory, at least, the wisest people in a society—people willing to make the effort to think—study human activities and determine which actions are evil, that is, those that degrade human beings and our environment. Then they draw up a law against it, with a proportionate punishment for those who still refuse to be human.

That's in theory. But the lawmakers themselves are human, subject both to an unwillingness to admit mistakes and an unwillingness to change. Creon did not want to admit his injustice against Antigone or to look like a fool for changing his mind. The same was true with the papacy in the Galileo case, with slave owners in the American South, with the presidency during the Vietnam War. Even today, it takes a great deal of money to be elected a lawmaker, and lawmakers cannot help but be swayed by the interests of the people who got them elected.

So, in the ideal order, people would evolve their own self-validated consciences and lawmakers would make only laws that point out which actions are human and which are not. But we live in the real order, where people are burdened with selfishness—whether they are the governed or the governors. There is only one way we can approach more closely to the ideal: to form young citizens who will reason out for themselves what actions are human and inhuman—and act accordingly—and pass judgment on the laws imposed on them, whether the laws are in fact just (true, human) or unjust (untrue, inhuman). That is the whole purpose of this book.

The superpatriot is usually no patriot at all. He or she believes the old cliche: "My country, right or wrong!" That is the cry of an unthinking person, the cry of a willing slave. If my country is genuinely, objectively wrong in choosing a particular policy or law, I do my country no service by simply going along with it. The government exists for the people, not the other way around.

There are two quite different sources of authority: political and moral.

Political authority is something *external* to the individual; it is imposed from outside. The king is anointed merely because his father was king, whether he himself is worthy of the job or even a good man. Lawmakers are elected; dictators seize power by force; mob bosses batter their way to the top. Such people command respect simply because they have the power to punish.

Moral authority is *internal* to the individual; it is not bestowed; it is achieved—by a great deal of thought and by successfully overcoming challenges to which the narcissism and inertia of less human persons would have yielded. Such people command respect not because they demand it but because they genuinely *deserve* it.

External political authority can be taken away—by coup, by impeachment, by assassination. Internal moral authority can never be taken away—not by solitary confinement or threat of torture or death. It can be surrendered but never stolen.

As we have seen before, there are two kinds of reaction to power that parallel those two kinds of authority: the utilitarian and the altruistic, or the self-protective and the self-giving.

Utilitarian = I want to win.

Altruisitic = I want to have character.

Even when utilitarians realize that authority has a valid reason for what it threatens to punish, they are constantly playing games with authority: How far can I go? Is a cop nearby? Is the punishment worth the rewards? Utilitarians have a great deal of common sense and are often quite successful. But they are not good citizens.

Altruists try to think as honestly as they can. They are open-minded enough to realize when their opponents' claims are genuinely more valid than their own. They refuse to bow to a statement merely because it comes from the mouth of a political authority; they want to check it out.

Altruists are patriots, but they also have a more profound allegiance to a higher cause than the country they truly love: the truth and the human family. Thomas More was such a person. So were Mahatma Gandhi, Martin Luther King, Jr., Harriet Tubman, and Mother Teresa.

Utilitarians are unable to fathom altruists' lack of common sense—which utilitarians identify with enlightened self-interest. Neither, of course, can they fathom their nobility.

DILEMMA

Graham Locklear is the CEO of a nationally known food-processing company that has eleven plants across the country. All the plants are making a comfortable profit except the one outside Renfrow, Ohio. There have been labor problems and agitation for higher wages; the local economy has been in a slump for five years; companies are being taxed disproportionately (in Locklear's opinion) to ensure essential services; the municipal government had long been in the hands of a "machine" that was only recently turned out of office by the impatient citizens.

Recently, representatives of a small city in northern Mexico contacted Locklear about opening a plant in their area, since the people are in terrible financial straits in a drought-ridden area. The roads are quite good and there is a seaport only fifty miles away; the land would be free; the operation would be tax-free for the first ten years; most important, while the Locklear Corporation pays American workers an average $6.50 an hour, Mexican workers would work for something closer to a dollar an hour. They are in desperate need.

A union delegation caught wind of the possible move and demanded a meeting with Locklear. They pointed out that Locklear was the only meaningful business in their small city and 3,000 families depended on the company for their livelihood. What's more, all the peripheral businesses— stores, gas stations, barber shops, restaurants— depend on the business of the Locklear workers. The municipal government showed great promise, even though there was criticism that it was too slow in showing results. Locklear reminded the union delegates that the Renfrow plant has been costing the company millions every year for five years. He is not running a welfare office. He has stockholders to whom he is accountable. He has legal rights.

▷ *Questions*

In what way does Locklear base his decision on the difference between the legal and the moral? Whom did his decision benefit? Explain whether you agree with his decision or not.

FAITH REFLECTION

Two other men, both of them criminals, were also led out to be put to death with Jesus. When they came to the place called "The Skull," they crucified Jesus there, and the two criminals, one on his right and the other on his left. Jesus said, "Forgive them, Father! They don't know what they are doing."

Luke 23:32–34

Both the men crucified with Jesus were law-breakers whom the law would not forgive. And yet Jesus forgave one and not the other. Why? Was it because Jesus didn't *want* to forgive both?

What is the difference between legal and moral? What is the difference between moral and Christian?

Our church reminds us that:

In addition to the effects of original sin, there is personal sin, committed by the individual.

Sharing the Light of Faith, 98

In our societies today, which are far more complex than in the simpler days of segmented towns and villages, it is difficult to pin the blame on individuals for huge injustices. Hitler could not have performed the atrocities of the death camps all alone; the men who pulled the triggers in the massacre at My Lai were "only following orders."

Does that complexity of "lines of command" absolve the individual citizen from blame when the whole society is committing injustice—with the full protection of the law?

TAKE AWAY LOVE AND OUR EARTH IS A TOMB.

ROBERT BROWNING

📖 FURTHER BIBLE READINGS

Skim the passages. Pick one that appeals to you and (1) summarize its main point, (2) tell how it relates to the chapter, and (3) list one or two thoughts that entered your mind when you read it.

- ◆ Law in Our Hearts   2 Corinthians 3:1–6
- ◆ Law Is a Curse   Galatians 3:10–14
- ◆ The Law and Mercy   James 2:8–13
- ◆ Judging Others   Mark 6:37–42
- ◆ The Heart and Mouth   Matthew 15:16–20

_____

_____

_____

_____

_____

✎ JOURNAL

In November 1989, either El Salvadoran government troops or government subsidized death squads entered the home of six priests whom the Salvadoran government believed were the masterminds of the guerrilla uprisings in El Salvador. The troops or death squads dragged the six priests, their housekeeper, and her daughter out into the yard, tortured them, then murdered them and removed their brains—as some kind of brutal symbolic act. The government that supported that effort was backed by the United States government with hundreds of millions of dollars in foreign aid. What would a good American citizen do about that?

REVIEW

1. Explain these statements:

    a. Laws are written for dumb people.

    b. Murder was evil long before there were laws and commandments.

2. What two factors in the makeup of humans render the devil at least unnecessary? Explain each factor. How are they an inevitable result within people who are not fully human people?

3. Explain why "original sin" is the only Christian doctrine you can prove from the information in the daily newspapers.

4. What is the difference between political and moral authority? Give an example of each.

5. What is the difference between utilitarian and altruistic motivation? Give an example of each.

DISCUSS

1. Winning is not the most important thing; it's the only thing. Is that true or false? Why?

2. One either expends the effort to evolve a personally validated ethic or becomes a lifelong victim. Why?

3. Loyalty—to my family, my school, my team, my country—is more important than truth. Do you agree? Why or why not?

4. Candidates for Congress need megabucks to be elected to office today. What effect has that on lawmakers' objectivity?

5. There is only one way we can approach more closely to the ideal society: to form young citizens who will make the effort to reason out for themselves what actions are human and inhuman, act accordingly, and therefore be able to pass judgment on the laws imposed on them. Why?

6. The super patriot is usually no patriot at all. Why?

7. Internal moral authority can never be taken away—not by solitary confinement or threat of torture or death. It can be surrendered but never stolen. Why?

8. Altruists have a more profound allegiance to a higher cause than the country they truly love. Explain.

9. In recent years, powerful lobbies have successfully argued the cases that burning the American flag, producing and marketing pornographic literature, and holding racist Nazi and Ku Klux Klan rallies are well within a citizen's First Amendment rights. What would a good American citizen do about that?

ACTIVITIES

1. Between classes every narrow corridor in the school is jammed with students. They are loaded with books and backpacks, rushing blindly from one end of the building and from one floor to another in the scant four minutes between classes, fearful they'll get detention if they're late.

    You and a group of fellow students sit down with the principal and, tactfully, propose a plan to add just one more minute to each passing time. The principal argues that your suggestion would lengthen the day and some students would miss public transportation and have to wait another hour for a ride home.

    You next suggest starting school ten minutes earlier. The principal counters that many students who come from a distance would have to get up too much earlier and that would be unfair to them. It's pretty obvious the principal's mind has been made up. Now what do you do?

    Role-play several endings.

2. Think of a character in a novel or film who is a victim of narcissism and utilitarianism. How is that revealed in the character's choices? How do those personality traits affect other people? What is the final result?

3. Divide into pairs. In each pair one partner is a utilitarian and the other is an altruist. Choose one of the following issues and debate it.

    a. Overeating

    b. Extramarital sex

    c. TV programming

    d. Violent cartoons

    e. Smoking

    f. Cheating on quizzes

    g. Selling drugs

    h. Building a house on the San Andreas fault

Relationship with Oneself

6. SELF-RESPECT

SURVEY

This survey is not an exercise for a grade, but a means to stir up interest, get an idea of varying opinions in your group, and focus on the topic. Circle the number on the rating scale under each statement that best reflects your opinion about that statement. On the scale

  +2 = strongly agree,
  +1 = agree,
   0 = can't make up my mind,
  −1 = disagree,
  −2 = strongly disagree.

Then share the reasons for your opinion.

1. Competition is a good way—if not the only way—to prove one's real self.

   +2 +1 0 −1 −2

2. Unless you keep up your guard constantly, people will take advantage of you.

   +2 +1 0 −1 −2

3. Few prices for being accepted by at least some of your peers are too high to pay.

   +2 +1 0 −1 −2

4. First impressions are critical.

   +2 +1 0 −1 −2

5. Sizing up a person's face, clothes, and posture gives you a good idea of a person.

   +2 +1 0 −1 −2

6. The more you care about people, the more they can hurt you.

   +2 +1 0 −1 −2

7. It is better to have a few trusted friends than many trusted friends.

   +2 +1 0 −1 −2

8. All we are as persons is the result of what other people have done to us.

   +2 +1 0 −1 −2

9. People who constantly "lose themselves" in music often avoid having a self.

   +2 +1 0 −1 −2

10. Two of the most wasted words in the language are *If only*.

    +2 +1 0 −1 −2

A FABLE
THE FLAKE'S PROGRESS

Once upon a time there was this king with three sons. Lance was blond, insultingly handsome, and bulgy-muscled; he was captain of the royal football team with scholarship offers from Oxford and Paris. Dirk had black curly hair, a face like a Greek statue, was captain of the royal basketball team, and combined SAT scores of 1600. The youngest, Ayrehead, was more or less normal except he had a head like a porcupine.

The king was getting pretty old and realized it was time for the usual heir tests. So, since the castle was drafty, he said whichever son brought back the finest robe by midnight Saturday would be his heir.

Well, Lance and Dirk had so many dates, games, college interviews, and TV programs to watch, they zipped off to K-Mart and were home in a jiffy with a couple of snazzy Taiwanese bathrobes with dragons on the back, and they had plenty of time to lift weights and admire themselves in the mirror.

Ayrehead—whose brothers called him "Blubber-brain," "Imbecile," and other unfeeling but not-far-from-the-mark names— wandered the forest. Then it began to rain, so he crawled into a hollow redwood and moped. "Where do I find a robe for father here?"

"A robe, you got," said a voice. "For a price."

Ayre turned his poor porcupine face down and saw a fat Black Widow scowling up from a silky froth of web.

"Anything," Ayre said, "but money. I'm broke."

"First," said the spider, "the tears. They're poking holes in the work. Then sort out these seeds for me. When you finish, you got a robe'd break Liberace's heart. So? Get to it."

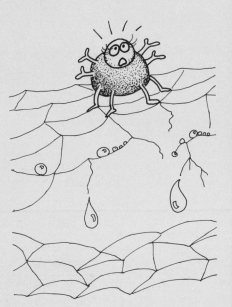

When Ayre saw the mountain of seeds, his heart plummeted. Sunflower, pistachio, lobelia, motherwort, smilax, love-lies-bleeding, Venus's-flytrap—among others. About a ton. But he set to sorting them into separate piles. Finally—about 11:45:20 Saturday night—he finished. And the spider gave him a glorious silk robe: "inside, lambswool; outside, the Bayeux Tapestries." Ayre ran home, and his father had no trouble deciding between Ayre's gift and the Taiwan dragons.

But the older brothers whispered in their father's ear about turning the throne over to a boy whose head had quills all over the outside and not much more inside. So the king proposed another test: Whoever brought back the most beautiful cup for the king's nightly knock would get the kingdom.

Well, Lance and Dirk ransacked their roomful of academic and athletic trophies and loving cups, picked the two most impressive, and gave them to the servants to polish; and Ayrehead got lost in the rain again. This time he ducked into a cave, met an old witch with a voice remarkably like the Black Widow's, but she was nearly deaf and spoke only Latin. It took poor Ayre the whole week, pointing at things and asking their Latin names. And, of course, there wasn't a cup in sight, right? Vases, glasses, ewers, beakers, ollas, urns, but not a single cup.

Finally, Ayre was about to give up. "If only my brothers weren't so callous!"

"Calix?" barked the witch and brought out of a cupboard a chalice covered with jewels that she insisted was the Holy Grail itself, even though it had "Tiffany" stamped right on the bottom.

The king was beginning to suspect Ayre wasn't such a ninny, but his brothers reminded the King of the quills, so he proposed a final test: Whoever brought home the most beautiful damsel before nightfall would get the throne. On that one, Ayre was a goner.

This test gave Lance and Dirk a problem. They had so many eager damsels to choose from that, in order to be sure of some gym time, they called a computer dating service and got two really spiffy girls. And Ayrehead was out in the rainy woods again. This time, a fat lady toad with a croak not unlike the spider's and the witch's came upon him and told him to follow her down an old rabbit hole. Easy enough for her, but it took Ayre the better part of the day to burrow in after her. When he finally got his head into the main chamber, there the toad sat in the firelight, bloated and baggy, and covered with nubs and knobs.

"Pop me in your mouth," she said, "and carry me home, and I'll give you a girl to die for."

Now Ayre had always been a laughably trusting soul, and his previous bizarre willingness to be hoaxed had saved him, so he popped the awful thing into his mouth and carried her back to the castle.

Well, they howled. Even stodgy old nobles. There stood Lance and Dirk with beauties to shame Ann-Margret and Elizabeth Taylor, and Ayrehead pulls out of his bristly mouth this big, fat, bumpy toad!

"Give us a kiss, then, luv," the toad whispered.

Ayrehead hesitated, then, to spite all the rest of them, planted a smooch on the toad's hideous cheeks.

Kabammo! That toad exploded into a damsel to splinter your wicked stepmother's mirror, and Ayre got transformed even more handsome than Wayne Newton.

Of course they were crowned king and queen and lived happily ever after. And Lance and Dirk grew old and fat as the managers of the Royal Gym and Massage Parlor in Ho-Ho-Kus, New Jersey.

▷ Questions

In the Olympics, only one person in each category can win the gold medal. Does that mean the silver and bronze medalists are both really losers? If so, then what about the men and women who spent eight or ten years training who didn't get a medal at all? And what about the ones who spent the same time and torment and didn't even make the cuts for the team?

Ask your parents if they can remember anyone from their high school years who they believed at the time was a "total loser"—and yet who later on surprised everybody.

What did Ayrehead have that his brothers did not?

A READING

The following song, "I Am What I Am" by Jerry Herman, from La Cage aux Folles *is sung by an aging transvestite in a gay night club. The man he has lived with for twenty years has, on a drunken spree, fathered a son whom the two have raised as self-sacrificingly as any regular parents. Now the boy is engaged and wants to bring his intended and her straight-laced parents to meet his father—but* not *his "mother." Before, the song has been sung in quick-tempo mockery. Now it is sung slowly and with fierce dignity.*

> I am what I am.
> I am my own special creation
> So, come take a look
> Give me the hook or an ovation
> It's my world
> that I want to take a little pride in
> my world, and it's
> not a place I have to hide in
> Life's not worth a damn,
> 'til you can say "Hey world,
> I am what I am."
>
> I am what I am, . . .
> and what I am needs no excuses.
> I deal my own deck,
> sometimes the ace,
> sometimes, the deuces. . . .
>
> It's high time that I
> blow my horn and sound my trumpet,
> High time, and if
> you don't like it, you can lump it.
> Life's not worth a damn
> 'til you can say "Hey, world,
> I am what I *am!*"

▷ Questions

The singer has come through a hell he did not himself choose and, at least according to his lights, has made the best of it. His situation is extreme and dramatic, and yet each of us is born into a family, a point in history, we did not choose. Each of us has been affected by others' choices and others' treatment of us. Can you face the fact that the singer is gay and see something that the song says to you?

The Serenity Prayer says: "God, grant me the serenity to accept the things I cannot change, the courage to change the things I can, and the wisdom to know the difference."

What are the things about yourself that simply can't be changed? What are the things that can be changed? How? When?

There is no birth of conscience without pain.
Carl Jung

68

THEME

CHARACTER > PERSONALITY

Each of us has a personality—the visible aspect of oneself as it impresses others and from which they make educated guesses about the person who resides within. Some people try to "work at" *being* a personality. Others hide within someone else's personality by imitating film stars or athletes or musicians. But most of us don't have to "work at" it; most personalities basically develop from our reacting to other people, especially to our parents in our earliest years.

The first child of very domineering parents, for instance, may react to them in fear, developing constant worries about not succeeding—even in situations where the parents are unaware or couldn't care less. First children carry that mind-set, that way of dealing with people, out into their neighborhood games with other children: they are fearful, afraid to compete, lest they be mocked. They carry it into school, into work, into marriage. They have developed a defensive personality.

The second child of the same parents may see what a sack of nerves the parents have made of the older sibling and swear by all that's holy and unholy they will not suffer the same fate. Second children sneer at the parents, stand up to them, and carry the same stiff-chinned, I-dare-you attitude into games, school, work, and marriage. They have developed an aggressive personality.

The unexamined life is not worth living.
Socrates

According to the ancient Enneagram—basic personality types—there are nine basic states of mind that children can form very early and that continue throughout their lives. Each type has a quality all its own; no type is better or worse; each has its advantages and liabilities that if the individual understands them, can help him or her to maximize advantages and curtail its liabilities. Resources on the Enneagram describe the nine types and suggest examples of each:

The Reformer: Organized and keen on justice, but can also become self-righteous and perfectionistic (William F. Buckley, Ralph Nader, Senator Joseph McCarthy).

The Helper: Caring and generous, but can also become possessive and manipulative (Eleanor Roosevelt, Bill Cosby, Jerry Lewis).

The Climber: Self-assured and competitive, but can also become narcissistic, self-absorbed, and hostile (Abraham Lincoln, Barbra Streisand, Al Sharpton).

The Artist: Creative and intuitive, but can also become introverted and depressive (Lawrence Olivier, Gerard Manley Hopkins, Blanche du Bois).

The Thinker: Perceptive and analytical, but can also become eccentric and paranoid (Albert Einstein, Howard Hughes, Doctor Frankenstein).

The Team Player: Likable and dutiful, but can also become dependent and masochistic (Rob Reiner, Robert Kennedy, G. Gordon Liddy).

The Sampler: Accomplished and spontaneous, but can also become excessive and manic (Leonard Bernstein, Peter Pan, Zonker Harris).

The Boss: Self-confident and forceful, but can also become combative and vengeful (Lee Iacocca, Sean Penn, The Godfather).

The Peacemaker: Serene and reassuring, but can also become passive and neglectful (Dag Hammarskold, Ronald Reagan, Neville Chamberlain).

Your basic personality just sort of "happens" as a result not so much of your own effort but of your own *reactions* to other people. Character is quite another matter indeed. Character you have to *work* to develop. It takes a great deal of exploring, pondering, and reasoning to discover a *personally* validated self. Character results from standing up to tough decisions when the most appealing option is definitely the wrong option. A person of character makes choices not as a result of what others—parents and teachers on the one side, media and peers on the other—believe to be true (the Superego), nor as a result of what one personally *wants* to be true (the Id), but as a result of what one personally *knows* from analyzed experience to be true (the Ego).

A person of character *deserves* respect not only from others but from himself or herself. To those without such self-confidence, those who genuinely have character seem to be arrogant—simply because, in a sheepfold, anyone with the courage and conviction to stand up and be counted (when the sheep wouldn't dare) looks arrogant.

The problem isn't with the valid self-respect within the person in question; the problem is with the cramped point of view of the one passing judgment. The self-validated person has gone through a great deal of painful soul-searching to be able to say, in all humility and honesty: "I am what I am. I am a good person. And I don't need anyone else to prove that to me."

The reason so few have the courage to accept their own basic goodness comes, I think, from something as trivial as a mistranslation of a word in the saying "Pride goeth before the fall! Those whom the gods will smite they first make proud." In each case, the word translated as "pride" or "proud" is the Greek *hubris,* which to a Greek did not at all mean a genuine pride in a job well done or a life lived as well as a flawed human being could hope for. Hubris is "arrogance," or narcissism: the refusal even to consider one's real flaws and faults and wickednesses.

Anyone reading these pages has the right to say: "Yes, I have my flaws; I make mistakes. But I'm a good person. And I don't need anyone else to prove that to me." Say it. I *dare* you. It's true. Are the people who love you crazy? Blind? Just tolerant? I'll bet they know the true you better than you know yourself. They are not as blinded by overconcern for your shortcomings as you are. Write a list of things you hate about yourself. Now divide them into two lists: one, the things that can't be changed; the other, the things that can be changed. Throw the list of the things that can't be changed into the fireplace and keep the other. And start doing something about them.

Be more concerned with your character than with your reputation, because your character is what you are, while your reputation is merely what others think of you.
John Wooden

The things that can't be changed are all the things you moan about that start "If only . . . ," "If only my parents hadn't been divorced; if only I were six foot six; if only I were white; if only we were rich; if only I hadn't lost my leg; if only. . . ." *If only* are the two most wasted words in any language because anything that comes after them is automatically and utterly impossible. Thus, to yearn for them to change is as useless—and frustrating—as wishing the sea weren't salty and that it rained only at night and that people weren't capable of making dumb mistakes.

Until you toss all the "If only's" overboard, you're never going to get off the ground. You're living in a world that doesn't exist. You'll never take possession of your own self—evolve a personal character—until you resolve to work only with what you *have.* Stop fretting over what you haven't got and start discovering what you have got. Then you have a chance. Till then, you're your own worst enemy.

Here are two ways to avoid developing character and self-respect: the defensive and the offensive (in both senses).

Many people would rather die than think. Most of them do. Bertrand Russell

Defensive Evasions

One defensive stance against self-respect is *scapegoating:* blaming everything you are on your parents, the economy, your skin color, your mean siblings, or unfair teachers. Of course you've been the victim of other people's unkindness and stupidity and insensitivity. Of course you have scars inflicted by others. We all do. But from today forward, take possession of what's left—scars and all. From now on say, *"I* take responsibility for who I am, what I do, and what I say. 'I am what I am'—And what I am *makes* no excuses."

Another defensive stance against self-respect is *minimalism:* settling for whatever you can get from the least input. Somewhere around second grade, when school stops being fun and becomes merely a drudge job or mindless imprisonment, you can pretty well start sorting any class into three groups: the self-starters who really want to achieve; the other-motivated who work their tails off to please their parents; and the majority who listlessly listen, cram at the end, and get by. Nobody with self-respect would settle for "the gentleman's 70." Nobody with self-respect would demean himself or herself to cheat for a few points on a test that in two weeks they'll forget they've even taken. Nobody with self-respect would give less than the best, not just on the playing field but also in the classroom and at the desk at night.

Still another defensive stance against self-respect is *withdrawal:* putting your head in the sand like an ostrich and denying there are any problems at all. Some withdraw into shyness, music, hobbies, a job. But the truth doesn't go away. You'll pay for the binge tomorrow; the credit card bills come at the end of the month; the SATs and the final get closer every day. In withdrawing from unpleasant realities, Id-dominated ostriches withdraw from precisely the conflicts one needs to conquer in order to have character, in order to have the *right* to self-respect.

Offensive Evasions

One offensive evasion of self-respect is *masks:* trying to cover up what you fear is a Big Nothing (you) with an aggressive facade that makes you look like someone who *is* Somebody—a rock star, a movie actor, a model. Some of the get-ups young people wear to attract attention would be laughable— if they weren't so pitiful. Those who wear the garish makeup and the leather-and-studs and the earrings and the Woodsman's Chic say they're "expressing themselves." Well, if "themselves" is nothing more than their clothing and their jewelry, then the "self" is purely surface. What the costumes cry out is: "There's nobody home inside!" Much of the external "self" is put on to get the approval of others. But why would anyone want to buy the friendship of someone whose judgment depended only on the surface "you"? Why would anyone crave the approval of a bunch of cliquish, condescending snobs?

Another offensive evasion of self-respect is *competition:* trying to purchase approval and respect from the outside to compensate for the lack of approval and respect on the inside. Competition is a fine thing, a good motivator, an exhilarating challenge to do better. But—like all other things on the face of the earth—it's a good servant but a very bad master. When a guy is willing to bet he can beat you at anything under the sun, when a girl has to keep asking her mirror, "Who is the fairest of them all?" there's something radically wrong. What's worse is that competition doesn't *prove* anything after the newspapers reporting the score or the prom queen are trashed. The person without *inner* conviction of self-worth or self-respect always has to go for another gold medal . . . and another . . . and then die.

Still another offensive evasion of self-respect is *perfectionism:* never being satisfied with what one has accomplished; always picking holes in it (before somebody else does). Of course it's good to learn from your mistakes, to try to do better next time, but not when it's going to make you feel lousy over a job you did your best at and have reason to take legitimate pride in. Some fathers, from the best of intentions, tell their sons that if they can't throw from home to second, aim for center field. All well and good, as long as when the kid can finally throw to second base he doesn't go on hating himself for not being able to hit center field. Impossible dreams are just that: impossible. Human beings are not perfectible; they're only endlessly improvable. Until you settle for that—for reality— you'll continue to be frustrated, fighting the truth. And you'll never give yourself the respect you genuinely deserve.

If a man has no enemies, he has no character.

Frank Sinatra

Character

Character—self-respect that refuses to demean itself—has need of two seemingly contradictory qualities: vulnerability and spine. On the one hand, you have to put down your guard against the truth and other people; on the other hand, you have to commit yourself firmly to what you know to be the truth and be willing to stand up and defend what you believe.

Vulnerability is essential to human growth. If humanity rises above animality, we are capable of knowing, loving, and growing, but there have to be *better* answers than the ones we've had so far. We can learn to love *more* people and on a consistently deeper level. To become more and more humanized, we have to be *humble* before the truth, wherever it leads, and humble before the other person who can open deeper and deeper levels of himself or herself to you—and in so doing open deeper and deeper levels of your self.

Every year I teach I have people play "Trust." It's a game in which one person reassures the person in front and then asks that person to fall back further and further. The person behind has only one purpose: to keep the person falling from getting hurt. Invariably, the person in front—even a hockey player who last Saturday fearlessly skated 90 miles an hour down the ice—will turn around and snap, "You're *there*, right? You're not gonna *pull* anything!" Paranoia, even among pals.

Nine times out of ten when you place your trust in others, they will reward your trust with new friendships. Of course one out of ten times you're going to be betrayed, and rather than risk that one-out-of-ten betrayal, you give up those other nine potential friends. Foolish, really, but very few people have the courage to be vulnerable.

Commitment, or spine, is also essential to the formation of character. If you're willing to accept everything, then you stand for nothing. Yet, especially nowadays when things change— or seem to—so often and rapidly, most of us balk at commitment. We prefer to "keep an open mind" in case something better comes along, not realizing the *most* open mind is an empty head. Chesterton said, "Art, like morality, consists in drawing a line somewhere." Unless you say, "Thus far; no further," you are only a walking reaction to other people's choices.

Once you reason your way to an opinion (not just mull it over, but gather the evidence, sift it, draw a conclusion), then you have to stand up and defend it—no matter what anyone else says. If they offer substantial and just criticism, then you go back and work the opinion over and try it out again. Having a personality is inevitable; having character takes work.

Most likely, sharks and tigers never suffer doubt. Only humans do. Like genuine guilt, genuine doubt is a hunch things aren't as right as they should be, that ideas you've been content with so far need retuning—or perhaps complete rethinking. No problem with that, as long as you sit down and figure out a better answer. It's what we were born for. Our humanity is an invitation to evolve an ever-richer self.

Humankind cannot stand too much reality.
—T.S. ELIOT

DILEMMA

Corlene Stewart is a very gifted black girl who has worked very hard in school, determined to be an attorney and pay back her hardworking, blue-collar parents for all they have sacrificed so that their five children could have a better life. Her father has worked two jobs for five years so that she could go to an academically and socially exclusive school. She has a very good chance of an Ivy League scholarship that is given each year to the student at this school who has the highest SAT score.

But most of the other students in the school have taken a high-powered preparation course for the SATs that Corlene's family simply couldn't afford. They have a definite and unfair advantage.

Corlene's boyfriend, Kamal, is a student at the same school and is probably as bright as she is, but Kamal turns his intelligence more to get-rich-quick schemes than to the books. On the afternoon before the SAT exam, the assistant principal had asked him and two other boys to carry the bundles of exams into the office. As the assistant principal put the exams in the safe, Kamal memorized the combination and purposely dropped a bundle so that the strap of one broke, though the exams remained sealed. That night he broke into the school, stole the exam, and gave it to Corlene. At first Corlene was reluctant to take it, but Kamal convinced her that this rectified the injustice of the others' unfair advantage. At about 4:00 A.M., he took the resealed exam back and put it in the broken bundle, locked the safe, and left.

▷ *Questions*

Corlene did in fact achieve the highest score in the school and did receive a scholarship. Now her conscience is beginning to trouble her. She can't eat or sleep or study. Did Corlene's "highest score" and scholarship contribute to her self-respect? Why can't she eat or sleep or study?

FAITH REFLECTION

In the earliest days of the Church there was a dispute between those converted Christians who had been Jews and those who had been Gentiles over whether Gentiles had to become Jews and undergo circumcision before they could become Christians—even though Jesus' openness to the Gentiles had been obvious. As you read the passage, recall that Paul was a Johnny-come-lately to the new community and that Peter was a peacemaker.

> *When Peter came to Antioch, I opposed him in public, because he was clearly wrong. Before some men who had been sent by James arrived there, Peter had been eating with the Gentile brothers. But after these men arrived, he drew back and would not eat with the Gentiles, because he was afraid of those who were in favor of circumcising them. The other Jewish brothers also started acting like cowards along with Peter; and even Barnabas was swept along by their cowardly action. When I saw that they were not walking a straight path in line with the truth of the gospel, I said to Peter in front of them all, "You are a Jew, yet you have been living like a Gentile, not like a Jew. How, then, can you try to force Gentiles to live like Jews?"*
>
> Galatians 2:11–14

Describe Paul's character—his confidence in a self he had painfully forged with God's help. How do his specific words and actions in this episode reveal that character correctly? Then describe a situation in which you were faced with a challenge that called you to exercise character and that also strengthened your character. Finally, try to explain what habits you have developed that give you an honest sense of self-respect.

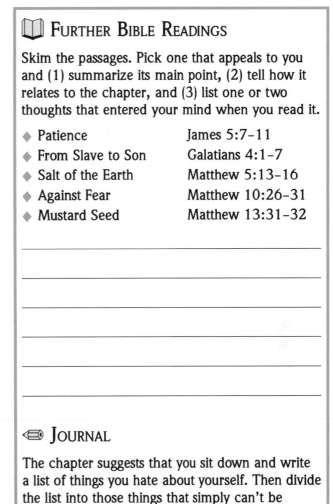

FURTHER BIBLE READINGS

Skim the passages. Pick one that appeals to you and (1) summarize its main point, (2) tell how it relates to the chapter, and (3) list one or two thoughts that entered your mind when you read it.

- Patience — James 5:7–11
- From Slave to Son — Galatians 4:1–7
- Salt of the Earth — Matthew 5:13–16
- Against Fear — Matthew 10:26–31
- Mustard Seed — Matthew 13:31–32

_____

_____

_____

_____

_____

_____

JOURNAL

The chapter suggests that you sit down and write a list of things you hate about yourself. Then divide the list into those things that simply can't be changed and those things that—with a great deal of effort perhaps—can be changed. Do it.

Understanding Self-Respect

REVIEW

1. What is the difference between character and personality?
2. Explain these statements:

    a. Personality we develop in antagonism to other people; character we have to fight for.

    b. A person of character *deserves* respect.

3. What is the difference between genuine "pride" and "arrogance"? Why is the refusal to perceive that difference so destructive of self-esteem?
4. Why are *If only* the two most wasted words in any language?
5. What is the difference between defensive and offensive ways of avoiding self-esteem?
6. Name some of the concrete ways one can avoid self-esteem, both defensively and offensively.
7. Explain why commitment is essential to the formation of character.

DISCUSS

1. If you had the choice, would you be the equivalent of gifted Lance and Dirk or the equivalent of the limited—but more challenged—Ayrehead? Why? Does being challenged honestly mean a great deal to you, or do you just like thinking that it does?
2. Why is vulnerability essential to human growth? Why is vulnerability so difficult, especially today?
3. What does competition prove about one's internal worth? It does prove something important, but does it *necessarily* cause a change in a person's *internal* self-esteem? Do you know anyone (no names) who is externally very successful and yet internally "empty"?
4. What are some of the concrete ways you see people on your grade level scapegoating? Minimalizing? Withdrawing? Wearing masks? Competing-for-the-sake-of-competing? Being a perfectionist? If you can answer those questions, you might lessen whatever unhappiness there is in your school.
5. Describe one time that you, however reluctantly, placed your trust in someone you certainly *dis*trusted and the wager paid off.
6. Describe one time that you trusted your*self* when you really felt you had no reason to trust yourself, and yet it ultimately paid off.

ACTIVITIES

1. Interview a person of your religious faith who you feel lives a genuinely fulfilled life. First, of course, you have to define for yourself what "genuinely fulfilled" means. Then ask the person why she or he seems to "have it all together." It might be a signpost for you to get it all together yourself.
2. Play the game Trust. Then describe the feeling in your gut when you finally let go and fell all the way, having placed your trust completely in someone else to break your fall. Why is placing that kind of trust in someone so difficult?
3. Look around the room and count how many people you have never had lunch with or have never spent ten minutes talking to. How long have you "known" them? Are there any students whose names you're unsure of? Why? Is there anyone in the room you're *certain* is unredeemably "nasty"? If you have identified someone, what objective evidence do you have to back up your opinion?
4. "Look, Ray," Vinnie said, "if the poor sap gave us a take-home, she *musta* known at least some of us would work on it together, no? I mean, is anybody *that* stupid?"

    "Vinnie, back off! Okay? Somebody's bound to find out. My old man'd kill me. She put us on our honor."

    "Ray-babe, listen. The sectionals are one week after the grades come out. I don't know diddly about this stuff; you're practically a world-class expert."

    "So? What about the essay parts?"

    "So we make a few mistakes. I can't be *too* good, right? She'd faint."

    "If you spent as much time with the books as you do with the ol' charm, Vinnie . . ."

    "Ya get more with personality, babe, than ya do with a lotta junk from books."

    "I don't like this whole thing, ya know?"

    "Ray, ya wanna lose the sectionals for us?"

    "Of course not."

    "And think about me! All the college scouts'll be there. Am I gonna get into college on my *grades?*"

    "I never did anything like this in my whole life, Vinnie."

    "So? It's like anything else. Once ya get usta it, ya can stop worryin' about it, right?"

    Role-play the continuation of the conversation. Choose the side you really believe has the stronger argument.

76

7. NARCISSISM

SURVEY

Circle the number on the rating scale under each statement that best reflects your opinion about that statement. On the scale

+2 = strongly agree,
+1 = agree,
 0 = can't make up my mind,
-1 = disagree,
-2 = strongly disagree.

Then share the reasons for your opinion.

1. The general "blah" feeling is caused not by bad people but by dull people.

   +2 +1 0 -1 -2

2. People wouldn't feel so helpless if they took charge of their own lives.

   +2 +1 0 -1 -2

3. As soon as you compromise with others, you start to sell out.

   +2 +1 0 -1 -2

4. In today's threatening society, it's wise to keep your guard up all the time.

   +2 +1 0 -1 -2

5. Admitting your mistakes to others is a sign of weakness.

   +2 +1 0 -1 -2

6. Nothing succeeds like the appearance of success.

   +2 +1 0 -1 -2

7. Most of the people on radio and TV talk shows are really worth listening to.

   +2 +1 0 -1 -2

8. Suicide, drug-addiction, and self-pity have a great deal in common.

   +2 +1 0 -1 -2

9. In modern society, surface personality is more prized than depth of character.

   +2 +1 0 -1 -2

10. Anyone addicted to the mirror is paralyzed from making any growth.

   +2 +1 0 -1 -2

A FABLE
THE LAST WORD

Once upon a time there was this boy named Narcissus. I mean, this kid was so beautiful one look would send Rob Lowe in panic to a plastic surgeon. He could hardly go out of the house without some damsel falling into a dead faint from the shock. Middle-aged women started to breathe so heavily when he passed by they thought they were having angina attacks—but worth the price. To Narcissus, that was pretty irritating.

Even though it had been happening since his cradle days, Narcissus was puzzled because he'd never seen his own face. At his birth an old soothsayer promised his mother that Narcissus would live to a ripe old age if he never saw his face. So his mother broke every mirror in the house and forbade him ever to look at one, on pain of his life. And Narcissus was not only obedient but very fond of living—even though it meant being pestered every moment by adoring young girls, lovely as flowers, swooning every time he walked down the street.

One of the many young ladies in constant pursuit of young Narcissus was a nymph named Echo who had been punished by Hera, queen of the gods, for telling long and zesty stories. Hera decreed that since Echo delighted in having the last word, she could have it—but not the power to speak the first. She could only repeat the last thing anyone else said.

One day when Narcissus was out hunting alone in the woods, Echo followed him, longing to speak to him, but unable to speak first. At last Narcissus began to suspect he was being followed.

"Is there anyone here?" he called.

"Here!" Echo answered.

"Come out where I can see you," Narcissus called.

"I can see you," Echo answered.

"Well, I want to see you."

"I want to see you!" Echo cried and ran out of the bushes, embracing Narcissus and covering his face with wet happy-puppy kisses.

Narcissus wrestled away from her and scrubbed at his cheeks, trying to bat away her sloppy advances. "I'll die before I give you power over me!" he cried.

"I give you power over me!" Echo pleaded.

But Narcissus was gone, and Echo sat there grieving, pining away till she was paler than smoke. In her heart she prayed that, one day, Narcissus would also fall in love with someone who refused to love him in return. And the gods were listening.

As Narcissus pushed angrily through the brush, his cheeks burning with shame at having been so rudely put upon, he came to the clearest crystal spring he had ever seen. It was so deep and pure it seemed to go down to the center of the earth. Exhausted, Narcissus dropped onto his belly and plunged his hot face into the cool water, slaking his parched throat. He pulled back onto his heels and wiped the water from his cheeks, watching the circles in the pool wrinkle out and away until they had quieted back into flat serenity. As flat and silver as a mirror.

Narcissus saw a face staring back at him. His heart nearly stopped. It was the most beautiful, the most perfect, the most flawless face he had ever seen. It must be some beautiful water sprite! Such golden curls! Such bright eyes! Such flushed, dimpled cheeks and perfect mouth! Trembling, he bent over to kiss this perfection, but the water wrinkled again and the creature fled. A moment later it was back, looking at him with exactly the same yearning he felt himself. He reached his strong arms into the water to embrace this vision; but, again, it fled.

For hours and hours he lay there, staring, in rapture, at that beautiful creature, his heart thudding dully in his chest, as lovelorn as Echo. Finally, he couldn't stand it.

"I must have you," he said, consumed in flame. "You are the only person in the world! You are all I need! I must. . . ."

And he tumbled headfirst into the water and went all the way to the bottom. And he never came back.

Echo, they say, came looking for him, helplessly, and found in the place he had lain only a single yellow flower, its tiny fluted buds curled and golden as Narcissus' hair. And she sat and wept and pined away, till there was nothing left of her but her voice. They say, too, that she still lives in caves and rocky places, condemned forever to have only the last word.

▷ Questions

Narcissus had everything any young man—or young woman—could yearn for in their most unrealistic dreams. But he was incomplete, unhappy. Despite all his gifts, what did Narcissus really lack? What was he reluctant to give or receive?

A READING

In this passage from The Great Divorce, *by C. S. Lewis, the narrator is watching people who have come from a Grey Town (which may be hell or purgatory) into a beautiful land so* real *that the grass hurts their feet. They are greeted by shining Solid People, who beg them to forget themselves, what they deserve, and stay to enjoy freedom from their hang-ups. The Bright People are living in a larger dimension than our own; the Ghosts are people more like ourselves.*

A moment later I heard the sound of feet, and one of the Bright People came in sight: one always noticed that sound there, for we Ghosts made no noise when we walked.

"Go away!" squealed the Ghost. "Go away! Can't you see I want to be alone?"

"But you need help," said the Solid One.

"If you have the least trace of decent feeling left," said the Ghost, "you'll keep away. I don't want help. I want to be left alone. Do go away. You know I can't walk fast enough on these horrible spikes to get away from you. It's abominable of you to take advantage."

"Oh, that!" said the Spirit. "That'll soon come right. But you're going in the wrong direction. It's back there—to the mountains—you need to go. You can lean on me all the way. I can't absolutely *carry* you, but you need have almost no weight on your own feet: and it will hurt less at every step."

"I'm not afraid of being hurt. You know that."

"Then what is the matter?"

"Can't you understand *anything?* Do you really suppose I'm going out there among all those people, like *this?*"

"But why not?"

"I'd never have come at all if I'd known you were all going to be dressed like that."

"Friend, you see I am not dressed at all."

"I didn't mean that. Do go away."

"But can't you even tell me?"

"If you can't understand, there'd be no good trying to explain it. How *can* I go out like this among a lot of people with real solid bodies? It's far worse than going out with nothing on would have been on earth. Have everyone staring *through* me?"

"Oh, I see. But we were all a bit ghostly when we first arrived, you know. That'll wear off. Just come out and try."

"But they'll *see* me.". . .

"An hour hence and you will not care. A day hence and you will laugh at it. Don't you remember on earth—there were things too hot to touch with your finger but you could drink them all right? Shame is like that. If you will accept it—if you will drink the cup to the bottom—you will find it very nourishing: but try to do anything else with it and it scalds.". . .

Almost, I thought the Ghost had obeyed. Certainly it had moved: but suddenly it cried out: "No, I can't. I tell you I can't. For a moment, while you were talking, I almost thought . . . but when it comes to the point. . . .You've no right to ask me to do a thing like that. It's disgusting. I should never forgive myself if I did. Never, never. And it's not fair. They ought to have warned us. I'd never have come. And now—please, please go away."

"Friend," said the Spirit. "Could you, only for a moment, fix your mind on something not yourself?"

▷ Questions

Narcissus was hung up on his own beauty. What is the Ghost in the passage hung up on? Narcissus had never really seen himself. What has the Ghost never seen? What is he or she most afraid anyone else might see? Don't answer too quickly; what is it, really? The last sentence that the Spirit speaks is very important. Very important. What is its importance?

THEME

LITTLE-LEAGUE NARCISSISM

In the last chapter, we saw that the root human fault is not genuine pride in one's life, but *hubris:* arrogance, self-absorption, narcissism. Narcissism is the exact opposite of genuine self-love. It has more in common with self-hatred and self-doubt than with self-esteem. Whether narcissists are hypnotized at the mirror by their flawless beauty or by their limitless shortcomings, they are locked into a cramped world in which the self looms way out of proportion.

Interestingly, the root of the word *narcissism* is the same as the root of the word *narcotic.* It means "benumbed," and both narcissists and addicts are numb to the world. Anyone and anything else is meaningless to them—except at times as a means to an end. When a group is high on marijuana, they all giggle away like crazy. But there's nothing funny; the drug acts on the nerves the same way tickling does. And they aren't enjoying one another's company; each one is cocooned alone. So, too, the narcissist: cocooned inside a mask of self-delusion.

Nowadays, because television makes the trivial important and the important trivial, image is far more prized than substance. All of us, without our even realizing it, have adopted the deadly standard of value Willy Loman had in *Death of a Salesman:* You become successful by making a good impression, by being charming, by having personal magnetism. Most of what is said by the charming "personalities" or celebrities on late-night talk shows is not worth recording even on tape, much less on stone. But somehow being a celebrity—being newsworthy—gives one a fake kind of credibility. At its worst, that newsworthiness is at the root of world terrorism: If we blow up a bus of school children, others will realize we've got to be taken seriously.

There are probably no world-class "genocides" reading these pages. Or nonaddicted pushers. Or Mafia hitmen. We get a kind of warm (at times smug) feeling that we are "not like the rest of men." We aren't responsible for the major evils of our time. But I wonder if we let ourselves off the hook too easily.

As we've seen before, we live in two connected ecologies, the biological ecology that we share with nature and the moral ecology that we share with all human beings. It's easy enough to see that although one candy wrapper dropped out the car window is not objectively that big a crime, twenty thousand candy wrappers dropped out windows adds up to a very big, ugly pile. It's harder to excuse ourselves for such a small act. But it's not as easy to see that one little lie—one little theft, one little attack on someone's reputation, one little grudge—adds up to a very big, ugly pile too. We may excuse ourselves too easily from:

- ◆ parking in a handicapped parking space because it's closer to the door.
- ◆ spitting chewing gum into a drinking fountain because the basket is down the hall.
- ◆ nudging in near the head of the line because the movie's about to start.
- ◆ snapping at customers because they're all faceless nothings in a long line.
- ◆ scratching graffiti on a wall to let everyone know that I was there.
- ◆ cheating for a few points on a quiz because there was a great program on TV last night.
- ◆ lying to my mother about what time I got in because it'll only provoke one more hassle.
- ◆ arguing with a teacher, long after I know she's right, because everybody will think I'm a coward.
- ◆ leaving the toilet roll empty for the next one to replace because I've got better things to do.
- ◆ nursing a grudge forever because it would be too humiliating to apologize.

None of those things is worth a life sentence. None of them is going to get your face on the cover of the *National Enquirer.* But they all add up to a pretty ugly pile, a pretty warped moral ecology, a pretty narcissistic society. Most often such minor misdemeanors are committed without any thought. They hardly seem worth even admitting. And there's the problem.

Without our realizing it, such seemingly insignificant acts say: *I'm* more important than *they* are. However petty, every one of them is an act of narcissism. Every one of them contributes to the ugly pile of narcissism our society is becoming.

Shoving in front of people because they're too sheepish to complain isn't in the same league as the Mob selling "protection" to small shop owners. But it's the same game. It's just that the Mob has bigger vision and more guts. Calling someone "spick" or "nigger" isn't in the same league as the Ku Klux Klan; destroying someone's reputation isn't in the same league as saturation bombing; quicksanding oneself in the "sulks" isn't in the same league with suicide. But they're all the same games.

We all have vague, ill-defined complaints about our lives. They result in the "blahs," the feeling that everything is a drag. If we could only *focus* our complaints, put them into words, and honestly accept our own part of the responsibility for things being so out of kilter, we might be able to *do* something about what bothers us and make the world a less impersonal rat race. But narcissists never apologize, never confess, never give themselves away—in both senses of that phrase.

One way to check ourselves—to focus our own particular little-league narcissisms—is to consider the nine personality types of the Enneagram we saw briefly in the last chapter and how their narcissism, their self-absorption, asserts itself.

The Reformer is well organized and keen on justice, but can also become self-righteous and perfectionistic. Is it possible you might be a touch too judgmental of others—peers, siblings, teachers, parents? Do you classify people too quickly into "us" and "them"? Are you just a bit too skilled at faultfinding? Are you willing to read—all sides—before you come to a tentative opinion? Do you feel every criticism of one of your opinions is a criticism of *you?* Are you humble enough to ask for help, or do you believe each job is all on your shoulders alone? Does the truth mean more to you than kindness? Do people whose judgment you trust ever suggest you might be a bit of a puritan?

The Helper is caring and generous, but can also become possessive and manipulative. Do you try too hard to please people so that they'll like you? Are you too "mothering" to your friends, too needful of "being needed"? At least occasionally, do you become too possessive and jealous of your friends? Are you "into" too many worthy projects? Do you, at least at times, get resentful that you've worn yourself out and nobody seems to care as much as you do? If one judges love only by the return on one's investment, it's closer to hatred than to friendship. Do people whose judgment you trust ever suggest you might be a bit of a sap?

Callous greed grows pious very fast.
LILLIAN HELLMAN

The Climber is self-assured and competitive, but can also become narcissitic, self-absorbed and hostile. Do you want to establish superiority over others by grades, scores, contests? Do you judge yourself by your looks, your possessions, your family's income? Do you establish self-esteem by having the "right" friends from the "right" places? Are you more interested in improving your inner self or only your external presentation of your image? Do you value things because of their intrinsic value or because they are currently "in"? Do you adjust your image to the demands of each particular "audience"? Do you find yourself sneering more than most people do? Do people whose judgment you trust ever suggest you might be a bit of a hustler?

The Artist is creative and intuitive, but can also become introverted and depressive. Are you unable to express your inner self right up front but only indirectly through the work you do? Are you secretly infatuated with some rock star or athlete, living a sort of illusion of friendship with him or her? Do you feel gloomy more than most other people, withdrawing into a kind of protective haze? Do you find it difficult to be easygoing and spontaneous? Are you lonely, feeling only "tolerated"? Do you find yourself "expressing yourself" in your clothing, jewelry, hairstyle? Do you spend a lot of time daydreaming of a self you would rather be? Do people whose judgment you trust ever suggest you might be a bit of a romantic brooder?

The Thinker is perceptive and analytical, but can also become eccentric and paranoid. Do you find yourself quantifying everything and taking it apart before you'll trust it? Do you collect and categorize things more than most? Were you an "ugly duckling" as a child? Is your mind far more important than your body? Do you often take refuge in intellectual games like chess and Dungeons and Dragons? Do you find yourself more involved in ideas than in objective reality? Do you avoid getting deeply involved with others because

people are cruel and unpredictable? Do you find yourself irritated or infuriated by complexity, wanting to reduce everything and everybody to clear categories? Are you more quarrelsome than most people? Do people whose judgment you trust ever suggest you might be a bit of a cynic?

The Team Player is likable and dutiful, but can also become dependent and masochistic. Have you always been known—and taken pleasure in knowing that you were known—as a "good" boy or girl? Do you usually wait till a majority of your friends agree on a particular decision before you "decide" yourself? Do you find you're only "really real" when you're with others? Do you take a high degree of comfort from being one of "us" rather than one of "them"? Do you have difficulty doing things on your own, making up your own mind, getting down to a job? Do you depend on authorities— parents, teachers, clergy, peers—to give you answers? Do you try to master your fears by facing them down with bravado? Do you "scapegoat" a lot? Do people whose judgment you trust ever suggest you might be a bit too much of a follower?

The Sampler is accomplished and spontaneous, but can also become excessive and manic. Are you perhaps too concerned about being "popular"? Are you just a bit too hyperactive and extroverted? Do you censor yourself as little as possible? In a conversation do you really listen or merely wait politely, thinking of what you're going to say next, while the other person chatters on? Easily distracted? When a job stops being fun and becomes real work, do you find something else to do as quickly as possible? Do you have a low tolerance for discomfort or inconvenience? Do you find a lot of "escapes"—drugs, alcohol, sex—that distract you from boredom? Do people whose judgment you trust ever suggest you might be a bit of an escapist?

The Boss is self-confident and forceful, but can also become combative and vengeful. Do you enjoy debating—not so much to find the truth but to win?

Do you really get a kick out of finding flaws in what a teacher says in class, knowing all the others are on your side? Do you strongly resent it when someone else is in charge? In a relationship, do you like to call the shots, dominate? Do you find it difficult or impossible to apologize? Do you hate softness in yourself and in others? Are you constantly on the lookout for weak points in systems and people so you can outfox them? Do people whose judgment you trust ever suggest you might be a bit of a bully?

The Peacemaker is serene and reassuring, but can also become passive and neglectful. Would you rather have peace than a challenge, even though the question is very important? Do you cling to traditions, tried-and-true methods, your parents' values rather than risk possible discomfort in rethinking those values, methods, and traditions? When an argument becomes heated, do you walk away or withdraw into some private place inside? Do you say "Yes, but. . . ." a lot? Do you tend to walk past any unpleasantness rather than try

to intervene? If you're forced to deal with a problem, do you go just as far as you absolutely must and then drop it? Do you put your serenity above other people's real needs? Do people whose judgment you trust ever suggest you might be a bit of a shirker?

Psychology and psychiatry sometimes give us the impression that we're not responsible for who we are. Rather, they suggest that we're merely victims of other people's treatment, led around by the Superego taped in our minds by our parents and the media and by the irrational urges of the Id. On the contrary, we can, if we choose, say no both to the untrue rulings of our Superegos and to the unacceptable promptings of the animal in us. However, if we don't *choose* to evolve a personally validated Ego, we automatically do choose to be victims. Rather than focus our guilt, accept it, and begin to do something to set things right again, we settle for formless anxieties. Being human—moral— is an invitation, not a command. We're helpless only if we refuse to help ourselves.

Character is destiny.

HERACLITUS

DILEMMA

In grade school, the kids always called Amelia "Miss Piggy," and even the most kind-hearted found it hard to disagree. She was more than merely pudgy; her body looked like a balloon about to burst. But her doting mother believed that it was healthier for her only child to be overweight than to be too skinny.

By the time Amelia reached ninth grade and began to notice boys, she felt even more left out than she had the previous years. The resentment against her mother built up to a frenzy, and she decided she was going to do something drastic to change her life. Without any advice from a doctor and to the consternation of her mother, Amelia drank nothing but a diet-preparation milk shake at breakfast and lunch and ate two grapefruits for dinner.

Within a few months, Amelia had lost all her baby fat and had become a relatively slender young woman—although there were dark shadows under her eyes—and she found herself listless, drowsy,

and unable to concentrate for very long. But she felt it was worth it to be "normal" at last. Her worried mother was relieved that it was over and began to plead with Amelia to begin eating normally again. But Amelia refused. She was not going back to that rejection again; boys were beginning to talk to her as if she were "a real person."

Her mother frantically sought the help of the student counselor, who talked patiently with Amelia, but the girl refused to budge. Her mother tried to force her to see a doctor but, again, she refused. She continued to quote the Duchess of Windsor: "You can't be too rich or too thin."

▷ *Questions*

One person plays Amelia, another her best friend or her new boyfriend. Whoever plays Amelia: dig in your heels. Think of every reason you can to deny whatever your friend says.

What do you do when you want to help and the person you're trying to help simply refuses it?

FAITH REFLECTION

Then the wife of Zebedee came to Jesus with her two sons, bowed before him, and asked him for a favor.

"What do you want?" Jesus asked her.

She answered, "Promise me that these two sons of mine will sit at your right and your left when you are King."

"You don't know what you're asking for," Jesus answered the sons. "Can you drink the cup of suffering that I am about to drink?"

"We can," they answered.

"You will indeed drink from my cup," Jesus told them, "but I do not have the right to choose who will sit at my right and my left. These places belong to those for whom my Father has prepared them."

When the other ten disciples heard about this, they became angry with the two brothers. So Jesus called them all together and said, "You know that the rulers of the heathen have power over them, and the leaders have complete authority. This, however, is not the way it shall be among you. If one of you wants to be great, he must be the servant of the rest."

Matthew 20:20-26

The mother seems to have a bit of gall asking for high positions for her sons in a Kingdom she doesn't even understand. And the sons—apostles and declared saints by the church—seem more than willing to go along with her ploy. What don't they understand about the real meaning of the Kingdom and the people who will "rule" in it?

"If one of you wants to be great, he [or she] must be the servant of the rest." Is that what your honest belief about "greatness" really means? If you had the choice to be a millionaire or a servant of the needy, which would you honestly choose? Give your reasons. Does your choice say anything about the effect of Catholic education and the media's brainwashing on you?

📖 FURTHER BIBLE READINGS

Skim the passages. Pick one that appeals to you and (1) summarize its main point, (2) tell how it relates to the chapter, and (3) list one or two thoughts that entered your mind when you read it.

◆ Pharisee and Tax Collector   Luke 18:9-14
◆ Self-Absorption   James 4:1-6
◆ Materialism   Matthew 6:24-34
◆ The Greatest   Mark 9:33-37
◆ Beatitudes   Matthew 5:1-12

_____

_____

_____

_____

_____

✏️ JOURNAL

Which of the nine personality types of the Enneagram "feels" closest to the way you approach (or escape) problems? All of the questions about the type don't have to be "on the mark," but which one rings most true? Write out the reasons you feel that type is closest to your personality. None of those ways of running from the truth is unchangeable. Do you honestly believe it's worth the effort to master your moods rather than be victimized by them?

Understanding Narcissism

REVIEW

1. Match each Enneagram personality type in the right-hand column with its most likely form of narcissism or self-absorption in the left-hand column:

a.	Image-conscious hustler	ـــــ The Reformer
b.	Possessive sap	ـــــ The Helper
c.	Judgmental prig	ـــــ The Climber
d.	Withdrawn coward	ـــــ The Artist
e.	Overdependent follower	ـــــ The Thinker
f.	Dominating bully	ـــــ The Team Player
g.	Romantic brooder	ـــــ The Sampler
h.	Aloof cynic	ـــــ The Boss
i.	Hyperactive escapist	ـــــ The Peacemaker

2. Each personality type on the Enneagram has not only liabilities but also strengths. Which of the personality types named above would most likely:

    a. come up with the theme for the prom?

    b. report a blatantly unfair teacher?

    c. mediate an argument between two friends?

    d. boost everybody's morale when they're down?

    e. organize a crew when the basement is flooded?

    f. keep an eye on the senior class budget?

    g. buttonhole patrons for the yearbook?

    h. sense that someone in the group feels left out?

    i. stay after and help clean up?

3. What do narcissism and narcotics have in common?

4. What can we do so that we are *not* merely victims of our prior programming, our Superegos?

5. Explain the statement: Unless we choose to evolve a personally validated Ego, we automatically "choose" to be victims.

DISCUSS

1. Why are the media strong contributors to our society's becoming a "culture of narcissism"?

2. When someone is hypersensitive to "me first," what is he or she actually *losing* out of life?

3. Brainstorm and list all the petty acts of narcissism that take place in your school every day. Identify those that are trivial in themselves but make your school a less valuable experience than it could be; for instance, cheating, shoving ahead in line, one-upping weaker people, and so on.

4. What are the ways narcissism can creep into a romantic relationship and make it a less fulfilling experience for *both* people; for instance, insisting on *my* way, jealousy, brooding over small acts of thoughtlessness? How can narcissism also creep into a marriage and ruin it?

ACTIVITIES

1. Pick nine people (or groups) who feel they know themselves well enough to know what personality type they are. Have them name what they might be able to contribute to a common school project; for instance, the yearbook or the prom. Have them also tell what negative qualities their coworkers on the project would have to watch out for in them. (The Reformer, for instance, often sees only one side to a question; the Boss, that he or she is part of a team and not the emperor.)

2. The door of the subway car rumbles open and a boy with a blasterbox enters. His chest bulges under a nest of gold chains and a T-shirt exhorting us all to take notice. The box is volcanic, spewing noise all over the car. From behind their newspapers, people are shooting lethal looks over at the boy—for whom the other people simply do not exist.

    Role-play this situation the way you suspect it would ordinarily work out in real life.

8. HONESTY

SURVEY

Circle the number on the rating scale under each statement that best reflects your opinion about that statement. On the scale

+2 = strongly agree,
+1 = agree,
0 = can't make up my mind,
–1 = disagree,
–2 = strongly disagree.

Then share the reasons for your opinion.

1. It's not as dishonest to cheat on a quiz as it is to cheat on a test.

   +2 +1 0 –1 –2

2. Lying to your parents is worse than lying to a stranger.

   +2 +1 0 –1 –2

3. People dumb enough to leave lockers open can't complain about thefts.

   +2 +1 0 –1 –2

4. Cheating the phone company is not stealing.

   +2 +1 0 –1 –2

5. To say "I love you" while being intimate with someone you don't care for is a lie.

   +2 +1 0 –1 –2

6. Everything that belongs to anyone in my family belongs to me.

   +2 +1 0 –1 –2

7. If I work hard for the minimum wage, I have a right to take a few things home.

   +2 +1 0 –1 –2

8. If a friend "copped" a copy of the final exam, I wouldn't look at it at all.

   +2 +1 0 –1 –2

9. People who lie to me once aren't likely to get my trust again very easily.

   +2 +1 0 –1 –2

10. When babysitting, I wouldn't hesitate to have friends over for a party.

    +2 +1 0 –1 –2

A FABLE
GREEDY GRETA

*Once upon a time there was this enterprising young girl named
Glumdalclitch whose parents were so embarrassingly poor that
she ran away to another town and passed herself off as Duchess
Greta, impoverished heiress to a kingdom far, far away. She had
been disinherited, she claimed, by a cruel father after an affair of
the heart. Greta shared the details of said affair with almost any
passerby who had a few coppers to part with for a half hour
of naughty stories. Greta told her tale so often and with such
embellishing relish she almost ended up believing it herself.*

*Business was brisk, and Greta's coppers grew to a purse
of gold. So she decided to set up shop as a fulfiller of dreams,*

which she intended to carry through—if only in a temporary way—
with the contents of a wagon of oddments she had won in a poker
game from a drunken, patent medicine salesman in Barney's Bar.

"Better watch yourself, Greta," Barney snorted. "Folks may
be dumb, but they ain't stupid. I seen you dealin' that salesman
from the bottom o' the deck."

"Naagh, Barney," Greta sneered. "There's a sucker born every
minute."

"When them wishes don't come true," Barney said, "they're
gonna come lookin' fer ya."

"Let 'em try to find me," Greta snickered. "I got a cottage
now. Deep inside the forest. They'd never find me. And I hired
me a bodyguard named Grunt. Big as a hippo. An' I'll be outta
here within a month. I got bigger plans than this no place."

So Greta rented a shop and stocked it with all the salesman's
wares: potions, creams, pills, elixirs, panaceas—the lot. Over the
door hung a sign: DUCHESS GRETA—WISHES FULFILLED IN A
MONTH! And Grunt stood just inside the door all day to check
that no angry customer came back before the month was over.

On the first day an old crone came into the shop, so horrible
even Grunt could look at her only through his fingers. Her
bloodshot eyes peered hotly from a face covered with warts and
whiskers and wens, and even the crow she carried on her shoulder
averted its eyes and whimpered.

"Hush, Ork," she gargled. "My name's Miasma," the old
woman croaked, "an' I got a dream!"

Good saleswoman that she was, Greta smiled and gave the
hag a cup of tea and let her pour out her woes. When Miasma
finished, Greta gave her a flask of "magic" lotion that, applied
faithfully morning and evening, would turn the old woman into
a desolating beauty within a month. But it cost fifty gold pieces.

Miasma whipped into her foul skirts, pulled out a bag, gave it to Greta, and hotfooted home through the snow to put on the first application.

Soon everyone in town was lining up at Greta's door to have their wishes come true. Dwarves from the forest filed in and departed with steroid pills; giants came in from the mountains for diet preparations; young girls came from far and wide to buy love potions; young boys came to buy foul substances to hasten the day of their inheritances; every village idiot in the territory came for elixirs to turn them into wizards. Soon the bag of gold had become a big trunk bound in iron hoops in the basement of Greta's cottage in the woods.

Toward the end of the month, Greta was having her beer at Barney's before Grunt escorted her home through the woods. All the patrons beamed at her, knowing that in just a few days all their dreams would come true because of this wonderful girl.

"I wouldn't stay around here too much longer, sister," Barney grinned maliciously.

"Thirty days," Greta snorted. "I got two more, Barney. Then me and Grunt are memories in this town." And she tossed off her suds and signaled for Grunt to follow her home.

Soon after, the door blew open and there stood Miasma, Greta's first customer, her face even more horrible in the flickering firelight. "Where is she?" Miasma snarled so loudly that the crow on her shoulder fluttered in fear. "Where's Greta, the imposter?"

The patrons were numb with fear. And then, just as they were recovering from the shock of this apparition, their jaws sagged again. "Imposter?"

"Ye-e-es," the hag hissed. "She told me I'd be beautiful within a month!"

"But. . . ," they stammered, "there's still two more days."

"Imbeciles!" he cried. "This is February! "We've all been had! Where is she?" And pretty soon everybody in the tavern was shouting, "Where is she?" Slowly, they all turned to Barney.

"Don't look at me," she said, easing toward the end of the bar. "She only told me she lived so deep in the woods nobody'd ever find her."

All eyes swiveled back to Miasma, who stood in the doorway pondering. Then her white brows narrowed into a knowing scowl. "Ork," she snarled. "Find!" And the crow winged off into the whirling snow.

Hardly half an hour later, he was back, cawing and fluttering, and the whole village followed him with torches out into the street and off into the forest—a host of dwarves and giants and damsels and young men and farmers and shopkeepers.

Grunt sat nodding at the door to Greta's cottage when suddenly the smell of burning pitch made his nose twitch. He looked up to see a line of flame coming through the woods. Shrewdly he remembered his feet and off he went into the curtains of snow.

"Come out!" the mob shouted.

A light flickered in the cottage, then died.

"Burn it down!" someone shouted.

"No! I want my money. . . !"

". . . my jewels. . . !"

". . . my deed. . . !"

One of the giants booted down the door, and the crowd surged into the cottage. They searched everywhere, but Greta was nowhere to be found.

"The back door!"

The crowd pushed through the back door, and there in the snow was a set of tracks: footprints and the runners of a sled. Furiously they ran into the trees, scattering great fans of snow; and they found her, exhausted and panting, clinging to her ironbound trunk like a shipwreck victim.

"If you'd left the trunk," Miasma cackled, "you could have saved your life."

Hunters and boy scouts are still finding bits and pieces of Greedy Greta to this very day.

▷ Questions

Advertising is good for the economy. It raises needs in us we never knew we had, and it keeps us working hard to improve our incomes so we can buy more and more—and more. But it also has very negative effects on the psychology and values of everyone in the country. What are they? For instance, we've all heard that "no toothpaste fights cavities better than X." Which is not saying that X is better than any other toothpaste; only that they're all the same. And who falls for that? We all know it's fake; but we all fall for it. What does advertising do to us?

A READING

In the following scene from A Man for All Seasons, *by Robert Bolt, Cromwell is an unscrupulous man in service to King Henry VIII. His task is—by any means—to secure the cooperation of Sir Thomas More in the King's divorce. At the moment he is meeting in a tavern with Richard Rich, a young man desperately seeking to improve his lot in the world. Cromwell is trying to convince Rich to betray his friend, More, by implicating him in a bribe—a cup that More refused to keep and gave to Rich.*

CROMWELL: Is this a good place for a conspiracy, innkeeper? . . . .

INNKEEPER: I don't understand you, sir. Just the four corners as you see. . . .

CROMWELL: When the likes of you *are* too tactful, the likes of me begin to wonder who's the fool.

INNKEEPER: I just don't understand you, sir.

CROMWELL: The master statesman of us all. "I don't understand." All right. Get out! *(Exit INNKEEPER.)* Come on. *(RICH enters.)* Yes, it may be that I am a little intoxicated. But not with alcohol. . . . With success!

RICH: Success? What success? . . .

CROMWELL: Sir Thomas Paget is—retiring.

RICH: Secretary to the Council!

CROMWELL: 'Tis astonishing, isn't it?

RICH: Oh no—I mean—one sees, it's logical.

CROMWELL: No ceremony, no courtship. Be seated. . . . Yes; see how I trust you.

RICH: Oh, I would never repeat or report a thing like that—

CROMWELL: What kind of thing would you repeat or report?

RICH: Well, nothing said in friendship—may I say "friendship"?

CROMWELL: If you like. D'you believe that—that you would never repeat or report anything et cetera?

RICH: Yes!

CROMWELL: No, but seriously.

RICH: Why, yes!

CROMWELL: Rich; seriously.

RICH *(bitterly):* It would depend on what I was offered.

CROMWELL: Don't say it just to please me.

RICH: It's true. It would depend what I was offered.

CROMWELL: Everyone knows it; not many people can say it.

RICH: There are *some* things one wouldn't do for anything. Surely.

CROMWELL: Mm—that idea's like these life lines they have on the embankment: comforting, but you don't expect to have to use them. Well, congratulations!

RICH: On what?

CROMWELL: I think you'd make a good Collector of Revenues for York Diocese. . . .

RICH: What do I have to do for it?

CROMWELL: Nothing. . . . Are you sure you're not religious?

RICH: Almost sure.

CROMWELL: Get sure. . . . Our job as administrators is to make it as convenient as we can. I say "our" job, on the assumption that you'll take this post at York I've offered you?

RICH: Yes . . . yes, yes.

CROMWELL: It's a bad sign when people are depressed by their own good fortune.

RICH: I'm not depressed!

CROMWELL: You look depressed.

RICH: I'm lamenting. I've lost my innocence.

CROMWELL: You lost that some time ago. If you've only just noticed, it can't have been very important to you.

RICH: That's true! Why that's true, it can't! . . . Collector of Revenues isn't bad!

CROMWELL: Not bad for a start. Now our present Lord Chancellor—*there's* an innocent man.

RICH: The odd thing is—he *is*.

CROMWELL: Yes, I say he is. The trouble is, his innocence is tangled in this proposition that you can't change your woman without a divorce, and can't have a divorce unless the Pope says so. . . . And from this quite meaningless circumstance I fear some degree of. . . .

RICH: . . . Administrative inconvenience.

CROMWELL: Just so. This goblet he gave you, how much was it worth? Come along, Rich, he gave you a silver goblet. How much did you get for it?

RICH: Fifty shillings.

CROMWELL: Could you take me to the shop?

RICH: Yes.

CROMWELL: Where did he get it? It was a gift from a litigant, a woman, wasn't it?

RICH: Yes.

CROMWELL: Which court? Chancery?

RICH: Court of Requests.

CROMWELL: There, that wasn't too painful, was it?

RICH: No!

CROMWELL: That's all there is. And you'll find it easier next time.

▷ *Questions*

Cromwell says of the innkeeper, "The master statesman of us all. 'I don't understand.' " What is the innkeeper's way of dealing with threatening situations? Is he honest?

Rich says he would never repeat the news of Cromwell's promotion, and yet he later yields and reports More's bribe. What are Rich's most basic principles?

Rich says, "I'm lamenting. I've lost my innocence." What does Cromwell's response imply about both his and Rich's "principles"?

"There, that wasn't too painful, was it? . . . and you'll find it easier next time." What does that statement imply about the effect of one small betrayal?

A MAN OF HONOR REGRETS A DISCREDITABLE ACT—EVEN WHEN IT HAS WORKED AND HE HAS NOT BEEN CAUGHT.
H.L. MENCKEN

THEME

HONESTY

In the scene, the innkeeper is "the master states-man of us all" because he has learned to withdraw into his self-protective cocoon: "See no evil." In what ways do we do that every day in school? How many Good Samaritan problems can we avoid by looking straight ahead and minding our own business? What effect does that have on the radius and depth of our lives?

Rich's basic principles are purely and simply utilitarian. At the outset of the play, there was some hope for him—if he took the advice of the clear-eyed More and became a teacher, that is, stuck to what he *was* rather than try to aggrandize himself narcissistically into a position of wealth, power, and fame that would "ratify" himself to himself but which he didn't have the moral fiber to sustain. How do Rich's ambitions parallel your own ambition regarding your career?

To Rich's shamefaced admission that he has lost his innocence, Cromwell replies, "You lost that [your innocence] some time ago. If you've only just noticed, it can't have been very important to you." Selling out one's innocence—integrity—*never* starts with major sellouts. It *always* starts with tiny, tiny sellouts and then ever so slowly snowballs.

Cromwell says, "There, that wasn't too painful, was it? . . . And you'll find it easier next time." When the snowball reaches strong enough momentum, the hope of turning back looks slimmer all the time. Like the little bit of litter, a little lie means objectively nothing, but it's hard to stop at one peanut or cashew. There is no virtue in honesty and no strengthening of the habit of honesty when you know all the answers and/or when you have a hawk-eyed proctor. But if you and your fellow students habitually lie and cheat when you have need and opportunity, you are—objectively—liars and cheats. What evidence is there that you will change your *habits* in college, in business, in dealing with your spouse and children? What happens, then, to our shared human (moral) ecology?

Cromwell says, "Now our present Lord Chancellor [More]—*there's* an innocent man." More has kept his integrity. How? By being *honest,* in tiny matters and in major matters, especially when it cost—which honesty often does. Rich replies, "The odd thing is—he *is,*" which implies that innocence and honesty are rare. It is difficult not to honor More, yet how many of us want to honor him by our imitation?

They tell a story (perhaps too good to be true) that George Bernard Shaw was sitting at dinner next to a beautiful woman. He leaned over and inquired, "I say, would you sleep with me for 100,000 pounds?" She blushed and said, "I rather think I would." Shaw twisted his moustache and said, "Would you sleep with me for 5 pounds?" The lady arched her brows, "*What* do you think I *am?*" Shaw snorted, "We've already settled that. Now we're haggling over prices."

It is impossible for anyone to be cheated by anyone but himself.

Ralph Waldo Emerson

If someone offered you full college tuition and a job starting at $80,000 a year to tell one lie on commercial television about a friend, would you do it? Don't answer too quickly.

The human ecology is a web of relationships connecting every human being on this planet, and the glue of that web is trust. I need to have at least some assurance that *most* of the people on the bus with me are not packing guns or knives. A quarterback has to have some basis to trust that the linemen he depends on are not going to lie down and let the opposition cream him. An actress who has finished her solo has to believe the people who are supposed to come onstage and continue the show will, in fact, show up and not leave her out there in front of hundreds of people, swinging slowly, slowly in the wind.

But trust dovetails right into honesty. If I have no grounds to believe what you are telling me is the truth—that the price you've quoted for your product is fair, that I can leave my children in your care without worrying all night, that your check won't bounce—the whole web caves in.

But in our day we've found reason to keep our guards up. There is a kind of all-pervasive, low-grade paranoia that convinces us: Everybody's got an angle; everybody's out to get you. What's worse, we begin to feel that the shrewd thing is to get the other person before he or she gets us.

If you think long enough, there are ways around just about everything. We all know that the ten-minute essay has got to get at least a 70. Right? So why kill yourself? We all know that seniors who graduate with a 64.6 average get exactly the same diploma as seniors with a 98.6 average. Right? We all know you can cut corners on taxes; we all know that people—especially good people—are willing to accept lies if they're told sincerely enough; we all know that everybody else is out for himself or herself. Right?

The absolute rock-bottom need is that each of us is genuinely honest with himself or herself. We tend to use words sloppily—and by that very fact dishonestly.

I WISH

> I were six feet tall.
> I hadn't done that.
> my parents were different.
> he (she) loved me as much as I love him (her).
> my family hadn't had that accident.

I WISH is a synonym for "If only." Anything after "I wish" is unfulfillable, a daydream. The difference between "I wish" and "I *want*" is the difference between illusion and reality.

*One in the wrong
may more easily be convinced
than one half right.*
Ralph Waldo Emerson

I FEEL LIKE

> bopping that guy on the "schnozz."
> dropping out of school.
> I ought to stop smoking.
> I should work harder at school.
> she needs a good talking-to.

I FEEL LIKE almost always comes before something that looks very appealing but that we know in our hearts we're never going to do because we're afraid of the price. The difference between "I feel like" and "I *want*" is the difference between wish-fulfillment and a resolution.

I WOULD LIKE

> to be a lawyer.
> to learn the guitar.
> to be more caring.
> to talk to my dad more.
> to finish this job off.

I WOULD LIKE, especially if there's a "really" in there, is a step closer to realization—unlike "I feel like," there's a real possibility *if* the price tag isn't too high. The object of "like" deserves serious consideration, but it could go either way. "I would like" is to "I *want*" as "maybe" is to "yes."

I WANT

> to make this team.
> to be kinder to my brother.
> to get into college.
> to pass this test.
> to do my best in the game.

I *WANT,* again especially with a "really" in there, may not be a total commitment, but it's "the first downpayment." As long as I keep genuinely wanting, the payments of time and effort will keep on coming. If I really want the *goal,* I really want the *means* to the goal. There is a first-class, foolproof test of whether I really want what I claim to want: What you *do* shouts so loudly I can't hear what you *say.*

Many students *say* they want a good education. How can you tell if they really mean it, that their "want" isn't just an "I wish" or "I feel like" or "I would like"? Easy. Just watch what they actually *do:* Do they get the work in on time? Are they constantly challenging themselves further? Do they read books even though they're not assigned? Do they actually *do* the summer reading—*before* they come back to school to be reminded? Do they go to plays, museums, planetariums? If they don't, then "I want" is the wrong pair of words.

If, on the contrary, a student consistently resorts to alibis, does the minimum, copies lab reports, asks for extensions ("Anybody do the math?"), then what she or he does shouts so loudly the claims to "want" an education are meaningless. There's objective evidence of that. Such students are dishonest—with themselves.

The most essential honesty is to be honest with *yourself.* If that's not true, the whole operation's a shambles from the start. If you can't tell the bald truth to yourself, you are living an illusion. What's more, you deceive everyone else as well, telling them what you genuinely—and totally wrongly—would like them to believe is the truth.

TRUTH IS THE SAFEST LIE.
YIDDISH PROVERB

"The truth will set you free" (John 8:32). But do you really *want* the truth? Do you really *want* to be free? Or do you just "wish" you could have the truth and be free or just feel you might "like" to have them? Again, you can get the answers to those questions by asking what you *do:* Do you drive yourself to learn more and more; gather the data and form a *personally* validated opinion; stand up and be counted? Or do you follow the crowd; do what everybody else does; slide by with the minimum? Proof.

No one ever said the truth would make you feel good, but just set you free.

Today, truth and freedom are acquired tastes, like martinis and anchovies. Children are painfully truthful and uninhibited. How freely they say, "Your breath smells funny; she has a moustache!" Then parents intervene with more messages for the Superego, and gradually they substitute politeness for truth and conformity for freedom. As Leo Rock says, "The mind's digestive system has to be carefully nurtured and developed if raw truth is to be palatable" again.

But only when you are honest with *yourself,* only when you know what you really *want,* can you ever be genuinely free. Knowing what you want *is* the truth that will set you free.

HONESTY WITH OTHERS

In order to survive in a complex society of unique personalities and wills, especially when people are more and more crowded together (and therefore more short-tempered), we have to *assume* that more people are worthy of trust than are not. Otherwise, no one would ever leave the house!

Think of the things no one would ever do, without at least a bit of belief that people are trustworthy and honest:

- Go into a subway.
- Walk down a street after dark.
- Write or accept a check or cash it.
- Loan money.
- Give your child the keys to the car.
- Accept what newscasters say.
- Believe any teacher is teaching truth.
- Get married.
- Agree to a downpayment.
- Pay for a concert ticket.
- Hire anyone without an FBI check.
- Turn your back on a stranger.
- Put a letter in the mail.
- Eat in a restaurant.
- Go to a doctor.
- Get on an airplane.

*Man is born broken.
He lives by mending.
The grace of God is the glue.*
Eugene O'Neill

100

Honesty and trust are what allow us to live together. Without them, the whole human web collapses into chaos.

"But you can get *away* with it!" But for how long? Look at Vietnam, at Watergate, at the Savings and Loan caper, at athletes who gamble or use drugs. The headsman finally caught up with Cromwell; Eliot Ness finally bagged Al Capone.

But even if they hadn't, both Cromwell and Capone were losers. They had lost their souls. Not that their souls were going to burn in hell; their souls were getting deeper and deeper into hell all the time. They had never "made anything" of their souls; they only made something of their bank accounts. They had never evolved; they were no more than high-level, nonhumanized animals with the added weapon of the cerebral cortex, which made them more monstrous than any beast is capable of being.

For each of you, personally, what does it really *mean* when you say, "I want to make something of myself"? What does "I *want*" honestly mean? What does "make something of myself" honestly mean?

If you're not totally honest with *yourself,* the game's already over, at least as far as you're concerned.

Then why be honest?

You tell me.

The tragedy of life is not so much what we suffer, but rather what we miss.
Thomas Carlyle

DILEMMA

Friday night Gordy Byrne had a first date with Anita Bonneville, Miss Just-About-Everything, whose father was a brain surgeon and who lived in a posh suburb several giant leaps above the Byrnes' two-family house in the city. No way could he show up at Anita's door in his father's beat-up Chevy. So he went to his best pal, Joey Vincent, and pleaded (practically on his knees) to borrow Joeys' parents' brand new Ford sedan since Joey's parents would be in Florida for another week. Reluctantly, Joey agreed.

The evening was perfect—up to the time Gordy had the first beer too many. After that, things began to slide. Anita began to steam and finally boiled over, left the party, and took a cab home. Humiliated, angry, and still muzzy-headed, Gordy got into the brand new Ford sedan and zoomed along the freeway toward Joey's house. Gordy was so nauseous and dizzy that he almost missed the exit; and as he backed up to make the turn, he smashed into a guardrail.

Shocked into momentary sobriety, Gordy got out of the car and threw up. Then he worked his way back to look at the right rear fender, completely crumpled. Gordy sat on the rail and was ready to cry.

Finally he got back into the car and drove to the nearest open filling station to see if he could get some estimate on the damages. "Probably about 500 to 600 dollars," the mechanic said. There was no way in the world Gordy could raise that kind of money in a week. His father would kill him. The only person he knew with that kind of money was Stu Masterson, who Gordy knew dealt drugs.

▷ Questions

List all the utilitarian options open to Gordy. Then give the only altruistic option.

FAITH REFLECTION

"You have also heard that people were told in the past, 'Do not break your promise, but do what you have vowed to the Lord to do.' But now I tell you: do not use any vow when you make a promise. Do not swear by heaven, because it is God's throne; nor by earth, because it is the resting place for God's feet; nor by Jerusalem, because it is the city of the great King. Do not even swear by your head, because you cannot make a single hair white or black. Just say 'Yes' or 'No'—anything else you say comes from the Evil One."

Matthew 5:33-37 (adapted)

Commitment—standing behind one's word—doesn't seem too popular nowadays. Nearly 50 percent of new marriages end up in divorce, even though some couples have stood in front of an intimidatingly large assemblage and promised to remain true to each other "till death do us part." What reasons do you think account for the rise in divorce over the last fifty or so years, a time before which divorce was not unheard of but surely not commonplace? What factors in our moral ecology have contributed to the acceptability of divorce—despite the anguish it causes the children?

Also, more and more, an unmarried couple who "lives together" does not shock people the way it did fifty years ago. What keeps such young people from wanting to say yes or no to marriage and stick to the responsibilities connected to their choice?

In a smaller but perhaps even more pervasive way, coaches and play directors find, far more than earlier in their careers, that young people will come to tryouts, make the team or cast, and then show up for practice only when it isn't particularly inconvenient. Or they simply drop out without even the courtesy of telling the coach or director. Why does that happen? What effect does it have on the school community—that small segment of the human ecology?

📖 FURTHER BIBLE READINGS

Skim the passages. Pick one that appeals to you and (1) summarize its main point, (2) tell how it relates to the chapter, and (3) list one or two thoughts that entered your mind when you read it.

◆ Build on Rock	Luke 6:46–49
◆ Hypocrisy	Luke 12:1–3
◆ Zacchaeus	Luke 19:1–10
◆ Truth and Bias	Ephesians 4:25–32
◆ Judas's Response to Truth	Matthew 27:3–5

_____

_____

_____

_____

_____

✏️ JOURNAL

Since this chapter calls for an effort to be completely honest with and about yourself and since your journal is completely confidential, how would you rate yourself as an honest person? If you do tend to give in rather quickly in tight spots or to a task or commitment that is not particularly appealing, what could you realistically do to change that? What does refusal to honor commitments do to your character, your self?

Understanding Honesty

REVIEW

1. Tell show how each character in the scene from *A Man for All Seasons* played fast-and-loose with the truth: the innkeeper, Rich, Cromwell.

2. Explain these statements:

    a. Betrayals of truth inevitably "snowball."

    b. There is no virtue in honesty and no strengthening of the habit of honesty when you know all the answers to an exam and/or when you have a hawk-eyed proctor.

    c. "One rotten apple spoils the barrel." If even one person in a class cheats, all are affected.

    d. Even if they hadn't been caught, both Cromwell and Capone were losers.

    e. If you're not totally honest with *yourself,* the game's already over, at least as far as you're concerned.

3. How did Thomas More hold on to his "innocence"?

4. Explain the point of the Shaw story: "We've already settled that. Now we're haggling over prices."

5. Explain how each of the following differs from "I *want*" and give an example in which each is used accurately:

    a. "I wish."

    b. "I feel like."

    c. "I would like."

6. Explain why if I really want the *goal,* I really want the *means* to the goal.

7. What is the first-class, foolproof test of whether what *I say I want* is really what I want? How can you tell if students are telling the truth (even to themselves) when they say, "I really want an education"?

DISCUSS

1. Why is trust intricately involved with honesty?

2. Why is pervasive paranoia the inevitable result of pervasive dishonesty?

3. Would young people be more likely to tell the truth—even when it is painful—to their best friends? Their steadies? Their parents? Their teachers? The police?

4. You come home late, way after the time you and your parents agreed on, and you give this "phony" explanation:

    "Yes, it was stupid, but everybody was having so much fun I decided to stay. I kidded myself that you'd rather not be wakened at two in the morning. So I didn't call. I'm sorry. Whatever you do, I deserve it."

What would your parents' reaction be the next time you give a true explanation, but it sounds phony?

5. In Number 4 we encounter a conflict between two very real values: getting out of a tight spot with a lie, in the short run; and having a reputation as a person of character and honesty, in the long run. No one is likely to deny that one's long-range reputation is objectively more important. But what is it in each of us that so casually goes for the short-run escape?

6. Othello says, "Who steals my purse steals trash, but he who steals my good name. . . ." What is Othello claiming? What evidence would he have to claim it?

7. Any game—poker, baseball, Monopoly—comes with a set of rules, and whenever a dispute arises, the players can appeal to the rules of the game to solve it. Where do you find the rules for the game of life together?

8. In Stephen Lawhead's novel *Merlin* a character says, "The man who does not know his own heart is a man to be feared." What does that statement mean?

9. What chance of success would there be if your school imposed an honor system for taking essay exams? What chance for taking objective exams? What does your response imply about your character and that of your fellow students?

10. Do we have to take it as a given that everyone—or at least the majority of people—can't be trusted?

ACTIVITIES

1. Divide into groups for playing board games. Make sure each member of your group knows the rules of the game you are playing. Then begin playing the game, and cheat at every possible opportunity. Is there a life-lesson to be learned from your experience? What is it?

2. You've found a wallet on the street. Nothing seems to have been removed: ID, credit cards, and $340 in cash. If you took the cash and returned the wallet, the owner would be grateful. Perhaps the owner would think that the wallet was pickpocketed, and the thief took only the cash. No one would ever know, but you.

    Debate what you very likely would do—and not what you should do. Give the reasons for your actions.

3. View the video of Paddy Chayevsky's *Network.* List all the things it satirizes about our society, its opinion makers, its members. What does it say about our society's values? About each of our own values? Where does our sense of value come from?

9. FREEDOM AND INDEPENDENCE

SURVEY

Circle the number on the rating scale under each statement that best reflects your opinion about that statement. On the scale

 +2 = strongly agree,
 +1 = agree,
  0 = can't make up my mind,
 –1 = disagree,
 –2 = strongly disagree.

Then share the reasons for your opinion.

1. In a free country, everyone can be free of any outside influences whatever.

   +2 +1 0 –1 –2

2. You can't make anyone love you more than he or she is able.

   +2 +1 0 –1 –2

3. Confusion and doubt are as inescapable and healthy as any other human hunger.

   +2 +1 0 –1 –2

4. Those who form a personal ethical code are severely limiting themselves.

   +2 +1 0 –1 –2

5. Parents should simply get out of the way of their adolescent children.

   +2 +1 0 –1 –2

6. Teenagers who reject family conformity merely turn to peer conformity.

   +2 +1 0 –1 –2

7. Teenagers are eager for the privileges of adulthood but not the responsibilities.

   +2 +1 0 –1 –2

8. Teenagers are eager to be free of parents' rules but not of their car keys.

   +2 +1 0 –1 –2

9. To be truly free, one has to make the effort to discover all the real options.

   +2 +1 0 –1 –2

10. When you exercise freedom and make a choice, you lose your freedom in that case.

    +2 +1 0 –1 –2

A FABLE
DECISIONS, DECISIONS

Once upon a time there was this orphan named Bucky who had been sold to a wicked miner far up in the mountains. The heartless miner worked Bucky all day, hauling great rocks and sifting for gold—without ever finding a grain. Well after dark, the miner dragged the boy to the toolshed, gave him a pan of cold beans and stale bread, and locked the door behind him.

One night, crying himself to sleep on the foul-smelling straw, Bucky suddenly heard a noise from the corner, and out from the dirt floor into the spill of moonlight popped a badger. The badger blinked, then shook his head in disgust.

"I've really gotta get a map," he snorted.

"Oooo!" Bucky said, his tears forgotten.

The badger's head snapped around, caught sight of Bucky, and backpedaled down into his hole. Then his whiskers reappeared, then his snout, then his eyes.

"What's wrong, child?" the badger asked. "Why are you out in this cold shed? Is that why you're crying?"

Bucky poured out his whole sad tale.

"There, there," the badger said. "Nothing simpler. We'll dig you out of here. Let's go."

"Wait!" Bucky said. "He's a light sleeper. And he's got a gun. What if . . . ?"

"Nothing ventured, nothing gained," the badger said and began burrowing along the back wall.

"Wait," Bucky said. "It's making too much noise."

"Well, grab that shovel and we'll do it quick."

"But. . . ."

"Look, you wanna stay here or be free? It's your choice, not mine. I'm already late for a date."

Well, the two worked as quietly as they could till finally the hole was large enough for Bucky to squeeze through and skeddadle down the mountainside. And the badger burrowed away to his doubtless angry sweetheart.

Bucky ran till he couldn't move another step and collapsed on the bristly floor of a pine forest. By the time he woke up, the sun was high and he looked around, not knowing which way was which or what he was going to eat. He sat for an hour or so, wondering if it might just be a good idea to climb back to the miner for a beating—but also a pan of beans. Slavery didn't look so bad compared with starvation.

Just then a robin perched above his head, cocked an eye, and chirped, "What's eatin' you, kid?"

"Nothing!" Bucky sniffed. "I mean I haven't eaten anything all day. My belly's growling like a bear."

"Hmm," the robin hummed, "fancy a few worms?"

"No," Bucky choked, "thank you. Is there a town nearby? I can work. Maybe some kind lady would. . . ."

"Follow me," and off she flew. And before Bucky knew it, they were at the outskirts of a village.

But the townspeople were as mean as the miner. Housewives set dogs on him. All the merchants broomed him down the street. When he stopped to beg at the stalls, vendors snarled, "Come back with some money!" Finally an old lady gave him a hunk of bread but warned him he'd better get out of the village quick.

Bucky sat in a field and was becoming more and more convinced mining might not be a half-bad profession at all. He heaved a deep sigh and prepared to get to his feet and trudge back up the mountain.

"Ey, uh, what's up sport?" a voice said, and Bucky looked down at a red fox leering up at him. So Bucky told his whole sad tale again.

"Listen, sport," the fox grinned. "I can set you up for life. You can go back and buy that town. Bit of a risk, but nothing ventured. . . ."

"What is it?"

"I know this guy, see? Well, we're not exactly pals. Ya see, he's this giant. And he lives on toppa that hill over there. And he's got this goose. And it lays golden eggs."

"Oh, no," Bucky said, "I don't think I. . . ."

Just then, quite by accident (this is a folktale, okay?), the badger popped his snout out of the turf and looked around, a bit dazed. He had a black eye.

"Hmm," he said, "You again. Was she mad!" He cocked a wary eye at the fox. "Who's your friend?" So Bucky described the fox's larcenous proposition.

"No problem," a voice chirped, and there perched the robin, who had been monitoring Bucky's lack of progress all day. "Do you want to go back to the mine or be free. And *rich?*"

"Well. . . ."

"Good," she said, "let's come up with a plan."

So the four mismatched friends set off for the giant's farm. When they arrived, the robin gave one wink and flew off to find berries to drop into the giant's beaker of beer at supper, a dosage she claimed would keep him asleep all night. A few moments later, she was back with a smug look to report that the giant was snoring like a tornado.

They crept through the enormous wheatfield to the windowless shed where the goose was wailing mournfully in the half darkness: "I simply can't do it again! Oh, the beast! He steals all my golden babies!" Immediately the badger and the fox began burrowing under the wall and in a jiffy were inside.

"Oooh, my," the goose squealed, "who are *you* two persons, and what are you doing *here?*"

"Forgive my intrusion, madam," they heard the badger say, "but we've come to set you free."

"Oh, my, my!" she squealed again. "How lovely."

"If you'll just follow us down this hole, . . ."

"Oh, I simply couldn't. *I simply hate, hate,* hate *dark places. And that sly fellow behind you looks remarkably like a fox to me. Oh, no. I simply couldn't* dream *of it. One* wasn't *born yesterday."*

In a flash, the fox was out. "She won't come."

"Well," the robin said. "You're just going to have to get the key from the giant, Bucky."

"You're out of your mind!" he whispered.

"We've risked a lot for you, Bucky," she said. And the red fox nodded. "Nothing ventured. . . ."

"Well, yes, but . . . it's very dark in there."

"There's a lantern by the door. And matches."

So, his heart thumping like thunder, Bucky crept into the giant's house, lit the lantern, and tiptoed across to where the giant snored like a buzz saw. He unhooked the big ring of keys and they jangled. The giant's snores turned to snorts. He was waking up!

Bucky ran across the yard with the lantern in one hand and the keys in the other. "He's waking up!" he croaked. "I thought you said. . . ."

"No time for that," the fox rasped. "Hook the lantern on my snout. Don't ask questions; find the right key." And off he went into the tall wheat.

Fumbling through the keys in the darkness, they finally found the right one and sprung open the lock.

"You can come out now," Bucky said.

"Is that fox still there?" the goose whimpered.

"No, he's gone. Honest. My name is. . . ."

Just then a roar came from the huge door of the giant's house as he saw his treasure about to depart. *"I'll stomp you all flatter than flounder,"* he bellowed and began to thump across the yard.

Suddenly the giant stopped, squinting this way and that, sniffing. Then his eyes flared with the realization.

"You've set fire to my fields!" he cried, and lumbered off to rescue what he could of his crops.

Well, the goose was so grateful that she begged Bucky to be her protector, champion, and broker. Bucky went back to that town and became the biggest banker in the kingdom, then chief advisor to the king, whom he convinced to outlaw all hunting and declare the whole country one big animal preserve.

▷ Question

Freedom is a strange thing: desirable and fearsome. Ironically, to be free costs. Go through the story once more and list all the things Bucky had to give up in order to be free. What did freedom cost Bucky?

A READING

Two roads diverged in a yellow wood,
And sorry I could not travel both
And be one traveler, long I stood
And looked down one as far as I could
To where it bent in the undergrowth;

Then took the other, as just as fair,
And having perhaps the better claim,
Because it was grassy and wanted wear;
Though as for that the passing there
Had worn them really about the same,

And both that morning equally lay
In leaves no step had trodden black.
Oh, I kept the first for another day!
Yet knowing how way leads on to way,
I doubted if I should ever come back.

I shall be telling this with a sigh
Somewhere ages and ages hence:
Two roads diverged in a wood, and I—
I took the one less traveled by,
And that has made all the difference.

—"The Road Not Taken," by Robert Frost

▷ *Questions*

We can take only one road at a time. Think of a major life decision you've made—one that really had you scared. Almost surely it didn't turn out as you'd "planned," but did it perhaps turn out better than you could have expected? If it turned out badly, is there still a chance you could go back to that first wrong turn and start over again? Or would that take too much vulnerability, too much effort, too much freedom?

You are free and that is why you are lost.
—Franz Kafka

THEME

FREEDOM AND INDEPENDENCE

Freedom is a reality riddled with ironies and paradox. First, you can define *freedom* (which is very positive) only by negatives: not bound, not coerced, not restricted. Second, freedom works only when you stop having it: When you stand in front of five doors and choose one, in that very act you deny your freedom to take the other four—at least for now. Third, freedom costs: The painful work of finding what all your options *are* before you can begin the even more burdensome process of deciding which is the right one. To be free, then, you have to commit yourself to a choice. Freedom is like money in your pocket: It's comforting to know it's there, but freedom has no real value until you *expend* it on something you want.

Finally there's a big difference between freedom *from* outside pressures and the inner freedom *to* make the choice you know is right. Consider yourself, for instance, sitting in your room tonight dutifully doing your homework. You have got a test tomorrow, and there's no way you can pass without a solid two hours of work. Then you hear your brother downstairs, howling, "This is the funniest TV show I've ever *seen!*" Are you free to stay in your room and do what you have to do, or—with all the freedom of iron filings in front of a magnet—"I hear and obey!"—do you stand up and go downstairs? Nobody's holding a gun at your head, forcing you downstairs. Then again, neither is anybody forcing you to stay at the desk. But are *you* free?

Much of the media hype leads us to believe we can be totally free. Not true. You'll never be free of the law of gravity, of your DNA, of your past. Not opinion; fact. You'll never be free of the natures of things: Fire burns. Dropped objects fall. All of us will one day die. Not opinion; fact. You can never be free of the fact that in a relationship that becomes intimate, there is not merely an animal, physical union established, but two human beings who lay claims on each other. Not opinion; fact. You may be free to get a divorce, but you'll never be free of those years of relationship nor free of your responsibilities for your children. You can never be free of the people you really love; faced with their needs, you will always be nearly helpless not to respond. Not opinion; fact.

Whoever offers you total freedom offers you a lie.

You are free to do anything you wish. But only within limits. You are free to walk off a tall building if you choose, but only once; free to withdraw into self-absorption, which negates all unpleasant realities; free to blow the whole planet to smithereens. But you—and those around you—are not free of the consequences. Nor are you ever free of your own past—not just of the "cards" dealt to you at the start (family, economic bracket, DNA), but also of the way you've played those cards so far. Nor are you free of the society in which you live, the moral ecology with which you must at times conform and compromise and contend. Your ideas and choices will come into conflict with the ideas and choices of others. You must decide—in each separate case—the price you're willing to pay to enjoy all the benefits that togetherness with others offers. And those benefits are many.

Freedom means you are unchecked either by forces outside you, which try to make you choose an option against your will; or by forces within you (narcissism, inertia, fear), which urge you to make the easier rather than the better choice.

Independence is something slightly different from freedom; independence means you can stand on your own two feet. You don't need crutches—even the crutch of approval from your peers. Independence means you can stand alone. And you can do that *only* if you have a personally validated character: an Ego, a conscience, an independent self.

The healthy Ego has at least five functions. First, reality testing, or discovering for *yourself* by experience, reflection, and reasoning, those actions which are objectively right and those which are wrong—rather than depending slavishly on what your parents, your teachers, or the media have told you.

Second, the healthy Ego analyzes as honestly as possible your own internal resistances to new insight: "Am I resisting telling my boyfriend that we ought to cool it because I'm afraid to hurt him, or am I afraid of his anger or of the hassle or of the fact that it'll be just too much trouble starting from nowhere with someone new?" Who chooses: you or your fears?

Third, the healthy Ego connects an act with its consequences: Is watching one TV program—no matter how funny—worth failing the exam tomorrow, especially if someone could tape it for you? The truly independent self can delay gratification because it sees, for instance, that drinking too much seems fun at the time—but not as much fun as a hangover is painful.

Fourth, as a result of connecting an act with its consequences, the healthy Ego establishes a vertical scale of value-priorities: Is dessert really worth the grief of eating the spinach? Is the time spent dawdling with the guitar really worth the agony of a test you're not ready for or the embarrassing grade or the parents' wrath? Which is more important to me: feeling good or being good?

Fifth, the healthy Ego rides herd on its own Id and Superego. My lower urges—moods, anger, lust—don't lead me around by the nose; nor do drill-sergeant commands laid on by parents, peers, and media. *I* choose what I will and will not do, independently of *any* outside or inside influences *except* the truth: the natures of things, the way things really are.

You can be free to be yourself only when you've made the effort to find out who that self is.

DILEMMA

Wanda Zitzkrieg mopes in her room. Her Fairy Godmother sprawls on her couch, disguised as a bag lady and puffing on her pipe.

WANDA: Gag! I feel so lousy. The weeks are twenty days long. If only I could get outta this place.

GODMOTHER: Well, till my wand gets back from the tune-up shop, you can't. Wanna go to a movie?

WANDA: Yes, but I'm not gonna pay those prices.

GODMOTHER: It's on me. Maybe you need a break.

WANDA: Yes, but I've got all this homework. If only tomorrow wasn't a school day.

GODMOTHER: Maybe I can give you a hand. Then we can go out and leave your guilt complex at home.

WANDA: Yes, but it'd take as long to explain it as it would to do it myself. If only I hadn't put it off so long.

GODMOTHER: So? Take the phone off the hook, unplug the TV, and get the mess outta the way. Start fresh tomorrow.

WANDA: Yes, but what if somebody important calls, like a *boy* or something? It's easy for you. You have so much energy. I'm always bushed.

GODMOTHER: Because you watch the late movie every night, sweetie.

WANDA: Yes, but I've got to have *some* time to relax, don't I?

GODMOTHER: Ya wanna be happy or griping all day?

WANDA: Yes, but. . . .

▷ *Questions*

What are the two phrases Wanda uses most? What is the real root of her dilemma?

114

FAITH REFLECTION

Someone will say, "I am allowed to do anything." Yes; but not everything is good for you. I could say that I am allowed to do anything, but I am not going to let anything make me its slave. Someone else will say, "Food is for the stomach, and the stomach is for food." Yes; but God will put an end to both. The body is not to be used for sexual immorality, but to serve the Lord; and the Lord provides for the body. God raised the Lord from death, and God will also raise us by God's power.

I Corinthians 6:12–14 (adapted)

The Genesis story shows that when God made everything, God saw that everything in creation was good. And God gave everything to human beings to be used to fulfill their function on earth: act humanly toward all creatures and one another. Nothing on earth is bad, but it can be *used* badly, that is, in defiance of the purpose God programmed into each creature when God made them.

The above passage from Corinthians says a very wise thing: "I am not going to let anything make me its slave." Everything on earth—food, sex, ambition, money, music, alcohol—is a good *servant* but a bad *master*.

Puritans, who had overly rigid consciences, condemned (and still do) even the legitimate use of sex, alcohol, and dancing. Relativists, who have overly flexible consciences, say, "Let 'er rip!" and go along with whatever mood possesses them at the time. Both puritans and relativists take good servants—moral integrity and fun-loving spontaneity—and make them into bad masters.

In the spectrum that stretches between the too rigid puritan and the too flexible relativist, where do you find your own conscience, your own general ways of governing your behavior? If you honestly believe you're too close to one or other extreme, what could you do about that? Don't talk in airy generalities. What could you do about it concretely, today?

📖 FURTHER BIBLE READINGS

Skim the passages. Pick one that appeals to you and (1) summarize its main point, (2) tell how it relates to the chapter, and (3) list one or two thoughts that entered your mind when you read it.

◆ Liberation	Galatians 5:1,13–15
◆ Confidence	Galatians 2:11–14
◆ Walking on Water	Matthew 14:25–32
◆ Widow and Judge	Luke 18:1–8
◆ Free and Slave	John 8:31–38

_____

_____

_____

_____

_____

✏ JOURNAL

Is the need to belong, to be accepted, simply too strong to allow you to make choices with genuine freedom, limited only by the truth? What are the principal external limitations on your true freedom right now? The principal internal limitations? Which are changeable and which are not? What reasonable steps could you take to change the limitations that can be changed?

Understanding Freedom

REVIEW

1. Explain the meaning of "to be free costs."

2. Why is it impossible for any human being to be totally free of *outside* influences on one's choices and behavior? List the elements in your life that the chapter says you can never evade for very long.

3. Why is it difficult—but *not* impossible—to be free of *inner* influences on your behavior? List five inner realities that can shackle your freedom. Are they all ultimately reducible to narcissism and inertia? If weaknesses are cured by their opposites, what are the opposites of narcissism and inertia?

4. Why is genuine independence completely dependent on finding one's own personally validated character?

5. List and explain each of the functions of the Ego that the chapter mentions.

6. As thoroughly as you can, write a definition of what *genuine freedom* really means.

DISCUSS

1. Most young people are eager to drive alone; some are eager to drink beer with their friends; all want to be treated like adults rather than like children. But when it comes to such responsibilities as taking care of the younger kids in the family, getting a job that contributes to college tuition (not just spending money), really learning rather than merely getting a diploma, many withdraw in a huff and say, "Hey, I'm only a *kid!* I'm only young once!" Why does that happen?

2. Ironically, real freedom and character require *commitment.* Freedom means that you commit yourself to one choice rather than dithering in front of all the possible choices. When the moderator of a group hands out a schedule, do you go over your calendar and identify where there are conflicts? Or do you just "wing it"? When you commit yourself to a project, can all the other people involved (the web of relationships) count on you being there every time you're needed? If not, why not?

3. One of the most obvious and continual encroachments on your freedom during this time of your life is your schooling. Other than such routine responses as "You need a good education to get a good job," what are your real motives for enduring all this for at least twelve years? Have you freely committed yourself wholeheartedly to your education? If not, why not? Now, how many of your reasons are valid and how many are hollow alibis?

4. Gratitude is also a legitimate limitation on your freedom. If I've gone out of my way for you, a real relationship comes into existence, one you've profited from at my "expense." Do you find—even against your better judgment—a real resistance to gratitude? Do you ever, for instance, come home and say, "Mom, is there anything I can do for you before I . . ."? Do you ever compliment a teacher after a particularly good class? Do you say thanks more than routinely?

ACTIVITIES

1. Choose a person of character you believe is truly independent. First, sketch out for yourself the evidence that gives rise to your opinion of that person. Then interview and ask that person what main principles guide her or his choices and behavior.

What's really important to that person? What guidelines does the person have when she or he faces inevitable difficult choices?

2. The Dunbars live in a very prosperous suburb of San Jose, California. George Dunbar has moved up the ladder to a very prestigious executive position with an international corporation. Susan, his wife, not only takes care of the home but has a ten-to-three job as a teacher of mentally retarded children who trust her and need her—even during the coming summer. Mickey, their son, begins 12th grade in the fall and, despite the fact he transferred to the school late this past year because of his father's recent promotion, he was selected last week a tri-captain of next year's football team. Cissy, who is going into 11th grade, has just fallen "eternally" in love.

Tonight, George has come home elated. The company has offered him a vice-presidency, a jump from $75,000 to $90,000 a year, plus a shot at the top. But it means another move, this time to corporate headquarters in New York City. He starts July first.

Role-play what might happen and be said at the Dunbar family dinner that evening.

3. List (at least try) all the things your mother has done for you since you were conceived—including the things you don't remember but that she must have done; for instance, the morning sickness, the labor room, the diapers, and so on. List all the things your parents did for you when you were a toddler, while you were in school, since you've grown up. What ideas does that suggest to you about your relationship with your mother and your father? About their requests—that encroach on your total freedom—to clean your room, pick up your little sister or brother, go to church? This activity might be not only an unnerving realization, but also a liberating one.

10. LEGITIMATE SUFFERING

SURVEY

Circle the number on the rating scale under each statement that best reflects your opinion about that statement. On the scale
+2 = strongly agree,
+1 = agree,
 0 = can't make up my mind,
-1 = disagree,
-2 = strongly disagree.
Then share the reasons for your opinion.

1. In a reasonable world, every day would be absolutely peachy.

   +2 +1 0 -1 -2

2. Parents' attempts to shield children from pain also shield them from growth.

   +2 +1 0 -1 -2

3. Parents should keep family financial problems from their children.

   +2 +1 0 -1 -2

4. A teacher who gives even a D to a top-of-the-head essay is not being kind.

   +2 +1 0 -1 -2

5. A game where neither side can lose is not worth playing.

   +2 +1 0 -1 -2

6. People who have never seriously suffered are the most boring people in the world.

   +2 +1 0 -1 -2

7. True happiness means feeling good and having no serious problems.

   +2 +1 0 -1 -2

8. Wisdom means humbling your mind before reality: the unchangeable.

   +2 +1 0 -1 -2

9. Every suffering invites us into a deeper life than we had planned on living.

   +2 +1 0 -1 -2

10. By the the time you are fifty, science will have solved most inner human problems.

   +2 +1 0 -1 -2

A FABLE
EROS AND PSYCHE

Once upon a time in ancient Greece there lived a king with three daughters. Many in the kingdom mistook the eldest for a man. The second daughter was cute as a Barbie doll and about as bright. Finally, Psyche, the third daughter, was so gorgeous that the castle turrets were aswarm with birds who came to sing out their souls to her, and so unworldly that all the country's saints sighed when she walked by: "A new goddess walks among us! A new Aphrodite!"

Well, the original goddess Aphrodite got wind of that little bit of exaggeration and was not one bit amused. You see, Aphrodite held something of a corner on oceanic femininity. She was also vain, conniving, lustful, unforgiving, and vengeful. And that was just her good side. So she decreed, under threat of all males in the kingdom losing their hair (for starters), that Psyche be chained

118

on a mountaintop to become the wife-victim of the Snake Monster. Then she sent her son, Eros, the most immature of an admittedly immature bunch of gods, to do the deed as soon as it got dark.

So the king, profusely sobbing but profoundly aware of his priorities, chained Psyche to the mountain and left her to die. But in the last bit of daylight, when Eros arrived to tear her to bits, he caught sight of this perfect maiden and sighed, "What a waist!" He then wafted her off in the darkness to this secret valley, where he nibbled sweetly on her earlobes in the dark, told her he wasn't really such a monstrous chap, won her heart, and . . . well, there's no need to go into details.

Things were very pleasant for a while. When her husband took off for work every morning, always before sunrise, Psyche woke all bubbly and giggly, and all day long invisible servants fulfilled her every whim—pleasant, but after a while a bit of a bore. So she invited her sisters to visit. Those two harpies were not for one moment ready to believe Psyche really was in love with this loathsome monster whose child she was carrying. "Ha!" they chortled, "if he's not horrible, why won't he ever let you look at him, eh? He's just waiting to gobble you up and your monster-baby too!" And they did a lot of very convincing squalling.

Well, among Psyche's many virtues, obedience had always been conspicuous, and thinking conspicuously absent. So she agreed to light a lamp to look at Eros that very night—and have a sharply honed knife there to lop off his ghastly head.

That night, when Eros began snoring, Psyche lit the lamp, picked up her stiletto, and looked. To her total bewilderment and guilt, Eros was even more beautiful than she was, if that was conceivable. She was so jolted that her hand shook and a drop of hot oil fell on Eros's perfect, pumped shoulder. With a yelp he was on his feet and bawling her out till sparks flew for disobeying his orders. And off he winged.

119

Psyche lay there and cried for about ten hours. But after a while, that became somewhat exhausting, not to mention swampy. So, to her own surprise, Psyche began to experience something she'd never experienced before: She began to think. Eros was burned, and yet she had to find some way to get him back—no help from her father, the price being what it was. Her sisters had proven fatally numb-headed, which left only one whisper of hope: old elemental Aphrodite.

Now, Aphrodite was surprised—and not at all unpleasantly— to see Miss Butter-Wouldn't-Melt-in-My-Mouth, come crawling for help. There might just be something to this little snip after all. But, of course, being a goddess and her mother-in-law, Aphrodite wasn't likely to tip her hand on that one. So she gave Psyche a nasty speech about being no better than a scullery maid and gave her several pretty degrading tasks. First, sort the compulsory Pike's Peak of seeds. Second, collect a bag of golden fleece from the ill-tempered and heavy-horned Sun Rams. Finally, descend to Hades and bring back the makeup kit of Persephone, Queen of the Underworld, without greeting anyone on the way down or back.

As you can guess, the tasks took more than a day or two, what with Psyche collapsing periodically from fatigue and despair. The seeds were child's play compared to the other two tasks. At first, watching the Sun Rams snarl and butt one another bloody gave her quite a turn, but Psyche kept her wits and waited patiently till they'd all butted one another blithery. Then she tiptoed over and pulled off the golden fleece that had caught on the bramble bushes during the battle.

The last was the most difficult of all. Ragged by now but toughened by adversity, Psyche didn't have much problem with the snappish ferryman, or the snarling three-headed guard dog, or snatching the beauty box, or even the screamies and ghoulies.

The hardest part was the cries of her fellow sufferers: "Oh, please! Come over here and help me! Please! Just one last cup of water!" But she kept on.

As she emerged triumphant from Hades, Eros flew to her, beaming with pride, and winged her off to Olympus where Zeus agreed that she had, indeed, performed like a true goddess and so made the rank official. Aphrodite raised no objections. In fact, some present there claim that her beautiful face radiated a kind of pride they'd never seen there before.

▷ Questions

At the beginning of the story, Psyche is not really a person. She is a dreamy, romantic beauty without substance, fit to be worshipped, but not courted—a goddess incapable of any deep, lasting human relationships. What precisely do her painful adventures *do* to her inner self? If that result is desirable in a fully evolved human being, then why do we shun even inconvenience—much less genuine suffering?

No man knows his true character until he has run out of gas, purchased something on the installment plan and raised an adolescent.

MERCELENE COX

A READING

His name was Gotama Siddhartha. "Buddha" is not a name but a title, like Messiah or Christ. It means "awakened one." He was born a prince, and his father the king kept him in the royal palace for years in order to win him over to the idea of being a king. For there had been prophecies at his birth that this child would become either the greatest king in India's history or the greatest world-denying mystic. Though Gotama's father did all he could to make kingship attractive, Gotama was a curious youth, and one night he bribed the charioteer to drive him outside the palace walls into the city, which his father had forbidden him to see. There he saw the Four Distressing Sights.

The first sight was a sick man. His father had allowed no sickness into the palace. "Why does that man cough and wheeze? Why is his face red?" "He is sick, O lord Gotama." "Can anyone get sick?" "Yes, my lord, even you." "Why do people get sick and suffer so?" "No one knows, O lord Gotama." "That is terrible! I must read this riddle." So Gotama spent the night in fruitless meditation and did not read the riddle of suffering.

The second night, the second ride, the Second Distressing Sight: an old man. His father had allowed no old men into the palace. "Why is that man leaning on a cane? Why is his skin all wrinkled? Why is he so weak?" "He is old, O lord Gotama." "Can anyone get old?" "Yes, my lord, even you will one day be old." "Why do people get old?" "No one knows, O lord Gotama." "That is terrible! I must read this riddle." So Gotama spent a second night in fruitless meditation on two riddles.

The third night, the third ride, the Third Distressing Sight: a dead man. Gotama had never seen such a thing. No motion, no breath, no life. "Why does that man lie so still?" "He is dead, O lord Gotama." "Will he rise again?" "No, lord Gotama." "Can anyone become dead?" "Nay, everyone, my lord. Life's one certainty is that we will all one day die." "Why? Why do we suffer and get old and die?" "No one knows." "Terrible! Terrible! The riddle must be read." But a third night produced no solution to the terrible riddle.

The fourth night, the fourth ride, the Fourth Distressing Sight: a *sanyassin,* an old Hindu mystic and holy man who had renounced the world and sought to purify his soul and find wisdom. An old man with a robe and begging bowl. "What is that?" "A sanyassin." "What is a sanyassin?" "One who has renounced all worldly possessions." "Why would anyone do that?" "To become wise." "What is it to be wise?" "To understand the great mysteries." "What mysteries?" "Why we suffer, and why we get old and die."

From *Making Sense Out of Suffering,* by Peter Kreeft

▷ *Questions*

Believers in a divine being have a difficult time answering the question: How could a good God allow innocent people to suffer? But, leaving aside the existence or nonexistence of God, even atheists have to face the undeniable fact of suffering. Prescinding from whether some human fault before history began caused human suffering and prescinding from whether human suffering will be rewarded after history is over, is there any positive value to suffering *now?*

If you suffer thank God! —it is a pure sign that you are alive.
Elbert Hubbard

THEME
LEGITIMATE SUFFERING

Suffering is used here in its broadest sense: not only physical pain and death, but also the natural crises that arise in our lives simply from growing. It also includes the suffering involved in losing something very good *in order* to get something better. Wind sprints cause suffering, but the athlete knows that the pain has a purpose. What, then, is the purpose of inevitable suffering in human life? What *legitimates* it? And, perhaps even more important, what happens when we run away from facing it?

Sigmund Freud discovered something in the human psyche that he called the pleasure principle: an inborn drive to attain pleasure and to resist pain. He said that each of us has within us two primeval, unconscious drives: *eros,* the life wish; and *thanatos,* the death wish.

Eros, the life wish, pushes us forward toward life—birth, growth, sex, parenthood, creativity— even at the cost of suffering. All things that make us grow—love, work, child-bearing, art—all require suffering: the loss of something very good in *hope* of something better. For Freud, the two most basic things in each of us that need to be fulfilled are love and work, both of which require suffering. But, according to Freud, every suffering *can* become a *birth* pain.

Thanatos, the other drive of the pleasure principle, impels us not forward but backward— back to the nearest place any human will ever know of paradise on earth: the womb. There we had everything we wanted supplied without our even asking: no problems, no doubts, no worries about the future—*because* we couldn't think. We resent life, Freud says, for ejecting us out into the cold and the noise, and we take revenge on life when we act destructively. This is the root of human aggressiveness, according to Freud.

Each individual, each culture, makes a fundamental choice between those two options: eros and thanatos. Heroism chooses *eros* and refuses *thanatos.* What Psyche suffered in her pursuit of Eros made her a complete person. All creation— especially creation of a self, a character, a personally validated ethic—involves suffering at great risk, leaving behind the known good and reaching precariously out for the better. That is why so many mythic stories, like *The Odyssey, The Aeneid, The Divine Comedy,* hinge on the hero's descent into hell. Because it is only in hell that one discovers his or her soul.

Now our culture seems at first glance, to be head-over-heels in pursuit of *eros* and pleasure. (But that wasn't what Freud meant at all.) Quite clearly, our society is not in hot pursuit of heroism but rather its opposite, *thanatos:* the achievement of the passive paradise of the womb, the painless, brainless utopia of *1984* and *Brave New World.* Not only are we unwilling to rise to the challenge of suffering, but we are even unwilling to submit too often to inconvenience—not without a lot of griping.

The Declaration of Independence declares that every human being has the inborn rights to life, liberty, and the pursuit of happiness. The greatest of all human questions is: Just what does *happiness* mean? Our culture believes *happiness* means "*feeling* good." But the Greek word for happiness is *eudaimonia:* literally, "a good soul." To be happy as a *human* is to be good. According to that definition men and women marching toward the gas ovens with their heads held high were happy; Hitler, capering at the humiliation of France, was not happy, just feeling good. *Being* good can live with suffering; *feeling* good cannot.

Life is difficult. Every philosopher starts from that fundamental and indisputable fact. Till you start there, you haven't started. But that is the one fact many adolescents are shielded from by well-meaning parents: suffering, without which human growth is impossible. What's more, even if you try to elude suffering, it is unavoidable. It will arise both from the imperfect way in which you are made and from your interaction with other different, self-willed, imperfect persons. The question is not whether life is difficult or not. That is a given. The question is whether you're going to try to understand that fact or just sit around and moan about it.

Psychiatrist Carl Jung wrote: "Neurosis [anxiety, obsessions, compulsions without objective cause] is always a substitute for legitimate suffering." To avoid facing the truths about life and about ourselves, we escape into games: one-upmanship, shyness, bullying. But if we avoid the truth, we also avoid discovering our own true selves. What's more, the neuroses we develop to avoid the pain of facing the truth are always *more* painful than admitting the truth!

There are three basic ingredients in coping with inevitable suffering: realism, responsibility, and delaying gratification. In the face of "the unfairness of things," take the filters off your glasses (realism), never point a finger except at yourself (responsibility), and get the homework done right away so it's not hanging over your head all weekend (delaying gratification).

◆ *Realism:* The truth, no matter how uncomfortable, is more important—more vital to your *self*-interest in the long run—than your comfort right now. You're free only when you see the truth, flat on—no illusions, distortions, prejudgments, or wishful thinking. You *did* make that stupid mistake; you *were* born to such-and-such family; she *doesn't* love you as much as you love her; you *aren't* the focus of everybody's attention; that person you loved *did* die; your parents *did* divorce. Now where do you go from there?

The truth sets you free not to hide anymore, not to get tangled in complicated nets of lies—especially to yourself. Lying is an attempt to deny the undeniable: Something's out of kilter. And it's going to remain painfully out of kilter until you stop feeling sorry for yourself and do something about it.

◆ *Responsibility:* You have to take responsibility for a problem *before* you can solve it. Maybe you didn't cause the problem; maybe it was foisted on you by a faceless fate, bad parenting, bad schooling, unkind people, or unfair teachers. But wherever it came from, it's in your lap now and it's going to stay there until you do something to get rid of it or overcome it. You're not responsible for the past actions of others, but you *are* responsible for your own future. Impotence comes only from surrendering your power to change your situation—by wasting all your time and energy trying to find someone to blame for it—and getting vengeance. Eldridge Cleaver has said it best: "If you're not part of the solution, you're part of the problem."

◆ *Delaying Gratification:* Do you get the painful jobs out of the way first so they're not hanging over you all the time? Do you get your homework done, or do you dawdle along with the guitar, then the TV, then the telephone, with the specter of homework, like an unexamined pain in the gut, nagging you all the time? Every minute you put off an unpleasant job, it becomes more detestable than it would have been had you gotten it done right away! And when you finally do get to it, at the last minute, you do a lousy job and hate yourself more. Whether it's taking out the garbage, writing the essay, or telling your parents about the traffic ticket, the unpleasant jobs won't go away. They're givens.

The truth will set you free, but first, it will make you miserable.
Anonymous

124

Psychiatrist Erik Erikson shows that our whole life is a predictable series of painful crises, or *disequilibriums,* that can be catalysts that draw our characters down into a deeper and richer level of meaning and widen the radius of our lives. Or if we evade these crises, they can strand us in a labyrinth of games and self-delusions and pitiful imitations of life. Some of the crises indentified by Erikson are:

◆ *Birth:* The first painful crisis, or shock, is birth itself. For nine months you lived as a fetus in mindless bliss in the womb; then suddenly you were ejected into the cold and the noise, ripped from paradise. And your very first birthday present was a hearty slap on the butt! But if you hadn't suffered that pain, you would never have learned to breathe; you would have died.

◆ *Childhood:* For the next two years, you were unconditionally loved; whatever you wanted, Mommy and Daddy supplied. Then, again suddenly and painfully, without your being able to understand why, the all-providing mother "rejected" you: weaned you, potty trained you. For the first time, in what had been an all-accepting life, you started to hear two words you'd hear for the rest of your life, in one form or another: *good* and *bad.*

When mothers cannot bring themselves to face inflicting the legitimate suffering these words bring on their children, their children never discover independence, but cling to their mothers—or to some "mother substitute"—for the rest of their lives.

◆ *Play years:* Then your mother again "rejected" you: forced you outside to play with the other children, even in the cold! If she didn't, you would again still cling to her. You'd never learn to socialize and discover how to work out problems without Mommy there as fairy godmother to solve everything.

◆ *School:* Then came that awful betrayal at the kindergarten door, when all-loving Mommy stranded you with all those strangers! The terror! The screams! The tantrums! Was this wicked "stepmother" abandoning you out in the woods like a Hansel and Gretel? In a sense, yes. Because you have to learn to handle problems on your own in ever wider and more challenging circles, or your life will be as narrow as a hermit's. And you have to learn industry and the skills to make a living and survive on your own.

◆ *Adolescence:* By the time you got to eighth grade, everything was more or less settled and acceptable again; you'd learned not only to cope with this wider challenge but to become at ease with it. Then, out of nowhere, secret distilleries in your body send out magic potions into your blood. Your limbs elongate and go gangly! Hair sprouts, like wolfman's at a full moon. And a lot of other animal urges start rumbling around; you thought you'd known all about S-E-X, but . . . wow! Your physical growth happens with no fault of your own, but you have to learn how to cope with this utterly new and surprising and at times painful change—or remain a little kid. It takes getting used to, but it's worth it. Your *psychological* growth, however, will not take place without your cooperation and a lot of painful reassessing of what "everybody says." If you don't take on the painful task of controlling your own animal Id, if you balk at going over all the commands on your Superego and test them one by one for truth, if you don't assume responsibility for your own self, someone sure will do it for you. And you'll be a victim the rest of your life.

Sakini, the little Okinawan interpreter in *Teahouse of the August Moon,* says: "Pain make man think. Thought make man wise. Wisdom make life endurable." Without pain, then, life is simply not endurable. To avoid pain is to avoid life. No pain, no gain.

DILEMMA

Keith Pulaski is your typical good-time-Charley, a natural born storyteller who never seems to have forgotten any joke he's ever heard. But he's not pushy. He yields the floor to anyone else who wants to top him and honestly listens and laughs with all the others; but he's always ready to keep a party moving when it threatens to sag. Everybody likes Keith.

This evening, he's sitting in his college dorm room looking at an intimidating stack of books and a pile of index cards with notes he's taken from them for a paper on "Shakespeare's Attitudes to Women," which is due tomorrow. This is going to be an all-nighter, but he wisely worked out in the afternoon, took a long nap, and he's ready to trot.

Keith's about an hour into the job, and his notebook is filling up with what he himself has to admit is "some pretty good stuff." He stretches and gets a soda from the fridge and settles back down at the desk. As he does, Artie Frawley sticks his head in the door.

"Hey, Keith! C'mon! We're all goin' down to Saki's for a beer."

"Sorry, Artie. No can do. I've got a paper for Baisley tomorrow."

"Go on. He's a sweetheart. He'll give you an extension."

"I don't want it hanging over my head. Besides, I was really making headway before you popped your ugly puss in here. Have a good time."

"C'mon! Just an hour. You-know-who's gonna be there. She says she wants to meet you."

"Yeah?"

"Let's go. An hour max. Then you can come back and push your 'cume' from 3.9 to 4.0."

▷ *Questions*

When Artie says, "an hour max," what's he really doing? Professor Baisley would, in fact, probably give Keith a day or two extension. Keith really does have a 3.9 cume. What would you do in his place? More importantly: What does it say about your character?

FAITH REFLECTION

"The hour has now come for the Son of Man to receive great glory. I am telling you the truth: a grain of wheat remains no more than a single grain of wheat unless it is dropped into the ground and dies. If it does die, then it produces many grains. Whoever loves his own life will lose it; whoever hates his own life in this world will keep it for life eternal. Whoever wants to serve me must follow me, so that my servant will be with me where I am. And my Father will honor anyone who serves me."

John 12:23-26

Jesus also said that we ought to love our neighbor as we love ourselves. Thus, he was certainly implying that it's all right to love oneself. Then what could Jesus mean here when he says, "whoever loves his [or her] own life [here on earth] will lose it? And is Jesus saying that unless we actually *hate* our lives in this world we'll never get into the Kingdom? Pause and reflect awhile before you read further. Try to find a reasonable meaning for what Jesus says here.

What Jesus is saying is that many people miss the whole point of human life—especially people who at the moment feel they're living life to the hilt! It is the same people who believe that happiness means feeling good, not being good. Just as Jesus did not condemn genuine pride but rather arrogance, so here he condemns not genuine self-love but rather self-absorption: narcissism. And when a Jew used the word *hate,* he or she often meant merely "love less." Jesus says that unless being good is more important to us than feeling good, we've missed the whole point of our being here!

Jesus makes the same point this chapter has made: Unless we, like the grain of wheat, undergo loss, we will never grow specifically as human beings. Every suffering we undergo—whether the natural and unavoidable crises of growing or the unexpected tragedies that often erupt into our well-planned lives—can become a birth pain.

That all sounds very uplifting. And everybody knows that it works in athletics: no pain, no gain. But do you really believe it is true in your everyday life: your dealings with parents, the embarrasing report card, the muffed pass, the steady who has found someone else more interesting?

You have already been asked to remember setbacks in your past that actually turned out to be blessings in disguise. Could it be that your present setbacks are also invitations?

FURTHER BIBLE READINGS

Skim these Scripture passages. Pick one that appeals to you and (1) summarize its main point, (2) tell how it relates to the chapter, (3) and list one or two thoughts that entered your mind when you read it.

◆ Wisdom and Suffering	James 1:2–8
◆ The Daily Cross	Matthew 16:24–28
◆ The Suffering Messiah	Isaiah 53:1–9
◆ The Price of Glory	Luke 24:25–27
◆ Childishness	Hebrews 5:11–14

_____

_____

_____

_____

_____

JOURNAL

In your own work to get an education, which of the two drives impels you most strongly: *eros* or *thanatos,* the life wish or the death wish? Do you really throw yourself into the jobs you're given, even the distasteful ones, or do you usually take the easiest way out? Most of us claim that we want to get the most out of life that we can. Do you? Really?

Understanding Suffering

REVIEW

1. Explain what Sigmund Freud meant by *Eros* (the life wish) and *Thanatos* (the death wish).

2. Our society seems very interested in the "erotic." How is that unlike what Freud meant by *Eros* and more what he meant by *Thanatos?*

3. How does our idea of happiness differ from the ancient Greeks' idea of happiness? What is the difference between "feeling good" and "being good"?

4. What did Carl Jung mean by "Neurosis is always a substitute for legitimate suffering"? What makes suffering "legitimate"?

5. The chapter says that three basic steps for coping with legitimate suffering are realism, responsibility, and delaying gratification. What meaning does the chapter give to each of those strategies, or steps, when it applies them to dealing with suffering? Why are they the basic ways to cope with suffering?

6. What are the first five stages Erik Erikson claims are part of the natural process of human development? What quality is each intended, at least, to foster in an evolving human being?

DISCUSS

1. Life is difficult; that is a given. If you haven't started there, you haven't started. How has that been true so far for you? Has unavoidable suffering ever proven, in the long run, to be surprisingly beneficial to you as a person? What's the difference in effect between merely *undergoing* suffering as an ox does, and *understanding* suffering as a human adult?

2. When parents ground their children for making dumb mistakes, when teachers give low grades, when bosses dock your salary for being late, they are doing you a good service in the long run. In such cases we again come up against the unpleasant conflict between the long run and the short run. Why is that conflict so unpleasant? Can anything be done to make it stop being unpleasant?

3. We've all read such futuristic novels as *1984* and *Brave New World* that promise a life where suffering has been eliminated by science. Would you want to live in such a society? Why or why not? And yet we all, quite naturally, want to avoid suffering. How do we resolve that contradiction? Is it resolvable with the left brain or only with the right brain? And what does that mean?

4. It is relatively easy (after a while) to admit that undergoing suffering is a way that helps us grow. But how do we resolve the problem of the innocent suffering: babies, old people, victims of terminal disease? Those who believe in a divine being depend on a larger context of eternity in which earthly suffering pales by contrast. How does someone who denies the existence of a divine being cope with the suffering of the innocent?

5. Someone wise once wrote that pain conquered is like forging a deep leaden keel for a boat. It allows such a person to sail through rough weather that would swamp shallower craft. What does that metaphor mean?

ACTIVITIES

1. If you can, interview someone who has suffered the great loss of a loved one, health, or hope for the future and yet seems to be nobly bearing up under it. How did the person cope with that burden? Some people manage to dredge up "something" from within themselves to keep them going. Others cannot and they dwindle into helpless despair. What is that "something"?

2. The big news in the corridors Monday morning is that somebody copped two terminals from the school computer lab. The assistant principal "rounded up the usual suspects," and the heavy money is on Tony Schmidt, who has been Public Enemy #1 for four years. He's "borrowed" cars from the school parking lot, for instance, and intimidated everybody—including you—into silence. Tony's very big, and he has big friends. In fact, you're pretty sure Tony was the one who lifted your $90 gym shoes. Then again, a lot of people have the same brand. And Tony is, after all, very large.

Only trouble is, you know it was your older brother who stole the two terminals to cover the overdue insurance on his car, the car you get a ride in every morning and afternoon.

Tony Schmidt is not only on the edge of expulsion, but because of his record pretty likely facing jail. It's your brother's first offense, but still. . . .

Role-play (1) you and your brother, (2) you and your best friend, (3) you and the assistant principal, and act out a conclusion to the episode.

3. Read through a daily newspaper and list the different modes of global, national, and local human suffering that are detailed there. Good news doesn't sell newspapers; bad news does. How does reading about suffering affect you? If we are repelled by personal suffering, why is the suffering of others so intriguing? Many young people today find themselves refusing to read the newspapers. Can you explain why?

Relationships
with
Others

11. FAIRNESS

SURVEY

Under each statement circle whether you think that statement, in your opinion, is fair or unfair. Discuss the reasons for your opinion.

1. Actresses like Glenn Close can't command the same salaries as actors like Tom Cruise.
   Fair   <u>Unfair</u>

2. Fifty of the largest American corporations pay no income tax.
   Fair   (Unfair)

3. A team's win/lose/tie record is a fair measure by which to judge its coach.
   Fair   (Unfair)

4. If you played golf with the Masters' Champion, he should give you a handicap.
   Fair   (Unfair)

5. In a race, someone physically impaired deserves a head start.
   Fair   (Unfair)

6. If someone arrives first at a counter, he or she should be served first.
   (Fair)   Unfair

7. "Why did you give it to him and not to me? I'm your own brother!"
   Fair   (Unfair)

8. Because you're trapped, airport concessions inflate their prices.
   Fair   (Unfair)

9. Strangers have legitimate claims on your money when they have a life-threatening need.
   (Fair)   Unfair

10. We said, "No strings." You've no right to be jealous.
    Fair   Unfair

A FABLE
PER ASPERA AD ASTRA

Once upon a time there was this girl named Cinderella. Well, Cinderella was just the happiest little girl ever. She had just the most perfect Mummy and Daddy, and all day she'd coo and gurgle and bite her toes in sheer bliss. But then one day her Mummy caught a heavy cold and, quicker than electricity, died. Cinderella was pretty upset, mind you. And she toddled to her Mummy's grave every day and wept and wept.

But not too long afterward, her Daddy—being only human— brought home a new wife, Malvooda. Well, this Malvooda turned out to be quite the hellcat. She refused not only to do windows, but also floors, dishes, cooking, or any household chores that might chip her nail polish. Ditto for her ugly daughters, Vomica and Hernia. All that, they left to poor little Cinderella who had to stand on a stool even to get to the sink and pretty soon had fingers like little albino prunes.

To make matters worse, Daddy was a traveling salesman and not around very much; and when he was home, he spent most of his time working on bills or with Malvooda, whose talents weren't limited to being mean and vicious.

One day when Daddy set off on a trip, he asked the girls if he could bring them back any gifts. "Ooooh!" Vomica squealed, "Pretty clothes, Daddy dearest!"

"Ooooh!" Hernia drooled, "Jewels, jewels, jewels, lovely Daddy!"

But Cinderella said, "Oh, just bring me back a twig or something, okay?" Not snotty, mind you, but by this time even a simpleton could figure out the cards were stacked.

True to his word, Daddy came home with designer clothes for Vomica, and a sack of emeralds for Hernia, and an old branch that had gotten caught on his fender for Cinderella. So, before Malvooda could use the branch to whip her, Cinderella planted it on her mother's grave and watered it with her tears. This she did every day in the few odd moments when she wasn't scouring pots or lugging out the ashes or giving her stepsisters pedicures.

That tree got a great deal of watering for the next ten years or so. Then one day, out of the long trailing green skirts of the tree, came a voice—which was about as startling in Cinderella's day, mind you, as it is in ours. Especially because the voice was remarkably like the voice of Cinderella's lovely Mummy, out of whose very grave the willow was growing. It was kind and gentle and understanding, and Cinderella spoke to her Fairy Godmother every day, at least when no one would eavesdrop and think her balmy.

Then, when Cinderella was fifteen, the king gave a great ball, in order to choose a bride for his son. Well, it goes without saying Vomica and Hernia went to the ball dressed to kill, right down to their size twelve shoes. But Cinderella had to stay home and clean the house from attic to basement to be ready when the prince arrived to whisk one of her hideous stepsisters off to her inevitable coronation.

Around eight o'clock, her rags smelling foully of oven cleaner, Cinderella lay moaning by her tree. Suddenly, her Fairy Godmother told her to stop feeling so darn sorry for herself and rattled off a list of pretty bizarre instructions: "Hollow out a pumpkin and bring six mice, one rat, and six lizards."

Well, Cinderella was used to crazy orders and well acquainted with rodents more delicate girls would faint at the sight of. She did as she was told, and the rest is history. She dazzled the daylights out of the prince three nights running, each time just managing to escape before her midnight curfew. But the third night her crystal slipper got stuck in some chewing gum on the main palace stairs. The prince started a house-to-house search for the slipper's owner, but no girl's foot was so perfect. Vomica and Hernia were ready to chop off their heels and toes, but to no avail. Of course, it slipped onto Cinderella's foot slicker than the rubber gloves she used to clean the oven. And she and the prince lived happily ever after, governing their subjects firmly and lovingly, and employing Malvooda and her two sourpuss daughters to muck out their royal stables.

▷ Questions

What had Cinderella done to deserve the bad treatment she got? How is she like people who live in ghettoes and poor rural areas, like street people, and children in depressed countries? Like Cinderella, they too are helpless through no fault of their own. Who can be a "fairy godmother" for those people?

Still, what had Cinderella done to deserve to go to the ball?

A READING

This selection is from A, B, and C: The Human Element in Mathematics, *by Stephen Leacock. The characters in the plot of a problem are three people called A, B, and C. The form of the question is generally of this sort:*

"A, B, and C do a certain piece of work. A can do as much work in one hour as B in two, or C in four. Find how long they work at it.". . .

Above all they revel in motion. When they tire of walking-matches—A rides on horseback, or borrows a bicycle and competes with his weaker-minded associates on foot. Now they race on locomotives; now they row; or again they become historical and engage stage-coaches; or at times they are aquatic and swim. If their occupation is actual work they prefer to pump water into cisterns, two of which leak through holes in the bottom and one of which is watertight. A, of course, has the good one; . . .

A is a full-blooded blustering fellow, of energetic temperament, hot-headed and strong-willed. It is he who proposes everything, challenges B to work, makes the bets, and bends the others to his will. . . .

B is a quiet, easy-going fellow, afraid of A and bullied by him, but very gentle and brotherly to little C, the weakling. He is quite in A's power, having lost all his money in bets.

Poor C is an undersized, frail man, with a plaintive face. Constant walking, digging, and pumping has broken his health and ruined his nervous system. His joyless life has driven him to drink and smoke more than is good for him, and his hand often shakes as he digs ditches. . . .

It seems that A and B had been rowing on the river for a wager, and C had been running on the bank and then sat in a draught. . . . A and B came home and found C lying helpless in bed. A shook him roughly and said, "Get up, C, we're going to pile wood." C looked so worn and pitiful that B said, "Look here, A, I won't stand this, he isn't fit to pile wood to-night." C smiled feebly and said, "Perhaps I might pile a little if I sat up in bed." Then B, thoroughly alarmed, said, "See here, A, I'm going to fetch a doctor; he's dying.". . . On the evening of the next day, as the shadows deepened in the little room, it was clear to all that the end was near. I think that even A was affected at last as he stood with bowed head, aimlessly offering to bet with the doctor on C's labored breathing. . . . The end came soon after that. C rallied for a moment and asked for a certain piece of work that he had left downstairs. A put it in his arms and he expired. . . .

▷ Questions

Are you an A? Or a B? Or a C?

If you're an A: Do you really understand how gifted you've been? How much of your talent and confidence came from yourself, and how much from others? Whom? Do you ever say thanks, or do you merely take them for granted? Are you sensitive to the objective fact that others aren't as gifted? Do you make allowances for them, give them handicaps, and share your strength with them—as others have shared their strength with you?

If you're a B: Do you let people take advantage of you too easily? Would their demands have to be obviously unreasonable before you stood up to the bullies? You have a right to be heard from, to refuse. What's keeping you from confidence in yourself?

If you're a C: Do the A's of this world make you bitter? Jealous? Why have you just taken it for granted that "that's the way it is"? You've been scarred, but scar tissue is the toughest. What would it take to make you stick out your chin and say, "Okay, that's *it!* I'm as much a human being as *any* body else. From now on, I'm gonna stand up and be counted!"

THEME
FAIRNESS

The ten previous chapters were about you, about forming a unique character and a personally validated ethic. The rest will be about you in relationship to an ever-widening series of concentric circles: our shared moral ecology. Or—to skew the metaphor a bit—the last chapters were about how to keep your personal vessel shipshape; the rest are about how to keep from colliding with all the other personal vessels. We are going to investigate what you ought to be able legitimately to expect from others and they from you—not as a matter of love or mercy or compassion, but in strict justice: fair play and harmony among the individuals who make up our society.

All human beings are created equal—red, white, yellow, brown, black; American, Indian, Pakistani, Russian. As Shylock says,

> *"Hath not a Jew eyes? hath not a Jew hands, organs, dimensions, senses, affections, passions? fed with the same food, hurt with the same weapons, subject to the same diseases, healed by the same means, warmed and cooled by the same winter and summer, as a Christian is?"*
>
> Merchant of Venice,
> Act III, Scene I,
> by William Shakespeare

Beneath all the surface differences of color, race, creed, ethnicity, or geography we all have the same *humanity.* In fact, what unites us is far more important than the trivial external variations of humanity that divide us.

DISTRIBUTIVE JUSTICE

From the very fact of someone's being human, he or she has certain rights that the Declaration of Independence says are not only self-evident (they neither can be proved nor need they be), but also inalienable (they not only cannot be sold or bought, but they cannot even legitimately be given away).

Those fundamental "givens" are: the right to life, the right to liberty, and the right to pursue happiness. Those rights are *not* bestowed by the government of the United States or by any other government, nor can they be taken away by the United States or by any other government. They are inalienable. If any power tries to deny or take away rights that come from our human nature, that power is—by that very act—evil.

Similarly, if someone tried to give away those rights, to offer oneself to me as my slave, to be treated with willing cooperation as a beast of burden, that person would be "evil" in surrendering himself or herself to slavery, and I would be evil for receiving that person into slavery. We both have cooperated in the *degradation* of a human: treating a human being as merely an animal. Just so, two people who engage in sex merely for sport, like two healthy young animals, without any psychological commitment whatever, degrade each other even if both enter the relationship willingly. Why? Because—objective fact—they are *not* merely two healthy young animals.

What's more, since every human being by nature has the right to life, every human being also has the inalienable right to those essentials without which life is impossible: sufficient food, clothing, and shelter to make sure life isn't impossible. Those essentials needn't be steak, sable, and Beverly Hills but they have to be sufficient enough to sustain life with at least basic human dignity. No one should have to grovel to get that basic right to life, nor should one have to apologize for exercising it. Each of us *has* inalienable rights, as our *birth* right, no matter who we are or where on earth we come from.

This is what is classically called distributive justice, (*distribuere:* "pass things around"). Distributive justice means that each of us, because we are equally human, has the right to our *fair* share of the pie when the pieces are being handed round.

Unfortunately, as George Orwell has said, "All animals are created equal, but some animals are more equal than others." Like A, B, and C, we are not all born equally talented, equally handsome, or equally advantaged financially. We all come into life, as into a Monopoly game, and take over the places of those who went before us; many of whom had more shrewdness—and luck—than others.

Nor are all humans equally honest, equally unselfish, or equally evolved from our basic animal roots. Some have had the advantage of consistent and genuine love, a relatively serene home life, the example of hardworking, law-abiding parents, and constantly monitored health care. Others—*through no fault of their own*—come into the game physically or psychically disadvantaged. They have had battling parents or no parents at all; lived in squalid homes or no homes at all; suffered from diseases before which their impoverished parents stand helpless because they either have no funds or no understanding of health care or both. Others may be street people, migrant workers, hill people, children of Third World ghettoes and villages.

"Yes, well," some may say, "when *my* ancestors came here, they didn't have a nickel either. And they didn't know the language either. But they *made* something out of themselves." Such a comparison itself is unfair because they were a different kind of people, and they arrived in a quite different kind of country. They did make something of themselves; but, so far, you haven't.

The forebears of present-day assimilated Jews, Poles, Irish, Italians, Japanese, and so forth, were a different kind of people. They all had a long and strong tradition of family loyalty, and for both good and bad, the unquestionable authority of the father. They came from a tradition of working their *own* land, wretched patches of dirt to be sure, but their own. There were no get-rich-quick lotteries. If you were going to make it, you made it with your own sweat. And, what's far more important, everyone in the family *accepted* that tradition. But today, even among the assimilated, tradition is a bad word for some.

More than that, immigrants in the past came to a country where cooperation was more in evidence than it is today in our ruthlessly competitive society. They also had a huge number of dedicated teachers whose sole purpose in life was to get children out of ghettoes. That is not true today. The best-intentioned disadvantaged young person simply can't succeed as well today when some teachers too often treat teaching as merely a job from which they get a paycheck. And when standards were lowered to allow everyone to pass, no matter what, the teachers' jobs became simply impossible.

Still more, our ancestors in the past came to a country without television. But even the poorest of us now have televisions. Our ancestors came to a country where *every*one, almost without exception, believed in the old-fashioned virtues of family, loyalty, thrift, and hard work. Now every ten minutes—poor children as well as rich children—are exhorted by the TV to believe that thrift is a vice, and greed is a virtue that is good for all of us.

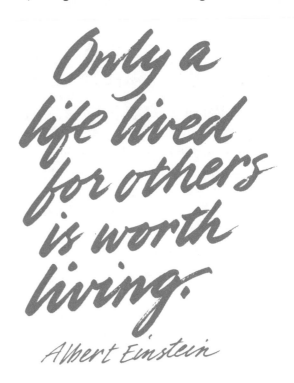

Only a life lived for others is worth living.

Albert Einstein

137

A STANDARD OF FAIRNESS

We've all argued; we've all heard others arguing. In fact, it's almost a given in human interaction: "Now, wait a minute! I touched the base *before* you tagged me!" "I gave you a piece of my orange; why won't you give me a piece of yours?" "Hang on there! I was here *first!*" "You have no *right* to do that! Wait a minute, buster! I know my *rights!*"

Without any of the quarreling participants realizing it, each is appealing to an unspoken *standard* of acceptable behavior. There are rules for baseball; and all players have to bow to them, even when it means losing out. There's a relationship set up when someone's been generous to you, and you can't treat that person as if she or he were a perfect stranger. Just so, you can't enter and walk around my house; you can't dump your toxic waste in my backyard; nor can you be intimate with someone and pretend you've never met. No matter what you think! I'm *here,* and I'm as much a human being as you are! As Linda Loman says about her failure of a husband, Willy, "Attention must be paid!"

That's an objective fact, no matter how inconvenient admitting it might be. "Do unto others as you would have others do unto you" is *not* the sole standard of any particular religion. It's the rock-bottom foundation of every religion and every political philosophy ever seriously drawn up: We have to treat other human beings as human.

Ah! "We *have* to." No. "We *ought* to." We must treat others as equal to ourselves *if* our moral ecology is to survive. And if it doesn't survive, each of us loses along with the rest.

But we are free not to.

In "Clue to the Meaning of the Universe," C. S. Lewis says,

I need only ask the reader to think what a totally different morality would mean. Think of a country where people were admired for running away from battle, or where a man felt proud of double-crossing all the people who had been kindest to him. You might as well try to imagine a country where two and two made five.

If morality changed at the whim of the beholder, we would have nothing to say to one another; and no cause to cry, "Hey, wait a minute! That's not *fair!*"

COMMUTATIVE JUSTICE

That standard of moral behavior is based on each human being's right to life and enough to sustain it (distributive justice). But every human being also has a right to liberty and to what liberty requires: private property (food, clothing, shelter) that no one else has a right to take or intrude on. This is called commutative justice (*commutare:* "exchange; pass back and forth").

Commutative justice means there is a give-and-take in human society: You can't take my private property without my permission and without reimbursing me. If I work for you for a week, you have to give me—in justice—a check in exchange for my time and effort. Conversely, if you pay me, it's simple justice that I give you an honest day's work for an honest day's pay. If you play a song I wrote and make money from it, it's only fair that you pay me a royalty. If you pay a teacher to make sure you get a good education, it's a matter of justice that you put in at least as much effort as the teacher. That may not be pleasant to hear, but it's an objective fact. Justice.

Once more, however, we run up against a most unpleasant but undeniable fact: Each of us has a separate, personal agenda that is often in conflict with someone else's agenda. We're competitive. Everybody wants to be a winner, but not everybody *can* win. We want to get the most we can—not just selfishly for ourselves, but for those who depend on us.

Owners want to make as much profit as they can for their shareholders; workers want to make as much as they can for their families. But the more money the company must pay its workers, the less it can pass on to its shareholders. That's where conflict arises. That's where we need an arbitrator: government.

SOCIAL JUSTICE

Hermits have no problems with social justice—the justice that arbitrates between the genuine-but-conflicting rights of individuals and groups within the web of our moral ecology. But if we want the advantages that come from living together, we have to pay for them.

Private property, for instance, is a right, but it's not an *absolute* right. There are times when that right has to yield to other, more important rights. For instance: If we're going to live together in relative security, we have to have police. But police deserve a fair wage. Where does that wage come from? It comes from us—from our private property—in the form of taxes. We need roads, a military, boats to dredge harbors, firefighters, and so on. Therefore, our right to private property has to be balanced with the government's right to get the funds it needs to give us what *we* demand of it.

What's more, there are many members of our shared moral ecology who, like Cinderella, have a great difficulty helping themselves—through no fault of their own—to get a job that would supply them with the essentials of life: food, shelter, and clothing. There are people who are physically and mentally challanged; there are people too old to work anymore and yet still need to eat; there are young women without husbands who can't merely leave their preschool children alone.

Some people are to some degree responsible for their difficult situations because of their own bad decisions. We, their fellow citizens, are not responsible for their being in the shape they are now in; but if we are to call ourselves people of character, responsible people, then we have an innate obligation to acknowledge a fellow human being who has a life-threatening need. We do not put the potential "suicide" victim out on the ledge, but we do have an obligation to try to talk him or her back to safety. If we have any awareness of the humanity people in need share with us, we can't just say, "You brought it on yourself. Starve."

Therefore, government—as our representative—has to intrude on our private property and help fellow human beings who, for whatever reason, are in need. Will some selfish people take advantage of their situation? Of course. But if you do some research, you'll find that studies show that fewer than 10 percent of the people on public assistance cheat the system. The rock-bottom question then becomes: Despite the flaws in our entitlement, or welfare system, should we take public assistance away from 90 percent of people in need in order to punish the dishonest 10 percent?

Every *is* involves an *ought.* If the instrument on my wall *is* a clock, it *ought* to tell time; if this person is my teacher, then she ought to do her best to help me learn. Just so, if I am a human being, I ought to act like one and be treated like one. And every other human being has exactly that same right.

There is a difference between feeling that you *want* to help and the feeling that you *ought* to help, whether you want to or not. That's called conscience. Look up *noblesse oblige.*

We are generally the better persuaded by reasons we discover for ourselves than by those given to us by others.
Blaise Pascal

DILEMMA

Bob is one of the most popular boys in the senior class: a plucky halfback on the football team, manager of the stage crew, the sort of kid teachers always nab when they've got something to be done that they have to be sure is done. Bob is not the smartest kid in the world, but a real sweetheart.

On a Friday evening in June, the last day of exams and one week before graduation, a bunch of the seniors went to a beer joint with apparent police immunity, laughing at all the craziness they'd shared and masking the sadness each of them felt because they'd never be the same again.

At about one o'clock Saturday morning, Anthony "Godfather IV" DiSalvo, who had had a school master key since sophomore year, proposed an innocent senior prank. They'd get a couple hundred plastic cups, fill them with water, and put one on every square of tile from the principal's office to the front door. There'd be no way for the principal to get to the office on Monday without emptying every single cup!

Everybody thought that was a truly inspired and marvelous idea, and off they went. But Bob tiptoed back through the minefield of cups toward the bathroom, giggling. Everybody held their breath, sure he'd knock over a few. He did.

"You *idiot,*" Tony hollered and moved through the mess to wipe the floor with his handkerchief. But he couldn't mop up what had gone under the door into the office and onto the brand new carpet.

▷ *Questions*

On Monday morning, the principal's secretary discovers the prank and is incensed. She says that if that boy graduates onstage, she will quit. A large number of the faculty agree. Do you agree or disagree with the faculty's stand? Give your reasons.

FAITH REFLECTION

"Do not mistreat or oppress a foreigner; remember that you were foreigners in Egypt. Do not mistreat any widow or orphan. If you do, I, the Lord, will answer them when they cry out to me for help, and I will become angry and kill you in war. Your wives will become widows, and your children will be fatherless."
Exodus 22:21–24

We have all been "foreigners," left out of the in-groups, picked on, ignored. Every one of us knows how that feels. But does that ever cross your mind when your pals are picking on somebody? Do you ever try, as the wise Atticus Finch suggests, to "get inside" that person's skin and walk around in it awhile? As the chapter says, "Do unto others as you would have others do unto you" is not the monopoly of Christianity. It is a matter of simple human decency.

God is sometimes pictured in the Old Testament as vindictive simply because God was viewed through the eyes of a very victimized people. But God doesn't have to be that dramatic. Think of the people you know who seem to "make a game" out of victimizing others. What are they like? Haven't they really punished themselves? Do you want to be like them?

Often even the best-intentioned of us go along with the hazing of the weaker among us simply because we're afraid that our friends will not like us any more if we stand up—as people of character—and say, "Stop that!" But at least now when you have some distance from a situation like that, consider: Do you really want to have the approval of a bunch of sadists?

FURTHER BIBLE READINGS

Skim these Scripture passages. Pick one that appeals to you and (1) summarize its main point, (2) tell how it relates to the chapter, and (3) list one or two thoughts that entered your mind when you read it:

◆ Fair Dealings   Exodus 23:1–9
◆ Fairness and Peace   Proverbs 3:27–35
◆ The Oppressed   Isaiah 10:1–4
◆ Mouth Control   James 3:1–12
◆ Blinder than Blind   John 9:35–41

_____

_____

_____

_____

_____

JOURNAL

In every grade, there is one person who is obviously "wounded," left out, perhaps even actively shunned. Without naming names, describe someone you know who is treated like that.

Whose fault is it? Perhaps you weren't responsible for that person being treated that way (or perhaps you were), but is there anything concrete you could do to help that person "heal"?

There is a different meaning to the word *responsible* when it is applied to the victims of other people's cruelty. What is that different meaning?

Understanding Fairness

REVIEW

1. Define the terms *distributive justice, commutative justice, social justice.*

2. When the real rights of one individual conflict with the real rights of another, what agency should—ideally—pass judgment on the conflict?

3. Explain these statements:

   a. The most basic human rights can't even legitimately be *given* away.

   b. Whenever two people argue, each one is appealing to an unchanging *standard* of justice.

   c. Every ''is'' involves an ''ought.''

4. What does the first statement in Number 3 have to do with two people who both want to have sex with ''no strings attached''?

5. List the reasons why the chapter says (whether you agree with the reasons or not) that it is unfair to expect present-day blacks (because of 300 years of slavery and 150 years of discrimination) or present-day immigrants (because of a different social milieu) to ''make it'' as ''easily'' as immigrants who came to the United States in the early part of our history.

6. What is the difference between the two statements ''we *have* to treat other human beings equally'' and ''we *ought* to treat other human beings equally''?

7. Did you look up *noblesse oblige?* What does it mean?

DISCUSS

1. Women have made great strides in achieving more justice than they had twenty years ago. But have women really achieved *justice?* Are they treated completely as equals with men?

2. Have all people of color achieved equality with others? Perhaps they have in the law books, but have they in the hearts and minds of most Americans of whatever color? All citizens are guaranteed equal opportunity, but what do nonwhites have to do to claim that equality that whites do not have to do?

3. No human being has to bargain for the right to live. But that basic and inalienable right has several other rights tangled around it. In order to live, one needs adequate food, clothing, and shelter—otherwise life is impossible. Therefore, the rights to food, to clothing, and to shelter are also inalienable rights.

But to have those three essentials, a person has to have money, and in order to have money one has to have a job. Therefore, is the right to a job as inalienable as the right to life?

4. The chapter says that a person has the right not just to ''raw'' staying-alive, but to a life of ''basic human dignity.'' What does that mean?

5. Go back over the first statement in Number 3 under ''Review.'' Attack its claims if you like. What evidence do you have to support your contrary views?

6. Selfishness is not always bad. Without a certain sense of what one deserves, a person becomes a doormat. But when does the right to private property have to yield to the rights of others who have life-threatening needs? What gives the government the right to intrude on your right to keep and use what you have worked hard for?

7. What are the advantages and disadvantages of being a hermit?

ACTIVITIES

1. ''Some of those helpless people because of their own bad decisions are to some degree responsible for their situation. Their fellow citizens are not responsible for their being in the shape they are now in. But if we are to call ourselves people of character, responsible people, we have an in-built obligation to help our fellow human beings who have life-threatening needs. (For instance, we did not put the potential suicide victim out on the ledge, but we do have an obligation to try to talk him or her back to safety.) If we have any felt awareness of the humanity the people with life-threatening needs share with us, we can't just say, 'You brought it on yourself. Starve.' ''

Do you agree or disagree with the views expressed in the story? Divide into pairs or teams and debate the opinions.

2. Most people in Maurice Dibble's own grade level don't even know who he is. In grammar school, he was the first one hit in every dodgeball game. In high school, he pulled back into a cocoon of anonymity. He ate his lunch quickly and alone and scuttled off to the quiet shelter of the library. By 3:00 every afternoon, Maurice is home with his books and ship models. He has a very high average and lots of scholarship offers. But his family is worried about him.

Get inside Maurice's mind. Tell in as much detail as possible how Maurice feels. Then role-play a dinner conversation between Maurice and his family.

12. LOVING

SURVEY

Circle the number on the rating scale under each statement that best reflects your opinion about that statement. On the scale
- +2 = strongly agree,
- +1 = agree,
- 0 = can't make up my mind,
- −1 = disagree,
- −2 = strongly disagree.

Then share the reasons for your opinion.

1. Love is a feeling totally uncapturable in words and concepts.

   +2 +1 0 −1 −2

2. Most times even strangers will repay your trust when it is given.

   +2 +1 0 −1 −2

3. The most profound way to express love is through sexual intercourse.

   +2 +1 0 −1 −2

4. Love requires far more than fairness to one another.

   +2 +1 0 −1 −2

5. What keeps us from loving more people is fear of what it might cost.

   +2 +1 0 −1 −2

6. Anything ugly, once it is loved, becomes beautiful.

   +2 +1 0 −1 −2

7. "Making love" means the same thing as "having sex."

   +2 +1 0 −1 −2

8. Love without commitment is a misuse of the word.

   +2 +1 0 −1 −2

9. "Love" in "I love Paris in the springtime" is a misuse of the word.

   +2 +1 0 −1 −2

10. "Love" in "love your neighbor" is a misuse of the word.

    +2 +1 0 −1 −2

A FABLE

BEAUTY AND THE BEAST

Once upon a time there was this poor, arthritic-fingered tailor whose three daughters were starving because no one would buy his wretchedly made clothes. Sick with guilt, he decided the only way to keep them alive was to sneak onto the grounds of the Duke's palace and shoot a deer in the Duke's personal stock. So in the dead of night, the tailor squeezed his skinny body through the iron bars of the fence, tripped over his own shoelaces, and went sprawling. He pawed blindly through the trees and bushes, and there, caught in a silver shaft of moonlight, stood a doe so beautiful that it broke the tailor's heart to shoot it. But if it was doe or daughters, the doe had to go. Sweat dripped from his brow onto his spectacles, and the tailor blinked as he shot. He wiped his eyes, put back his spectacles and looked. The doe was gone. And he had shot himself in his own foot.

Before he could get breath to say "Ouch," the Duke's gamekeepers were upon the tailor, pinioning his arms and hustling him off to the Duke's chambers, dripping blood all the way.

The Duke's palace was so sumptuous—crystal chandeliers the size of oak trees, gilded mirrors big as ponds, wall hangings big enough to carpet the Colisseum—that the tailor gaped, oblivious of his pain. The gamekeepers hurled the little tailor to his knees before a great desk so high he had to pull himself up by his fingers and peer over the edge.

There before him sat a personage more hideous than any ghoul from his worst nightmares. The Duke's body was admirably proportioned, but atop that perfect body a boar's head bristled with fur, black-marble eyes, a flat snout big as a stove plate, and on either side of it two yellow tusks curled like truck springs.

"Oh!" said the tailor.

"Oh, indeed," said the Duke, covering his piggy grin with a gold-lace handkerchief.

"Forgive me, your grace," the tailor whimpered. "It was not for myself. My daughters are starving."

"Yes," said the Duke. "I've watched you and your lovely daughters from my window as you went to church."

"If there is anything I can do to make amends, . . ."

"Oh, there is," grinned the Duke. "I will set you free. And I will bestow on you an annual pension. . ."

"Oh, my, your Grace!"

". . . if you send me your lovely youngest daughter, Rosalinda. It's so terribly, terribly lonely here. She will have everything . . . everything provided for her. And you will escape with your neck."

Well, soaked with terror and blind with relief, the little tailor immediately saw the wisdom in that proposal and heartily agreed. At which the Duke snapped his fingers and the gamekeepers bore the tailor off, treated his wound, and took him home in a gold carriage just after sunrise.

The tailor limped shamefacedly into his little house where his three daughters stood gaping through the door at the carriage. He explained his plight and turned regretfully toward Rosalinda.

She was lovely as dawn, hair hanging in honeyed braids at either side of a face so sweet it gave the room a greater glow. Her skin was tawny as peaches, and her eyes glinted amethyst. Rosalinda bobbed her head once to her father and walked out to the carriage just as she was, in her clean patched dress.

When she arrived at the palace, maidservants whisked her to her luxurious rooms, bathed her, perfumed her, arranged her hair, dressed her in a brocade gown, and crusted her with jewels. Then they led her off to meet the Duke for luncheon.

"Ah," the Duke sighed, "you are lovelier than light or music. Please. Please sit down."

Rosalinda sat at the end of the huge table and looked shyly at the golden plates and the crystal goblets and the silver tableware. Then, slowly, she looked the long length of the table to where the Duke sat. Without wanting to, she gave a tiny gasp.

"Yes," the Duke grinned sadly. "I apologize."

"I'm sorry," Rosalinda whispered.

"So am I," he said. "And sorrier still that I had to inflict myself on you like this. Your poor foolish father. What was I to do? I couldn't punish the poor man, not after he'd shot himself in his own foot. But the whole county would be prowling my park if he'd gotten away with it. I don't mind that at all, but . . . well,

it would give them bad dreams if they ever saw me. I'm afraid," the Duke sighed again, "you are the sacrificial lamb, my dear girl."

So, every day at noon and in the evening, Rosalinda joined the Duke for luncheon and dinner. Each time he plied her with questions about the village and her friends and family, and he regaled her with fascinating stories of his adventures on the Crusades. Soon Rosalinda hardly noticed the Duke's deformity, and her tinkling laughter set even the grim-faced servants smiling, and the Duke beamed with delight.

One evening, a month or two after her arrival, Rosalinda cleared her throat and said, "Your grace, do you mind . . . do you mind if I bring my food down to your end of the table." She chuckled. "I feel I'm speaking to someone in another county."

So the servants moved her place down to the Duke's right, and the two ate and drank and chattered away, like children delighting in their games. Finally, one evening, Rosalinda cleared her throat again. "Your grace, don't think me rude. But it pains my heart. . . ."

The Duke smiled. "How I came to be as I am? Only a friend—or a mean-spirited boy—would dare to ask that. And you are neither mean-spirited nor a boy."

"Well, of course I am your friend," Rosalinda sniffed, as if that ought to be obvious.

The Duke sat back and sighed, lacing his hairy fingers together. "In the Crusades, Rosalinda, men were cruel. Inhuman. And . . . and I not the least of them. I left men—and young boys—more deformed than this hideous face you see. One day, after a more monstrous battle even than we'd become used to, I sat in the midst of the destruction and gore, almost satisfied, almost proud of what we had done that day. Just then a bent old monk stood there, his shadow falling across me. I couldn't even see his face, but from the shadow of his cowl came a voice of limitless sadness.

"'You know not what you do,' the monk said. I tried to bat him away, but he persisted. 'You have become a brute,' he said. 'And you will show the mark of the beast on your face, so all can see the man within, until the day you know true love.'"

Tears trickled down the Duke's warted cheeks, and he lowered his head onto his hands at the edge of the table. Rosalinda's eyes and mouth went wide, and she rose from her chair and moved to the Duke's side.

"But, your grace," she said, caressing his hideous head, "I love you." And she leaned down and kissed the Duke's forehead.

In that instant, the Duke's whole body began to glow, and Rosalinda backed away in amazement. The blaze shimmered and then gradually faded, and sitting in the Duke's chair was the handsomest young man she had ever seen. And they lived happily ever after. More or less.

▷ Questions

What statement in the opening survey best captures the theme embodied in this story?

One day I was visiting a hospital unit devoted to nothing but babies who had been born deformed. It was a place to tear anyone's heart out, so many helpless, hideous innocents. I said to a nurse, "It must be difficult for you. How do you keep your spirits up?" She looked as if I'd spoken gibberish. "But we love them," she said.

What did she know that I did not? What does love do to ugliness? And how does it do it?

A READING

In the following speech from A Tale of Two Cities, *by Charles Dickens, Sydney Carton is about to be executed by rebels in the French Revolution; but Carton is not Charles Evremonde, the aristocrat who has just been condemned, nor is he even French. He is a dissolute Englishman who loves Evremonde's wife, Lucy, and knows that she loves Charles and not himself.*

They said of him, about the city that night, that it was the peacefullest man's face ever beheld there. Many added that he looked sublime and prophetic.

One of the most remarkable sufferers by the same axe—a woman—had asked at the foot of the same scaffold, not long before, to be allowed to write down the thoughts that were inspiring her. If he had given utterance to his, and they were prophetic, they would have been these:

"I see Barsad, and Cly, Defarge, The Vengeance, the Juryman, the Judge, long ranks of the new oppressors who have risen on the destruction of the old, perishing by this retributive instrument, before it shall cease out of its present use. I see a beautiful city and a brilliant people rising from this abyss, and, in their struggles to be truly free, in their triumphs and defeats, through long years to come, I see the evil of this time and of the previous time of which this is the natural birth, gradually making expiation for itself and wearing out.

"I see the lives for which I lay down my life, peaceful, useful, prosperous and happy, in that England which I shall see no more. I see Her with a child upon her bosom, who bears my name. I see her father, aged and bent, but otherwise restored, and faithful to all men in his healing office, and at peace. I see the good old man, so long their friend, in ten years' time enriching them with all he has, and passing tranquilly to his reward.

"I see that I hold a sanctuary in their hearts, and in the hearts of their descendents, generations hence. I see her, an old woman, weeping for me on the anniversary of this day. I see her and her husband, their course done, lying side by side in their last earthly bed, and I know that each was not more honoured and held sacred in the other's soul, than I was in the souls of both.

"I see that child who lay upon her bosom and who bore my name, a man winning his way up in that path of life which once was mine. I see him winning it so well, that my name is made illustrious there by the light of his. I see the blots I threw upon it, faded away. I see him, foremost of just judges and honoured men, bringing a boy of my name, with a forehead that I know and golden hair, to this place—then fair to look upon, with not a trace of this day's disfigurement—and I hear him tell the child my story, with a tender and faltering voice.

"It is a far, far better thing that I do, than I have ever done; it is a far, far better rest that I go to than I have ever known."

▷ *Questions*

How does one explain unselfish love? Not with the analytical left brain, surely. There is a nobility—almost a sacredness—about unselfish love that defies reason. As Pascal said, "The heart has reasons that reason knows not of."

Before going further in the chapter, set the book aside and try to write out for yourself what *genuine love* really means. We all use that expression incessantly. Do you really have any clear idea at all what it means?

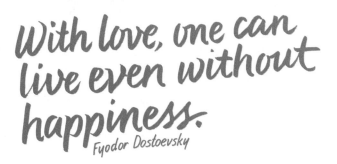

With love, one can live even without happiness.
Fyodor Dostoevsky

THEME

LOVING

Probably no word in any language is so misused and bandied about as *love.* It is trivialized even more than the word *value.* Every day you hear it trivialized: "I'd *love* a drink right now." "I just *love* what you've done to this room." "I'd *love* to give that jerk a poke in the mouth." Exactly the same word that you use for your love for your mother or your best friend is used for a soft drink, a roomful of furniture, and hatred.

And yet we do it because we're lazy. Inertia, again. It's too much effort to analyze our feeling down to what we exactly mean—and then use the right word: *enjoy, admire, take wicked delight in.*

Thus in TV movies when two people are boiling over with sexual tension, they say, "Let's make love." Wrong words; no thinking. They've used the same words two people use who have the right to use them: people who have shared miscarriages, kids with flu, soiled diapers, frayed tempers, unpayable bills; yet still say, "I'm yours; you're mine; no matter what." There is something slovenly, even obscene, about using the word *love* to describe two people taking advantage of each other. To give the Rolling Stones their due, they never said, "I want to make love"; they said, "I want *it!*"

People we respect never tire of telling us love is the most important reality in human life, more important than one's own comfort, or food, or even life itself. But though we are taught to factor quadratic equations and diagram sentences, we are rarely taught what love even means. Perhaps it's time to rectify that.

We have an infinite capacity to kid ourselves, especially when love is involved and *especially* when sex is involved. The reason for that is: Love is a very self-enriching experience, but it is often difficult to find out which of the two selves involved is uppermost, myself or the other person.

One of the sinister self-deceptions regarding love is: Where's the line? How far can I go? I've given my 50 percent, now where's yours? Real love doesn't draw lines. Lines are for lawyers, not for lovers. As soon as you ask those kinds of questions, you're not talking about love anymore; you're talking economics, justice, and fairness—a game.

Don't get me wrong. Justice and fairness are intimately bound up in loving—whether it's the pale, thin love of the anonymous neighbor or the deep, vibrant love of sexual intercourse. Even if I only share my lunch with you, I have a greater claim on your courtesy and concern than a casual stranger has. If I have any sense of honor, I can't claim we've never met. How much more claim on another's attention and concern if someone shares his (or her) body with her (or him), intimately and secretly? Trouble is, we can share bodies without sharing selves, open our clothes

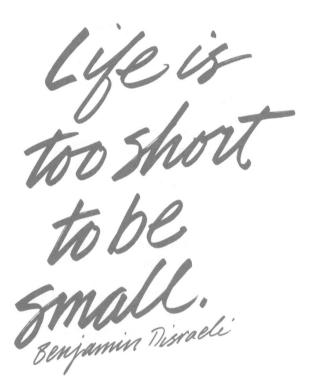

Life is too short to be small.
Benjamin Disraeli

without opening our hearts. Love isn't like that. In love, you "give yourself away," in both senses of that phrase.

One readily accessible example of genuine love is the love of truly good parents. Over and over they discipline their children, even when their children don't have the perspective to see the rightness of the penalty. Parents are, in effect, saying, "Look, I'd rather have you hate me right now than have you get hurt." Parents spend twenty years of their lives feeding, clothing, sheltering, worrying about, and cleaning up after their children *in order that* their children will one day say, "I've found someone I love more than I love you—or at least in a different way."

That's the real article. If you want to test whether a relationship is truly a loving one, try asking: "Is what I call my love for you the same disposition my parents have toward me? If you honestly believe that someone else can make you happier than I can, that's what I want."

No matter what one's religious convictions or lack of them, it is difficult to find fault with this explanation of love given by the Apostle Paul:

Love is patient and kind; love is not jealous or conceited or proud; love is not ill-mannered or selfish or irritable; love does not keep a record of wrongs; love is not happy with evil, but is happy with the truth. Love never gives up: its faith, hope, and patience never fail.
1 Corinthians 13:4–7 (adapted)

Genuine love is not just passing back and forth between the two people involved; but it is so powerful that it bursts out and enriches the lives of everyone around them.

Genuine love, real love, is life-giving. In fact, that might be another handy test of whether what we claim is love is actually real love, or just a self-deceptive word for something less than love or even opposite to love. Is this love truly *eros*: life-seeking and life-sharing? Does it actually enliven other people not directly involved in it?

If you love something, set it free. If it comes back to you, it is yours. If it does not, it never was.
Anonymous

Does it make each of the two people more patient, more kind, more willing to overlook mistakes and forgive? Does it make them more yielding to others, more trustful, more enduring?

Or is this love really a wrongly chosen name for *thanatos:* a creeping back to womb security? Does it make the two people more cranky, thin-skinned, faultfinding? Are they jealous of each other's friendships outside this one or given to alibis and lies or resentful of advice? Does it make them more unyielding?

Nifty test.

Perhaps one word, *yielding,* sums up the meaning of genuine love about as well as any other. Love does *not* mean the mindless yielding of a doormat or a barber chair. There are two free and independent selves involved here. The wife and mother, for instance, who defines herself *solely* in reference to her husband and children is not, strictly speaking, loving them; she is instead enslaved to them. But one lover yields to the other when yielding enriches *both* of them. Two heads—and wills—are better than one: "Gee, I never looked at it that way." "Maybe your way *is* better than mine." "To see you that happy was *worth* missing my bowling night!"

Yielding in genuine love, of course, requires vulnerability: an openness to and free acceptance of not only the other's virtues but also the other's shortcomings, sensitivities, and blindspots. Love means loyalty to the other, even when the chips are down—especially when the chips are down. Love is dependable.

Love is *not* a feeling; love is an act of the *will.* Love takes over when feelings fail, when the beloved is no longer even *likable.*

As with any act of freedom, love includes a *commitment* to the other, a sacrifice of freedom—even at times a painful sacrifice. But as we have seen before, love often involves a loss in the hope of something better.

Another word that might capture the elusive reality of genuine love is *understanding.* Again, that does not mean merely left-brain cognition of causes; it means right-brain *empathy* with the person loved.

A parent or spouse or sibling or friend who says, "I would never do that myself and I'm saddened that you did, but because I know where you're coming from, I understand why you did it. And I still love you," treats those he or she loves not as a protector or judge. They treat them as a wise and understanding counselor or psychiatrist who has no vested interest in the case except to help the pain.

Of course I feel hurt when someone I love does something foolish or disgraceful or mean—especially to me. But the crucial test of whether this is really love is: Which pain is most important at the moment, mine or my friend's, or my spouse's or my child's?

It is not enough for parents to understand children. They must accord children the privilege of understanding them. MILTON SAPIRSTEIN

Before the mistake—and before the inevitable shame and anger that complicate the issue—there is no problem with handing out rules: Look both ways. Don't get into fights. That dress is too short. *After* the mistake, though, it is—or ought to be—quite different. The wise parent, the devoted spouse, the loving sibling, the good friend first puts his or her arms around you, saying, "I know. I've done stupid, cruel, hateful things, too." That's love.

We will return to love when we discuss romance and sexuality, but it is worth noting here that the love that comes to most of our minds—again from media brainwashing —is not love at all. Just as the media have convinced us *happiness* means "feeling good" rather than "being good," they have also convinced us *love* means "feeling exhilarated" by those we love rather than "feeling empathy, or compassion" for those we love. The exhilaration is not love but being—*in*—love: romance.

Genuine love is far less dramatic, far more commonplace: diapering-the-baby-love, cutting-down-on-the-drinking-love, letting-go-of-the-grudges-love. Again,

> *Love is patient and kind; love is not jealous or conceited or proud; love is not ill-mannered or selfish or irritable; love does not keep a record of wrongs; love is not happy with evil, but is happy with the truth. Love never gives up: its faith, hope, and patience never fail.*
> 1 Corinthians 13:4–7 (adapted)

If love doesn't *cost*, we're talking about something else entirely.

Justice is washing your own dishes. Love is washing someone else's.
Anonymous

153

DILEMMA

"Mom," Amy Castellano said to her mother who sat at the table grating parmesan cheese from a smelly, yellow hunk, "is it okay if I go to the movies with a bunch of the kids tonight?"

"Now, Amy, you know I've been working all day on this meal. And your aunt and uncle are coming."

"Yes, but I'll be here for most of it."

"Most of it? You mean stuff a couple of meatballs between two pieces of bread and run out, 'So long, everybody. I've got more important things'? No."

"But, Mom. . . ."

"You heard me, young lady. Now go do some homework."

"But it's Friday afternoon."

"I don't care. Do you see me goofing off because it's Friday afternoon? Besides, you're going to get that scholarship to Nazareth College."

"But, Mom, I want to go *away* to school. All the teachers say it's an experience nobody should miss. Becoming inde-. . ."

". . . Independent? My goodness, just take a look at your room. You'd live in a pigsty if I weren't here to keep it clean. Besides, you're too young to be off on your own at some school with a lot of boys. Hah, don't tell me about boys. There's only one thing they're interested in, and they're not getting it from you."

"Mom, there are a lot of decent boys."

"Right. Till they drink a few beers."

"I've got to make my own decisions *some* time."

"Yes, and that'll be the day you get your college diploma. Your father and I haven't worked ourselves ragged so that you can go off to some school and come back a couple months later and telling us you're . . . in the family way. Now go upstairs and study. And if you're too uninterested in your own future, start making a salad."

▷ *Questions*

What does the dialogue between Amy and her mom say about their "love" for each other? Role-play the situation. Change the dialogue if you think it is necessary—to "show" genuine love.

FAITH REFLECTION

"My children, I shall not be with you very much longer. You will look for me; but I tell you now what I told the Jewish authorities, 'You cannot go where I am going.' And now I give you a new commandment: love one another. . . . If you have love for one another, then everyone will know that you are my disciples."

John 13:33–35

We've all heard that Scripture passage so often that we hardly even hear it when it is read yet again. And yet it is the most radical statement in Scripture.

The Id in us wants precisely the opposite of that: "Take care of old Number One; this is *my* turf; get outta my face!" A large part of the Superego is also sheerly utilitarian: "Be polite so that people will like you; don't take someone else's stuff or they'll get you back; when someone has paid a debt, you have to forget it."

Love—Christianity—goes much further than mere justice, morality, or ethics. Love forgives *before* the perpetrator has made amends! Skim through the four gospels and see whether, when a sinner came to Jesus, he ever made the sinner grovel, list every single sin, and do some kind of penance as an act of atonement. Not once. Then that's what Jesus meant by "love." That's what Jesus meant distinguished Christians from others.

That doesn't mean Christians are suckers and patsies, although we may look like suckers and patsies to Id-dominated utilitarians. If someone has stolen my goods or my reputation or my work, I have a right to restitution—in justice, before the law. But the gift a Christian gives to the perpetrator is surrending the bitterness and hatred and demand for more than justice, than vengeance.

Do you have any grudges? Are they doing your "enemy" any harm? Are they doing you any good?

 ## FURTHER BIBLE READINGS

Skim these Scripture passages. Pick one that appeals to you and (1) summarize its main point, (2) tell how it relates to the chapter, and (3) list one or two thoughts that entered your mind when you read it.

◆ Loving	1 Corinthians 13:1–13
◆ Loving Enemies	Matthew 5:43–48
◆ Sharing Burdens	Galatians 6:1–5
◆ Compassion	James 3:13–18
◆ Only One Commandment	Romans 13:8–10

_____

_____

_____

_____

_____

JOURNAL

This chapter claims that genuine love is yielding and understanding. Consider your relationship with your parents. In what ways do you yield to them? Is it grudgingly or willingly? Do you ever take time to try to understand what they say and do from *their* point of view? If so, in what concrete ways? If not, do you think that they deserve an attempt on your part to understand them as they are, at least in gratitude for what they've done for you since you were conceived? Feel free to ramble on this one.

Understanding Loving

REVIEW

1. Choose the description of *love* in the left-hand column that most accurately describes the relationship in the right-hand column. Match the columns.

a.	Unconditional friendship	_____	Spouses
b.	Horny selfishness	_____	Parents for children
c.	Considerate respect	_____	Children for parents
d.	Graciousness	_____	Siblings for siblings
e.	Blood comradeship	_____	Pals
f.	Enjoyment	_____	Boyfriend, girlfriend
g.	Amiability	_____	Friends
h.	Fondness	_____	Acquaintances
i.	Contentment	_____	Strangers
j.	Protective devotion	_____	The easy pickup
k.	Loyal affection	_____	Vacation
l.	Romantic friendship	_____	Beer on a hot day
m.	Affectionate gratitude	_____	Your dog
n.	Self-esteem	_____	Your car
o.	Pride	_____	Yourself

2. Explain these statements:

   a. Justice and fairness are intimately bound up in loving.

   b. In love, you "give yourself away," in both senses of that phrase.

   c. Love is not a feeling; love is an act of will.

3. How does love go beyond justice and fairness?

4. Show two ways in which good parents give love worthy of its name.

5. In what ways is love an encroachment on one's freedom?

6. In what ways does love yield? In what ways does love refuse to yield?

7. Explain what the chapter means by "love as understanding."

8. What is the most profound way of showing love?

DISCUSS

1. How does the love described in the chapter differ from the way love is put forward by TV programs and pop lyrics? The media are certainly in many ways good for our lives. But in many ways they are also not good for our lives. What can you, for your own personal integrity, do about that?

2. Explain why genuine love is far less dramatic and far more commonplace than emotional, romantic love; for instance, diapering-the-baby love, cutting-down-on-the-drinking love, letting-go-of-the-grudges love. Give other examples from your own life.

3. Before you can love or be loved by another person, you have to share a great deal of trust—and sacrifice—with him or her. Before that, you have to give that person some time and you have to talk, just in order to be known. Even before that, you have to notice him or her. How defensive do you think you (and your friends) are against noticing, or knowing, or loving more people than you do now?

ACTIVITIES

1. Choose two people you know who seem clearly to love each other genuinely—unselfishly, yieldingly, understandingly—and whose love for each other spills over into all their other relationships. Ask at least one of them what loving means to him or her.

2. Give those two people (or two others) the following list. Ask them to rank each quality in its order of importance in their relationship. Then ask them to give their reasons for the ranking:

_____	Trustworthiness	_____	Sense of humor
_____	Honesty about me	_____	Honesty about self
_____	Playfulness	_____	Creativity
_____	Sexuality	_____	Hard work
_____	Good looks	_____	His/her friends

3. If you can, get a video of an old episode of *The Waltons*. View it and tell how life is different today from what it was (or appears to be) on the episode, which takes place during the Depression. What values have been lost—and to gain what? How did families, neighbors, and even strangers deal with one another in those days that we would find perhaps "naive" today? What would we have to give up today in order to get those values back?

13. MARRIAGE

SURVEY

Circle the number on the rating scale under each statement that best reflects your opinion about that statement. On the scale

+2 = strongly agree,
+1 = agree,
 0 = can't make up my mind,
−1 = disagree,
−2 = strongly disagree.

Then share the reasons for your opinion.

1. "Happily-ever-after" is as fragile as "being-in-love."

   +2 +1 0 −1 −2

2. A bridal couple doesn't *know* their marriage will work out; they are betting it will work out.

   +2 +1 0 −1 −2

3. A wife's career should always yield to her husband's career.

   +2 +1 0 −1 −2

4. Family values would be worth sacrificing for the advantages of urban life.

   +2 +1 0 −1 −2

5. The competition pervading our society is not good preparation for marriage.

   +2 +1 0 −1 −2

6. A marriage is a moral relationship because it involves two human beings.

   +2 +1 0 −1 −2

7. Few people admire an adulterer or an adulteress.

   +2 +1 0 −1 −2

8. Divorces often happen because the spouses are too busy to remain best friends.

   +2 +1 0 −1 −2

9. Divorces are more common among people who gauge self-worth by external standards.

   +2 +1 0 −1 −2

10. Divorce has a more long-lasting effect on children than a parent's death does.

    +2 +1 0 −1 −2

A FABLE

Hopefully Ever After

Once upon a time Cinderella and Prince Charming settled down to live happily ever after. Well, it was sheer paradise. They never argued, not once. They just twittered around like a pair of parakeets. Then one day Cinderella felt this definite kick in her tummy, as if the squab she'd eaten had just reassembled itself therein, and she ran to the royal purgatory and was royally ill. Well, the quarrelsome Royal Academy of Physicians all agreed the unsettling disturbance in the royal tummy was none other than a bundle of joy: five-to-ten—a prince.

Cinderella and Charming were ecstatic and resolved that this little heir would have everything, and both his Mummy and Daddy would share in every phase of his upbringing. And Charming's father, the king, decided that—now that this new heir gave the dynasty an iron-clad guarantee—he'd retire to the South Seas.

For months the palace was aflutter with preparations, and as Cinderella began to get a bit portly, she put aside her crystal slippers, which were making her back ache. But she supervised all the palace doings and was happy to work because King Charming was now busy far into the evening with affairs of state and also because it reminded her of her childhood when she fell asleep each night smelling of Murphy's Oil Soap and Brasso. Cinderella was so busy-busy she often forgot to fix her hair and lacquer her nails until Charming reminded her, gently, when he came home late from the office or an execution. To mask his youth in dealing with other kings, Charming had begun to affect a beard of which Cinderella was not overly fond; but overall, she was sublimely happy and at the year's end she delivered a boy child.

Bells rang and the riotous peasants whooped and threw their sweaty caps into the air and cried out, "Long live Prince Ledouze (Twelve)!" Many mistakenly shouted "LeDouce (Sweet)," thinking he was so named because he was so cute—actually, it was because the new prince had six fingers on each hand. Not even King Charming was troubled. After all, his son would have the best spear-grip in the kingdom. And King Charming went back to complete involvement in more important affairs.

Hardly a season had passed before Queen Cinderella felt another quite definite boot in the tummy, and almost before Quasimodo could get up the belltower, the sweaty peasants were throwing their caps in the air once more and shouting, "Long live Princess Mantissa!" The new princess was so named because her first words, delivered shortly after her birth, were "The area of a circle equals Pi-r-squared." This caused her royal father not a moment's anxiety, owing to the fact he had missed the blessed event and her christening and first two birthdays, conquering three other kingdoms to add to his children's patrimony. And, he said, to find himself.

As the royal children grew, they became something of a puzzle to their royal father when he had a moment free to think

159

about them. Prince Ledouze showed a marked disinterest in fencing, hawking, or bearbaiting and preferred to spend his time at the pianoforte and lute where, it is not surprising, he was able to play some pretty fulsome chords. And Princess Mantissa had polished off spherical geometry by the time she was three and turned her childish attention to brewing mysterious mixtures in her little golden tea set.

Their royal father, on his rare returns from the wars with a great deal of what looked like lipstick on his collar, hardly spoke of it, involved as he was in more important affairs. He now affected a perpetual scowl, and Cinderella noticed that his once alabaster body was now covered with dark hairs and his canine teeth seemed considerably longer. "Ah," she found herself sighing, "Where did 'happily-ever-after' go?"

With her husband continually off to the wars and the children happily occupied in their own interests, the Queen found herself devouring too many chocolates and Silhouette novels. Finally she enrolled in a sporting club where she played at tennis and learned Turkish belly dancing with other women nearly of her station: a drowsy minor princess named Beauty, the lovely Duchess Gretel, a ravishing blonde who claimed to have once been a harp but now was married to a fabulously wealthy man named Jack, and Lady Red Hood who kept trying to remember someone from her past of whom King Charming always reminded her.

After their invigorating games of tennis, the women sat in the club and drank frozen daiquiris and discussed all kinds of forbidden subjects, like sex. But mostly they ran bake sales for such worthy causes as the new Dragon Sanctuary. Most women merely brought pastries their servants had made, but Queen Cinderella always made her cakes with her very own hands— which the other women found only a whisper short of disgraceful, though all the Queen's confections were sold before she even got them out of the boxes.

160

Then one day when she was tipsily tiptoeing from the tennis court, the Queen encountered a most hideous crone with a corncob pipe poking out between her warty corncob nose and her whiskery corncob chin. "Ag, ag, ag," snorted the witch, for so she was.

"I beg your pardon," hiccuped Queen Cinderella. "Were you addressing us?" and she leaned on a big old oak to clear her royal headache.

"I said, 'Ag, ag, ag,'" the witch sniggered and handed the Queen a foaming beaker.

Dazed, Cinderella downed the draught and pfft! went her headache. "Thank you," she said. "That worked like magic. I seem to have forgotten myself for a moment."

The witch blew her nose disdainfully into the hem of her skirt. "Fiddlesticks! You fergot yerself longer'n a minute, sweetheart." And the Queen stood there silent while the witch hobbled away up the road.

For nearly a week, Queen Cinderella locked herself in her chamber, weeping and pacing. Then late Sunday night when the whole castle was asleep, her door opened and out she strode like a galleon into a gale, and headed straight for the kitchen. All night long she labored, feeling the good clean dough between her fingers and smelling the sweet perfumes of cinnamon and vanilla. About an hour before dawn, humming to herself, she went out to the royal stables and hitched up a wagon, loaded all her cakes and pastries in it, and trundled off to the fair.

By noon Monday Cinderella was back with supplies and bustled into the kitchens, firing orders right and left. Tuesday all the royal wagons set off and were back again, empty, by noon. The Queen set the brightest girls in charge of specialties like spun-sugar swans and leaning towers of pizza. All one afternoon she and Mantissa huddled over maps and a crisp new ledger, planning out new markets, costs, and profits. Duchess Gretel, who had some experience with ovens, took over production. And Ledouze and his musical friends went with Mrs. Jack, the former harp, from village to village tootling their enterprise, *Royal Confections*. Before the year was out, the whole palace was singing at work and the treasury doors were cracking with the weight of the gold behind them—which was only petty cash, since Mantissa had diversified them into an agricultural-timber-marketing-transportation cooperative, *Royal Enterprises*. And 10 percent of the overall profits before division were marked off for a great school for all the children in the land.

Then King Charming came home.

The wars had not fared well, and the army crept home from one defeat after another. The king slumped into his chair. "First thing," he growled, "Ledouze takes over the eastern front," and he held out his boot for Cinderella to pull off.

"No," said the Queen, from a great height.

"Second," the king went on, "Mantissa marries King Gorboduc. We need his troops."

"No," said the Queen, again.

"Third, I've heard about this business. I need all we've got to rearm my troops and get some big guns."

"You've spent too much time with big guns," the Queen said. "It's made you deaf."

The king looked up, slowly. "What did you say?"

"The Kingdom is yours," she said quietly. "But not the children. Not the money. Not me."

The king towered over her, and she rose to look at him eye-to-eye. "I've done this for you and the children!" he shouted.

"No," she said, "I do this for me and the children. What you do, you do for yourself."

The king glowered, turned on his heel, stormed out of the castle, leaped on his horse, and rode off in a cloud of dust.

For the next weeks morale was pretty low through the castle and town. But gradually a lad here began to whistle and a lass there began to hum as Cinderella kneaded her dough. Then, nearly a month later, King Charming returned. On foot. Clean-shaven.

The queen and the king met alone in the silent courtyard, both staring at the hard earth. Slowly the king brought from behind his back a pair of new peasant sandals. "Here," he said, and held them toward her. "I traded my horse for them. They're not crystal, but they were the best I could afford."

And Queen Cinderella wrapped her arms around King Charming; and he wrapped his arms around her, and they wept together for a long while. And "happily-ever-after" seemed possible once again.

▷ Questions

What happens in a marriage relationship when the honeymoon is over?

Even physically, Charming and Cinderella changed—How and why? Neither of their children turns out "as expected." Anything seriously wrong with that? How do their parents' reactions to their "differentness" contrast?

How at first is Cinderella's marriage like Psyche's (Chapter 10)? What has Cinderella lost from her earlier hard life? Why?

What brings the family—except the father—together? When Charming comes home from work, he doesn't notice any differences. Why? And he just assumes that he's still in charge. Why? What lesson has he learned by the end of the story? What does he give his wife that he's never given her before? And I don't mean shoes.

What does the story say about marriage? What glue keeps the marriage relationship together? What attitudes and habits inevitably make it fall apart? What is the only way to glue it back together again?

Singing for no reason occurs a lot in the story. What does that signify?

A READING

In this scene in a nonrealistic play, The Skin of Our Teeth, *by Thornton Wilder, George and Maggie Antrobus and their children, Henry and Gladys, are at a convention on the boardwalk in Atlantic City. George has just come from a "conversation" with an attractive young floozie named Sabina Fairweather.*

MRS. ANTROBUS: *(calmly, almost dreamily)*
I didn't marry you because you were perfect.
I didn't even marry you because I loved you.
I married you because you gave me a promise.
(She takes off her ring and looks at it.) That promise made up for your faults. The promise I gave you made up for mine. Two imperfect people got married and it was the promise that made the marriage.

ANTROBUS: Maggie, . . . I was only nineteen.

MRS. ANTROBUS: *(She puts her ring back on her finger.)*
And when our children were growing up, it wasn't a house that protected them; and it wasn't our love that protected them—it was that promise.

▷ Questions

Maggie (Mrs. Antrobus) cuts through all the important but inessential aspects of marriage: attraction, house, even love itself. What *one* reality separates a so-called trial marriage (living together) from true marriage? A marriage is not in the words or in the marriage certificate; it's in a commitment of the heart, the gift of one's freedom. What elements of life—foreseen and unforeseen—does that promise and commitment entail?

What does Maggie's ring embody for her? No matter what her husband intends to do, what does her putting her ring back on symbolize?

Marriage is three parts love and seven parts forgiveness of sins.

Langdon Mitchell

THEME

PARTNERSHIP

Adolescence, fortunately, needn't be an incurable disease—though sometimes it is. Erikson believes that the healthy adult must move on from the fifth stage of finding a self—an Identity (Adolescence)—to a new and just as painfully achieved stage of Intimacy (Young Adulthood), and share the newfound self with another so that the interplay between the two selves can keep both selves growing.

But if adolescence is the greatest disequilibrium in a person's life, the commitment to marriage comes a pretty close second—despite all the "happily-ever-after" stories and songs. We are no longer talking about an individual's relationship with his or her self. We are talking about *two,* quite *different,* selves finding not only peace, stability and accomodation with each other, but also preparing a strong nurturing environment for the next stage: Parenthood.

Most marital problems arise because neither of the two selves in the relationship has, in fact, achieved a healthy, positive self-image—chosen a personal map, forged a keel that will take the self through life's inevitable storms and conflicts. After the euphoria of the honeymoon wears off, such a couple goes back to playing the same old games they played in childhood—laying off blame on the other, demanding that the other show qualities one lacks, and put-downs—because their union is not just physical, but also psychological. And two inadequately comprehended selves are headed inevitably for collision. (You can't honestly deal with another self if you've never honestly dealt with the self you have.)

Romance is an absolute requisite for marriage. Without the breathless blindness that makes him into a god and her into a goddess, no one in his or her right mind would ever make a commitment so enormous with so few guarantees—and most often sworn to! In front of hundreds of witnesses,

Govern a family as you would cook a small fish—very gently.

Chinese Proverb

a couple will say, "I promise to be true to you, in sickness and in health, till death do us part." But how many men and women would walk up to a relative stranger, someone they've known for only a year and say, "You seem like a nice, trustworthy person. Here's all my money"? Yet people who won't speak to strangers in elevators, who won't risk raising their hands in class, who won't commit themselves even to choose a college till the last minute are betting their very lives in marriage! "Ya gotta be a little crazy to walk into something like that, right?" Yet perhaps 95 percent of people do it—some more than once.

Marriage is a *calculated* risk. But the more calculation beforehand, the greater likelihood the marriage will work out; the less calculation, the more risk. And there we find the dark underbelly of the rosy clouds of romance: Cinderella and Charming are so juiced up to leap into love that they very often don't look first.

But if his great dream is to be a high school English teacher and her great dream is to belong to a country club, the two ought to do some serious thinking. If she sets her sights on becoming a surgeon and he is climbing in a company that frequently uproots executives and moves them around the country, one or the other has to yield. Perhaps love truly does heal all wounds. But being-in-love hasn't that strength; and it is simply too wounding to ask either to give up the dream or the career for the other. Far better to face the wound of a break-up before the wedding than to live a whole life with an unfulfilled dream and a short-circuited career. Even real love isn't always strong enough to heal that.

Most lovers would probably find it demeaning to their love to take the very practical step of sitting down with a pad, drawing a line down the center, and writing out the things they love about the other on the left side and the things they very strongly dislike on the right. If there are no—or very few—items on the right, the scribbler is very, very blind. So each partner risks joining hands with a near stranger and together leaping off a cliff into the dark. They may call it "blind faith." To my mind, blind faith is a synonym for "idiocy."

Even when the two selves are about as healthy as they can get at their stage of development and about as sure as two sensible people can be that the other is "right for me," conflict is inevitable: Do we sleep with the window open? Do we put in the toilet roll overshot or undershot? Do we smoke, watch the Super Bowl, eat liver? Unlike school or business or athletics, where every policy and penalty is spelled out, the two selves in marriage are left to improvise and compromise. Unlike any competitive activity for which they've been so carefully trained for their entire lives— school, business, athletics—the object of this enterprise is *not* to win. If either self wins, both lose.

Everyone would like a peachy little handbook with all the answers for every clash of wills in marriage. Sorry. The best anyone can offer is a driver's manual. No one can anticipate the curves and detours and collisions a couple will encounter. This is one more map you have to draw—and redraw—for yourself. And this time, it's two wills making the choices, not just one.

To my mind, one of the worst things that has happened to marriage and the family in the last generation was the success of TV programs like "The Waltons." This program presents a form of marriage and the family that had in fact existed for most of history for most families up to World War II, the time at which the series was set, but no longer exists. Even stripping away the program's dewy-eyed idealization where everybody forgives everybody else within an hour (and makes every viewer's actual family look lousy by contrast), it raises expectations that the present economic division of labor simply cannot fulfill: Pa working just out back, ready to run into the house for any crisis, teaching the boys skills they'll need when they move in with their wives just down the road; Ma producing clothes, canned food, and on-the-job training for the girls. The workplace and family

One would be
less in danger
From the wiles
of the stranger
If one's own kin and kith
Were more fun
to be with.
Ogden Nash

166

place were the same then. And the whole Walton family's story is linked up to an even longer story by the supportive presence of the grandparents. The family's circle of friends was limited to the town, but it was filled with very intense personal relationships. And there was no TV to tell them what they were missing.

All that changed; in many ways, for the better. But at a very real price. For many families, at least after the first child arrives, workplace and family place are separated by more than an hour's commuting. The whole governing ethic of the two places is completely different—if not completely opposed to each other: It's a jungle out there, where dog-eat-dog world is the rule; home is a hedged-in haven, where love is the rule. And Dad is in charge of the dog-eat-dog and must, by some miracle, change from werewolf to loving father when he gets in the car for the ride home. And, in many cases, Mom stays at home and is both Ma and Pa Walton at the same time.

That's difficult enough. But once children can be separated from the mother at least for day care, it becomes even more so: Many women join their husbands in the marketplace. There is the very real advantage of two incomes; and, like Cinderella, the mother gets a sense of her self back, but the housekeeping still has to be done. Studies show that in such homes the wife still does 80 percent of that work *after* she's finished a work day that is just as taxing as that of her husband, who, understandably, wants to come home and relax. But so does she.

In just the last fifty years, the chances of conflict between spouses have increased by geometrical proportions. How does a couple not only survive the conflicts but keep on growing together? There is one rock-bottom difference between a marriage and a love affair: a promise. If romance were all that were required for happily-ever-after, then the promise would add nothing.

Being in love is a beautiful fantasy. Loving is realistic, a commitment: "I promise to be true to you in good times and in bad" even when you don't seem lovable at all. That promise is the reason that, even with the escalating divorce rate, the family is still the toughest human institution in history. In a good marriage, the will takes over when the feelings fail.

As Robert Johnson says:

"Stirring the oatmeal love" is a humble act— not exciting or thrilling. But it symbolizes a relatedness that brings love down to earth. It represents a willingness to share ordinary human life, to find meaning in the simple, unromantic tasks: earning a living, living within a budget, putting out the garbage, feeding the baby in the middle of the night— discovering the sacred in the midst of the humble and ordinary."

And if *both* partners don't engage in all those ordinary tasks—for which nearly all girls but hardly any boys are trained to do for twenty years—then there's trouble.

However, marriage needn't be "the ultimate trap" either for the husband or for the wife. It needn't mean that the two—especially the woman— have to tailor their expectations of life nearly to zero, negating the self in total submission to the other and to the children. But, unlike romance, love does take work. Love takes openness with gripes; and it takes forgiveness, independence, flexibility, and compromise without grudges; and most of all, it takes creativity. Love means that— quite unlike romance—the two people have to remind themselves to think up ways to *surprise* each other, even when most of their days are filled with activities that are only remotely connected to the other person.

When longtime, happily married couples were asked what kept their marriages alive, almost unanimously the reason given was that their spouse was my best friend, sacred to me, constantly interesting, and, most importantly, interested in me. We laugh together; we're in this together; we *listen.*

Once a couple stops doing those things, their marriage begins to die, either halfway down to a dull and unfulfilling routine where grudges simmer and wait to explode, or all the way down to divorce.

DIVORCE

No one is really pro-divorce, any more than anyone is really pro-war or pro-abortion. In each of those cases, there is a desperate response to what at least appears to be a problem that cannot be solved in any other acceptable way. And yet half of all new marriages now end in divorce. In a 1978 survey, when couples who lined up to get marriage licences were asked whether they expected to be married for the rest of their lives, 63 percent said no.

Statistics consistently show the same reasons for divorce. Spouses have to work much harder for a lasting marriage, for instance, if one or both is the child of a broken home, was married before the age of twenty, has only a high school education, or they are in a very high or a very low income bracket, and have no children.

Psychological factors in either or both spouses are also critical. Divorce is more common among people who are defensive, directed by others, gauge their personal worth by standards outside themselves, shift responsibilities onto others, or are oversensitive and temperamental. In short, divorce happens most often between two people one of whom at least has never evolved a personally validated self. (Another good premarital checklist.)

In a divorce the "Child" in one or both spouses takes over and there is displacement, projection, one-upmanship. The marriage that has divorced was most often contracted in the first place, by the starry-eyed "Child"—the incomplete self believing the other *is* fulfillment and also that "what one feels" is more important than "what one is and does." Such a "Child" who marries feels bound only by a legal, not by a moral (human) obligation; the "Child" understands a fifty-fifty contract, but cannot understand a commitment by which one accepts unlimited liability for the other. What the "Child" expects out of the marriage is what most people expect from psychotherapy, that the other heal their own lack of wholeness.

Divorce happens when the two are no longer romantically in love; and unless one or both healthy Egos take over from the snarling Ids, it is highly unlikely either spouse will ever be able to achieve realistic love—much less adulthood, no matter how many times they remarry.

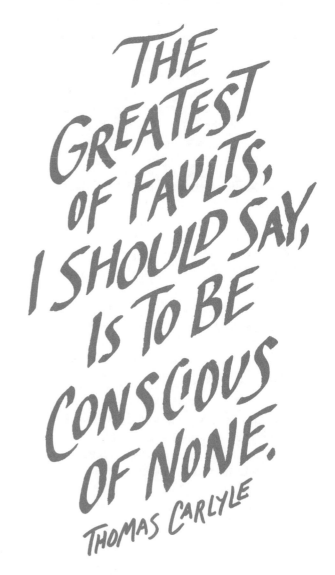

THE GREATEST OF FAULTS, I SHOULD SAY, IS TO BE CONSCIOUS OF NONE.
THOMAS CARLYLE

There are many arguments *against* divorce, that are not religious. One is the rejection of the shared story that has given meaning to two lives for a long time. Another is the sense of failure. Still another is that it is much more difficult to develop a completely new story with someone new at an older, less flexible time in your life. But the primary and most obvious reason against divorce is the children. Yet there are one million children-of-divorce every year. One-third of all children under eighteen will have lived at least for some time with a divorced parent—and some of them not for the first time.

A child needs both a father and a mother and all the balancing factors that nature and nurture have bred into the male and the female. But a child also needs a sense that the parents are somehow fused, complementary to each other. If parents are divided, the child will experience both a division within himself or herself, and a confusion that a child, no matter what age, is incapable of resolving. The single most common cause of depression in children is the experience of their parents' divorce.

For many children, their parents' divorce is a source of trauma that they feel for the rest of their lives. This trauma is often greater than the trauma experienced by children who suffer the death of a parent, because a bereaved child realizes that he or she could not possibly have been responsible for the parent's death. Most children of divorced parents say that their parents' divorce was the most painful experience of their lives—except for those who were later divorced themselves, in which case their own divorce assumes that place.

There is also evidence that continued intense conflict between parents who remain together is an even worse experience for children. Yet, Miriam Van Waters discovered that most children of "bad parents," given the choice between custody in a foster home or custody by their own parents, preferred to return even to their own "homes in shambles." This "incurable loyalty of children to unworthy adults," although it was "the despair of the social worker," nevertheless suggested to Van Waters that a child's "own home gave him or her something that the mere kindness and plenty of the foster home could not furnish, and that all the social workers in the world would fail to supply." Whatever that "something" is, the child of divorce is not even given the choice of the abused child. Further, the child-of-divorce must cope not only with his or her own pain and loss but also with the misery of the two parents as well.

As with war and abortion, the need for a painful but acceptable solution of divorce to a shattered marriage usually becomes evident only after all acceptable solutions are impossible. The answer becomes evident long *before* the tragic impasse: before the enemy launches missiles, before the woman is pregnant, before the couple even gets married. The only road to both a successful marriage and to a successful human life is to forge a self that has all the qualities *opposite* to those listed above that contribute to divorce:

◆ to become open to honest criticism,
◆ to be self-directed,
◆ to gauge your worth not by standards outside yourself but only by those you yourself know to be true,
◆ to accept the full blame for anything for which you are objectively responsible, and perhaps most important of all,
◆ to be able to laugh at yourself.

In our age, where image often outweighs substance, such self-possession is relatively rare—even among presidents who would rather save face than face the music. If you find another self who has all the qualities listed above and who looks sort of godlike, I'd suggest you put down this book and head to the Marriage License Bureau. If he or she has only the godlike qualities, it's probably better to keep on reading.

DILEMMA

Matt Grimes and Missy Elkins have been going together for four years. It's a chaste, genuinely loving relationship: fun, understanding, honest. But Matt wants to get married. The two of them have good jobs, and both of them eventually want children; but they are both just short of thirty and Missy's childbearing years are narrowing down.

"Honey," Matt says, "I just figured we've been going together for fourteen hundred and forty days. How many times have I proposed, excluding leap year?"

"Maybe fourteen hundred and thirty-nine. . . ."

"Make that forty."

"Oh, Matt. You know why. . . ."

"Look, honey. Your dad's been sober for nearly three years. He's found a very nice lady who's a recovering alcoholic too. They're *made* for each other. They're happy; maybe they'll get married. But you're twenty-nine years old. Don't you have the right to have kids of your own, instead of treating your dad like your child?"

"Matt, you just don't know what it's like to live with a recovering alcoholic."

"Missy, I've lived with a recovering alcoholic for the last four *years!* Your dad's practically as much *my* father as he is yours! Okay, wait a minute. I'm getting too ticked off."

"Yes. You are."

"Honey, do you ever think that he might *want* you to back off, stop playing his parent?"

"I don't want to talk about this any more."

"I know you don't. But I *do.* I love you. I want to marry you. I want to start having kids."

"So do I."

"No, you *don't!* What you *do* shouts so loud I can't *hear* what you say."

"You're raising your voice again."

"Yes. I know. I was just hoping that, for once, you might hear me."

▷ *Questions*

Matt says to Missy, "I've lived with a recovering alcoholic for the last four *years!*" What do you think Matt was saying to Missy about their own relationship? How was it affecting their relationship? How do you think it might affect their future marriage?

Matt was trying to deal with a real problem he and Missy were having. What was that problem? Did it reveal any other problems?

Where would you suggest Missy and Matt go from here? Continue their dialogue in a role-play activity.

FAITH REFLECTION

Then the Lord God made the man fall into a deep sleep, while he was sleeping, God took out one of the man's ribs and closed up the flesh. God formed a woman out of the rib and brought her to him. Then the man said,

> *"At last, here is one of my own kind—*
> *Bone taken from my bone, and flesh from my flesh.*
> *'Woman' is her name because she was taken out of man."*

That is why a man leaves his father and mother and is united with his wife, and the two become one.

> *The man and woman were both naked, but they were not embarrassed.*

Genesis 2:21–25 (adapted)

This fanciful story most likely never literally happened. We at least know that the biblical writer was not an eyewitness because writing hadn't even been invented yet. But nonetheless, like the fanciful stories that open each chapter of this book, this story also tells a great deal of truth.

The "woman" is no less human than the "man"; both are totally different from the mere animals around them. Also, despite centuries of male domination, the "woman" is an equal partner with the "man," not merely a companion, sexual partner, and means of production. Still, there is no getting away from the fact that the Genesis story does come from a society in which male dominance and female subservience were taken for granted; and thus the story cannot help but be colored by that prejudice.

It is interesting to see the great deference with which Jesus treated women. Many women were his disciples; the adulterous woman and the Samaritan woman at the well who had had many husbands get nothing but respectful courtesy from Jesus. The gospels also say that other than "the disciple that Jesus loved," no other male had the courage to stay at Jesus' crucifixion, and only women were privileged to be the first witnesses of his resurrection.

If you are a male, do you treat females with the respect they deserve? If you are a female, do you treat yourself with the respect you deserve?

📖 FURTHER BIBLE READINGS

Skim these Scripture passages. Pick one that appeals to you and (1) summarize its main point, (2) tell how it relates to the chapter, and (3) list one or two thoughts that entered your mind when you read it.

◆ Husbands	Ephesians 5:25–33
◆ Wives	Proverbs 31:10–31
◆ Faithfulness	Proverbs 5:15–23
◆ Happy Marriage	Hebrews 13:1–6
◆ Yahweh and Israel	Isaiah 54:5–10

_____

_____

_____

_____

_____

_____

✐ JOURNAL

Think of three couples you believe have a quite happy and fulfilling marriage. Concretely, how does that *show* to an outsider, that is, what made you settle on these three couples? Again concretely, what do they *do* that probably keeps their relationship growing? If you are able, ask them.

Understanding Marriage

REVIEW

1. We have previously discussed the first five stages, or crises, in Erik Erikson's study of human growth. What are they? What is the desired effect of each crisis? What are the sixth and seventh stages that were introduced in this chapter? What is the desired effect of each?

2. What is the most basic cause within spouses for their inability to weather the conflicts of marriage together? Why are so many people today incapable of accepting and holding to what Maggie Antrobus insists is *the* bedrock of a marriage? Think back to what we said earlier about commitment.

3. Explain why romance is an absolute requisite for marriage.

4. Why *should* marriage be a *calculated* risk? What kind of probing would go into that calculation?

5. Why is conflict absolutely inevitable in marriage?

6. Why does the chapter assert that one of the worst things that has happened to marriage is "TV family sitcoms"?

7. What positive and negative effects on marriage has the two-income household brought about?

8. List five factors that should make both partners look more carefully before "leaping" into marriage.

DISCUSS

1. If both spouses don't engage in doing ordinary, undramatic household chores, there will likely be trouble, unless the wife (or husband) is a willing slave. Why is it that girls are trained from their childhood to do household chores and most boys are not? And if the wife chooses to become a willing "slave" (because she believes that is what her husband wants), what happens to his respect for her?

2. In marriage, no matter how busy the two partners, a key to success is to keep surprising each other. What kinds of things could spouses do to keep themselves interesting to each other? Don't be general; give specific things they could do.

3. Explain what happens in both marriage and in divorce when the "Child" in each partner makes the decision. In the event of divorce, what has *not* happened within each partner?

4. If there is any single factor at the root of broken marriages and a shattered childhood, it is this: The parents are simply too busy to take time to sit alone together and figure out just what they're doing. If a marriage fails, it is because genuine communication has failed. How do you avoid that?

5. No one is really pro-divorce, any more than anyone is really pro-war or pro-abortion. Explain why you agree or disagree with that opinion.

6. What does the high divorce rate in the United States have to do with the general breakdown of trust, which glues together our overall moral ecology? One little marriage out the window doesn't make any real difference, or does it?

ACTIVITIES

1. You are married with two children, a girl, age 12, and a boy, age 10. You and your spouse both work; your combined income is $80,000 a year; you have a suburban home with a heavy mortgage, which your income (with care) can handle. Other than the expectable differences of opinion, your family life and the personal life of each family member are pretty serene.

   Today two of your most trusted friends, independently of each other, have given you unquestionable evidence that your spouse has been having an affair for about five months.

   Continue the episode by role-playing with your best friend, then with a member of the clergy, and finally with your spouse.

2. Check the library (the librarian will be glad to help) for statistics and information on: the age group in which most divorces occur today, the age group in which the fewest divorces occur, some of the reasons for those statistics.

3. This activity will take some tact, and it's wise not to undertake it without the advice of your parents. Interview someone you know who has been divorced. What reasons can he or she give you to help you make a wiser choice about your marriage?

14. FAMILY

SURVEY

Circle the number on the rating scale under each statement that best reflects your opinion about that statement. On the scale

    +2 = strongly agree,
    +1 = agree,
     0 = can't make up my mind,
    –1 = disagree,
    –2 = strongly disagree.

Then share the reasons for your opinion.

1. No great harm is done to infants when mothers return to work six weeks after their infants' birth.
   +2 +1 0 –1 –2

2. Better to be too lenient with children rather than risk being too strict.
   +2 +1 0 –1 –2

3. Boys should be trained to be fathers as girls are trained to be mothers.
   +2 +1 0 –1 –2

4. Children need privacy but not *too* much privacy.
   +2 +1 0 –1 –2

5. Teenagers should begin to contribute financially to the family.
   +2 +1 0 –1 –2

6. A teenage girl should not have to secure parental consent for an abortion.
   +2 +1 0 –1 –2

7. As with divorce, family problems usually arise from lack of communication.
   +2 +1 0 –1 –2

8. Suicides of teenagers from affluent families often result from impossible expectations of life.
   +2 +1 0 –1 –2

9. The highest rate of suicides is in the 75 to 84 age range.
   +2 +1 0 –1 –2

10. Doctors should be allowed to hasten the deaths of brain-dead victims.
    +2 +1 0 –1 –2

A FABLE

NUDGED FROM THE NEST

Once upon a time at the edge of a huge forest lived a woodcutter, his wife, and their two children, Hansel and Gretel. Famine stalked the land like a herd of white wolves, howling in the bellies of the starving peasants. At night the woodcutter tossed and turned and moaned to his wife, "What shall become of us? How will we save our poor Hansel and Gretel? Not to mention ourselves."

His portly wife grunted, "Nothing simpler, husband. We'll take them out tomorrow and pretend we're going into the trees to cut wood. Then we'll just walk away and be shed of them."

The woodcutter gagged, "Oh, I wouldn't have the heart! Wild beasts will come and tear them apart!"

His wife snorted, "Perhaps you'd rather I feed myself to beasts then?" And she gave him no peace till he consented.

Because of the hunger boiling in their bellies, Hansel and Gretel couldn't sleep either, and they heard every word their parents said. Gretel wept, but Hansel said, "Hush, Gretel. I'll take care of us." And he crept out into the moonlight and filled his pockets with white pebbles that lay there like silver coins. Then he crept back into bed and waited for the dawn.

Next morning the family set off into the dark woods, and as they went Hansel slipped the pebbles from his pocket onto the path. When they reached the dark heart of the forest, they built a fire, and their mother said, "All right, children. Lie by the fire and stay warm. We must chop some wood." So off they went.

At noon the children ate their bread and then fell asleep. When they awoke, it was dead dark and the wind whipped the trees into a frenzy. "Oh," Gretel sobbed, "bears will eat us up!"

Hansel patted her shoulder. "There, there," he said. "Wait till the moon comes up." And when it rose they found their way home, following the pebbles glinting in the moonlight.

Imagine their Mama's surprise when she saw them on her doorstep the next morning. "You naughty children," she lied, "we were worried sick." And she shot a look at her husband that said the story wasn't over yet. And Hansel knew that if Papa had given in once, he'd give in again. He just didn't know when.

A few weeks later their mother came into their bedroom before dawn. "Up, you lazy lumps. We need to cut wood again. Here is your bread. Get cracking." What could the children do? Their mother would see Hansel picking up pebbles. So off they went, their hearts heavy, when suddenly Hansel got an idea. As they walked, he broke bits from his bread and dropped them along the way so he and Gretel could follow them back as they had the pebbles.

The parents left the children by the fire and went off, they said, to cut wood. At noon Gretel shared her bread with her brother, and the two fell asleep again. They woke in the dead dark and waited for the moon; but when it rose over the frightening treetops, Hansel couldn't find his breadcrumbs. Birds had come and eaten them all up. "Never mind," Hansel said, not too convincingly, "we'll find a way." But they didn't.

They walked and walked till their legs were stiff as andirons and their bellies churned like disposals, when suddenly there appeared out of the forest the most astonishing little house. Its walls were bricked with brownies, the roof was nubbly peanut brittle, and the moss on the eaves was cotton candy. So, with astonishingly bad manners, Hansel broke off a slab of roof and Gretel began gnawing hungrily on the delicious walls.

Suddenly in the doorway stood a pretzeled crone with long wispy hair and eyes like poached eggs squinting from under tufty white brows. Her skin was dusky and crinkled as dead leaves, and one spiky white hair snorkeled from the black wart at the tip of her sweet-potato nose. "We-e-e-el!" the old hag cackled. "Children! *How* lovely! *My* name is Virago, my pretties. Oh, come in, *my* dears! Come in, come in! You're so thin! We must fatten you up, mustn't we?"

So Virago clucked over them, fed them blueberry pancakes and butter and syrup, and led them to two little beds with crisp white sheets, and Hansel and Gretel crawled in and thought they'd found heaven.

But as soon as they had fallen deeply asleep, Virago swooped on Hansel and carried him, still dazed with fatigue and his heavy meal, out into a dark, dark shed where she clanged him into a cage. And the witch, for so she was, scuttled back to her house, which had returned to its original horrifying shape. Green slime oozed from the walls, and rats skittered through the rotting straw roof. She shook Gretel like a dustmop. "Up, idle hussy!" she rasped, her breath like an open sewer. "Stir up the fire! We'll cook *your pretty little brother a delicious dinner and fatten him up! And when he's nice and plump, I'm going to eat him!" And she honked like a donkey with its tail on fire.*

Day after day Gretel toiled at stove and oven, cooking steaks and potatoes and chocolate cakes and banana cream pies for Hansel, and all she had to eat was scraps and her tears. Three times each day Virago pawed her way into the dark, dark shed with Hansel's meals; but before he could eat, she always hissed, "Put out your arm, boy. I want to feel if you're getting plump." But after the first time, shrewd Hansel poked through the bars a hambone he'd gnawed clean.

"Rats!" said the witch. "More starch!" And off she went to beat Gretel for being a lousy cook and then went down in the cellar to count her gold and jewels to see if the lazy little minx had gotten into them while she was out.

After four weeks Virago returned from the dark, dark shed, her white brows knotted like thunder clouds over her flaring eyes. "Enough!" she cried. "Heat the oven, you scurvy scamp! Plump or skinny, I'm going to eat your wretched little brother today!"

Poor Gretel didn't know what to do. Sobbing, she tried to fumble the wood and drop the matches till she could think of a plan. "Stop horsing around," Virago shrieked. "And bag the tears! It'll do you no good. Get cracking, or I'll heat the oven myself and eat you first!" Her brow knitted and she cackled as if she'd had an idea. And Gretel suspected what that idea was.

Finally the fire was roaring, and Gretel called to the witch. "The oven is ready, but there's a terrible smell coming from it. I think something's inside."

Virago shouldered her aside. "I don't smell anything," she snarled. "But then I've got a bit of a cold."

Gretel swung open the big, iron door. "There," she said and sniffed and made a face. "Something rotten."

Again Virago sniffed and scowled. "Imagination," she spat, but she didn't relish being poisoned. So Virago leaned far into the oven and sniffed again. As she did, Gretel shoved her with all her might, slammed the iron door and bolted it fast. The witch howled inside; and within moments there was, indeed, a most powerfully rank smell coming from the oven.

Gretel ran to the dark, dark shed and banged open the cage with a rock. She and Hansel ran into the sunlight, capering for joy. Then they went into the cellar, scooped up gold and jewels, and found their way home, where their parents were only too delighted to see them again. Not to mention the gold and jewels.

Until they discovered that Hansel and Gretel had no intention of staying.

▷ Questions

Unlike other folktales, the villain in this one is not a stepmother but the children's own mother. If you took the story literally, it would be monstrous: two parents stranding their kids out in the forest so they can save themselves. But think of the day your mother or father "stranded" you at the kindergarten door. How did you feel about your parents at that moment?

Remember that these stories are told from the child's-limited-point of view. What does the story say about the role parents have to play in their children's growth—even when it's painful to the parents? What indispensible lesson did the children learn by being stranded out on their own?

A READING

Beth and Calvin Jarrett had two sons, Buck and Conrad (the "him" both parents speak of in this scene from Ordinary People, *by Judith Guest). Buck, his mother's favorite, died in a boating accident, and Conrad, sick with guilt that it was his fault, tried to cut his wrists and was in a mental hospital for eight months. Beth is a club-woman, chic, and controlled; she did not cry at Buck's funeral. Calvin is a lawyer, sensitive, trying to break Conrad's painful defenses. The two are at the home of Beth's brother, Ward, and his wife, Audrey.*

"Why don't we finish it?" he [Calvin] asks.

She [Beth] looks up. "Finish what?"

"What you started out there tonight."

"I started? How did I start it? By suggesting we go away together on a vacation? And I didn't stop it, either, you did. You were the one who walked away from me, remember?"

"What the hell was I supposed to say to that? The old song and dance, I overprotect, I breathe down his neck.". . .

"Why are you so obsessed?" she snaps. "God, I am sick of talking, talking, talking about *him!* He controls you, even when he's not around, even when he's two thousand miles away."

"Oh, stop it. We haven't exchanged a dozen words about him in months—that isn't the problem. *He* isn't the problem."

"Isn't he?"

"No! So let's talk about what's really bothering you."

"Oh, no, let's talk about what's bothering *you!* That's what you want, isn't it? That's why you go around moping and depressed—just the way you used to! As if it helped, being half-alive, dragging everybody else down with you!". . .

He struggles for control, his senses blurred. Important. This is important, don't screw it up, don't get off on old songs, old dances. "I am asking you to tell me," he says slowly, "what I've done that's made you so angry with me."

"It's not what you've done," she says. "It's what you think I've done.". . .

"I don't know what you mean, I don't think you've done anything."

"Oh, you liar," she says bitterly. "You do, and you know it. You blame me for the whole thing."

"For what whole thing?"

"That whole vicious thing! He made it as vicious, as sickening as he could! The blood—all that blood! Oh, I will never forgive him for it! He wanted it to kill me, too!"

And suddenly she is crying. . . . Bewildered and frightened, he goes to her, kneeling beside her chair, . . .

> *Without forgiveness life is governed by... an endless cycle of resentment and retaliation.*
>
> ROBERTO ASSAGIOLI

"Beth, I love you, honey, please let me help.". . .

"Help? What do you mean, help? I don't need it. Not your kind of help. I can help myself.". . .

Ward and Audrey are standing in the doorway.

"Hey," Ward says softly, "I'm sorry about this. We don't want to butt in.". . . .

Ward moves toward her. "Honey."

"I don't know what you want from me anymore, Cal. I don't know what anybody wants from me!"

"Honey, nobody wants anything from you," Ward says. "We all just want—Cal and Con and everybody, we all just want you to be happy."

"Happy!" She looks at him. "Oh, Ward! You give us all the definition, will you? But first you'd better check on those kids. Every day, to make sure they're good and safe, that nobody's fallen off a horse, or gotten hit by a car, or drowned in that swimming pool you're so proud of! . . .

"And then you come and tell me how to be happy."

> ▷ *Questions*

The tension in this relationship has been building for a long time. Notice Calvin is the one who wants whatever is spoiling their marriage out in the open. What is Beth's reaction? You sense it as soon as she says, "Finish what?" Can you find the precise words for her strategies in this scene?

The source of Beth's anger is the same as the source of her cool distance from Conrad (she never visited him in the mental hospital). "Oh, I will never forgive him for doing it!" What did she believe Conrad was doing to her with his suicide attempt? Do you sense she has empathy for her son?

Beth says, "I don't need it. Not your kind of help. I can help myself." What does that say of her personality?

In her long speech beginning with "Happy! . . ." what does Beth tell of her understanding of the relationship between parents and their children?

What one healthy character trait have we seen over and over that is almost completely lacking in Beth Jarrett?

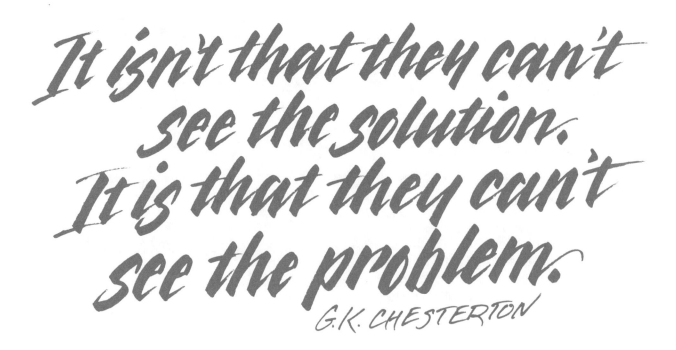

It isn't that they can't see the solution. It is that they can't see the problem.

G.K. CHESTERTON

THEME

FAMILY

An old Chinese proverb says, "It is easier to be in charge of a kingdom than of a family." Why?

There are books about family life, but no rule book that can surface the hidden wounds deep within each parent or the unpredictable differences in the children or their completely different reactions to the same set of parents and siblings. Nor are there any guidelines that tell how to cope with the accidents that are inevitable in life and different for every family—and for every unique individual in that family.

Perhaps the two words, *yielding* and *understanding,* we saw in the last chapter on marriage might serve as at least tentative guidelines for a healthy family. Both of these approaches require not only empathy and vulnerability to each of the unique others, but also the ability to communicate understanding—and have the other members hear and respond to it.

As the wise Atticus Finch says in *To Kill a Mockingbird,* "You never really understand a person until you consider things from his point of view—until you climb into his skin and walk around in it." But that is *very* difficult to do, especially for people who don't yet know the person walking around in their *own* skin.

How do parents, for instance, put aside for a moment all the principles they have wrestled with for a lifetime —to say nothing of the blind biases many of them cannot even admit, much less critique—in order to understand and forgive a son who declares in anguish that he is a homosexual or a daughter who is pregnant? How do parents lay aside the wound inflicted on *them* by their child's wounds? How does a son or daughter lay aside the confusion and hurt to understand and forgive a parent who has gone off to marry someone else or is an alcoholic? How does a brother or sister understand and forgive a sibling who has betrayed his or her trust? How can the elderly understand and forgive the young for being too fast, too loud, too new-fashioned. And how do the young understand and forgive the elderly for being just the opposite?

Communication is an easy word to bandy about, and counselors use it often. But like the valves of a physical heart, the channels between family members may have been silting up for years because each of them—old and young—have been busy about things that to them, at the moment, seemed more important than communicating with one another.

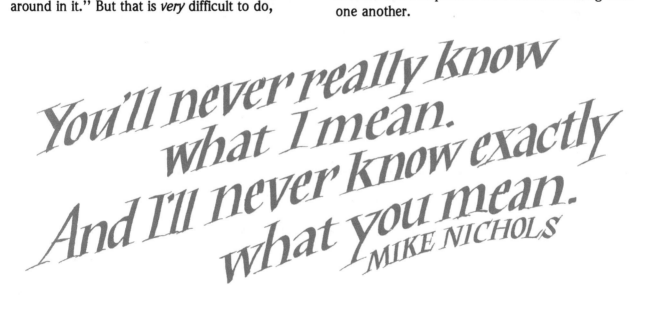

You'll never really know what I mean. And I'll never know exactly what you mean.
—MIKE NICHOLS

At times the understanding and forgiveness are there, but the words are not. At times the shared truth is too enormous for words (as at a wake) and the only answer might be "arms around one another and mute tears." The family in which members have a barrier against touch and tears will find their mutual life far more difficult than families more comfortable with sharing their mutual vulnerability.

That, of course, is what a liberal education is, or should be, for: to give people the ability to read books, to climb inside other people's skins and walk around in them for a while, and to give the words to embody the understanding. But too often education is merely a sentence served in numb servitude to a job certificate.

What also makes family life difficult is that family relationships involve not only the legitimate rights of the self, but the legitimate rights of the others. A family is a microcosm of our human ecology. Parents have obligations to their children, but they also have obligations to their own still-growing selves. Parents must be vulnerable to their children, but they are also flinty places against which to hone their children's growth to adulthood. The children must not only be obedient and loyal to the family, but in search of a unique self. The aged deserve respect, but they also need to yield to change.

There, then, are at least a few lodestones for a family, four words, *yielding, understanding, forgiveness, communication*—often expressible only by touch, picked up like four lucky pebbles on a path.

By the accident of birth—and thousands of hours of bonding that forged sharing the "slings and arrows of outrageous fortune"—we become a family. Every "is" involves an "ought." Even against our wills we share a web of human relationships in a family, which is by that very fact a moral relationship. The cliche remains true: "Home is where, when you go there, they *have* to take you in."

PARENTS TO CHILDREN

Erikson's seventh stage of natural provocation to growth is Generativity: establishing and guiding the next generation. When that stage fails, there is a regression into a sense of stagnation and impoverishment. Many childless couples turn their natural need for generativity onto other nurturing activities, like caring for dogs and cats. Without children to keep throwing adults curves, the adults can become very dull, unless they're really willing to work at staying alive specifically as human beings.

For the first half-dozen years, parents are in a relationship with their children that is pretty much one-way. If the child's popping eyes and goo-goo smiles are not endlessly fascinating and worth all the effort a child requires of parents, and if one or both parents do not have a healthy grasp of their own self, tragedies can begin slowly to brew—for both parents and children. If the parents cannot forget themselves, the parent-child relationship can become a "curse and cursed."

There are two extremes to governing, whether in a nation or in a home: individualism and the totalitarianism. Every other way falls somewhere between the two.

Individualism lets things go to wherever the Id points: Growth is an opportunity to experiment and a result of finding things out for oneself; but it is also chaotic. No parent, no matter how open-minded and iron-nerved, is utterly flexible in regard to cleaning up after a willful child. And some children go through a lot of unnecessary pain that their parents' experience and courageous intervention could have prevented. Very often, discipline says: "I love you so much I'd rather have you hate me for a while." But often it is more difficult for parents to carry around rightful guilt without punishment than it is to carry around the brief pain of disciplining a child.

Totalitarianism nails down every corner exactly as the parental Superego wants it: Things are very orderly, very peaceful. But the totalitarian's approach is also inhuman; no child can grow *without* making mistakes. A child must never be allowed to believe punishment is rejection or anything more than a temporary matter. And a child must begin to realize Mommy and Daddy have feelings too.

Once the child is two or three (often earlier), many mothers will have to go back to work, whether they want to or not. About two-thirds of all mothers work; about half of them work full-time. The Census Bureau has reported that half of all mothers with infants return to the job before the child's first birthday, and 51 percent of women with children under age three work; a figure that has now grown to 63 percent with "absolutely no signs of leveling off." Some children will receive day-care that often does not have a single, constant, reassuring caretaker's presence, but a confusing series of different voices and attitudes.

We also have the phenomenon of the latchkey kids who come home from school, read the instructions on the fridge, and often just turn on the TV. If the issue is survival, as it sometimes is, survival is a burden the child has to bear and grow with. But if having two working parents is just an issue of a better life style, then something else ought to give, rather than the child's mental health.

As children move into adolescence, many parents who have done a superb job—while their children were still dependent on them—become completely ineffective. Some parents might even think, "It's like Martians switched kids on me. She was such a sweet little thing; now she's turned inna some kinda hellcat." For all the dumb simplism of that statement, there's a certain amount of truth there.

On the one hand, the parents haven't been as aware as they should have that the change in the "little girl" has been going on for some time. She is, in fact, no longer theirs, nor little, nor just a girl. On the other, if parents haven't been reading anything outside of their own fields—and the newspapers—they're not aware the little girl grew up in a world much different from the one they grew up in. There's a truth to the snappish response: "You were never my age."

As children naturally begin to reach for more freedom, parents still have only a "driver's manual"—if that—to guide them and they must take the curves as they come upon them. But parents must have some time of peace (no matter how hectic their lives) to read, to consult, to analyze together not just how their children are progressing but how their own marriage is progressing.

If there is any single factor at the root of broken marriages and shattered children, it must be: Parents are simply too busy making a living, making a home, keeping up with the Joneses, living up to what they think are their kids' expectations, providing, and "intending"—to have time to sit down alone together and figure out just what they're doing.

So, to *yielding, understanding, forgiveness, communication,* and *touch,* add *time together.*

Basically, the parents' job is to render themselves unnecessary, to help a child *interiorize* the reasons for being a good human being. Parents must both have lives of their own, to keep on growing themselves—if only as a gift to each other and the children they serve. But they are also

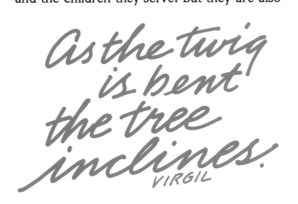

As the twig is bent the tree inclines.
VIRGIL

preparing future parents, men and women who won't have to be on the phone all day asking their Superegos what to do.

The release of the children to their own freedom can't be abrupt; adulthood is not a thermostat that clicks on either at puberty or at college graduation. Nor is it merely a stage a kid drops into, not to be heard from in any meaningful way until age twenty-two. Young people need the challenge, daily, to start fulfilling a meaningful role as adults. That is why every youngster ought to have a job, and put half the salary into the bank—not for personal expenses in college, but for tuition.

"I worked a lifetime so my kids wouldn't have to wade through all the grief I had to wade through to get where I am—hating the other kids for their cars and their clothes and their summer homes. So, I did it. The only thing I didn't give them is what I *got* from wading through all that grief: spine."

Nor is adolescence a process of turning the children into new, improved editions of "the Old Man" and "the Old Lady." Adolescence is an experiment in freedom; and when you honestly give freedom, the results can be surprising. He may want to be a clown; she may want to be a Marine. There is the "genius" of the good parent: knowing instinctively when the occasion calls for flint and when for vulnerability, and having the courage honestly to apologize when one has used the wrong tack. Socrates and Atticus Finch provide good guidelines: hearing the raspy questions and snotty comebacks, feeling the jutted chin or the tears from *inside* the sender. Any parent of an adolescent has to become as sensitive to signals as a secret agent—or the mother of a newborn baby.

Sex is one serious issue between parents and adolescents. If parents are not vulnerable and honest in communicating about that issue, their children surely won't bring parents any questions that are more important. If a father can be vulnerable enough to say, "I had problems when I was standing in front of a rack of soft-porn magazines too," or a mother say, "I was stupid-blind-crazy about a boy once too," there would be fewer communication problems in a family. The worst thing parents could pretend to be—believing it is for the children's sake—is flawless. They're not. And time will prove that true.

(If you want to give this to your parents and ask them to read it, feel free.)

There are only two lasting bequests we can hope to give our children. One of these is roots; the other, wings.
HODDING CARTER

CHILDREN TO PARENTS

There is no problem when young people ordinarily respect their parents' opinions and believe them to be right—except, of course, when the opinions are objectively wrong. Problems arise when the teenager believes the parents to be dead wrong about things: drinking, sex, curfews, questionable friends, grades, religion.

The answer is, I think, the Atticus Finch test again: Get inside your parents' skins and walk around in them for awhile. But honestly, probably the toughest three words for you to say are "I was wrong." When you genuinely are wrong and can't or won't admit it, don't say that's pride refusing to bend; it's arrogance—narcissism. Get inside your parents' heads and see the question from *their* point of view, which often includes perspectives larger than you're willing to admit. If you're willing to mouth the cliche "Experience is the best teacher," admit that your parents have had a whole wagonload more experience—and pain which has been overcome and assimilated—than you have.

A good touchstone for arguments between parents and children is to divide questions into matters of principle (religion, politics, morality) and matters of experience. Matters of principle deserve a real honest rake-over. That's what you have brains for: to govern your own Id and to critique your own Superego. But in matters of experience, nine times out of ten your parents will be right. They know more than you do about sex, about money, and about getting along with people. They were adolescents too, remember, and they have outlived it. It's hard to believe, but your parents do—honestly—know more from *experience* about sex than you do. They'd be willing to talk about it, I'm pretty sure, if *both* sides weren't so shy of each other. Sad, really—so much experience that could have helped someone else.

A discussion between parents and children at least ought not to be a battle, yet quite often it is. As with spouses, if either side wins and shows up the other, both sides lose. Is that all you want, to belittle the other side? To stand over the other with your sword raised? Dinner table battles over religion, like the battles in the Near East and Northern Ireland, have less to do with religion than they do with *power*. If "standing over the other side" has become a given in your life, sit back and ask: "Is that what anyone wants? Does it do any good?" All it does is rile and hurt the two people without whom you wouldn't exist.

Yielding, understanding, forgiveness, communication, touch, time together.

There is—or ought to be—nothing you can't tell your parents when you're confused or depressed or despairing. That's what they're there *for.*

But you may get the idea (especially if communication stopped a long while ago—no matter who stopped it) that your parents are too busy, too judgmental, too out-of-it. How do you know that unless you've tried to talk with them again, not as child-to-adult but as emergent-adult-to-adult?

If a problem is so bad that it ties you up in that kind of knot, it wouldn't be something you'd take to a *kid* for advice, right? You should take it by rights, to your parents. But if it can't be taken to them, then it ought to be to *some* adult whose life seems to give you reason to trust him or her. My hunch is that most of the too-many teenage suicides could have been prevented if the kids involved had been vulnerable—trusting—enough to find one vulnerable adult to talk to.

What can be done when "negotiations have broken down and all ambassadors have been withdrawn"? Ideally, it should be the mature adult parent who sets up peace initiatives. But that is not always the case. If two or three people are living in the same house in a state of war, there are only two alternatives: Escalate, or make peace no matter what the cost. Get the parent into the car, on any excuse, and pull off to the side of the road and talk: "Now. Let's make peace."

My wise Aunt Gladys one time said to me, "You're ashamed of your parents, aren't you?" I denied it, vehemently. But Glad saw though me. "Just remember, Mister College. If it weren't for those two dumb people in there, you'd never be where you are now."

Probe the earth and see where your main roots run.

HENRY DAVID THOREAU

SIBLINGS TO SIBLINGS

Without our realizing it, family is the twenty-year laboratory where youth discover how to cope with the way the web of society works: getting along with people.

The Enneagram shows nine basic personality types, but using the Enneagram is only a handy way to *begin* narrowing down what a person is like inside. Each person in each Enneagram type is as uniquely different from every other person in that type just as each person's DNA is uniquely different. Children of the same parents are uniquely different; each child came into the family at a different time, under different circumstances, with different reactions.

With such variances, there are bound to be conflicts of goals and wills in a family—just as there are in the outside world. Your big brother won't let you hang around with his in-crowd; your little sister itches to paw through your stuff; your sister borrows your sweater and starts to think it's hers; your brother spends an hour a day in the "john" admiring his muscles or counting his acne, and calls you a wimp.

Again, there are only two ways to deal with conflict, in the family or in society: Escalate, or make peace. We all want peace, but we all want our pride too. We also want power—or at least not to be power*less*. There is only one painfully simple question: Is dominating more important than belonging? Which do you want more? You will face that choice no matter what the society.

One useful gimmick when you contemplate "fratricide" or "sororicide" is to force yourself to be calm for a moment and picture your brother or sister lying in a coffin. Morbid? Perhaps, but it is going to happen some day. We don't realize how precious people are to us—under all the hassles— until we realize they are only "borrowed on time." Death is grim, but it is a reality; and acknowledging it puts our petty problems with one another into perspective.

These people are—or could be—the most precious in your life if only you'd get your perspective back and shake hands. *Yielding, understanding, forgiveness, communication, touch, time together.*

THE AGED

Commercials are a far cry from reality. For instance: They picture Grandma chattering away with the children on the phone, or Grandpa walking with a boy along the lane to the fishing hole. Perhaps that's true for some families, but not for all and not forever.

People get old, and in our society people are living longer. It is the family's obligation that they live longer with as much dignity as possible.

Retirement can often be a new lease on life. But what has to concern a family about retirement is when its elders suddenly find themselves at a loss without the tyranny of a schedule. One big answer is to force them back into activity: Enroll them in "Elderhostel." Or take them to the movies or a ballgame or to bingo, even if you find it frightening, and even if you feel you have "more important things to do." Surely this is as much a genuine obligation for grandchildren as for their parents, at least if the grandchildren want to be considered adults.

If grandparents are in a nursing home, the obligation to reach out to them falls not just on their children but on their grandchildren as well. Sometimes visiting with older family members is not pleasant; you're not sure how much you say is getting through. But you have to be there, if not for the old person's sake, for your own. You have a responsibility to a person without whom you would never have existed.

You are an emergent adult; your sense of responsibility will not click on automatically on the morning of your twenty-first birthday. What's more, remarkable things can happen—for both little children and for old people—when even grammar school children are taken once a month to visit them in retirement homes. Our aged *deserve* our respect and attention.

Yielding, understanding, forgiveness, communication, touch, time together.

SUICIDE

Surprisingly, the highest suicide rate in our country is in the age group from seventy-five to eighty-four. Obviously, many elderly people find themselves purposeless, friendless, and unable to cope with pain any longer. Others are without families, or with families too busy to pay them much attention. Again, young people can make a difference to elderly people. There are so many needs and so little time that even the best-intentioned can pick only one service to offer people in need. Perhaps reaching out to the elderly is the one for you.

Suicide seems a strange topic in a chapter on family, and yet it is a rending of the moral web that binds the victim to the rest of the family. Suicide is the ultimate divorce, and just as with divorce, we often become aware of the symptoms of suicide after it is too late. The answer, then, is to be more sensitive, especially to our own families—and resolutely courageous in intruding. It is appalling how many suicides are abetted by a family's shyness or fear of embarrassment or reluctance to intrude. Politeness hamstrings love.

If anyone you care for shows prolonged symptoms of the blues, withdrawal, or snappishness, don't hesitate to say, "Okay, just give me a minute. I don't want to stick my nose in. But there's something wrong. Don't tell me there isn't. I know you. Now you don't have to talk to me. I want to, if you do. But you've got to talk to somebody. Please. I love you."

It's not overdramatic.

Yielding, understanding, forgiveness, communication, touch, time together.

EUTHANASIA

Ending the life of someone incapable of recovery is a family moral problem too. Certainly there is no moral obligation to take extraordinary and impoverishing means to keep a person alive when the best medical advice says there is no reasonable hope of recovery. Although one might think the rights of family members who have known the terminally ill all their lives should supercede the rights of outsiders, sometimes the state or special interest groups intervene and insist extraordinary means be used to continue someone's life. That situation can be averted if a person in sound mental health signs a living will expressing his or her desire that such an intrusion not be allowed. Without that living will, the family can be impoverished both by medical bills, and by legal fees trying to challenge the courts. It is an iniquitous state of affairs, especially because well-intentioned people are not prolonging life but prolonging death.

Sometimes, however, as in the Karen Quinlan case, the patient who is taken off a respirator and heart-lung machine continues to survive. That is the thorniest question. Common decency dictates that the patient at least be given nourishment and be kept clean and comfortable. But some would go further and defend the right of the patient's family—whatever the anguish—to cut off nourishment or even to induce painless death.

One can only state the objective facts: Any human entity has the inalienable and self-evident right to life, which in turn guarantees the right to nourishment without which life is impossible. To deny that right is to kill a human entity, which is undeniably premeditated homicide. The question each person in this quandary—as in war—must face is: Is this a justifiable homicide or not?

However, in the event of an attempted suicide where the victim's personal will and certain intent is to end his or her own seemingly unbearable life, common decency would induce any onlooker to try to intervene. How much more, then, a blood relative?

DILEMMA

"My name's Michelle Cassidy. I've got a problem. My parents. They are one *big* problem. I mean, why can't they mind their own damn business? 'Who were you with? When did you get home? Were you drinking?' I mean, I'm grown-up, right? I mean, why can't they let me mind my *own* damn business?

"It's not as if I'm some kind of tramp or anything. 'That skirt's too short! You're not going out of this house dressed like that!' Don't they know that *everybody* dresses this way? Why can't they think back when they were young?—if they ever were.

"I happen to know, from my Aunt Doris who they won't have anything to do with, that my mother was pregnant with me *before* the two of them got married. How d'ya like *them* apples? Why is it that *I've* gotta be purer than white soap, and *they* did 'it' long before they tied the knot? Where's the justice there? I mean, is that *hypocrisy* or what?

"What *right* do they have to know what I do when I'm out with Jamie? It's like reading somebody else's mail or listening in on the phone— which I think they do too. How do I get through? How do I get them to back off? What am I, some kind of kid in grammar school?

"I mean my mother goes, 'I don't want you to make the same mistakes I did.' What am I, a *mistake?* What am I supposed to make out of that? *They* got through all this bilge—I'm ready to throw up when I hear about it all again. What makes them think they know what me and Jamie can't?

"You're somebody I trust. What do I do?"

▷ *Questions*

Michelle really feels that she is "grown-up," but her parents don't seem to think she's that "grown-up." Michelle and her parents are in conflict. What is that conflict? What is causing it?

What do you think needs to be done *by all* to resolve it? How would you answer Michelle's reaching out to you, "You're somebody I trust. What do I do?"

FAITH REFLECTION

You have heard that people were told in the past, "Do not commit murder; anyone who does will be brought to trial." But now I tell you: whoever is angry with his brother or sister will be brought to trial, whoever calls his brother or sister "You good-for-nothing!" will be brought before the Council, and whoever calls his brother or sister a worthless fool will be in danger of going to the fire of hell. So if you are about to offer your gift to God at the altar and there you remember that your brother or sister has something against you, leave your gift there in front of the altar, go at once and make peace with your brother or sister, and then come back and offer your gift to God.

Matthew 5:21–24 (adapted)

Judging from the many occasions in which Jesus dealt with people who had done far worse things than call a relative a bad name, he is not implying here that such an action is a one-way ticket to hell. What he says at the end of the quotation shows that such sins can easily be forgiven—but only if one *asks* forgiveness. Often, that can be very difficult indeed.

Sometimes, when you have hurt a member of your family, the person's anger makes her or him refuse to accept your apology, or you feel so humiliated at your own stupidity that you kid yourself into thinking the other person would refuse your apology. But there are only two alternatives: an apology or a cold war, in the same house.

There are brothers and sisters, parents and children, who haven't spoken to one another in years. More often than not, they would be hard-pressed to remember just why the rift had occurred in the first place; and if they can remember, nursing the old grudge has often blown the original cause out of all proportion.

The point is: How can anyone call himself or herself a Christian when he or she nurses a grudge against a family member? According to Jesus, the punishment for that kind of self-absorption and hard-heartedness is very severe indeed. Regardless of hell, both the perpetrator and the victim go on suffering right here and now—when all it would take is a sentence to cut loose the anchor from both their souls.

📖 FURTHER BIBLE READINGS

Skim these Scripture passages. Pick one that appeals to you and (1) summarize its main point, (2) tell how it relates to the chapter, and (3) list one or two thoughts that entered your mind when you read it.

◆ The Family Bond   Ruth 1:1–22
◆ Joseph and His Brothers   Genesis 37:1–37
◆ Forgiving Peter   John 21:15–19
◆ The Aged   1 Timothy 5:2–7
◆ Settling Disputes   Romans 6:1–6

_____

_____

_____

_____

_____

_____

✏ JOURNAL

Name and describe each of your brothers and sisters. Describe how each enriches your life. Show where you come in conflict with each, and how you usually resolve the conflicts.

If you are an only child, describe how being an only child has been an advantage *and* disadvantage.

Understanding Family

REVIEW

1. Why is it easier to govern a kingdom (or any civic entity) than a family?

2. Explain the difference between the two extreme methods of governing a family, the individualist and totalitarian.

3. Give the six "lodestones" the chapter suggests for keeping a family's relationships healthy and life-giving. Show how each affects the relationships of parents to children, children to parents, siblings to siblings, and the aged.

4. What happens to our growth as human beings if we reject or shirk Erikson's seventh stage, Generativity?

5. What's wrong with the sentimental old song, "And she's Daddy's . . . little . . . girl"?

6. Explain these statements:

   a. The parents' basic job is to render themselves unnecessary.

   b. Adulthood is not a thermostat that clicks on either at puberty or at college graduation.

7. Why is the responsibility for caring for grandparents as much the grandchildren's responsibility as it is the responsibility of the grandchildren's parents?

DISCUSS

1. Why is it often easier to be vulnerable with friends—or even with strangers—than it is with your own family?

2. Why will the family that has set up barriers against touch and tears find its life together far more difficult than families more comfortable with and who share a mutual vulnerability?

3. A liberal education should give people the ability to read books, to climb inside other people's skins and walk around in them for a while, as well as the words to embody understanding. But too often school is merely a sentence served in numb servitude to a job certificate. Why does that happen?

4. Parents must not only be vulnerable to their children but also be flinty places against which children hone their adulthood.

5. "I worked a lifetime so my kids wouldn't have to wade through all the grief I had to wade through to get where I am—hating the other kids for their cars and their clothes and their summer homes. So, I did it. The only thing I didn't give them is what I *got* from wading through all that grief: spine." Why is that conclusion—no spine—true?

6. Any parent has to become as sensitive to signals from their adolescent son or daughter as to those of a newborn baby.

7. Why is it true that dinner table battles over religion—like the battles in the Near East and Northern Ireland—have less to do with religion than they do with power?

8. If two or three people are living in a state of war in the same house, there are only two alternatives: escalate or make peace—no matter what the cost. Why?

ACTIVITIES

1. As a group or as individuals, visit a nursing home. Be extraordinarily alert to details: Watch how the people hold themselves; listen to the kinds of things they talk about to one another and to you; sniff. Then come back and write a *detailed* report of your visit.

2. Role-play one or all of the following, with one person playing the parent and another the child:

   a. "Don't ever bring a black kid (or any other member of a group a family might be prejudiced against) in this house again!"

   b. "Your brother thinks you're smoking grass."

   c. "All those lousy Democrats do is raise my taxes to feed no-goods on welfare."

   d. "I'm pregnant."

   e. "I'm going to drop out of college."

   f. "I'm gay."

   g. "I'm not going to church anymore."

3. Get a copy of a living will. Probably a lawyer friend could supply one. What does it ensure? What does it cost? Would you feel comfortable signing a living will yourself?

15. SEX/GENDER

SURVEY

Circle the number on the rating scale under each statement that best reflects your opinion about that statement. On the scale

    +2 = strongly agree,
    +1 = agree,
     0 = can't make up my mind,
    −1 = disagree,
    −2 = strongly disagree.

Then share the reasons for your opinion.

1. Selfishness is bad; but total selflessness isn't so good either.

   +2 +1 0 −1 −2

2. Males who offhandedly touch each other are quite likely homosexual.

   +2 +1 0 −1 −2

3. Most women go to college, just waiting till they get married.

   +2 +1 0 −1 −2

4. If your teenage son asked for ballet lessons, you'd have cardiac arrest.

   +2 +1 0 −1 −2

5. Males may *feel* more sexual, but females *are* more sexual beings.

   +2 +1 0 −1 −2

6. Female inequality in jobs is based entirely on pervasive male chauvinism.

   +2 +1 0 −1 −2

7. Boys are, by their nature, more competitive and analytical than girls.

   +2 +1 0 −1 −2

8. Schooling should make boys more "masculine" and girls more "feminine."

   +2 +1 0 −1 −2

9. Industrial society is a "jungle" because it is exclusively "masculine."

   +2 +1 0 −1 −2

10. To advance in the professions, a woman must be tougher than most males.

   +2 +1 0 −1 −2

A FABLE
A Head Saved by a Tale

Once upon a time in a place called Samarkand, there was this Sultan who was fabulously rich and supremely powerful—but not overly adult. He trusted women less than rabid dogs. Two basic reasons. First, growing up in a harem with 217 mothers all of whom wanted their own sons to succeed to the throne over him even by recourse to poison, bribes, and other unfair means, left him a bit wary. Second, he discovered that since he had become Sultan, every one of his many wives had betrayed him with the slaves, delivery men, newspaper boys, and even (some averred) the palace eunuchs.

Well, that made the Sultan pretty furious. Not to mention depressed. He made up his mind no woman would ever do that to him again. I mean, a man's got his pride. Still, after his dog-eat-dog, nose-to-the-grindstone, shoulder-to-the-wheel, rat-race day in the royal hall, a man deserves a little diversion. So the Sultan had this terrific idea: Every night he'd sleep with a virgin; and when dawn came, off went that virgin to have her pretty little head lopped off. It was a clever and efficient solution to the Sultan's problem—even though, as I said, not very adult, nor very popular with the virgin population.

After a few months, there just weren't any virgins left—except for the beautiful Scheherazade, daughter of the prime minister, who wasn't keen on his daughter's one-night stand with the Sultan but who did value his job rather highly. This Scheherazade was not only a dutiful daughter but a very guileful girl. She decided she was not only going to survive, but also wean the Sultan from this quite childish and uncivilized treatment of his female subjects who had begun to cut their losses and offer their virginity to any passerby.

So after the Sultan had had his way with her, they were lounging in the (now deserted) harem with Scheherazade wiling away the hours till dawn when she was to be taken off for dismemberment. The small talk, understandably, began to wane; and the Sultan began to yawn and talk vaguely about calling it a day. But since "calling it a day" meant something considerably different to Scheherazade than it did to the Sultan, she said, "Ahem! I can tell a story." And she started to tell the Sultan about the adventures of Sinbad the Sailor, and the Sultan really got caught up in it.

Just at dawn, Scheherazade stifled a yawn. "Well, really been nice meeting you, your majesty," she said and rose to begin the long walk to the chopping block.

"Wait!" the Sultan said muzzily. "You haven't finished the story. Come back tonight and finish it for me."

Scheherazade curtsied politely and headed for a well-earned rest, unable to keep her lovely fingers from straying to her lovely neck, which still connected her lovely head to her lovely body.

Well, that Scheherazade was one smart odalisque. She kept breaking off her stories just at dawn for a thousand and one nights, which, if you're not too good at math, is nearly three years. Actually, the Sultan wasn't as dumb as it first appeared. Just deeply ego-bruised and bulldog-stubborn.

After a while, he looked forward each evening even more to being with Scheherazade than to hearing her fascinating stories. He was beginning to soften. And Scheherazade began to notice how really attractive the Sultan was, which in turn added a considerable surge of warmth, vigor, and spice to her narratives, to the pleasurement of both parties. She became more interested in saving the Sultan from his depression than she was in saving the new crop of virgins that had managed to survive due to her cunning. The Sultan and Scheherazade had managed, pretty obviously, to fall in love.

So, amid great jubilation (especially among the country's virgins), the Sultan and Scheherazade wed and became one. Or so we are given to understand.

▷ Questions

Who is more Id-dominated, the Sultan or Scheherezade? Who is more Superego-dominated?

The two are incompletely human; what do each of them lack? Neither one supplies what the other lacks, but rather provokes the other into discovering something within and into bringing it to the surface. What is that, for each of them?

What happens when someone, no matter what sex, focuses seriously on someone *other* than his or her self?

What does the story really mean when it says "they wed and *became one*"? That fusion means something more than a mere literal marriage.

A READING

The following scene from another not-quite-realistic play Who's Afraid of Virginia Woolf, *by Edward Albee, takes place after a gin-soaked, bitter, emotional orgy in which Martha and her husband, George, have raked not only each other over the coals but also their younger guests, Nick and his wife Honey. George, a professor—bookish, controlled, icily witty—has left the house, and Martha and Nick are glumly talking after an unsuccessful attempt at sex together.*

NICK: Everybody's a flop to you! Your husband's a flop, *I'm a* flop. . . .

MARTHA: You're all flops. I am the Earth Mother, and you're all flops. I disgust me. I pass my life in crummy, totally pointless infidelities . . . *would*-be infidelities. Hump the Hostess? That's a laugh. A bunch of boozed-up . . . impotent lunk-heads. Martha makes goo-goo eyes, and the lunk-heads grin, and roll their beautiful, beautiful eyes back, and grin some more, and Martha licks her chops, and the lunk-heads slap over to the bar to pick up a little courage, . . . and they bounce back over to old Martha, who does a little dance for them, which heats them all up . . . mentally . . . . while Martha-poo sits there with her dress up over her head . . . suffocating—you don't know how *stuffy* it is with your dress up over your head— suffocating! . . . There is only one man in my life who has ever . . . made me happy. Do you know that? One!

NICK: The . . . the what-do-you-call-it? . . . uh . . . the lawn mower, or something? . . .

MARTHA: No; I didn't mean him; I meant George, of course. Uh . . . George; my husband.

NICK: You're kidding.

MARTHA: Am I?

NICK: You must be. Him?

MARTHA: Him.

No indulgence of passion destroys the spiritual nature so much as respectable selfishness.
Geurge Macdonald

195

NICK: Sure; sure. . . . .

MARTHA: . . . George who is out somewhere there in the dark . . . George who is good to me, and whom I revile; who understands me, and whom I push off; who can make me laugh, and I choke it back in my throat; who can hold me, at night, so that it's warm, and whom I will bite so there's blood; who keeps learning the games we play as quickly as I change the rules; who can make me happy and I do not wish to be happy, and yes I do wish to be happy. George and Martha: sad, sad, sad.

NICK: Sad.

MARTHA: . . . whom I will not forgive for having come to rest; for having seen me and having said: yes; this will do; who has made the hideous, the hurting, the insulting mistake of loving me and must be punished for it. George and Martha: sad, sad, sad.

NICK: Sad.

MARTHA: . . . who tolerates, which is intolerable; who is kind, which is cruel; who understands, which is beyond comprehension. . . .

NICK: George and Martha: sad, sad, sad.

MARTHA: Some day . . . hah! some *night* . . . some stupid, liquor-ridden night . . . I will go too far . . . and I'll either break the man's back . . . or push him off for good . . . which is what I deserve.

NICK: I don't think he's got a vertebra intact.

MARTHA: You don't, huh? You don't think so. Oh, little boy, you got yourself hunched over that microphone of yours. . . .

NICK: Microscope. . . .

MARTHA: . . . yes . . . and you don't see anything, do you? You see everything but the goddamn mind; you see all the little specs and crap, but you don't see what goes on, do you?

▷ Questions

Martha says, "I am the Earth Mother." What connotations from primitive religions does that title carry? What kind of rites did they perform? In its way, this play is a similar rite: sacrificing someone you love for personal reprieve.

Look carefully at the words Martha chooses and the subjects she focuses on; what do they say about her personality *as* a woman? How does she challenge the feminine stereotype? What does she let out which most women don't?

If she's telling the truth (and in this play, you can never tell), Martha has frequent affairs with strangers like Nick; and yet George and she are still together. Can you guess why two such antagonistic personalities keep going? If you can, explain her statement: ". . . the hurting, the insulting mistake of loving me and must be punished for it. . . ." Martha says that some drunken night she will get rid of George one way or another "which is what *I* deserve," not what George deserves. Can you explain what she means?

Explain: "You see everything but the goddamn mind; you see all the little specs and crap, but you don't see what goes on, do you?"

What others think of us would be of little moment did it not, when known, so deeply tinge what we think of ourselves.
George Santayana

196

ME TARZAN, YOU JANE

At the outset of the Scheherezade story, both of the characters have pretty good control of their wits, at least in the sense that each knows how to use cunning. But the Sultan is a caricature of a pouting, childish, power-mad, macho male: a lion with brains and loins but no heart. And Scheherazade seems a caricature of the noble, self-sacrificing, submissive, saintly female: a lamb with brains and heart but no loins. Surely, there's nothing of Martha in Scheherazade's known self. It's only through their gradual fusion that they become one: completely human. The lion lies down with the lamb; she becomes enlivened by his royal vigor and he becomes enobled by her generous vulnerability.

In simpler stories, the male is the clear-eyed and clear-thinking, noble, muscular knight; and the female is the muddle-headed, helpless damsel-in-distress. (Probably because most such stories were written by males.) Not so in this story, and not so in this life.

In the Scheherezade story, it's the male who is in distress and the female who is the rescuer. And in this life, each of us—no matter what our sex—is both. Despite the solely left-brain (therefore half-witted) assertions of such eminences as Luther, Hegel, Freud, and Henry Higgins, males are not singularly sterling chaps nor are females merely brood-sows, their heads "filled with cotton, hay, and rags."

Far too easy—therefore the usual procedure—to stereotype males as muscular, competitive, autonomous, and analytical; and females as pliant, cooperative, dependent, and intuitive. "Everybody knows" males make good business leaders and scientists; females make good homemakers and nurses. Males think; females feel. As so often, a single- (therefore simple-) minded theory blinds us to the observable truth. There are some crackerjack female heads-of-state, astronauts, and brain surgeons, and most of the world's musicians, artists, and chefs are male.

Still, witless theories die hard. We like our distinctions and categories iron-walled and consolingly certain. Thus even a father who prides himself on an open mind finds something at least a bit "unseemly" when his boy plays with dolls too long or asks for ballet lessons. Similarly, a "normal" mother feels a twinge when her girl can throw a baseball better than any of her boys or wants to learn auto mechanics. Perhaps "tomboy" is a passing phase; the number of lesbians, after all, is relatively small. But "fag" seems a lifelong stigma that has to be fought with even brutal means. "They," after all, seem to be sprouting up all over nowadays, even in impossible places like the National Football League.

The mere use of *normal* and *unseemly* shows we have some kind of "standard" of what males and females ought to be. The question is whether it is an objective standard based on the unchangeable *natures* of males and females, and therefore a moral question; or merely a subjective preference based on no more than changeable whims of a particular individual or society or century, and therefore morally completely indifferent.

Do you not know I am a woman? When I think, I must speak.

William Shakespeare

On one hand, male priests hurled female virgins off cliffs to placate the gods, fathers sold or drowned less desirable female babies, officials noted for fervent religious practice neutered males to do guard duty in harems or to have more beautiful singing voices for papal choirs. On the other hand, French kings wore weird hairdos, Joan of Arc led an army, Madame Curie discovered radium, Scotsmen wear skirts, contemporary men get their ears pierced, and more than half the doctors in the Soviet Union are women. Both males and females are human beings. As such, both have absolutely equal rights, not only to the needs of physical, animal life, but also to the needs of intelligent, human life. No one can legitimately treat any human, either male or female, in the same way as he or she treats a rock or a turnip or a goat. The objective humanity in the potential victim commands respect, no matter what her or his sex.

But even little children playing doctor discover that, although males and females are equal, they are not the same. The sole objective physical difference between males and females is in their reproductive organs. Genitally speaking, as the philosopher Rousseau wrote: "The male is only a male now and again, the female is always a female, or at least in her younger years." A male experiences his sexual difference only in the act of copulation; but a woman experiences her sexual difference not only in copulation but also in menstruation, conception, pregnancy, labor, and nursing. Macho males may *feel* more sexual, but any woman *is* more sexual.

Outside of sexual intercourse a male may be reminded of his sexuality by an often pleasurable nocturnal emission, but a woman is reminded of her sexuality every month by her menstrual cycle, which is not pleasurable at all. If any objective inequity exists between the sexes, it is precisely there: Although the sexual act may be pleasurable to both males and females, the events leading up to and following the act of intercourse are in no way equal. But since that inequity antedated the

caves, no one can blame it on any male-dominated society or any culturally imposed custom or tradition. It is a natural, objective fact that can be blamed only on God or some faceless Fate or the quirks of evolution. An unsatisfying explanation? But also undeniable.

Outside of matters explicitly sexual, males and females are—and should be treated as—equal. Women are as (or more) intelligent, as (or more) resilient, as (or more) decisive. With advances in technology, even some physical and muscular differences are becoming no longer really differences: A woman can start a harvester or operate a crane or press a rocket button as well as any man. However, it's unlikely science will soon devise a way that a man can conceive a child and carry it.

Despite their human equality with men, there are situations where a woman's sex does in fact work against her, particularly in the marketplace where a woman often faces job and wage discrimination, not to mention out-and-out "pig-ignorant" chauvinism. But I'm concerned here only with getting an honest picture of the basic differences in male and female psychology—independently, for the moment, of further issues.

Each of us is an intelligent self, but each of us is also an *embodied* self. Our bodies have an effect—sometimes justified, sometimes not—on our psychology, our way of looking at life and at ourselves. Those differences affect—not objective morality—but our *viewpoints* on morality. Skin color, disfigurement, wasting disease, or a loss of limbs have a stunning impact on the mind and soul, but they do not make us less human. Often, in fact, they have precisely the opposite affect. But they do change a person's viewpoint.

The same, I think, must be true of our sexual differences. Since sexuality is such a radical physical difference, I cannot help but think that, by nature and not by custom, males and females must view life from different points of view—not unequal, mind you, but different. That difference may be *amplified* by customs (like dolls or footballs) sheerly external to it; but the radical difference, I think, is there.

I cannot believe there is not a marked psychological difference between a person who has accustomed herself to the monthly bleeding of menstruation and a person who has not. There must be a difference in her sensitivity to pain and to her compassion for those who undergo pain. (This does not mean that only women should be nurses; it does imply that they might be naturally better at being nurses—and perhaps better at being doctors and clergy.) Far more, I cannot believe a woman who has actually conceived, carried, nursed, cared for, cleaned, fed, and coddled even a single child would not be profoundly affected by those experiences, and sensitized in a way no male, no matter how well-intentioned, could ever be. All women don't react to either menstruation or to childbearing in the same way. But no man has ever had even the opportunity.

Given that difference and its resultant natural (not society-induced) potential for compassion, is there any further natural, significant difference between the psychology of females and males *before* puberty has activated their genital differences?

Because parents know that more or less all female children grow up to be mothers and homemakers creating protective, civilizing space and that more or less all male children grow up to be fathers and breadwinners climbing the beanstalk and bringing home the golden goose, parents more or less assign roles along with the "proper" toys and games—tea sets and dolls and jump ropes; baseball gloves and video games and submachine guns—long before the genital differences of boys and girls are activated. Again, the word *proper* implies that the standard (normal) little girl is a peaceful homebody and the standard (normal) little boy is an aggressive go-getter—by *nature.* But is that true?

NATURE/NURTURE

The nature/nurture controversy has been around as long as the chicken/egg controversy. Whether you believe boys are "aggressive" and girls "adaptive" because of the way they are made (nature) or because of the way they've been brought up (nurture) depends pretty much on which psychologist you have read last. But whichever is the cause of such characteristics (or if both are), until the definitive answer arrives from Delphi and the appropriate changes are made, we have to take children as we find them.

Many psychologists maintain that because a male child grows up with a mother of the opposite sex, he develops his individuality by separation from her; a female child, however, experiences herself as "like her mother," and, therefore, doesn't feel this separation. Thus, they say, the female individuality develops by vulnerability, by relationships and connections with other people; while the male individuality develops by invulnerability, by establishing more defensive ego boundaries.

Further, psychologists claim girls experience themselves as less differentiated than boys: their internal worlds are more continuous with the external world and have fewer ego boundaries. Finally, since masculinity is defined through separation while femininity is defined through union, male gender identity is threatened by intimacy, while female identity is threatened by separation.

This, psychologists claim, comes from nature, not from being nurtured in any particular society. To an extent, I can accept that. But I would think, a little girl, just as a little boy, feels the same necessary maternal abandonment at being weaned, potty trained, put outside to play, and left at the kindergarten door as boys do. Nor can I accept that a boy, by his *nature,* brushes away maternal (or paternal) caressing and stroking "because it's sissy." Sissiness, like all prejudice, has to be taught. If boys—and older males—resist physical forms of affection when they are a genuine sign of the love we all claim is the purpose of human life, I cannot believe that such resisting is "natural" but rather that it is "societally induced." Nor can I imagine that females find solitary confinement any more painful than males do.

Peer groups are a major factor in socialization (nurture), and playtime is the major agent of a child's socialization. Janet Lever found that boys play outdoors more than girls do; boys also play more often in large groups of broader age-range, play more competitively, and for longer periods of time—not because the games require more skill, but because disputes arise more often among boys and boys seem to enjoy the debates as much as the games themselves. In contrast, girls are more tolerant in their attitudes to rules, more willing to make exceptions to include the clumsy and unskilled, and more easily adaptable to innovations than boys are. Rather than elaborating rules for resolving disputes, girls would rather stop the game, because they find the game itself less important than the friendships.

The girls want to play; the boys want to win.

Thus, Lever says, the male model of playing games fits the requirements for modern corporate success, while the care for feelings that girls show in games has little market value and can in fact impede professional success—unless a female learns to out-tough the male. She has to learn to play like a boy.

Ironically, however, though academic education seems to be square in the stereotypically "male" arena, most school teachers are females. Thus a boy is left to think that education is girl stuff, while a girl who stereotypically should be taking nothing but home ec, health, and checkbook-keeping, is forced to take trigonometry and physics. Something skewed there if the natural stereotypes are correct in even the flimsiest way.

For two years, Erikson studied one hundred and fifty boys and one hundred and fifty girls at play constructing a scene with toys on a table as if they were setting up a shot for a movie. Erikson found that the girls emphasized "inner" space while the boys emphasized "outer" space. The girls' scenes were most often interiors, sheltering people and animals, having low walls and elaborately inviting doorways. The boys' scenes were almost exclusively exteriors, having high walls with towers, and had more moving pieces, more accidents, more ruins, more policemen. Ruins, in fact, were exclusively boys' constructs. From his studies, Erikson concluded that, by nature, children's games in some way subconsciously mirror the children's own genital structure: the boys with external, the girls with internal genitals.

Differences in play skills and interests might possibly be rooted somewhere in nature. However, just as the methods (and motives) of competitive professional athletics filter down to university and high school athletes, so, too, the methods of competitive business filter down to children at play and to adolescents choosing career courses—subtly expressed to the child through inadvertent scowls and grins from parents, through the jeers and cheers of the peers, and most especially through role models on television.

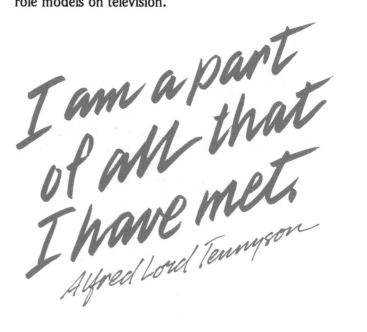

I am a part of all that I have met.

Alfred Lord Tennyson

GENDER: MASCULINE/FEMININE

Just as a definition can't completely exhaust all facets of the reality it tries to define (that is, box-in), so there are also limits to all psychological schemes, whether developmental or behaviorist, Freudian or Jungian. On the one hand, the very nature of our minds forces us to categorize, to group objects into classes so we can understand them better by studying properties the objects have in common. But, on the other hand, each object—each snowflake, puppy, human being—although remarkably similar to others of its grouping remains unique. We want our definitions as sharp-edged as cookie-cutters.

Unfortunately, reality doesn't usually conform to our desires. Therefore, it would be foolish to believe that because one has slapped a generic label on a person, one has understood the person. *Male* and *female* are matters of observable fact; they are definitive, either/or categories. But *masculine* and *feminine, analytical* and *intuitive,* or even *heterosexual* and *homosexual* are no more a matter of either/or than *conservative* and *liberal* are. They are not definitive; they are approximative: more/less.

Once we are out of the womb, there is no great difficulty separating males and females. All Mommy and Daddy have to do is lift the diaper and look. Differentiating sex (male/female) is easy and clear: completely an objective, left-brain operation. Differentiating *gender* (masculine/feminine) is not so easy or clear: it implies more subjective, right-brain operation. A lot of problems arise, however, when we fail to see that the two—sex and gender—are *not* the same.

Unlike a person's sex, gender is an approximative, either/or judgment call. Gender is not a matter of definition (as sex is), but a matter of *connotations;* that is, resonances a word sets up in the listener—as in the fact the word *home* has warmer connotations than *house,* and *steed* has more romantic connotations than *nag.* Slovenly thinking, unfortunately, has constricted the words *masculine* and *feminine* into nearly equivalents of *male* and *female.* So if you say a female writer's work is very masculine or a male's reaction to someone in need was very feminine, you'd better be prepared to defend yourself.

Masculine means, roughly, all those character qualities we wrongly associate solely with males, not *manliness* and *virility* that deal with sexuality, but attitudes and preferences: logic, analysis (taking apart), tough-mindedness, decisiveness, competition. *Feminine* means, roughly, all those character qualities we wrongly associate solely with females, not *womanliness* and *mothering* (sexuality), but attitudes and preferences: intuition, synthesis (putting together), openness, patience, cooperation.

Critics who bristle at applying those words and qualities to the wrong sex, seem to have no problems applying the masculine qualities to the mental viewpoint of Greek thinkers: "The Western Mentality"; and the feminine qualities to the mental viewpoint of Hebrew thinkers: "The Eastern Mentality."

The Greeks were people of very incisive minds and were dedicated to clear definitions and rigid logic in seeking the truth: To know = to define. Their viewpoint survives today in Western scientific method, computers, efficiency reports, assembly lines; it also has its dark side: quantitative judgments of people (the SAT's), deification of competition, the rat race.

The Hebrews, on the other hand, were people of very intuitive minds. Their sense of the truth was more relational than logical: To know = to trust. For instance, the Hebrews had no concept, as the Greeks did, of something just existing. The Hebrews asked, "What did it exist *for?*" *To be* meant nothing by itself. Something had *to be with,* or relational. For the Hebrew the epitome of knowing was sexual intercourse in which a person "knew his or her spouse," which, you will agree, has very little whatever to do with analysis or definitions. The Hebrew viewpoint survives today in Eastern mysticism, meditation, calm acceptance, absorption into the "All"; it also has its dark side today: fatalistic acceptance of the status quo, passivity, and, to some, fuzzy-headedness.

This does not say the Greek or the Hebrew approach to truth is *better.* Both are good, and in order to have a fully-rounded assessment of the truth, one must use both approaches.

One's approach to the truth has its impact on interpersonal (moral) relationships. For the Greek-Western-Masculine mind, knowledge is associated with certitude: A proposition is proved by logic, as one proves a formula; *perfection* has connotations of being both flawless and needless of further growth. For instance, abortion is, objectively, premeditated homicide.

In contrast, for the Hebrew-Eastern-Feminine mind, knowledge is associated not with certitude but with trust: A proposition is proved not by logical formulations but by experience, as one person proves herself to another; *perfection* has connotations not of completeness but of organic wholeness capable of growth. For instance, abortion (like war) has to be judged not only against some iron vertical scale but also by its effects on persons—including the perpetrators.

Carl Jung has made a strong case that the human self is *androgynous;* that is, whether male or female, each of us has both masculine and feminine qualities—just as men and women secrete both male and female sex hormones. The masculine qualities in the female, Jung called the *animus;* the feminine qualities in the male, he called the *anima.* Like the yin and yang of Chinese psychology, they complement each other, but only when there is a *conscious* synthesis of the two—which is a feminine undertaking.

If a male exhibits only his masculine traits, his feminine traits (anima) become unconscious and remain primitive as the Sultan's would have if he hadn't met Scheherazade: the macho man who weeps for mercy. If a female exhibits only her feminine traits, her masculine traits (animus) also remain unconcious and primitive as Scheherazade's would have if she hadn't found the Sultan as exciting as her cause: the pretty little featherhead princess who juts out her jaw to be lopped off for nothing.

Thus, both the female's animus and the male's anima have real, positive power. In order to survive—in fact, to be fully human—a female needs the so-called masculine qualities of logic, analysis (taking apart), tough-mindedness, decisiveness, and competition. In order to survive and be fully human, a male needs the so-called feminine qualities of intuition, synthesis (putting together), openness, patience, and cooperation.

Both animus and anima have a dark side: In either a male or a female, feminine feeling without masculine strength is wooly sentimentality; masculine power without feminine love is brutality

The finest people marry the two sexes in their own person.

Ralph Waldo Emerson

(like Martha in *Who's Afraid of Virginia Woolf*). On the one side, there is the tyrant male and the temptress female; on the other side, the nerdy male and the dewy-eyed damsel.

Nowhere is this more obvious than in business, politics, and government. The "System" is, by its capitalist, competitive nature, predominantly—at times exclusively—masculine. Uncontrolled and uncritically accepted, the exclusive pursuit of power, prestige, and accomplishment impoverishes us (male or female) in that it drives out all the feminine, anima values. It becomes not the pursuit of excellence, as it's so often miscalled, but the pursuit of brute dominance. That pursuit is one reason for the metaphors dog-eat-dog, rat race, and jungle (that is, nonhuman).

Even when the feminine is called into play in business (by males or females), it is sometimes prostituted in the name of conquest: "Because you're my friend, I'm gonna make you a deal." "Mommies who really love their children give them chocolate cake and sugar cereals and candy bars."

What's more, individuals project the repressed, primitive animus/anima on others; that is, blame someone else for having the very traits they're ashamed to admit they have themselves. The underfeminized macho male goes out and beats up "queers"; the undermasculinized doormat female thinks all successful business women are "butch"—little realizing they're saying more about their own impoverishment than they are saying about the people they are criticizing.

It is our feminine qualities that humanize, civilize, give meaning to *human* life: relatedness to others, the ability to soften power with love, awareness of inner feelings and values more important than merely winning, respect for the earthly environment rather than for making the quick buck, the introspective quest for inner wisdom. It is not just making a living, but knowing what living is for.

Carol Gilligan quotes Dostoevsky's *Crime and Punishment* to show the difference between the masculine and the feminine approach to morality—whether in males or females. Raskolnikov has murdered an old woman, meaninglessly, only to "prove" himself. Sonia, his lover, will not turn him in to the police even though she loathes his crime. Because she loves him, she persuades him to turn himself in, but not because a crime has been committed and must be "paid for"—the masculine demand that the books be balanced again. The masculine judge in Sonia sees the crime; the feminine lover in her sees beyond that to the criminal. She convinces Raskolnikov to turn himself in so that he can redeem himself. Mere punishment does nothing to change the victim or the perpetrator. Freely accepted, legitimate suffering does.

Sonia's answer is not better than a judge's just because she is a woman. It is better because she is fully a human being.

Let the final word go to Mother Teresa of Calcutta, who is every inch a lady, but as unstoppable as a Sherman tank:

> *It is not very often things that people need. In these twenty years, I have come more and more to realize being unwanted is the worst disease any human being can ever experience. For all kinds of diseases there are medicines and cures. But for being unwanted, unless there are willing hands to serve and there's a loving heart to love, I don't think this terrible disease can ever be cured.*

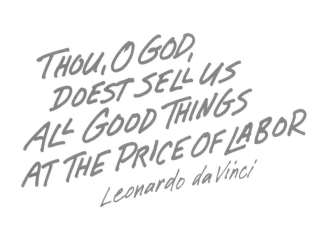

THOU, O GOD, DOEST SELL US ALL GOOD THINGS AT THE PRICE OF LABOR
Leonardo da Vinci

DILEMMA

Kenny Lindner sat at the opposite end of the couch from his hockey coach, Packy McGuire. Packy was the only guy he could have told about Becky, about how much he loved her, and about what they'd done, and then, about Becky coming to him in tears, and about the clinic, and what they had done with the baby.

Kenny's face sagged as he turned to the bulldog face of his coach. "Do you think we . . . do you think. . . ?"

Packy's sad face mirrored the boy's pain. He sighed, "It doesn't matter what I think, Kenny. You feel, deep down, that it was something terribly, terribly bad. That's what matters."

Suddenly the boy's big shoulders began to quake, and the tears spilled hotly down his cheeks. He was filled with grief and shame for what he and Becky had done, for crying like a kid in front of his coach. It wasn't manly.

He felt Packy's weight shift on the couch and the old man's arms come round him and the big paw stroking his shoulder. Kenny turned his face under the coach's chin and sobbed.

"There, there, son," Packy said. "It'll heal."

Suddenly Kenny's body went rigid, realizing. He jackknifed to his feet, scrubbing his eyes with the heels of his hands. "Thanks a lot, coach," he stammered and hurried toward the door. "I'm sorry. I'm really sorry."

"Kenny, are you sure you're gonna. . . ?"

But the boy was already in the hall, his face burning, his lungs dragging for air, panicking at the thought that he'd have to turn in the old "queer" to somebody. But to whom? His parents? The principal? Kenny shuddered, feeling soiled.

▷ Questions

Is there any shred of objective evidence for the conclusion Kenny came to? What's behind his belief about his coach? What factors in his life influenced his opinion? How is his life impoverished by that unexamined belief?

FAITH REFLECTION

"A healthy tree bears good fruit, but a poor tree bears bad fruit. A healthy tree cannot bear bad fruit, and a poor tree cannot bear good fruit. And any tree that does not bear good fruit is cut down and thrown in the fire. So then, you will know the false prophets by what they do."

Matthew 7:17–20

In the Acts of the Apostles, the Rabbi Gamaliel gave the Jewish Council similar advice when it was persecuting the new Christian community, which it considered a heretic sect of Judaism:

"I tell you, do not take any action against these men. Leave them alone! If what they have planned and done is of human origin, it will disappear, but if it comes from God, you cannot possibly defeat them. You could find yourself fighting against God."

Acts 5:38–39

The will of God is expressed in the natures of the things God has made. Therefore, to condemn anything that is natural is automatically to condemn the will of God. Too often we leap to judgment about other people—men who are sensitive, women who are ambitious—when there is nothing whatever unnatural about them. Too often, too, we leap to judgment about others from only the slightest evidence: the way they walk or dress, their opinions and choices, the people they hang out with. There is only one important judgment: What kind of *human being* is he or she?

Considering what has been said about being human—moral—in this book, how would you judge a person not by his or her external behavior but by the kind of "fruit" he or she bears? Hint: It has something to do with knowing and loving.

Think about the types of people you simply can't abide. Picture some of their faces in your mind. Now, how do you think Jesus—or one of his followers—would deal with those people?

 ## FURTHER BIBLE READINGS

Skim these Scripture passages. Pick one that appeals to you and (1) summarize its main point, (2) tell how it relates to the chapter, and (3) list one or two thoughts that entered your mind when you read it.

◆ Immorality	1 Corinthians 6:15–19
◆ A Shrewd Woman	Exodus 2:1–10
◆ A Sensitive Man	John 8:1–11
◆ Joseph	Matthew 1:18–25
◆ Judith	Judith 13:1–12

 ## JOURNAL

Don't answer each of these questions separately. Just mull them over awhile and then write.

Female: Do you have a real interest in some area like math or sports that you "shouldn't" have? When the family is talking politics or business, are you seen and not heard? When you have a personal problem, do you sit down and work it out on paper or talk it over endlessly with friends? Do males—especially confident males—intimidate you? Do you stand up to them, argue with them, call their bluffs? What kind of wife would you like to be?

Male: Do you do housework about as much as the females at home do? Do you know how to cook? Do you have a kind of itchy resistance to things like poetry, plays, or soft music? When you have a personal problem, are you reluctant to talk about it with a friend? Do you ever go for long walks alone and just look around and muse? Think about your best male friend, somebody you'd give your last dollar to. Can you say, even in the silence of your own soul where no one can hear, "I *love* him"? What kind of husband would you like to be?

Understanding Sex/Gender

REVIEW

1. How are George and Martha precisely the opposites of the Sultan and Scheherezade? What has each of the four over-developed and underdeveloped?

2. Describe the stereotype of a male and female. What is objectively wrong with the stereotypes?

3. "Objective morality changes from age to age." Why is that statement false?

4. Explain why the mere use of the words *normal* and *unseemly* in our descriptions of males and females shows we have some kind of *standard* of what males and females ought to be. Is that standard objective or merely subjective?

5. Explain these statements:

   a. Macho males may *feel* more sexual, but any woman *is* more sexual.

   b. Unlike sexuality, gender is an approximative, either/or judgment call.

6. Explain the objective differences between the terms: *nature* and *nurture; male* and *female; masculine* and *feminine; Animus* and *Anima; punishment* and *rehabilitation.*

7. Give three reasons why some psychologists believe that male dominance and female inclusiveness are based in objective *nature.*

BONUS: Anybody look up *odalisque?* What does it mean?

DISCUSS

1. Without much or any thought, we attach such "killing" labels to people as "fag," "nerd," "bitch." What effect does such common character assassination have on the web of our moral relationships? Is anyone else degraded besides the victim?

2. How would you feel and what would you say or do if your son asked for ballet lessons or your daughter asked to be an auto mechanic? Give objective evidence to support your stand.

3. What do these statements say about our moral relationships?

   a. Since genital inequity between the sexes antedated the caves, no one can blame it on any male-dominated society or any culturally imposed custom or tradition.

   b. It seems impossible that there not be a marked psychological difference between a person who has accustomed herself to the monthly bleeding of menstruation and a person who has not.

c. It would be foolish to believe that, because one slaps a generic label on a person, one understands the person.

4. Why does a female need logic and analysis (taking apart), toughmindedness, decisiveness, competition in order to survive—in fact, to be fully human? Why does a male need intuition and synthesis (putting together), openness, patience, cooperation in order to survive and be fully human?

ACTIVITIES

1. You are the personnel director for a large computer corporation. Role-play interviews with each candidate. Each has an excellent record and has first-rate recommendations from their previous supervisors:

   a. a young, unmarried woman

   b. a male recovering alcoholic

   c. a single-parent woman with two children

   d. a man who seems somewhat effeminate

   e. a Kathleen Turner type woman

   After the interviews, vote on who gets the job. Tally the ballots. Who won?

2. Ask your "little" brother or sister (or a relative's or neighbor's "little" boy or girl) the following questions. Then write a report on the topic:

   a. What would you like to be when you grow up? Why?

   b. Did you ever think you might like to be (boy) a nurse or (girl) an astronaut? How come?

   c. If you were in a race just for fun and there were a disabled person in the race, would you give that person a head start? Why?

   d. When you're choosing up sides, are there people always picked last? What do you do about that?

   e. Do you ever play (boy) house or (girl) cowboys and Indians?

   f. When you feel gloomy or alone and left out, whom do you go to, your mom or dad, to get some comfort?

   g. Do you have any heroes or heroines? Who are they? What do they have that makes you admire them?

   h. What's your favorite subject in school? What's your least favorite? Can you say why you like the one and don't like the other?

16. L*O*V*E P*O*T*I*O*N*S

SURVEY

Circle the number on the rating scale under each statement that best reflects your opinion about that statement. On the scale

  +2 = strongly agree,
  +1 = agree,
   0 = can't make up my mind,
  −1 = disagree,
  −2 = strongly disagree.

Then share the reasons for your opinion.

1. Authentic love sets the other free genuinely to love others as well.

   +2 +1 0 −1 −2

2. Romance (being-in-love) can last forever if the couple guards it carefully.

   +2 +1 0 −1 −2

3. Romance is so explosive for teenagers that parents should guard against it.

   +2 +1 0 −1 −2

4. Sex is too intoxicating for teenagers to handle level-headedly.

   +2 +1 0 −1 −2

5. Love is not blind; being-in-love is blind.

   +2 +1 0 −1 −2

6. Family quarrels would be lessened if parents remembered their own experiences when they were young.

   +2 +1 0 −1 −2

7. Falling out-of-love is a chance for real love— with the same person.

   +2 +1 0 −1 −2

8. Many "steady" relationships are more exclusive than most marriages.

   +2 +1 0 −1 −2

9. A good marriage is not 50–50 but 100–100, with nothing kept for the self.

   +2 +1 0 −1 −2

10. Very often, being-in-love has many aspects similar to chemical addiction.

   +2 +1 0 −1 −2

A FABLE
TERMINAL ADOLESCENCE

*Once upon a time at the tail end of England there was this
kingdom called Cornwall. And in this kingdom there was this
fabulous knight named Tristan whose board scores weren't top
drawer, but who was all-Cornwall in every other field, from sword
to harp. He had, despite his youth, set some pretty impressive
records along the giant and dragon lines. Tristan was the nephew
of Mark, King of Cornwall, and the most precious thing in the
king's life, not only because he was making dragons an endangered
species, but also because he was the only child of Mark's dead
sister, Blanche-fleur; and Mark himself was unmarried and
childless.*

*As will happen when one seems unfairly gifted, Tristan's
enviability stirred up envy. Four barons, miffed that the best they
could ever hope for were silver medals, went to King Mark and*

demanded he produce an heir. Nothing against Tristan, mind you, but there, uh, had been some talk about the king's . . . well, call it "timidity." King Mark roared for a while about that one, but finally he saw they had a public relations point. So he sent Tristan off to Ireland with a by-no-means insulting bribe to fetch Princess Iseult the Fair, who from all reports made pious monks foreswear their vows when she just genuflected.

The Irish King found the bribe much to his liking, but Iseult the Fair wasn't that keen on spending what looked like a very long life as the bedmate of a grumpy, old barbarian who couldn't get a single girl in all of England to marry him. Tristan, like all bearers of ill tidings, was automatically hateful by association. As it turned out, Iseult's mother was not only a queen but also a sorceress, so she slipped a flask filled with one part wine to fifty parts l*o*v*e p*o*t*i*o*n to Iseult's maid. On the wedding night, the maid was to be sure Iseult and King Mark took a substantial dosage just before retiring, which would make happily-ever-after a better bet than death and taxes.

Alas, the best-laid plans even of sorceresses often fail to factor fate into the formula. On the sea journey to England, it got hotter than the hubs of hell; and Tristan and Iseult poked around for something to slake their thirst. "Oh, la!" says Iseult. "I found a flask of wine in my maid's suitcase." And . . . ka-zappo!

Well, they tried their best. They both really loved their relatives and were very loyal to their kings and all, but they were, remember, very young, and even the wisest of us finds that the Superego doesn't have much of a chance against an Id-laced l*o*v*e p*o*t*i*o*n. They went through agonies.

"I will die without you," Tristan gargled.

"Life is meaningless without you," Iseult gurgled.

That went on for three days until . . . well, who's not human, right?

Perhaps if they'd had more brains than beauty, they'd have headed the ship for Majorca. But they returned to Cornwall where King Mark was most pleased with his new wife and there was a riotous wedding.

From the start things were a bit edgy—what with lightning lasers of lust lancing from Iseult to Tristan and zapping back again. Even blind old pensioners felt the hot tingle when they groped their way through the electric field between their eyes. So for months they met to do what they felt helpless not to do, and, of course, they were caught. King Mark raged like a savage, and sent Iseult off to pleasure a band of lepers and Tristan to be burned very, very slowly at the stake. He loved them both dearly, but fair's fair.

But on the way, Tristan leaped off a cliff, used his cloak as a parachute, and landed without a scratch. He found the lepers, frightened them off with his sword, and ran into the forest with his beloved.

For three years Tristan and Iseult camped out in the forest in relative bliss. Passion, as we all know, is a thriver; and even though their bellies howled like standpipes sucking air and they didn't bathe too much because all the lakes had gone stiff as lucite with cold and they got on one another's nerves more often, they grinned till their faces hurt.

Then one day they met an old hermit named Ogrin who bawled them out, up, down, and crosswise: "Traitress to your husband! Traitor to your king!" Tristan and Iseult found their consciences leaning toward that. And their bodies leaning toward a nice, hot bath. So Ogrin interceded with King Mark, who forgave them and welcomed them back. So they returned, and everything was just fine again. For a while.

But once they started eating more than earthworms and stopped smelling like a pair of sewers, the old love potion started juicing up their batteries again and the atmosphere in the castle was once again sparking. They agonized. "Life is barren," she moaned. "Life is death," he groaned. So they made what the less puritan among us might call certain concessions.

But they were both getting older, and the potion seemed to be neutering down, and conscience was beginning to act as an uncomfortable antidote. So rather than continuing to betray Mark, Tristan bade Iseult a pretty hot-and-heavy adieu and fled to France, and Iseult settled down to make a proper wife and queen.

All went well. Iseult did make an admirable queen, wife, and mother. Tristan went from one victory to another in France, met a fine friend, Kaherdin, and married his lovely sister, Iseult of the White Hands. Happily-ever-after finally had a chance for both.

Only one problem: Tristan had spent so much time being faithful to Iseult the Fair—even above friendship, patriotism, sportsmanship, and at least half the Ten Commandments that he couldn't, ahem, make Iseult of the White Hands a proper husband—if that isn't being too confusingly delicate. Kaherdin got wind of the situation; and, after Tristan spilled the whole story, potion and all, Kaherdin proposed that the two of them return to Cornwall. If Iseult the Fair had transferred her affections to her lawful king and husband, Tristan could return to Iseult of the White Hands and get down to the serious business of happily-ever-after. If not, well, there was always therapy.

But Iseult the Fair had heard of Tristan's marriage and, though she'd almost forgotten him till then, went into a nearly terminal pout. When Tristan and Kaherdin showed up, she drove them off with a broom like a pair of pushy peddlers. So much for that.

Iseult of the White Hands, though a model cook, housekeeper, embroiderer, and furnace tender, was just not Iseult the Fair. So Tristan tried to heal his wounded heart in battle, where he got really wounded with a poisoned arrow. Nothing could cure him. Only the touch of Iseult the Fair. So he sent Kaherdin to fetch her from Cornwall. If she agreed, he was to bring her in a ship with a white sail; if she refused, he was to fly a black sail, and Tristan would turn his face to the wall and his back to the world, and buy the farm.

Iseult of the White Hands, ordinarily busy at that time of day sprucing up the palace powder rooms, had been, uncharacteristically, eavesdropping. And was she *mad! So,* a month later when she was puffing up Tristan's pillows, she looked out the window and said, "Oh, my stars, just look. There's Kaherdin's ship."

And Tristan croaked, "What . . . (cough) . . . color . . . (cough) . . . sail?"

And Iseult of the White Hands smiled down and said, "Why, a black *sail, lovey. Why do you ask?"*

Without a cough, Tristan turned his face to the wall and his back to the world, and bought the farm. Too bad, really. Because the sail really was white, and when Iseult the Fair burst into Tristan's room and saw him colder than Novaya Zemlya, she and the other Iseult exchanged a pair of scorchy looks. "My only one!" she squalled, and ran for one last kiss. Alas, due to Tristan's quick-freeze passing, there was still a rather lethal dosage of poison on Tristan's lips. Smooch, went Iseult. And turned her face to the wall and her back to the world, and bought the farm.

And that was that.

▷ Questions

If Tristan really loved Iseult the Fair, why wouldn't he rather she be a queen, happy in a palace, rather than miserable with him out in the woods? If she really loved him, why would she feel so betrayed when she learned he'd finally found someone who might be able to make happily-ever-after possible—as she, from years of experience, knew she simply couldn't do? Tristan and Iseult truly believed they loved one another. Did they?

Isn't it strange that both of the women in Tristan's life had the same name? Was the author too lazy to think of another one? What is the significance?

A READING

In this song, "Do You Love Me?" from Fiddler
on the Roof, *by Jerry Bock and Sheldon Harnick,
Tevye and Golde reflect, somewhat in surprise,
that they've been married twenty-five years. Their
marriage had been arranged by their parents.
Oddly, in all those years, they'd never had time
to ask each other—or even themselves—if they
loved one another.*

TEVYE: Golde, I'm asking you a question—do you
   love me?

GOLDE: You're a fool.

TEVYE: I know—but do you love me?

GOLDE: Do I love you?
   For twenty-five years I've washed your clothes,
   Cooked your meals, cleaned your house,
   Given you children, milked the cow.
   After twenty-five years, why talk about Love
   right now?

TEVYE: Golde, the first time I met you
   Was on our wedding day.
   I was scared.

GOLDE: I was shy.

TEVYE: I was nervous.

GOLDE: So was I.

TEVYE: But my father and my mother
   Said we'd learn to love each other.
   And now I'm asking, Golde,
   Do you love me?

GOLDE: I'm your wife.

TEVYE: I know—but do you love me?

GOLDE: For twenty-five years I've lived with him,
   Fought with him, starved with him.
   Twenty-five years my bed is his.
   If that's not love, what is?

TEVYE: Then you love me?

GOLDE: I suppose I do.

TEVYE: And I suppose I love you, too.

BOTH: It doesn't mean a thing,
   But even so,
   After twenty-five years,
   It's nice to know.

▷ Questions

How is Golde and Tevye's love drastically different
from Tristan and Iseult the Fair's? Golde and
Tevye's love is certainly a real factor in their lives;
it's supported them through many trials. Why
haven't they been able to *talk* about it? Because
it wasn't important?

Think of the themes that keep recurring in
modern love songs. What are they? Do they reflect
a relationship more like the one between Tristan
and Iseult the Fair or the one between Tevye and
Golde? Are most modern love songs really "love
songs" or just "being-in-love songs?"

*When we are young, we drink
   from thirst, or to get drunk;
it is only later that we occupy ourselves
with the individuality of our wine.*
   Isak Dinesen

THEME

BLISSFUL BLINDNESS

No need to ask why happily-ever-after was short-circuited from the start between Tristan and Iseult the Fair. Like so many heroes and heroines, they are, for all their gifts and advantages, children of inner poverty. Tristan—and King Mark—are men too long deprived of their own inner feminine: the gifts of human relatedness, the ability to soften power with love, the ability (as every good parent understands) to realize that true love means setting free the beloved. Like Psyche, Iseult the Fair is lovely, pampered, and spineless. These two lovers are incapable of loving. They are capable only of romance—of being-in-love.

The word *romance* comes from the Old French *roman,* which means a "tale or novel." Romance is, then, "story-book love," the kind celebrated in movies and songs: "You're my everything . . . You and me against the world . . . I would give my very soul and not regret it," and on and on. Those aren't really love songs; they're being-in-love songs. There are, in fact, very few true love songs like Tevye and Golde's. People who *really* love each other are most often too busy to think about it much. People *in* love can't seem to think (or talk) about anything else—Good clue, there.

Two people *in* love (though it is a very wonderful and beautiful thing) don't really love the other person as much as they love the being-in-love, though the love potion makes them think this is "true love." Each is *in* love with his or her *projection* onto the other. Projection not only overlays the other with one's own image of the perfect member of the opposite sex but also filters out any evidence to the contrary—something that would be obvious to a more objective viewer. What's more, too often a male "dumps off" his inner feminine (anima) on the female, and she "dumps off" her inner masculine (animus) on the male. You hear it all the time: "The little woman pretty well takes care of the church-going for me,"

and "Oh, my husband makes all those really important decisions."

Being-in-love is a truly enriching experience; so is loving. The difference between the two is like visiting the Alps and living there: When you visit the Alps, you spend the whole time in awe at their breathtaking beauty; when you live there, you pretty much take the beauty for granted and go on about the business of living. Being-in-love has one thing grating against it: reality—the objective and prickly uniqueness of each of the lovers, the rightful demands of outsiders, and, perhaps most of all, the inevitable erosions of time.

It was not mere laziness that kept the original authors of the Tristan-Iseult tale from finding a different and less confusing name for the second woman in Tristan's life—nor why later centuries of retellers refused to do it either. The two Iseults are the same person, the girl Tristan fell in love with and the woman he found himself married to. Later, the first Iseult becomes the "girl in the office" who makes Tristan feel all-Cornwall again. Tristan is the hunk Iseult the Fair adored as a girl, and Mark is the real husband she woke up next to twenty-five years later. Illusions versus realities.

When two young people are intoxicated with love potion, they lay claim to a special exemption from the law that governs ordinary folk: reality. "Things are different with us." Standards others invoke are naive, old-fashioned, not for people "in heaven."

But old Ogrin inevitably shows up. The reason the old-fashioned standards finally start getting through at last is that the standards finally begin to make sense. Why? The first factor is simple burn-out. You just can't go on very long living at that intensity without some breathing room. The second factor is that it's no longer as easy to make allowances as it was when the beloved's whim was one's command: "You and your bowling! (Or: Your night school!) I've got a few things that are important to *me,* too, y'know!"

The best definition of real loving I ever heard came from a seventeen-year-old boy who had been very much in-love. As will happen, the girl he was in-love with began to feel attracted to one of his friends. And he said to her, "If you really think that he can make you happier than I can . . . that's what I want."

That looks like the genuine article to me.

ILLUSIONS VS. REALITY

Being-in-love is like being in the womb. Both are wonderful—in fact, essential—places to visit. But, all in all, you really wouldn't want to live there. And Freud had some pretty negative things to say about people who wanted to get back to the womb: *thanatos.*

During adolescence you face all the old childhood battles all over again, as if you'd never fought them before. Instinct wars against reason again; the id resents the superego corset; skepticism undermines trust. Parents, who always seemed more or less able to understand before, don't anymore; perhaps they never really did. Same for teachers, pastors, and any other adult who doesn't act as confused as an adolescent. Unconfused equals arrogant—or insensitive.

What romance gives is trust again, hope again. Each person in-love begins to lower his or her ironclad, defensive ego boundaries again, to rise above (at times to soar above) the routine and humiliating smallnesses of the day, above the commonplace. At least for a while he or she finds that there just might be an ultimate meaning to life after all: a superhuman intensity to being alive that lifts two people out of the ordinary.

Suddenly people in-love are liberated from self-centeredness; in a frenzy of freedom, they smash all the critical mirrors; they look at someone else other than themselves. And that is a very, very good thing. They are freed from "pseudo-cool," the pretense of invulnerability that is laid over their exposed nerves like steel armor over the coward's

skin. All at once the fantasy virtues of childish stories seem possible in the real world again: honor, faithfulness, nobility. There is, at last, something—someone—to hold truly *sacred.*

But invariably—although those in-love would deny it to exhaustion—the bliss of romance is temporary. Like all things subject to the laws of thermodynamics, the intoxicating love potion wears off. Cinderella is back in the kitchen; Ayrehead has prickly skin. Being in love was, for a while, a regression back to infancy where one was utterly united with mother. At the height of the experience, the two had no ego boundaries at all (at least between each other), as close to Nirvana as any human can hope to be, outside the womb.

But just as the womb does, just as the good mother does, being-in-love finally creates a natural, disruptive, rejecting disequilibrium. That is true not only in adolescent love but in married love too. Invariably, wills come into conflict: He wants to have sex, she has a headache; he wants a new car, she wants a microwave; she hates his friends, he hates hers. So both begin to entertain the possibility that they are not one with the beloved, that the beloved will continue to have his or her own desires, tastes, prejudices, and timing—different from the other's. Gradually the ego boundaries shoot back up; gradually they fall out of being-in-love. At that point they begin either shredding the ties that bind or begin building real love.

If we only wanted to be happy,
it would be easy.
But we want to be happier
than other people,
which is almost always difficult,
since we think them
happier than they are.
Montesquieu

The house—reality—always wins.

First, being-in-love for too long is too stifling; one or the other partner is going to begin feeling trapped. Why? Because for a while, their relationship was perfectly natural, like being in the womb. But if it goes on too long at the same passive level, it becomes unnatural. In many "steady" arrangements, the relationship is *more* monogamous than the best of marriages! "I don't mind you having friends of your own sex, but take one serious look at a member of *my* sex and you'll be looking for a dental surgeon!" When partners believe they are "meant for each other," they imply that they were not "meant" (in any profound sense) for anyone else outside the relationship. In fact, *relationship* is not the right term; *mutual absorption* would be closer.

If the two egos reject meaningful enrichment from outside themselves, the pair begins to become pretty thin fare, since neither partner brings anything new to the other—like a snake devouring its own tail. If there are no other deep attachments to others of the opposite sex (including their own parents), the two egos begin to wither, like Tristan and Iseult alone out in the forest. And if these two ever decide to marry, how truly *free* would that choice be? How can one be free when there is only one choice he or she honestly knows of?

Second, being-in-love is self-sabotaging. It nearly always degrades into egotism. Once the honeymoon is over, whether in a marriage or going steady, the partners begin to take each other for granted, like some old, married people may do. As Toni Morrison says, the partner becomes like "the third beer," not the first one that jolts you or the second that makes you at peace with the world, but the third one you take because . . . well, it's there, isn't it? Such self-sacrifice becomes a self*less*ness. And who can love a self who isn't really "there" when you're not there? If your goal is to be loved, you have to be a recognizably *separate* self worthy of being loved, and not merely a tissue that's handy when you feel the need for it.

Third, as we've seen before, no one can find any true, long-lasting self-validation from outside oneself—whether it's a paycheck or stardom or being loved. The beautiful result of falling-in-love in adolescence is that, after quite a spell of feeling confused and unlovable, you find that that is simply not true. Somebody *does* love you! Once you can take that for granted, then you can go back to building up the *self*-confidence that comes from *in*side and that cannot be taken away by any loss from the outside—even the loss of the beloved. This does not imply you are *using* the beloved in a kind of self-improvement course. Rather, he or she is the motive for making a self that will be an even better gift to him or her.

Fourth, when being-in-love goes on too long, the individuals stop developing as persons. In fact, the last thing they want is to change, to upset the blissful equilibrium each has given the other. But first, without disequilibrium, you stagnate. Second, disequilibrium is going to come whether you want it or not: He goes off to college, and she doesn't; or she writes poetry, and he goes out to shoot Bambi. Third, there are the abrasive demands of friends, parents, and jobs.

Whether as two steadies or two married people, we fall under the illusion—brainwashed into us by the being-in-love songs—that once romance is gone, love is gone too. Hardly true; we don't feel erotic love for our same-sex friends or parents or children, and yet we do truly love them. Either the relationship turns into real (realistic) love or it dies. Only what is separated can be joined.

God and goddess have to die so man and woman can be born. "She's my soul!" you say. No, your self is your soul. You may give your soul to her (or him), but before you can, it has to be yours—an entity *you* are responsible for and no one else. The reason the story of Tristan and Iseult has been retold for a thousand years is that every generation has found it true.

Being-in-love lasts only if the two people actually are perfect. If you both are, the last few pages were a waste of time.

"Love" is not a noun. It's a verb, and an *active* verb not a passive one. Passion is passive; in fact its Latin root means "to suffer."

Love finally separates itself from the sentimental (self-serving) froth our culture leads us to believe "love" will always be. Love separates itself from id-wants. It has realistic expectations. If you truly love, you accept responsibility for your *own* happiness or unhappiness; you neither expect the beloved to make you happy, nor do you blame your beloved when you're unhappy, nor do you need this relationship in order to be whole. The key is that each of you—you and your beloved—gives the other the most difficult gift of all: freedom to be a self.

Realistic love is not at all comfortable; it is, in fact, a risky business. It means risking intrusions on your plans. It means risking confrontation: "In this case, I'm right and you're wrong." And when the other says "What gives you the right to say that?" you answer, "Loving you gives me the right." In the end, realistic love means risking that you must one day let the other die. And you go on—because there is still a self left.

EXTRAMARITAL SEX

You knew this was coming, right?

Teenage fascination and experimentation with sex is not something that started when you personally passed puberty. It's been going on (at least) since the caves. But in the process of our civilization—humanization—we've become smart enough to treat sex in a more sophisticated way than hominids (just one step up from the apes) did. We see now that, just as human life is objectively more sacred than animal life, human sex is objectively more important than animal sex. That just stands to reason. Trouble is, each generation has to go back and learn the whole darned thing over.

If you read everything men and women have written about sex since writing began—and before that when folktales passed on the tribe's wisdom—you'd find exactly the same truths that young people in love today vehemently protest is *not* true about sex. Boys I teach think *Catcher in the Rye* "really tells it like it *is!*" They're surprised that it was written forty years ago when *I* was Holden Caulfield's age—and their age. There's nothing new under the sun about growing up—or sex. Oh, the surfaces change: One era is puritan, another is prurient; girls wear twenty petticoats, girls wear bikinis. *Attitudes*—subjective opinions—about sex change; but the objective truths about sex don't

TO FALL IN LOVE IS TO CREATE A RELIGION THAT HAS A FALLIBLE GOD.
JORGE LUIS BORGES

change any more than the moon changes or the laws of physics change or human beings change.

You don't really want to go back and read everything men and women have written about sex, do you? My hunch is you'd rather go with what you *feel,* rather than with what you know—which means that you're sure to make the same mistakes men and women have made for 300,000 years. So the only thing you learn from history is: You learn nothing from history.

Human beings are a quantum leap up from animals. That's an objective fact. Therefore, human sex is—objectively—also a quantum leap up from animal sex. Ah, but subjectively we're free to deny that objective fact and to act as if the truth weren't true—but to our peril. If we act *as if* human sex is no different from animal sex, then the sex act becomes—in our inner system of values—no better than an animal act.

Both animals and humans have a physical encounter in the sexual act. But only human beings are capable of also having a *psychological* encounter in the sexual act. Most animals meet, couple, and walk away; as far as we know, no orangutan feels guilt over coupling with his mate's girlfriends. Humans do feel guilt, or ought to. Animals don't perform sex acts behind closed doors; humans do. Why, if it's only a healthy animal act? Because, unlike animals, caring (evolved, adult) humans lay claims on one another, feel shame, look at one another as more than mere means to lessen sexual tension.

Therefore, there are two—and only two—questions about extramarital sex: Is it sex with no psychological relationship? Is it sex with a psychological relationship—whether it be between adolescents or grownups, inside marriage or outside?

When people who are ostensibly human beings don't feel anything, don't *commit* themselves to their sexual partners, they're inhuman. If their sexual encounters are merely "animal," they are

by that very fact immoral, because immoral *means* "less-than-human." Denying that or ignoring that or not wanting that to be true doesn't change the truth.

"Yeah, but if she wants it, too, then who's getting hurt?"

Well, if somebody were willing to be your slave, would that make that particular case of slavery moral—human? If someone begged you to help her or him commit suicide, would that person's eagerness make your help moral?

You've probably seen a man looking a woman "up and down." That lusty stare tells the whole story. The woman (or man) is no more than an object, or worse, a commodity—no longer a human person.

Sex is a statement. Body language "speaks." Twisting your body into knots when I'm speaking to you "tells" me you're being defensive. A sneer ("I didn't *say* anything!") also tells me something; so does putting your head down on the desk during class—and not a word was spoken. Sex also "says something." It is impossible to think of any way in which a human being can be more vulnerable than being stark naked. The very situation *says:* "I surrender my *self* to you, totally." If you don't mean that, then your sexual act may give pleasure but it's a lie.

Perhaps the reason religions try to curb casual sex is not that they want to keep people from having fun. Religions have been around a long time and have seen, time and time again, that casual sex takes something that is very important and makes it commonplace. What's more, religions realize that sex valued solely for its own sake has no reference to the future—not merely to having babies, but to continuing the relationship itself. Two people who "make love" with "no strings" give up the right ever to be jealous. Their communication is laced with lies. And someone almost inevitably is going to get hurt.

218

A second and far more serious problem arises when there is, in fact, a genuine and growing psychological commitment: "But you don't understand! We *love* one another." But to those who have had the long and painful experience of love, "love" is a pretty mercurial label. It's hard to be sure "love" is the right label, especially when there is such a heady personal return on a relatively minimal investment.

Love isn't a feeling; being-in-love is a feeling. Love is an act of the will. Love takes over when the feelings fail, when the beloved is no longer likable.

If, in fact, there is a deepening psychological involvement between two sexually active partners and there is no intention or possibility of a permanent commitment, at least for a long, long time, then the two are drifting blindly into very hazardous waters. Not inevitably—but pretty close to it— somebody's going to get hurt.

Further, if you can't marry because you have to go to college first, then college is *more* important than your sexual relationship. Objective fact.

Illusions versus truth; attitudes versus reality.

Sexual indulgence is now like air pollution or city noise or litter; we hardly notice it unless it's especially blatant. *Playboy* and its host of imitators not only provide a feast of perfectly airbrushed bodies but also of enlightening articles, like "What Co-Workers Think (and Say) About Your Office Affair" and "The 30-Minute Orgasm." Everybody sleeps with everybody on the daytime soaps. Ads ("Remember last night?") assume that, if you enjoy someone's company, sleeping together is as natural for humans as for hamsters. Rock lyrics make the same assumption. One Rod Stewart lyric is typical: "I don't want to challenge you / Marry you, or remember you. / I just wanna make love to you." At best, that's a self-deceptive use of the word *love*. Making condoms easily available in schools is an open admission that society believes the young too

far gone to be convinced that abstinence is even an option.

In the last thirty years, our society has turned 180 degrees from where it had been heading. Today, there is heavy pressure from the media and peers to indulge early in sexual activity. With what result? In 1986, the House Select Committee on Children, Youth, and Families estimated that we annually have a minimum of one million teenage pregnancies, half of them aborted. According to the National Center for Health Statistics, of the 3.7 million children born each year, 700,000 have unmarried parents: That's one-fifth of the children born each year in our country.

John Gasiorowski reports:

- ◆ intercourse before eighteen—56 percent boys, 43 percent girls;
- ◆ acceptability of coitus with someone for whom you have no affection—27 percent of both sexes;
- ◆ "I feel premarital sex is immoral" — (1965) 33 percent boys, 70 percent girls, (1980) 17 percent boys, 25 percent girls.

Things haven't changed much despite 300,000 years of experience with sex.

Never give a sword
to a man
who can't dance.
Gaelic Proverb

Along with a large percentage of the adult population, the young are at least half-convinced the Pill has broken the link between sex and love. In the old days, casual sex was taboo because the girl could end up having a baby—no other reason whatever. Now that consequence seems easily avoidable. And parents who were themselves trained before the Pill existed are unable to give their children any other reason to abstain from sex before marriage than the one they were given: the curse of unmarried pregnancy.

What is odd—and tragic—is that, despite open and wholesale talk of birth control and its easy and unquestioned availability, there were 828,124 unwanted births and 1,368,987 abortions in one year in the U.S. alone—and those only the reported ones—and most of them to younger women. That means that at the very least two million couples believe "it can't happen here."

The cause of those tragedies, I think, is that—although the facts and the results are objectively undeniable—even entertaining the *possibility* that the facts about extramarital sex might be true would mean the couple would have to consider giving up something they like very, very much. Like any pleasurable thing—food, alcohol, music—sex can become *addictive* and preoccupy your whole mind and blind you to objective reality.

MANY A MAN HAS FALLEN IN LOVE WITH A GIRL IN A LIGHT SO DIM HE WOULD NOT HAVE CHOSEN A SUIT BY IT. MAURICE CHEVELIER

The short-term pleasure of uncommitted sex denies its long-term—and unavoidable—results. It ignores the centuries-old practice of friendship and courtship. It prevents the couple from getting to know each other as *persons* before they "give themselves" to each other. How can you give a self you don't really know yet to another self you don't know either?

In a very real sense, a couple engaging in uncommitted sex are having their "honeymoon" *before* the marriage. Then what will happen *after* their marriage? The real honeymoon, which carries the couple through a lot of life adjustments, will be "more of the same." In the last thirty years more and more couples have lived together before making a commitment. In the last thirty years divorces have skyrocketed, so that nearly one-half of new marriages end in divorce. Is it possible that there's a connection? Is it possible—contrary to what many claim—that active uncommitted sex actually *gets in the way* of genuinely knowing each other?

You can't talk reason to two people in an extramarital sexual relationship any more than you can talk reason to a bulemic or alcoholic. There is the crucial difference between being-in-love and love. One is blind; the other isn't.

The acid test of real love is the visible results of what is claimed to be "love." Does this genuine, genitally expressed love result in two people becoming more openhearted, honest, and joyful with other people outside the relationship? Or does it result in two people becoming more under-handed, cranky, and thin-skinned? Nifty test. And the evidence is as objectively verifiable as the numbers on a Geiger counter.

Illusions versus truth; attitudes versus reality. The first step toward wisdom is calling a thing by its right name.

220

DRUGS AND BOOZE

This might seem an odd—not to say unfeeling—place to introduce such a jarring subject. And yet I suspect it is precisely the right place. Both sexual involvement without a chance of long-term commitment and addiction to drugs or alcohol both become dependencies. Neither is a relationship between equals, but a relationship between master and slave.

For a while the love potion is intoxicating; you feel "out of this world." There are no ego boundaries. There is, to all intents, no ego at all. Whether it is a sexual obsession or a "high" for a moment, you feel at least that you've had a brief glimpse of Nirvana. Illusion versus reality.

Almost all young people come into adolescence passive and dependent on parents, friends, grades, and the assessments of others. Young people are prime candidates both for being-in-love and for drugs. The "high" does not come from a genuine, lasting cause: Jack climbing the beanstalk or Psyche descending into hell and returning. Nor does the "high" come from a real spiritual growth that comes only after a painful expenditure of self. It comes from taking.

The teenager in need of a being-in-love fix and the teenager in need of a chemical fix are suffering from the same lack of a self. They feel a terrible sense of isolation, a breakdown of their inner "story," a sense of shame for being unable to live up to all the expectations, an inability to get any sense of accomplishment from any activity, and—most basically—a mistrust of everybody else. Exactly the same could be said of the teenager who commits suicide.

As Mother Teresa has so wisely said, feeling unwanted is the worst disease any human being can ever experience. Perhaps your being-in-love is only a temporary lift, until you can feel solid ground under your feet again. But, unlike drugs, no one ever died of being-in-love—only of expectations of what being-in-love can do.

We run carelessly to the precipice, after we have put something before our eyes to prevent us seeing it. Blaise Pascal

DILEMMA

Eileen Worth and Jim Jacobsen began dating when they were sophomores in high school. At first, it was always with a "gang" going to the movies, bowling, and basketball games. But after a while Eileen and Jim wanted more time alone together; and it was a heady experience for both of them. For the first time since they were kids, they knew that someone was actually *listening* to them and caring about what they said. Most of the time the content of their endless conversations wasn't worth etching on bronze, but the time they spent together was more precious than anything else in their lives.

Then they began necking pretty heavily, though Eileen always backed away when things began to go too far. Jim was insistent, sometimes pouty, sometimes downright angry. Finally Eileen gave in, and although it was very painful for her, she lied to Jim and told him she was just fine. Gradually the pace of the sexual involvement increased, and now they have sex every two or three days.

Eileen still doesn't like it. Not only is Jim in such a hurry that nothing "happens" for her, but she is afraid: afraid of becoming pregnant even though Jim always takes steps to prevent it, afraid of AIDS, afraid of being caught, even afraid that Jim might be bragging about it to his friends. The whole thing has her nerves ragged.

Their whole relationship has changed from a happy, romantic, fun thing into something deadly serious that is always aimed in the direction of the bedroom. It's as if Jim "owned" her—slavery. Eileen is not really a person, just a . . . convenience. And she's noticed the way he looks at other girls now. But she's also afraid that if she stands up to him, he will drop her and find someone else more pliable.

▷ *Questions*

What is Eileen going to do? How did she come to know that this is not real love but an illusion? What changed Eileen and Jim's relationship with each other?

222

FAITH REFLECTION

Love must be completely sincere. Hate what is evil, hold on to what is good. Love one another warmly as Christian brothers [and sisters], and be eager to show respect for one another. Work hard and do not be lazy. Serve the Lord with a heart full of devotion. Let your hope keep you joyful, be patient in your troubles, and pray at all times. Share your belongings with your needy fellow Christians, and open your homes to strangers.

Romans 12: 9–13

The kind of love described in that passage is love for the long haul. Nothing about instant gratification there, simply because love and instant gratification are totally incompatible. Being-in-love is impetuous, as children are impatient and impetuous. Genuine love is patient, willing to wait.

Two people in an "in-love" situation ordinarily show exquisite patience and kindness—with each other. But the energizing power of genuine love should spill over into other relationships as well, as the love of a married couple spills over to their children. It should make the two people better for everyone else to be around—family, friends, and fellow workers.

In any exclusive relationship, however, there is not only a tendency to be hypersensitive to intrusion from the outside—to criticism, and to suggestions, but also to sharing the beloved with others. That exclusivity and sensitivity almost inevitably lead to the jealousy the passage from Romans says is absolutely incompatible with genuine love. Could anyone really say they love someone when they don't want that person to be enriched by other relationships?

Further, Christianity teaches that your love should spread even beyond the attractive people you find it easy to love. Does that love—nourished by the being-in-love—spread out even to strangers? Does it make you more sensitive to the cafeteria personnel, the check-out person in the supermarket, or the busdriver? If it does, it's the genuine article.

FURTHER BIBLE READINGS

Skim these Scripture passages. Pick one that appeals to you and (1) summarize its main point, (2) tell how it relates to the chapter, and (3) list one or two thoughts that entered your mind when you read it.

◆ The God and Goddess   The Song of Songs 2:8–14

◆ Jacob and Rachel   Genesis 29:9–30

◆ Joseph and Potiphar's Wife   Genesis 39:1–20

◆ Samson and Delilah   Judges 16:4–22

◆ David and Bathsheba   2 Samuel 11:2–16

_____

_____

_____

_____

_____

JOURNAL

Describe a time when you were very much "in-love," even though reality later stepped in. What did it feel like at first? How did it finally break up?

If you're romantically involved now (no need for confessions), how do you know that this is the real thing? What makes this different from all the temporary crushes and infatuations in the past? How do you know if this is real love and not a wonderful illusion?

If you don't have a steady relationship now, how does that make a difference in your life? The first step toward finding even friends is to notice others, then to spend time and talk with them, then for two selves to begin slowly opening the two selves to each other. What are ways you could at least begin that process?

Understanding L*o*v*e P*o*t*i*o*n*s

REVIEW

1. What is the meaning of *romance?*

2. What do romance, extramarital sex, and drug addiction have in common?

3. Give three unavoidable factors that guarantee the burnout of romance.

4. Explain these statements:

   a. Being-in-love is like being in the womb.

   b. Total self-sacrifice becomes self*less*ness.

   c. "Love" is not a noun. It's a verb.

   d. Religions have been around a long time and have seen, time and time again, that casual sex takes something that is very important and makes it commonplace.

   e. Two people who "make love" with "no strings" give up the right ever to be jealous.

   f. The crucial difference between being-in-love and love is: One is blind; the other isn't.

5. What are the dangers of a friendship being too exclusive?

6. What is the basic difference between human and animal sexual intercourse? What are the effects in people who don't acknowledge that difference?

7. What dangers occur when having sex actually deepens into a psychological relationship, but with no possibility of a permanent commitment?

DISCUSS

1. Why is it that two people *in* love don't really love each other as much as they love the being-in-love, though the love potion makes them think this is "true love"?

2. When two young people are intoxicated with love potion, they lay claim to a special exemption from what governs ordinary folk: reality. Give examples.

3. The image of male as a "god" and female as a "goddess" must die so man and woman can be born.

4. Each generation denies most everything we have learned about sex in 300,000 years. Why?

5. "Yeah, but if she wants it, too, then who's getting hurt?"

6. Sex is a statement.

7. Despite open and wholesale talk of birth control and its easy and unquestioned availability, why were there in one year 828,124 unwanted births and 1,368,987 abortions in the U.S. (those were only the reported ones) and most of them to young women?

8. Why can't you talk reason to two people having an extramarital sexual relationship any more than you can talk reason to a bulemic or an alcoholic?

9. Why are the teenager in need of a being-in-love fix and the teenager in need of a chemical fix suffering from the same lack of a self?

10. Why has the "pill" broken the link between sex and love?

ACTIVITIES

1. Bring to class several magazines of all types: men's, women's, sports, music—excepting perhaps religious magazines and those that only appeal to an older audience. Examine the ads. How many ads (no matter what size) are there in each magazine? How many use sex in even a remote manner; for instance, "this sexy European car"? (Read *Subliminal Seduction.*)

2. Tonight watch the TV programs you usually watch and on a note pad list each commercial. Tell what it advertises and whether or not it depends for its effectiveness on sex, looks, acceptability by others.

3. Both Christy and Jeff are in their late 20s. Christy is head window designer for a large department store, and has received hints of being promoted into the clothing design department. Jeff is an accountant and has strong possibilities of moving up. They are both attached to their own apartments. They have never lived together, but they have an active sex relationship.

But then even their most dim-witted friends begin to notice their increasing strain: quick, hurt looks, raised voices, slammed doors. One evening while at dinner together, Christy and Jeff talk it all through, not without a lot of tears. They do love each other as good friends, but all the thrill has evaporated. When they leave the restaurant, partly because of the feelings they still have, partly because of the wine, they follow the advice of the song: "make believe you love me one more time—for the good times."

Six weeks later, Christy calls Jeff—to tell him she is pregnant.

Role-play the telephone conversation between Christy and Jeff. Then Jeff's conversation with his parents, best friend, and a member of the clergy; then Christy's conversation with her parents, best friend, a member of the clergy.

17. WORK

SURVEY

Circle the number on the rating scale under each statement that best reflects your opinion about that statement. On the scale

  +2 = strongly agree,
  +1 = agree,
   0 = can't make up my mind,
  −1 = disagree,
  −2 = strongly disagree.

Then share the reasons for your opinion.

1. A job gives a person's life a consistent meaning and focus.

   +2 +1 0 −1 −2

2. One can't rightly have true self-esteem unless he or she works to capacity.

   +2 +1 0 −1 −2

3. The main satisfaction in work is not the pay but the chance to help others.

   +2 +1 0 −1 −2

4. At work one has a responsibility not only to the job but to people as well.

   +2 +1 0 −1 −2

5. When you're employed, you owe an honest day's work for an honest day's pay.

   +2 +1 0 −1 −2

6. In school I give my parents an honest day's work for an honest day's pay.

   +2 +1 0 −1 −2

7. Overall, I'm genuinely proud of the way I work at schoolwork.

   +2 +1 0 −1 −2

8. When I write an essay, I usually first make a very thorough outline first.

   +2 +1 0 −1 −2

9. Most of the time I'm a self-starter; I don't need to be prodded to work.

   +2 +1 0 −1 −2

10. I wish I were a better student, but I can't find any effective motivation.

   +2 +1 0 −1 −2

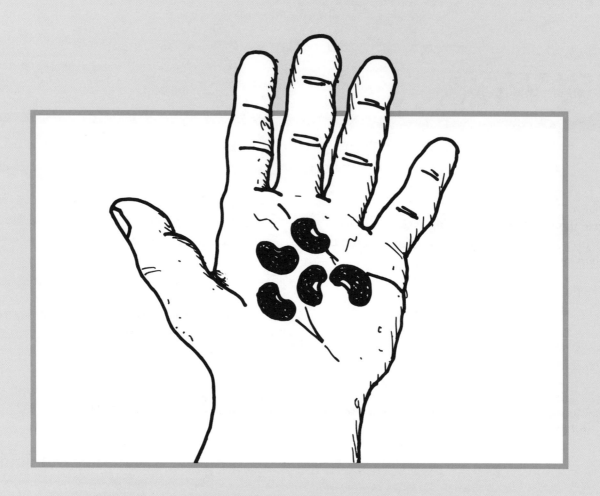

A FABLE

BEYOND UPWARD MOBILITY

*Once upon a time there was this boy named Jack, whose mother
was a very poor widow. (The catty neighbors hinted, however,
that Jack's debt-ridden and henpecked father had taken off with
a wench from the local tavern.) Jack himself had tried to find
work, but to no avail—much to his mother's irritation.*

*To make matters worse, the cow that had dutifully provided
sustenance since Jack was born suddenly went drier than a TV
tube, so Jack's mother sent him off to the fair to get as much as
he could for the poor old thing. Along the way, Jack encountered*

a stranger who looked and spoke and even smelled remarkably like his one-way-or-other departed father. The stranger proposed a swap: the spavined old cow for a handful of beans that, even considering the arid state of the cow, was a bad bargain, except that the stranger assured Jack these seeds were magical.

Well, you can imagine how Jack's poor old Mum reacted. She mocked Jack's seeds and winged them out the window. Then she took a stick to Jack's behind and, for good measure, sent him to bed without supper. Lying there in the dark, Jack started to steam. He'd just grump and be wretched for a whole week; that'd make her miserable. All in all, running away seemed the most appealing alternative. While he lay there pondering ways to revenge himself on his Mum's refusal to appreciate his enterprise, Jack thought he heard a grump and a thump and a long, long hiss outside his window, as if a huge snake were waking and uncoiling from sleep. But he probably was dreaming.

Nope. Sure enough, next morning, the magic seeds had shot up into this really spectacular beanstalk that disappeared up, up into the clouds. So without even brushing his teeth, Jack crawled out the window and began to climb—which turned out to be a considerable effort through a considerable distance, but Jack refused to turn back. Up he climbed until finally he stepped off in front of a castle that made the Pentagon look like a pigeon coop.

Jack scooted across the drawbridge, through the courtyard, and opened the huge oak door into a room big enough to house the entire population of Ohio. And the furniture looked like the New York skyline. Since he'd become a pretty accomplished climber by now, Jack managed to shinny up a chair to the tabletop and peered over the edge. What he saw made his eyes pop. There was a sack of gold, a hen that kept clucking and plopping golden eggs, and a golden harp that hummed lovely tunes.

Not wanting to make the acquaintance of the owners while he divested them of their property, Jack tiptoed over and picked up the harp, but it began lovingly to sing, "Someday he'll come along, the man I love." Nice, but a lot louder than Jack would have preferred. So he set it down and it went back to humming sorrowfully. He lifted the hen; it squawked. So just as he'd resolved that his best bet was the bag of gold, a huge woman suddenly loomed over the edge of the table. But the massive lady gave him a big smile and cooed and said what a handsome boy he was and smooched Jack wetly and gave him a great deal to eat.

Suddenly in the distance there was a rumbling at about 20 on the Richter scale. The jolly giantess went pale, murmuring that it was her ogrish husband who'd gobble Jack up like a limp french fry if he caught him. "Meal!" roared the ogre, who was about 99 percent id. So the kindly giant lady plopped Jack, kaplooey, right into her teacup, which was about as deep as your everyday whirlpool bath and awash with lukewarm tea but no damper than Jack imagined the ogre's gullet might be.

So Mrs. Ogre set a roasted side of beef on her hairy hubby's plate and he gnawed away, pausing only to slurp Niagaras of beer and belch volcanically. Finally, the giant lurched into his bed and snored so loudly that the screws popped out of half the furniture. Jack climbed slowly up the side of the cup and thudded onto the table, well tanned from the tea. He skittered over, grabbed the gold, and hightailed it out of the castle and down that beanstalk faster than a firefighter.

For some time Jack and his mother lived very well, but the sack wasn't bottomless. So after a while Jack decided it was time to venture back up the leafy pathway to solvency again, but this time for a more permanent source of income—the hen that kept on laying those golden eggs—and with full awareness of what he was getting into. Not to worry. The sweet giantess helped him once again.

The third time Jack was not drawn up the beanstalk either by need or by greed. That old hen sat inside a bank vault all day, clucking away and booping out those ovoid ingots. Partly, Jack was pulled by the sheer adventure of it. But also something quite mysterious in his soul felt the sweet bewitchment of the singing harp, not because it was gold but because it made such lovely music.

Well, just as Jack ran across the stadium-sized table under the ogre's cannonade of snores and picked up the harp, it started to sing! And not just "Brahms' Lullaby," mind you. Not even "Goodnight, Sweetheart." Oh, no. That harp was so glad to see Jack, she started singing "I'm Gonna Wash That Man Right Outta My Hair," fortissimo, louder than the Mormon Tabernacle Choir. Louder even, alas, than the ogre's full-throttle snoring.

Jack ran to the beanstalk, the thunder of the ogre's feet toppling trees all around him. As he started down the stalk, hugging the harp, which had switched to "Hey, Big Spender," he shouted down to his mother, "Ma! Get the axe!"

Off Jack's mother went to fetch the axe, but when she looked up and saw a set of legs the size of two Washington Monuments coming down the beanstalk, she froze. Jack handed her the harp, which now was happily belting "Zing Went the Strings of My Heart," grabbed the axe, and started whacking away at the beanstalk. Fortunately, the ogre was high enough that, when the stalk finally gave way, he hit the ground so hard that St. Patrick's Cathedral shifted from Fifth Avenue to Scranton, Pennsylvania. And, of course, the harp turned out to be an enchanted princess, she and Jack were happily married. And that hen is contentedly booping out golden eggs for them to this very day.

▷ Questions

This story can be read, in Freudian terms, as an outline of what it is like for a boy to begin puberty. The symbols are so obvious that no one need underline them. But it can also be read as an outline of what any man or woman working into the business world has to go through. And if that's difficult for a man, it's even more difficult for a woman.

According to the story, if you're going to get to the top and grab the hen that lays the golden eggs, with whom are you going to have to wrestle? What steps would you have to take to prepare for that kind of match, which will *be* a great part of your life? At this time in your life, are you genuinely preparing for it? If not, when do you start? There are guys and gals out there right now who are really training to be giants. How do you get ready? When?

When Jack (or Jill) goes up the beanstalk the third time, there's no financial reason. He (she) has everything anyone could want: an endless supply of golden eggs. What, then, does the harp signify? It's not important because it's gold; Jack has loads of that. Nor is it important because it's female—though it may be important because it symbolizes something feminine. What does Jack (Jill) need that is more important than financial success—something symbolized in all stories of battle by the harp?

A READING

In this selection from Rabbit, Run, *by John Updike, Harry "Rabbit" Angstrom is twenty-six, 6'3", and lives and works in Mt. Judge, a grungy town outside the fifth largest city in Pennsylvania. Eight years ago Rabbit had been the best basketball player in his high school and was famous throughout the county. Now he demonstrates Magi-Peel Vegetable Peelers in five-and-dime stores. His wife has stopped being pretty; now she is pregnant again and alcoholic. It's Friday night. And on his way to pick up his son, whom his wife has dumped at his mother's, Rabbit simply takes off in his old car.*

Route 23 works west through little tame country towns, Coventryville, Elverson, Morgantown. Rabbit likes these. Square high farmhouses nuzzle the road. Soft chalk sides. In one town a tavern blazes and he stops at a hardware store opposite with two gasoline pumps outside. . . .

"Couldya fill it up with regular?"

The man starts to pump it in and Rabbit gets out of the car and goes around to the back and asks, "How far am I from Brewer?"

The farmer looks up with a look of curt distrust from listening to the gas gurgle. He lifts a finger. "Back up and take that road and it's sixteen miles to the bridge."

Sixteen. He has driven forty miles to get sixteen miles away.

But it was far enough, this was another world. It smells differently, smells older, of nooks and pockets in the ground that nobody's stirred yet. "Suppose I go straight?"

"That'll take you to Churchtown."

"What's after Churchtown?"

"New Holland. Lancaster."

"Do you have any maps?"

"Son, where do you want to go?"

"Huh? I don't know exactly."

"Where are you headed?" The man is patient. His face at the same time seems fatherly and crafty and stupid. . . .

"Check the oil?" the man asks after hanging up the hose on the side of the rusty pump, one of the old style, with the painted bubble head.

"No. Wait. Yeah. You better had. Thanks." Simmer down. All he'd done was ask for a map. Damn dirtdigger so stingy, what was suspicious about that? . . .

The man lets the hood slam down and smiles over at Harry. "That's three-ninety on the gas, young fella": the words are pronounced in that same heavy cautious crippled way.

Rabbit puts four ones in his hand. . . . The farmer disappears into the hardware store; maybe he's phoning the state cops. He acts like he knows something, but how could he? . . . Switching off the lights in the hardware store as he comes, the farmer comes back with the dime and the man pushes it in with his broad thumb and says, "Looked around inside and the only road map is New York State. You don't want to go that way, do you now?"

"No," Rabbit answers, and walks to his car door. He feels through the hairs on the back of his neck the man following him. He gets into the car and slams the door and the farmer is right there, the meat of his face hung in the open door window. He bends down and nearly sticks his face in. His cracked thin lips with a scar tilting toward his nose move thoughtfully. He's wearing glasses, a scholar. "The only way to get somewhere, you know, is to figure out where you're going before you go there."

At one time, basketball had supplied meaning to Rabbit's life. Then, for a while, his marriage had. But now he's aimless. Why? There is a clue in the gas attendant's homespun remark: "The only way to get somewhere, you know, is to figure out where you're going before you go there."

Do you have any focused idea of where you're going? Or is it just "Onward!"? Most people seem to just fall into their lives, based pretty much on what everybody knows. Everybody knows you've got to go to college and get a job and get married. Why?

What does *success* mean to you as an individual—don't answer in airy generalities like "to achieve my goals." Nobody can achieve a vague goal, no more than you can buy a map until you know where you want to go.

Not many high-school students have a specific career goal as yet; but unless you at least begin to narrow down the possibilities, you will get to the last semester of college and have to take whatever job you can *get* because your parents are going to disqualify you from the family welfare program.

Most people, like Rabbit, end up in sales in some way. No problem with that, so long as you freely *choose* it. If you don't get around to making a reasoned choice of a career, you're going to be aimless, unsuccessful, and unhappy—like Rabbit. And the key to understanding that is right there: You have no *aim,* no goal to give meaning to your life. To live, you have to eat; to eat, you have to work. Your work can give meaning to your whole life. But not if the work itself, like Rabbit's, is meaning*less.*

What do you want to be "when you grow up"? Or, more precisely, when you achieve adulthood, since you already are grown up.

THEME
CAREER/CALLING

In the expanding circles that form the web of relationships in our moral ecology, we begin with the self, then with the spouse, then with the family, and expand outward to relationships in the workplace. Freud said that there are only two things a person needs for a sense of fulfillment: love and work. Work, the common task and the people with whom we share it, is the background against which we judge at least some of our value—not our internal, personal worth, but the degree to which we are "contributing." Our job, our work, ought not answer the question "Who am I?" (Though, sadly, it often does.) Rather, it should help answer the question "Where do I fit in?"

If your job becomes merely a way—any way—to get a paycheck in order to survive, your whole life will be nothing more than that: mere survival.

It is unnerving for adolescents (especially the way they are treated today) to begin even vaguely to narrow down a career. Adolescents now resent any intrusions on their freedom: "You're only young once, and then it's all over." That will, unfortunately, be absolutely true for you unless you begin to take charge of your own life, your own self. Now.

The suffix *-escence* is inchoative; that is, it describes a process that has begun but has not yet been completed, as in *convalescence.* Adulthood, as we have often seen, does not click on either at puberty (as many young people think) or with the issuance of a college diploma (as many parents think). Nor is adulthood a kind of coma you slip into at twelve, like Snow White in her crystal coffin, and from which you emerge only ten years later.

Adol*escence* is inchoative adulthood: a process that has to be worked on every day, like lifting weights or practicing to be a dancer. You are—or ought to be—practicing every day to be an adult. It doesn't happen without your cooperation and effort, which means, alas, encroachments on your freedom. But to be truly free, you have to *expend* your freedom by finding, choosing, and committing yourself to a map.

Though it may not seem to be, choosing a career is a genuine moral question. You *owe* it to yourself to begin narrowing down the way you will spend a great part of the one life you have. It also is an obligation arising from your objective relationship with your present family and with what will soon enough become your relationship with your future family. In evolving an adult self, you're really preparing a future parent. What kind of parent do you want your kids to have?

ACHIEVING/STRIVING

In every Olympic event, every competitor gives years of total effort, and yet all but three walk away empty-handed. Some students do a totally committed job on every assignment and get a C+, while others breeze along and pull down A's without ever seeming to open the book. " 'Tain't fair." Right. 'Tain't.

All the teachers and coaches and parents who ever told you that if you really put out the effort, you'd attain success, meant well. But, unfortunately, they forgot all the times they themselves tried with all their hearts to win—and lost. Just because a goal is concrete—a gold medal, a scholarship, the boss's job, stardom—it doesn't mean you can, in fact, achieve that goal. There are all kinds of other variables, besides your own effort that are involved, for instance, others' effort, for one, not to mention others' superior talents or stamina or luck or connections or unscrupulousness. There, I think, is the great flaw of the American school system and, in fact, of the entire American mind-set: training people to achieve rather than to strive. If your life-*goal* is meaningful to you—no matter what it is—your *life* will be meaningful, whether you're number one or not.

Achievers have lots of trophies; they've marked goals out for themselves and come home with tangible proof that they've captured them. Achieving (and not always merely material acquisition) is another name for The American Dream—success, but only insofar as that success has been validated by external referees. American literature is filled with such characters: Rabbit Angstrom, Budd Schulberg's Sammy Glick, Eve Harrington in *All About Eve.* But there also are many who longed for that external validation and, like Arthur Miller's Willy Loman, missed it. And there are many who we have seen who achieved in spades, and yet committed suicide.

In contrast, strivers content themselves with trying to do the best job they can; and if they come home with a medal or two or a raise in pay, that's just fine. Such men and women used to be the staple of American literature, from the settlers of the West to the lone, unpaid detective. But such characters no longer appear so frequently. They perhaps seem even a touch naive.

The pitfall for the achiever is that there are a *lot* more people who yearn to achieve than there are winners; only a few win. But what is an achiever without achievement? For the striver, the struggle itself is reward enough.

Perhaps you see this most clearly at events like the Academy Awards. Who wouldn't want to stand up in front of fifty million viewers and receive a statuette that proclaimed that you are—beyond dispute—the (current) best? What a boost to your career, to say nothing of your ego! And yet not a few nominees do not show up for the ceremonies. Some of the absentees even win, and the audience feels a bit cheated of their tears and boring litanies of people to thank. Pretty selfish of them, no? Perhaps not.

In the first place, it is somehow demeaning to turn an actor's struggle to inhabit another human being's soul into a kind of commercial competition like the World Series. Who is to say one actress's portrayal of a hillbilly singer is better—more important, more successful—than another's portrayal of an aged bag lady? That is at least somewhat similar to saying your father's job at the office is more important than your mother's job at home because money is involved. Are oranges better than apples? Do you decide the difference in objective value by a vote?

Every actor—like every doctor, teacher, executive, student—has a career to think about: a set of vertical, achievement-oriented goals, along with choosing means to achieve those goals. Is this role—or residency, or school, or corporation, or course—something that will advance me up the pecking order and salary scale? Or is it a momentarily appealing opportunity that will either stall my advancement or even send it into a tailspin? Anyone who fails to take those considerations seriously is a fool.

The professional who thinks only—or at least primarily—of his or her work as a career may (or may not) achieve success. But the professional who thinks of the work as a *calling*—the kind of person who says, perhaps a touch romantically, "I'd do this even if they didn't *pay* me!"—can't help but achieve success, a different kind of success to be sure, but a very meaningful success nonetheless.

Again, the connotations that cling to the word *career* depend almost totally on factors *external* to the individual (others' talent, connections, luck, judges' prejudices), as well as on rewards (medals, raises, broken records) that are not only external but also temporary. Someone else will break the record, and there's always someone with a higher salary. On the contrary, the actor absorbed in the work, the doctor who cares for broken people, the teacher who challenges minds, the student who wants simply to learn—people who do their jobs, surely, for a salary, but far more as a fulfilling challenge—are paid doubly, win or lose, as "wage earners" and as human beings.

Here, as elsewhere, there is an unstated—and unquestioned—standard. Which is more important: a country doctor who for generations has brought people through heart attacks or a celebrated heart-transplant surgeon who has his picture in *Newsweek;* a woman who doubles the assets of a national corporation or a woman who raises two children who are healthy, happy, and honorable; the president of the United States or the president's staff; Annie Sullivan, who taught Helen Keller to communicate, or the actress who won an Academy Award for portraying her? It seems silly even to ask, but does anybody honestly know what *important* really means?

The focal difference between the pairs is not a question of value. All of those people are, without exception, admirable and valuable. The sole difference is a matter of publicity, and how publicity makes one person *seem* more important than another.

You have merely to look around at the ordinary school setting to see what the future holds for most. For those to whom education is just another job, what evidence is there on which to base a hope that life in the real world will be any different?

How much are the educated superior to the uneducated? As much as the living are to the dead.
ARISTOTLE

234

The goal of the upwardly mobile American Dream is the middle class. There is hardly a reader of these pages who does not assume—with some kind of blissful blind faith—that he or she will be living a life at least as comfortable as his or her parents even though he or she doesn't plan practicing to be an adult till age twenty-two. What's more, the achievement-oriented are climbing a mountain with no real top. How many million bucks would be enough? And, at forty, when it becomes clear that you never really will make the top, what happens to your sense of personal worth?

If career is the gauge of a person's worth, only a few will make it to the top—and even they will still be flexing to climb restlessly higher. The absence of a sense of calling in one's work is the absence of a sense of meaning in one's life.

The difference between a career and a calling was very well demonstrated to me by a football player who came up to me after a musical I had directed, the first one he had been in. "I can't believe it," he said. "In a show, *everybody* wins."

Once the tryouts are over and the parts assigned and the hurt feelings start to heal, all the competition is gone from a play. Everybody gets down to work just for the sheer enjoyment of the work and of the people you work with. It's a team endeavor in which if the chorus is out of sync, it doesn't make any difference how good the leads are; and if the leads are at one another's throats, the whole enterprise fails. Everyone is important; nobody is essential. You take the part you're given, and you play it to the hilt—not for yourself but for the others and for the audience.

Similarly, real professionals—professional surgeons or professional street sweepers—see themselves as providing a service for others, providing the community with healthier lives and a cleaner environment in which to work and live. Whenever you encounter someone surly and mean-tempered—a salesclerk, a lawyer, a subway changemaker, a member of the clergy, a plumber—you've run up against someone who does the job for the paycheck

and nothing more, someone whose work and life have no more meaning than the paycheck.

There is only one choice: Be an autonomous person or a paid automaton.

SPECIALISTS/GENERALISTS

It's obvious we need specialists. It's the rarest of individuals who is an expert on business, gardening, taxes, auto mechanics, history, plumbing, and physics. Not too many physicians can keep up with the flood of literature even about the brain, much less with the best new methods to control heart disease, liver ailments, and tennis elbow. The president of General Motors can't waste time answering his own phone, and his secretary shouldn't have to clean the office in her spare time. A division of labor is essential, both for those with special qualifications and for those without them.

But there are many tasks that can be effectively performed only by men and women who have kept some capacity to function with a broader perspective: generalists. It is such people who will be the advisors, the planners, the innovators, the communicators, the teachers. Too much specialization—too restricted a viewpoint—diminishes a person's versatility.

A specialist can't neglect the generalist's viewpoint without lessening the effectiveness of even his or her specialization. A good physician doesn't treat patients as mere biological puzzles, nor does a good advertising executive treat audiences as potential suckers, nor does a good legislator treat constituents as people who can throw her (or him) out of a job. They treat others like fellow, many-faceted human beings.

In a world of accelerating change, there is a need for people with a broader viewpoint, people whose knowledge of history, sociology, politics, and psychology enables them to *anticipate* the direction we're all moving in. People who refuse to be mere functionaries or cogs-in-the-wheel or interchangeable units on an assembly line, have to understand complex relationships, to reconsider assumptions, and have a skeptical eye for "we've always done it this way." They have to be flexible, critical, constantly learning about fields that were not even invented when they were in college, and able to handle problems no textbook even envisioned.

To most graduate school admissions officers, whether in medicine or business or engineering, the young man or woman who has specialized too soon is a real liability—no matter how skilled he or she has become in the narrow specialization. Even though courses in philosophy, history, and literature may not seem to be marketable skills, they are indeed. Specialists may get a better job right out of college than the generalists will. But they will more than likely be still at that same job or at a slightly higher level in that job for the rest of their careers. The people who will get to the top are those who are *curious*—in both senses of that word.

WHAT ABOUT NOW?

Perhaps you have agreed with most of what the chapter has said so far. It's really true. For other people. For older people. For you, maybe four or five years down the line. But what about now?

Students often say, "When I get out into the real world, . . ." No. The moment you passed puberty, the moment you began adol*escence,* you began to live in the real world. Perhaps you don't *feel* as if you've begun to have the role and responsibilities of an adult in our shared moral ecology, but you do. Illusion versus reality. If you want to learn how to drive by yourself, you'll have to learn how to contribute too.

Just as family is a microcosm of our society, so is school. High school, though, can often be a *false* microcosm. It doesn't prepare you for anything but conformity, willingness to do meaningless drivel, and the ability to sleep with your eyes open. Most of the data you so passively copy off the

chalkboard you will not only not remember but you will also never find any use for it. Then why do you do it? Because "everybody says." You accept a prison sentence of twelve years, or sixteen years, or more, without ever asking, "Why?"

If all your parents want for you from your education is good discipline, you'd have done better in the Marines—to say nothing of prison. If all you're learning is more and more unmemorable and unusable data, you deny the existence of libraries. Thomas Edison, Henry Ford, and Mark Twain never even graduated from *grammar* school, but each one managed to make his mark. You don't need to know calculus or irregular French verbs to run a very lucrative French restaurant or live in a posh suburb or buy the Yankees. All you need is basic literacy (which you already have or you wouldn't be reading this book), basic arithmetic, guts, the willingness to work hard, and the savvy to take advantage of your breaks. All the rest is overkill.

Real education means learning how to learn, and it takes *consistent* effort to discover how to deal with ever more complex data and relationships. Real education means learning:

◆ to be curious, to distrust what "everybody knows," to smell rats;
◆ to be humble before the evidence, down no matter what unpleasant paths it happens to lead;
◆ how to think, not just have thoughts, *how to reason:*
  —gather the data,
  —sift the data to find what's essential,
  —put the data into some kind of logical sequence (an outline), so you can
  —draw a conclusion, and
  —put it out for someone to critique;
◆ how to care for the people around you;
◆ to have the courage to stand up and be counted.

There it is: everything your parents and all those taxpayers are laying out all that dough for you to learn. It's not the data you memorize that's important; it's what working on the data does to your ability to handle more and more complex problems. But every time you wing a fifteen-minute essay filled with wind, you're impoverishing yourself, writing trash no *human* being should ever *de*grade himself or herself to write—or justly ask any other *human* being to read. When you copy a lab report or homework, when you refuse to research or to do a careful outline or to rewrite, you short-circuit your own learning-how-to-learn. You *waste* your education.

Whenever I ask students why they (most) don't work up to potential in school, they almost automatically answer, "I'm lazy." Nothing is further from the truth. All you have to do is look at those same kids playing handball at recess or shaking it up at a dance. They're not lazy at all; they're *unmotivated.* Give them a reason, give them a *cause,* and they'll work their fingers to the bone. Hockey? Yearbook? Mischief?

What, then, are the reasons for your working, right now, in *this* "real world"?

1. There's an old saying: "As grows the twig, so grows the tree." If you learn how to beat the system in high school, you'll beat the system in college. No problem. But you won't beat the system when the boss is paying you money to think.

2. There's also the lowest of motivations: "My parents will kill me." If the only reason you're at least passing is to keep your parents off your back, why not be rid of this god-awful servitude, have them give you the $60,000 more they're ready to waste on college, and use it to set yourself up in business?

3. On a slightly higher level of motivation, you are subsidized for at least $15,000 a year—tuition, clothes, food, heat, insurance, and what-have-you. To take the fifteen grand without giving an honest day's work—every day—is grand larceny! You're a felon and have no right to feel good about yourself. Whatever number of people cheat on welfare, even in the most generous states, they rob the government of only about $5,000 a year. Unless you're really working at school, best not to shake any fingers at welfare cheats. You're one too. "That's *different!*" Right. It's your parents. It's worse.

4. It may *seem* far in the distance, but in about five or six years you'll very likely have another human being dependent on how well you can think. Perhaps more than one. When does the responsibility thermostat click on? First year of college? Doubtful. Last year of college? What evidence do you have, even now, that that will happen? "As grows the twig, . . ."

5. Pride. How can anybody go to bed content with his or herself when the best he or she has done all day is survive, cope, endure? Oh, in a prison camp, yes. But in a situation that is an *opportunity,* no! Again, don't poke fingers at the folks on Mediterranean Avenue and say, "Why don't you make something of yourselves?" when you have all the opportunities in the world and are not rising to the challenge.

6. Control! People who have never learned how to think clearly and honestly are victims. They haven't the ability to think logically or the words to express their honest convictions. The reason you study math and vocabulary is *not* so you can ace the SATs and get into Harvard! But you can lose the forest for the trees, and mistake the means for the end! The reason you plough through the formulas and word lists is not just to pass the exam (short-range, long-range) but to learn to handle more and more complex problems *without fear.*

DILEMMA

Connie Cepeda has never been more than almost average at anything. Her mother tells Connie she's pretty, but no boy ever has. She's never been asked on a date, except by boys she neither trusts nor respects. At school she tries her best, but no one ever showed her how to study, or if they did she must have been into one of her endless daydreams about being a movie star or a model or someone important on TV. The only ones that teachers seem interested in are the smart ones or the very slow ones or the troublemakers.

All the stuff in school seems meaningless to Connie. She factors equations as well as she can, but she keeps wondering who ever would use that at work. Her English teacher assigns novels that make no sense either. Though Connie has been in America for five years and her English is more than passable, the pages of the books always blur into another daydream about home when she was a child, where a woman's place was to cook and work the fields and have babies. *Pride and Prejudice* is as far from Connie's reality as Mars is. As for Shakespeare and chemistry, the teachers might be talking in Chinese.

▷ *Questions*

Last week Connie's cousin Maria offered her a full-time job in her beauty shop to learn the trade. Connie's mother is strongly against it. "Why come to America to get a dead-end job?" she argues. "At least wait two more years for the diploma, then maybe a secretarial school. Besides, the women who go to Maria's to get their hair done are . . . not nice." But to Connie the job begins to look more glamorous every day. Who is right? Connie? Her mother? What might Connie do about her "career opportunity?" Is it a real opportunity?

FAITH REFLECTION

Our brothers and sisters, we command you in the name of our Lord Jesus Christ to keep away from all brothers and sisters who are living a lazy life and who do not follow the instructions that we gave them. You yourselves know very well that you should do just what we did. We were not lazy when we were with you. We did not accept anyone's support without paying for it. Instead, we worked and toiled; we kept working day and night so as not to be an expense to any of you. We did this, not because we do not have the right to demand our support; we did it to be an example for you to follow. While we were with you, we used to tell you, "Whoever refuses to work is not allowed to eat."

2 Thessalonians 3:6–10 (adapted)

Many young people today have at least part-time jobs, but survey after survey shows they do not use their salaries to help pay their families' expenses but for personal spending money either now or in college. Is that an adult way of behavior? Or is adolescence in America merely a protraction of childhood and childishness? Think about it honestly.

Not too many adolescents like to hear that they are being subsidized, and yet that truth seems, in many cases, to be undeniable: They get away with the minimum at "work" (school) and feel no sense of guilt at cheating their "employers" (parents). Nonetheless, some adolescents live in comfortable homes with what even Turkish princes would have considered unimaginable luxuries.

Few adolescents are lazy or mean-spirited. But are a lot of adolescents . . . spoiled? Other than a sense of genuine and deserved self-esteem, what are the motives you might have for giving your parents an honest day's work for an honest day's pay? Of offering to bank at least some of your salary to pay, say, half of your college tuition?

What would happen in your family if "whoever refuses to work is not allowed to eat?"

📖 FURTHER BIBLE READINGS

Skim these Scripture passages. Pick one that appeals to you and (1) summarize its main point, (2) tell how it relates to the chapter, and (3) list one or two thoughts that entered your mind when you read it:

◆ The Servant Jesus	Philippians 2:5–11
◆ Striving	Philippians 3:12–16
◆ Cooperation	1 Corinthians 3:4–9
◆ A Peaceful Mind	Ecclesiastes 5:10–12
◆ A Proud Worker	2 Timothy 2:14–17

_____

_____

_____

_____

_____

_____

✏ JOURNAL

One way to narrow the field of jobs is to list all the subjects in school you hate and all those you like. If you hate math, for instance, you can eliminate astrophysics, computers, economics, accounting, and a whole host of other jobs. Not to decide *is* to decide. Many vaguely aspiring writers end up selling Magi-Peel Vegetable Peelers in five-and-dime stores.

Your guidance counsellor has a list of careers. Photocopy the list and cross out the jobs that definitely do *not* appeal to you. Then go back and circle the jobs you feel so-so about. Finally, write about the general area you feel, at present, you might like to work in.

Understanding Work

REVIEW

1. Define *inchoative.* What does it have to do with the difference between *grown-up* and *adult?*

2. What connection is there between finding meaningful work and achieving self-esteem?

3. Why is it important that adolescents at least begin to focus in high school on a particular career?

4. What is the difference between achievers and strivers? Why do strivers win even when they lose?

5. What makes a calling more fulfilling than a career?

6. What is the *concrete* content of "The American Dream"? Does it mean something internal or sheerly external to the individual? What is its value as a motivator?

7. What are the virtues of specialization and of generalization in education? Why are specialists more likely to be lucky in the short run and generalists more likely to be lucky in the long run? Explain why the people who will get to the top are those who are curious—in both senses of that word.

8. Explain the statements:
   a. No adolescent is lazy.
   b. High school can often be a *false* model of society.

9. What are the five elements the chapter claims are the core of genuine education? How would you rate your school and your self in fulfilling them?

10. What are the five steps in the reasoning process—the only way to solve *any* problem, ever?

11. Give at least three solid reasons for your starting to work seriously at your education, right now.

DISCUSS

1. If you don't get around to making a reasoned choice of career, like Rabbit in *Rabbit, Run,* you're going to be aimless, unsuccessful, and unhappy. Why?

2. Freud said that there are only two things a person needs for a sense of fulfillment: love and work. Is that true? Why?

3. You are—or ought to be—practicing every day *to be* an adult—not just *acting like* an adult. Why is that true?

4. When does your "future" start?

5. Many young people go for a long time without much to show for their effort. Why shouldn't they just quit? What's the benefit of just striving on?

6. When you get away with the minimum, beating the system, what do you do to yourself as a learner? As a trustworthy son or daughter? As a future parent?

7. Which is more important: Annie Sullivan who taught Helen Keller to communicate, or the actress who won an Academy Award for portraying her? Explain.

8. There is only one choice: Be an autonomous person or a paid automaton. Why?

9. Even though courses in philosophy, history, and literature may not seem to be "marketable skills," they are, indeed. Why?

10. Perhaps you don't *feel* as if you've begun to have the role and responsibilities of an adult in our shared moral ecology, but you do. Why?

11. Every time you wing a 15-minute essay without putting forth any real effort, you're impoverishing yourself and writing trash no *human* being should ever *degrade* himself or herself to write—or justly ask any other *human* being to read. How might admitting the truth of that statement force you to change the way you do things?

ACTIVITIES

1. Interview three people you consider to be not only financially successful but also happy with their lives. Ask them: How did you happen to choose your career? At what time in your life did you "know" that was it? How does your career affect the meaning of your life and your self-esteem?

2. Have you ever had a job you'd almost be willing to do even if you didn't get paid for it? Poll the group to see how many have. Then discuss what that job did to your days and your weeks.

3. Give a situation when that old adage "If you just put in the effort, you're bound to succeed" proved to be definitely untrue. Did anyone learn anything from the disappointing outcome?

4. In the two years since his promotion, Al Degnan has been a very unhappy man, despite his new raise from $60,000 at a job he loved to $85,000 a year. He's now snappish with his wife and growls out of the house every morning and does not return till well after 7 P.M. from a job he loathes. Al's best friend, Ken Silvio, handed him a scotch, a bit warily. "But you were happy once. You couldn't wait to get to work on Monday. Just go to the Old Man and say, 'Sir, I'm grateful, but I'd like the old job back.' "

"Hey! That's 25,000 bucks!"

Role-play a continuation of the episode.

18. COMMUNITY

SURVEY

Circle the number on the rating scale under each statement that best reflects your opinion about that statement. On the scale

   +2 = strongly agree,
   +1 = agree,
    0 = can't make up my mind,
   –1 = disagree,
   –2 = strongly disagree.

Then share the reasons for your opinion.

1. Wherever "society" is located, "it" dictates most of our values.

   +2 +1 0 –1 –2

2. We crave a heart-based community but we settle for a profit-based society.

   +2 +1 0 –1 –2

3. In most of us, idealism is killed by the more concrete rewards of materialism.

   +2 +1 0 –1 –2

4. Society—school, family, media—does not encourage us to be "somebody."

   +2 +1 0 –1 –2

5. Society is impersonal; community is interpersonal.

   +2 +1 0 –1 –2

6. What I would have to surrender for community is too costly to my self-interest.

   +2 +1 0 –1 –2

7. It is a travesty to call my school a real community or family.

   +2 +1 0 –1 –2

8. I suspect most of my fellow students lead smaller lives than they want to.

   +2 +1 0 –1 –2

9. People of other races, homosexuals, and nerds have legitimate demands on me.

   +2 +1 0 –1 –2

10. I would honestly like to crack open my teflon cocoon, but I'm afraid.

   +2 +1 0 –1 –2

A FABLE

THE DAY AFTER THE LAST DAY

Once upon a time, after the Old Days, when the Simpletons had begun the Great Simplification, there was a young girl named Hope. She had no clear memory of her parents or where she was from or, for that matter, where she was at the moment. Hope had been playing alone in her secret cave, deep in the side of the mountain, the day the Great Lights fell and everything went dead.

When Hope had come to the mouth of her cave to go home for her supper, she gaped out over what had been a valley carpeted with farms and forests. As if some otherworldly vacuum had sucked up all the green, the valley had gone russet desert, the barns and farmhouses melted away, the crops and trees sifted to sand.

Far off, the wind lifted dust devils like empty promises into the hot air. A dream. She would wake soon. But she didn't wake. And she could feel the angry sun savaging her skin. It was no dream. And Hope had wandered out into it.

She crept down the mountainside toward what had been the highway. Off in the heat-haze she saw a dark figure moving. As it focused itself out of the mirage, it seemed to be a woman with black skirts billowing in the gusts of sand, her face hidden by a black veil against the dust. A nun! "Sister!" Hope cried and ran through the stinging wind. "Wait!"

The figure stopped and turned slowly toward Hope. The shock of a voice lowered the woman's guard, and her veil dropped from her face. The toothless mouth was open in horror; great goiters of flesh looped around the one-eyed face, drool dripping in long plastic strings from the anguished mouth. The figure crossed herself. "There but for the grace of God," she muttered and scurried on her way.

Hope squatted against the bleached pink of a soda machine, its contents spewed onto the asphalt of the devastated gas station. She popped a can and slaked her thirst with the warm, fizzless fluid. Far off where the muffled woman was disappearing in the haze, a bicyclist came toward her, pedaling furiously, skirting what Hope had thought was a nun on the opposite side of the road.

Hope ran to the center of the road and wagged her arms furiously. The cyclist slowed to a halt a few yards away. He put his hands in the air. "No food!" he cried. His face was a clot of wens and knobs, his eyes steel splinters embedded in putty. His crooked mouth yowled open as he glared at the girl. "Unmerciful God!" he cried, and humped onto his bicycle and wheeled furiously past Hope, sprawling her in the dust.

She struggled listlessly to her feet and began to trudge after the cyclist. No direction was as good or bad as any other. Time meant nothing. The sun seemed locked overhead. The earth stood still.

Then up ahead something like a sign focused itself and unfocused itself and then began to focus itself again out of the haze. "Villain Hell Haven," it seemed to say. But as Hope came closer it said, "Victims: Help Given." An old, black man sat rocking under a tattered piece of canvas, a drippy empty pipe angled from his battered mouth. His face was like melted mahogany, all shiny red-brown planes, like a face sculpted in slick layers with a trowel. "Oh, my Lordy, you poor child," the old man said, rocking to his feet. "You just come with me. We'll fix you up jus' fine."

So he took her by the hand and led her up the dusty wash to a raw-board cabin. "Ah, got one!" he gasped, scrabbling up the cindery path. "Lord, 'a mercy, I got one!" In a weary daze, Hope followed.

Inside, the cabin was dark and cool, and Hope could hardly discern the grotesque faces half-hidden in dark cowls. Hands pale as parchment reached from long baggy sleeves and touched her sunburned face delicately, as if her skin were spiderwebs. "Perhaps," said a voice, hesitantly.

"A very good chance, I think," said another.

"Come here, child," said still another. "Don't be afraid. We can help you."

The hooded figures led her to a cot with a filthy mattress, and Hope lay on it gratefully. "Here, little sister," and the voice's shadowy hands reached a tin cup to her. "It will help you sleep." Hope drank and slowly sank back onto the cot into a daze, and into black sleep. One of the figures brought a scabby case to the table next to the bed and opened it. The faint light filtering through the torn shade winked on the long sharp knives.

For days Hope swam in dark sleep. Whenever she woke into the lighter darkness, groggy and numbed, one of the dark figures was there to soothe her with a caressing voice and to hand her another drink from the tin cup that eased her back into healing oblivion.

Finally Hope eased back into full awareness. But she could see nothing. Perhaps it was night. No. She couldn't open her eyes. She reached out and felt the rough blanket. And then her own face. It was covered with gauze.

"There, there," said a voice. "Be patient, my dear. It will only be a few more moments."

Hope sensed there were many of them huddled around her, hunched and expectant. A pair of hands touched the bandages on her face, gently unwinding them. Finally the bandage was gone, and Hope opened her eyes.

Figures solidified in the pale light and the horrible faces appeared ashen in the shadows of their cowls. Hope looked from one to another, and the faces sagged in disappointment.

"Oh," said the figure next to her. "Oh, no."

The others edged forward, peering down at her, muttering sadly.

"Tragic," a voice said. "She's still. . . ." The voice fumbled for the word, as if it were long forgotten or repellent to the tongue. "She's still . . . beautiful."

There are aboriginal tribes who, even today, still scar their faces as a sign of adult beauty. Month by month Ubangi mothers insert larger and more painful plates in their daughters' lower lips to stretch them into huge loops; others put more and more rings on their daughters' necks to stretch them to great lengths. "Beauty," the cliche says, "is in the eye of the beholder."

The Western man sees a woman in Bombay as not up to standards—her hooked nose pierced with a gold nugget, her hair greased, her body too lumpen. But to a man from Bombay, the Western woman is "not up to standards," her leprous white skin daubed with paint, her skeletal figure cinched into a dress too scandalously short for any man of honor to look at twice.

What does *beautiful* mean? Where do we get our norms for it? From Greek statues? Surely today our ideas of what is beautiful are formed before we were able to think by the faces and bodies we see on television and in magazine advertisements. Men and women spend fortunes on makeup, workouts, plastic surgeons. Why are we so envious of others' faces and bodies and so discontent with our own? Who or what has convinced us that the way we look is even that *important?*

Think of some people you know who seem genuinely at home and at peace with themselves. Do they seem to be people who worry much about their looks?

List all the other things that divide us from one another: race, ethnic background, religion, sex, private property, income, clothes, hobbies . . . certainly, if you take a moment, you can think of more.

Why are the things that divide us more important than the things that unite us? Or, more precisely, why do they *seem* to be?

A READING

Maycomb is a rural county in southern Alabama. Its caste system is rigid: white merchants and professionals, white farmers, blacks, and no-account white trash. In this selection from To Kill a Mockingbird, *by Harper Lee, Tom Robinson, a respectable black man, has been accused of raping Mayella Ewell, a white girl whose family respectable whites consider lower than blacks. Atticus Finch, a white lawyer, has taken Tom's case simply because "it's the right thing to do." But his willingness to defend Tom has earned him the town's wrath, threats on himself and his children. Atticus has proven Tom could not have committed the crime, and he is concluding his summation to the jury.*

"One more thing, gentlemen, before I quit. Thomas Jefferson once said that all men are created equal, a phrase that the Yankees and the distaff side of the Executive branch in Washington are fond of hurling at us. There is a tendency in this year of grace, 1935, for certain people to use this phrase out of context, to satisfy all conditions. The most ridiculous example I can think of is that the people who run public education promote the stupid and idle along with the industrious—because all men are created equal; educators will gravely tell you, the children left behind suffer terrible feelings of inferiority. We know all men are not created equal in the sense some people would have us believe—some people are smarter than others, some people have more opportunity because they're born with it, some men make more money than others, some ladies make better cakes than others—some people are born gifted beyond the normal scope of most men.

"But there is one way in this country in which all men are created equal—there is one human institution that makes a pauper the equal of a Rockefeller, the stupid man the equal of an Einstein, and the ignorant man the equal of any college president. That institution, gentlemen, is a court. It can be the Supreme Court of the United States or the humblest J.P. court in the land, or this honorable court which you serve. Our courts have their faults, as does any human institution, but in this country our courts are the great levelers, and in our courts all men are created equal.

"I'm no idealist to believe firmly in the integrity of our courts and in the jury system—that is no ideal to me, it is a living, working reality. Gentlemen, a court is no better than each man of you sitting before me on this jury. A court is only as sound as its jury, and a jury is only as sound as the men who make it up. I am confident that you gentlemen will review without passion the evidence you have heard, come to a decision, and restore this defendant to his family. In the name of God, do your duty."

▷ *Questions*

In his address to the jury, Atticus also speaks of "the evil assumption" that all people are the same. We all like to think of ourselves as fair-minded people; we all feel disdain for narrow-minded bigots. But is there any group of people you simply can't stand, whose mere presence makes your skin shrivel—not because of their proven wickedness but because of what they *are?* For instance: Kids scarred with acne? People who can't understand English? Jocks? Girls dressed garishly? Homosexuals? Street people? Clergy? Native people in the *National Geographic?* Retarded people? Puritans? Don't read any further until you've actually *focused* one such person in your imagination.

Pause for a moment and force yourself to do what Atticus tells his daughter, Scout: Climb inside his or her skin and walk around in it awhile. What does the world look like from in there? What do *you* look like through that person's eyes and perceptions of what's important? What things do you think may have happened in that person's childhood to make him or her that way? Hear someone say aloud what you yourself merely think of that kind of person? Look up the word *compassion.* What does it mean?

Atticus accuses certain people of using the phrase "all men are created equal" out of context to justify stupid decisions, the most ridiculous of which is promoting students when they have no objective claim to it. As George Orwell wrote, "All animals are equal but some animals are more equal than others." In what ways do you feel more equal than others? List them on a piece of paper. Now go back over the list and check the ones that you have personally achieved, and then circle the ones you owe to someone else and can take no legitimate credit for, for instance, looks, brains, parents' achievements, and so on.

But there is one place, Atticus says, in which all people *are* equal. Where? Why? Under all the differences that create blind bigotry, under all the differences of talent, brains, and money, by what objective reality are we all genuinely equal?

Crucial to Atticus' argument is his final statement: "A court is only as sound as its jury, and a jury is only as sound as the men [and women] who make it up." Why is that inescapably true? How is Atticus' statement also true of any group: family, team, school, community, city, or nation?

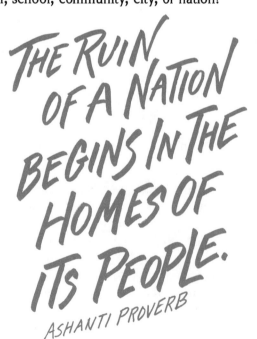

THE RUIN OF A NATION BEGINS IN THE HOMES OF ITS PEOPLE.

ASHANTI PROVERB

THEME
CONGREGATIONS AND COMMUNITIES

The last chapter said that the goal of genuine education is to make emergent adults continuously learn: (1) to be curious; (2) to be humble before the evidence; (3) to reason; (4) to care for one another; (5) to stand up and be counted. This chapter will concentrate on "to care for one another (caring) and "to stand up and be counted" (confidence). Without these two, no real community can exist.

Later in *To Kill a Mockingbird,* when Atticus' sister is worried about what the town's mean-spiritedness is doing to him, a wise friend says to her, "Whether Maycomb knows it or not, we're paying [Atticus] the highest tribute we can pay a man. We trust him to do right. It's that simple." Just as Atticus trusted the jury to do right, even if it cost him.

All that's needed for evil to triumph is that good people be silent. Like the mad TV prophet in Paddy Chayevsky's *Network,* we're all "mad as hell, and we're not going to take it anymore!" And yet we do. We all expect that sooner or later *some*body will do *some*thing. Who if not you? When if not now? No one asks *big* greatness of you, just greatness of soul.

"Leave me *alone!*" Does anybody ever really mean that?

Our lives are a paradox, caught between two conflicting tensions. On the one hand, I want to be a self, known and owned. I want a valid sense of self-esteem. I want a room of my own with my own specially selected "junk." I have a need to be *some*body. I have a right to private property. On the other hand, "it is not good for the man [or woman] to live alone" (Genesis 2:18). The worst punishment short of death—and sometimes worse— is solitary confinement. I have a need for solidarity with others, for validation from outside to prove that my self-validation is not self-delusion. I'm willing to give up the right to some privacy in return for the right to share. I want not just to be "Who am I" but also to know "Where do I fit in?"

Like it or not, my self-esteem is tied up with others and depends on them. It's not enough for me to think well of myself; I also need to *be* esteemed.

We all need external and palpable symbols to shore up our belief that our lives are not meaningless: a paycheck, a report card, a medal, a birthday present. We need applause, stroking, approval. Sadly, too many of us base our sense of value *solely* on external validation, but even the healthiest of us cannot go too long without *any* external validation. We need at least a couple of people who are nearby and are significant in our lives who will, a few times a week, reassure us that we're not only "there" but worth some attention. Otherwise, we melt into anonymity.

Whatever in us dreads solitary confinement also yearns for human interaction, affirmation from family and friends. Some people crave it in the extreme: men and women who sweat under the hot lights in concert in theatres or in arenas to be buoyed up by the surge of applause from out in the darkness. We all secretly crave that too; and yet only a small number are willing to risk even trying out for a high school play. But we can't be affirmed if we're afraid to allow ourselves even to be *noticed.* We can't fly, bright-winged, unless we forsake the warm security of the cocoon.

Since standing up for oneself and joining oneself to others both cost—even if they are enriching— many lower their expectations both of themselves and of the community and submit to "solitude-in-the-crowd." They settle for one or two trusted friends, rather than caring and being cared about by more and more people. As a result both individual and community are impoverished.

The difference between a community and a "congregation of strangers on a bus" is the same as the difference between love and politeness. *Community* means "us"; *congregation* means "us among them."

Community is an internal thing, a highly personal commitment we usually associate with family, the old-time town, or neighborhood. In a community everybody not only more or less knows everyone else's business, but also *cares* about everybody else. They are the kind of people you know you can call on when you need help, even when it's inconvenient. And the price you willingly pay is that you, too, have to be ready to help, even when it's inconvenient. There is a unifying *spirit* in a community.

A congregation is an accidental grouping of people in a single place, each person cocooned within his or her own self-interest, for instance, travelers in an airport lounge, recruits dumped into the same platoon, students trying out for the same team or play. For a short time their personal needs or destinations just accidentally happen to coincide with others in the same location. Nobody came into the group in order to meet the others, and quite often each would just as soon *not* get mixed up with the others. It is not concern for the other people that unites them (as with a community) but self-interest.

Somehow, such easily mouthed phrases as "our Madison High *family*" and "our Savanarola *community,*" which proliferate in brochures and graduation speeches, strike me as being a blatant and self-serving misuse of the words. So too, no matter how often it echoes from the pulpit, does applying the word *community* to the usual group gathered to worship together on a Sunday. Worshipers most often do not even know one another. Most at least do not seem willing to be called on to help, say, for building a barbecue or helping with teaching English as a second language, even when helping is not inconvenient.

The first step toward wisdom is to call a thing by its right name. And until we stop using the word *community* for a group of strangers who are quite content to leave things that way, we'll never roll up our sleeves and begin doing something to change that.

Community at least seems easier for girls; girls are more vulnerable, inclusive, ready to adapt; boys are more defensive, competitive, cautious. If the team is a real community, a boy knows he can definitely count on all his "brothers." If it is not, it's every man for himself; the others are only necessary adjuncts to each one's personal self-improvement. But even with teams that seem to be well-knit communities, the player who scores often tends to forget he couldn't have done it alone. The opposite is also true: when the team loses, it was "*all* his fault," a judgment that denies that the team loves the man enough to forgive.

The game of Trust exposes the root reason why life-giving (*eros*) communities are so rare and sterile (*thanatos*) congregations are so commonplace. Players who seem the most "in control" are angrily wary just before they fall back: "If you *try* anything, . . ." When the worst that could happen if the partner slipped would be a broken fall—on a rug! You can sum up the difference in one word: *control.*

When the hockey player is skating, he's not dependent on anyone else except *himself.* In any competition, whether it's Monopoly, baseball, or war, it comes down to every person for himself or herself: it is the survival of the fittest, whether you're wearing boxing shorts or tattered jeans or a designer suit. Competition gives rise to using the human mind almost exclusively on the level of animal cunning in social, business, even school relationships: "Keep your guard up; watch your back; don't talk to strangers." Not a very promising situation for building community.

We also get a measure of control—or at least a lessening of our feeling of helplessness—when we cultivate "us" against "them": us blacks, us rednecks; us bikers, us cops; us jocks, us brains. The list and the antagonisms are nearly endless.

Even within the relatively small population of a school, groups are so honeycombed into cliques and segmented by nasty names that a school sometimes seems like a congregation of hermits with their huts grouped together for mutual protection. Not a very promising situation for building community.

Competition is a wonderful motivator; but not when it enters every single area of our lives, not when we become low-grade paranoids thinking that everybody's "out to getcha."

Like the journey theme, the theme of a mismatched group of strangers—a congregation—slowly evolving into a community is a staple of literature. We read about the victims trapped in the crashed plane or the overturned ocean liner, the gaggle of recruits forged into a devoted military unit, the wagon train, fellow patients in a psychiatric ward, even a group of pilgrims wending their way to Canterbury. Studying how strangers can slowly evolve into a community might help improve the accidental groupings we happen to be in, and help us enrich one another and ourselves.

The first step is to *notice* one another. Walk along the corridor some day at recess and actually count the number of faces that make you say, "I have *never* seen her before, even though she looks as if she must be at least a junior." Not a very promising situation for building community.

Grief can take care of itself, but to get the full value of joy you must have somebody to divide it with.
Mark Twain

We set up protective filters so we won't be distracted, intruded on, forced to get involved. Self-impoverishing. How many clubs have you dared to get involved with? If school is a way to learn how to succeed in the real world and the real world is a nearly infinite variety of people you're going to *have* to get along with, you're wasting a good part of whatever money's being spent on your education if you're not in extracurriculars. What's more, you're going to be like a Martian when you get into the marketplace.

The next step is to take *time* and *talk.* Right now, if you happen to be reading this in a study hall or library, look around and count the people you have *never* talked to or worked with or even eaten lunch with. Not a very promising situation for building community.

We become secure and content—in control— with a small group of friends. We become so worn down by our daily hassles that we'll settle for civility, politeness, and basic unruffled discipline rather than find ways to break down self-protective (and self-impoverishing) barriers, to strip away the shyness, and to see that behind all the macho and prom-queen masks—the guido boots and the garish earrings, the running shoes and the loafers—we all want the same things: to love and be loved.

Male or female, ugly or gorgeous, hunk or nerd—beneath all the deceptive surfaces, we all want to be known. The most repellent among us still have dreams, hopes, hearts. We all want to succeed. We all fear failure and rejection and pain. We've all cried, mourned, despaired. We all have people who are precious to us, and every one of us could use more.

If only we could all see—and admit—that enlightened self-interest isn't enlightened at all: it's *against* our own genuine self-interest! If we could take the steps to make a school a genuine community of people who cared for and about one another, we'd all profit. We'd have to worry less about stealing. We'd hear fewer soul-shriveling names. We'd have a better chance of peace. And if not here in school, what hope have we of peace outside of it?

If only we could see that we impoverish ourselves when we deny our selves to others.

The more you give yourself away, the richer you are! If you are not a constantly emerging adult, when do you begin to live in the real—endlessly variegated—world? In college? Doubtful. You'll hang around with the same limiting "types" you hung around with in high school.

When, if not now? "Excuse me. Is anyone sitting here? Thanks. My name's. . . ." Who knows? This person could become another best friend. Your best friend *was* a perfect stranger once. She or he could become your spouse! And meanwhile, what a place that school would be! A place you *wanted* to get to every morning! A place where every day you met a new, enriching friend, where every day you became more fully human.

What's stopping *you* from standing up and being counted, from making a difference, from making this place less a prison and more a family? Dr. Martin Luther King, Jr., said that anyone who had nothing worth dying for didn't deserve to live. But if you and those around you haven't the courage even to put up your hands in class, I doubt you're at present a promising candidate for the Nobel Peace prize. In order to make a difference, you have to be different from the rest of the sheep. In order to be useful, you have to be used. As Eldridge Cleaver said, "If you're not part of the solution, *you're* part of the problem." Shyness is robbing you of a far fuller life. If your school is only a dull congregation of sad, shy people, there's only one person who could begin to change that.

Guess who?

DILEMMA

Denny Reid has been a very popular English teacher and the director of plays at Quigley High for twenty years. For a great many of those years, the high points of his life were the fall play and the spring musical, as every year he took on more difficult, taxing plays and produced bigger and more complicated musicals: *My Fair Lady, Fiddler on the Roof, Man of La Mancha.*

But more than the satisfaction of doing a big job well, even with complete amateurs, the biggest satisfaction of Denny's after-school job was seeing the kids come alive. He could remember the days when those old black-and-white movies said anybody could put on a show. He felt a genuine sense of camaraderie that both called on the individual's loyalty and in turn fed the individual's sense of identity and personal worth. In the past the students were *committed,* and the alumni kept coming back to tell him how important taking part in those plays had been in their growing.

But in the last few years things began to change. The kids were becoming more inaccessible, more reluctant to commit themselves. It was almost as if they were in the show only to get to the big cast party. Students who survived the cuts now show up for practice only when it's not too inconvenient. Even the leads say, "I had a dentist appointment; I didn't know I was up yesterday; I forgot." What's more, their parents try to wheedle exceptions to have it both ways: "But he wants to play hockey too. He won't miss more than two or three rehearsals a week." Lately, when a play is rehearsing, Denny wakes up with a knot of barbed wire in his gut: "I wonder who will not show up *today.*"

▷ *Questions*

Denny is only forty-two, but he's beginning to wonder if it's worth the anguish. Is It? What do you think?

FAITH REFLECTION

My brothers and sisters, what good is it for someone to say that he [or she] has faith if his or her actions do not prove it? Can that faith save him or her? Suppose there are brothers or sisters who need clothes and don't have enough to eat. What good is your saying to them, "God bless you! Keep warm and eat well!"—if you don't give them the necessities of life? So it is with faith: if it is alone and includes no actions, then it is dead.

James 2:14–17 (adapted)

What you *do* shouts so loudly that we can't even hear what you *say.* We were all baptized Christians without our consent, but most of us ratified that choice at our confirmations. When Christians sign into a hospital that asks for one's religious affiliation, we write Catholic, Methodist, Lutheran, and so on. We assure ourselves that we are trying to live the best Christian lives we can. But is it just possible that we might be kidding ourselves a bit too much? If, for instance, being Christian were outlawed and Christians were being hunted, what *concrete* evidence could they get against you?

Further, one must not read the gospels with materialist eyes, as if the only real poverty were the literal poverty mentioned in this passage. There are many people right at our elbows who are "naked" to other people's nastiness, who are "hungry" for some kind of attention, respect, or approbation. Do you in some vague way "wish them well" but do nothing concrete to help them?

C. S. Lewis wrote that it is much easier to pray for a bore than to go visit him. What do you think? Do you more often pray for others than act to help them? "If [faith] is alone and includes no actions then it is dead." How "alive" or "dead" are you as a Christian?

 ## FURTHER BIBLE READINGS

Skim these Scripture passages. Pick one that appeals to you and (1) summarize its main point, (2) tell how it relates to the chapter, and (3) list one or two thoughts that entered your mind when you read it.

◆ Different Gifts	1 Corinthians 12:4–11
◆ Generosity	2 Corinthians 9:6–15
◆ 70 x 7	Luke 17:3–4
◆ Joseph and His Brothers	Genesis 45:1–8
◆ A New Standard	2 Corinthians 5:16–19

_____

_____

_____

_____

JOURNAL

This is going to sound like a repetition of a previous question (Psst! It *is.*) Perhaps you've grown since the last time it was asked.

Think of the one person in your class who is the greatest outcast, someone who raises in you a reluctant compassion. Don't name names. Describe how he or she makes himself or herself difficult to take.

Like the Wolfman at full moon, feel yourself changing into that person. Describe a typical lunch period for him or her (from *inside* his or her skin), and contrast it with your own.

Finally, write not what you *could* concretely do for that person in the next week, but what you *will* do! Harking back to the previous time this question came up, have you actually made an attempt to make that person feel more "at home"?

Understanding Community

REVIEW

1. Explain Miss Maudie's statement: "Whether Maycomb knows it or not, we're paying [Atticus] the highest tribute we can pay a man. We trust him to do right. It's that simple." What is the radius of people who can count on you to "do right"? Does it go beyond your family and closest friends?

2. Explain why all that's needed for the triumph of evil is that good people be silent. What evidence do you have that there are more good people than bad in your community?

3. What is the basic "polar tension" regarding self and community the chapter says each of us has to struggle with at the depths of our being? Explain. What do you gain from living in community? What do you give up?

4. Explain these statements:

   a. Some people depend too much on approval by others for their self-esteem, but none of us can get along without any external validation at all.

   b. The difference between a community and a congregation of strangers on a bus is the same as the difference between love and politeness.

   c. If only we could all see—and admit—that "enlightened self-interest" isn't enlightened at all, that it's *against* our own genuine self-interest!

5. Why does relating in community at least seem easier for girls than for boys? Where are the exceptions?

6. How does an individual's need for control affect the possibility of community? Why is control so important for all of us, even the apparently weakest?

DISCUSS

1. Brainstorm all the things that divide your group. Be as painstaking as you can. Now, what concrete steps could the group realistically take to become less a mere congregation and more a caring community? Would it be worth it to take those steps?

2. We all secretly crave applause, and yet only a small number of people are willing to risk even trying out for a high school play. Why is that true?

3. The first step toward wisdom is to call a thing by its right name. And until we stop using the word *community* when we mean a "group of strangers" who are quite content to remain that way, we'll never roll up our sleeves and begin doing something to build community. Why is that true?

4. Competition is a wonderful motivator, but not when it enters every single area of our lives and we act as low-grade paranoids thinking, "Everybody's out to getcha." Do you agree or disagree?

5. If school is a way you learn how to succeed "in the real world," and if the real world is a nearly infinite variety of people you *have* to get along with, are you wasting a good part of whatever money's being spent on your education if you're not in any extracurricular activities?

6. In small groups brainstorm: Who are the people who *always* eat lunch together—every day? Without losing the very real value eating lunch together has, how can you do something to spread that value around?

7. How would you feel if your parents forgot your birthday? How would they feel if you forgot theirs? Write down the birthdays of everyone in the group. Now, what are you going to do with that list?

8. Why is one sure-fire gauge of a healthy community how it treats its "outcasts"?

ACTIVITIES

1. Research responses to the following questions:

   a. What are the salaries for whites and blacks in the highest fifth of each income bracket?

   b. What is the average salary a woman earns? What is the average salary a man earns? Contrast the two. Why is there a difference between the two?

   c. What percentage of whites, blacks, and Hispanics finish college? Why is that true?

   d. How many males and females finish college? Why?

   What damage does the evidence your research discovered do to the opinion: "You've got to have a college education to get a good job"?

2. Gather and form a circle. Each person names each other person in the circle. Then each one says where each other person lives. Then (this is the tough one) each one tells what color eyes each other person has. Eye color isn't important, but what does recognizing it and remembering it say about our receptivities to others?

19. SOCIETY

SURVEY

Circle the number on the rating scale under each statement that best reflects your opinion about that statement. On the scale

+2 = strongly agree,
+1 = agree,
 0 = can't make up my mind,
−1 = disagree,
−2 = strongly disagree.

Then share the reasons for your opinion.

1. Slavery is impossible if citizens are willing to read and think for themselves.

   +2 +1 0 −1 −2

2. Women, blacks, hispanics, and people living in poverty have fair representation in Congress.

   +2 +1 0 −1 −2

3. Corporations have stronger influence on public policy than any group of citizens do.

   +2 +1 0 −1 −2

4. Government cannot interfere with what citizens do and view privately.

   +2 +1 0 −1 −2

5. Government can interfere with what citizens can't avoid seeing and hearing.

   +2 +1 0 −1 −2

6. If crime and the economy run wild, a president like Hitler could be elected.

   +2 +1 0 −1 −2

7. Homosexual or lesbian teachers should be outlawed from teaching students of their own sex.

   +2 +1 0 −1 −2

8. The mandate of the Supreme Court is to legislate citizens' morality.

   +2 +1 0 −1 −2

9. Capital punishment has been proven a deterrent to crime.

   +2 +1 0 −1 −2

10. Only those declared "persons" by the Constitution or by law have legal rights.

    +2 +1 0 −1 −2

A FABLE

THE ONCE AND MAYBE FUTURE KING

Once upon a time there was this pretty-much nerd named Arthur. He was really a nice, likable boy, but most often that isn't enough in itself, as we all know. He was sort of spindly and not too hot for hacking the heads off chickens and poking pigs with spears and savaging sparrows with hawks, as real boys were rightly expected to be. Worse, he read books! And he wasted a lot of valuable sports time hanging out with this old wizard named Merlin, who by all reports was working with a few mental circuits unsoldered. To make matters worse, Arthur was also—well, uh, illegitimate.

Anyway, just before the king died—childless, as everybody but old Merlin believed, he took his great sword, Excalibur, and thrust it into a big boulder. (It was a magic sword, you see.) And on the rock he wrote, "Whoever pulls this sword is king." Well, knights from as far away as Vladivostok showed up to try to pull out that Excalibur. They really tried. Sweat gushed in gallons from their brows, and their biceps bulged big as beachballs, and several had to be stretchered off to the wise woman to tend to hernias the size of pumpkins. Finally, during a joust among the knights still able to see and sit on a horse, Sir Kay, Arthur's foster brother, broke his sword and sent Arthur to fetch a fresh one. You guessed it, right?

Well, that Cornwall Arthur took over was one pretty dog-eat-dog-it's-a-jungle-out-there-every-man-for-himself kind of operation. I mean, you talk about competitive. To prove who was the better man or the better clan, these knights used to dress up in these enormous iron boilers and ride full-tilt at each other with steel-tipped vaulting poles. And if one was imbecile enough to get up after being knocked off his horse, the other had to render him all-the-way comatose with cleavers and rotisserie spits. All clean fun while there were referees to declare one or other stone cold dead and stop needless barbarism; but some knights took the competition out into the real world, where, as we all know, there are few referees.

Once every twenty minutes in Cornwall, some knight took a fancy to another's castle or horse or wife and undertook to prove he had a greater right to it by the fact that he was the better man—since he could shorten the other knight down to his kneecaps. That is not world-class savagery, but in a kingdom approximately the size of Rock Island County, Illinois, some sob sisters deemed it excessive. And Cornwall was only one small kingdom. That whole island of England was a pretty laissez-faire kind of place.

Well, King Arthur decided that things had gone well beyond far enough and that he was going to do something about it so everybody all over England could live in peace and harmony ever after, the way they were supposed to. Now, peace and harmony are rather, uh, feminine qualities; and a few more belligerent, not to say unintelligent, knights began to say uncomplimentary, not to say treasonous, things about their sovereign—words like sissy, gutless, and pansy, to quote only some of the printable ones. But several knights with higher-wattage brains agreed with Arthur that peace at least deserved a chance, and they hammered the opposition into grudging agreement.

It seems Merlin and Arthur had invented this new thing called "Justice," which they said was the road to peace; and Arthur started his reforms with the knights themselves. In his castle at Camelot, Arthur set up a Round Table at which no knight—not even the king—had a place of dominance. And he sent out his knights to stop rape and pillage and slander, and to assure the rights of every man, woman, and child.

Well, before you knew it, people began to feel truly safe for the first time in their lives, and they began to turn their minds from the war news and tournament stats to caring for their land and families, which they found they enjoyed even more. And they started to use their hands to help their neighbors back to their feet rather than to knock them off of them. There was no longer the pleasant jolt of violence; but this peace and justice that now dominated Camelot lasted longer and was a great deal more comfortable.

But something persnickety in some people makes them noticeably uncomfortable when nothing's going on but growing. And all the bad guys in the kingdom had either been converted to the cause or were long since staring up at the undersides of potatoes and carrots. So, because the young bucks were getting restless, Arthur invented a new thing called "The Search for the Holy Grail," which was really the search for something a lot more complicated than peace—or even for the cup Jesus used at the Last Supper. It was the search for things called "Nobility" and "Honor" and "Integrity," which hardly anybody had ever felt before, much less been able to define. Even though Arthur suspected most of his people might not yet be quite ready for such nonprofit inventions, he decided to risk it. Who knows when a whole country's ready to grow up, right?

Well, it did work for a while. But it's easier to convince the young to fight against something negative and evil than to fight for something positive and good. So, a few fights broke out here, a few hackings there, and gradually, like the first rumblings of a volcano, it began to boil over again. And Arthur wondered whether people were more incurably animal than he'd thought—that maybe they really weren't meant to be human after all. Finally, civil war broke out between Arthur and his son, Mordred, who was also a b-----d, but in both senses of the word. Sadly, more people seemed to want Mordred's return to brutal competition than Arthur's progress from competition to peace and wholeness.

At the end, Whatever-in-Us-Resists-Civilizing moved toward victory. Broken, defeated, Arthur trudged slowly away, the last battle in fiery shambles behind him. He stumbled across the beach toward a dark ship, and three cloaked maidens ministered to his wounds and bore him off on the tide to the mystic isle of Avalon.

That, Mordred believed, was the last they would ever see of Arthur and his sort. Such starry-eyed, womanish idealists have no notion of what real life and real people are made of, of what they really want. It took a hard-eyed, stiff-spined, iron-willed man of the world to determine that. In the long run, we're all best off without doomed dreams.

Yet some claim Arthur never died at all, that he's merely waiting for a time when people might seem ready for peace and maybe even for nobility and honor and integrity—or at least less hostile to them. There are some still childish enough to believe there will come a time when men and women are willing to grow up.

Some, quite naively perhaps, report that even now Arthur is on his way.

▷ Questions

Hermits have no problems with the id-savagery in every human being: the incompletely evolved animal that snarls at every real or imagined encroachment on its turf. But when we live together in families, communities, cities, and nations, there is bound to be conflict.

What is the link between private property, fences, boundary lines, "*my* rights" on the one hand, and family spats, factions, gang wars, hockey battles, racism, rage over welfare taxes, and hostile corporate takeovers on the other hand? There is one.

What about William Golding's *The Lord of the Flies?* Is it merely a pipe dream that human beings can ever evolve into the reasonable, tolerant, wise, and just entities that our cerebral cortexes suggest we were intended to be? What objective evidence, at least, suggests there might still be hope for us to become fully human?

A READING

In 1852, the government of the United States inquired about buying tribal lands from American Indians for use by the wave of immigrants flooding into the country. Chief Seattle wrote this in his letter of reply:

The President in Washington sends word that he wishes to buy our land. But how can you buy or sell the sky? The land? The idea is strange to us. If we do not own the freshness of the air and the sparkle of the water, how can you buy them? . . .

The shining water that moves in the streams and rivers is not just water, but the blood of our ancestors. If we sell you our land, you must remember that it is sacred. Each ghostly reflection in the clear waters of the lakes tells of events and memories in the life of my people. The water's murmur is the voice of my father's father. . . .

Will you teach your children what we have taught our children? That the earth is our mother? What befalls the earth befalls all the children of the earth.

This we know: the earth does not belong to us, we belong to the earth. All things are connected like the blood that unites us all. We did not weave the web of life, we are merely a strand in it. Whatever we do to the web, we do to ourselves.

One thing we know: our god is also your god. The earth is precious to God and to harm the earth is to heap contempt on its creator.

Your destiny is a mystery to us. What will happen when the buffalo are all slaughtered? The wild horses tamed? What will happen when the secret corners of the forest are heavy with the scent of many people and the view of the ripe hills is blotted by talking wires? Where will the thicket be? Gone! Where will the eagle be? Gone! And what is it to say goodbye to the swift pony and the hunt? The end of living and the beginning of survival. . . .

We love this earth as a newborn loves its mother's heartbeat. So, if we sell you our land, love it as we have loved it. Care for it as we have cared for it. Hold in your mind the memory of the land as it is when you receive it. Preserve the land for all children and love it, as God loves us all.

As we are part of the land, you too are part of the land. The earth is precious to us. It is also precious to you. One thing we know: there is only one God. No one, Red or White, can be apart. We *are* brothers and sisters after all. (adapted)

▷ *Questions*

Though it was written only one hundred and fifty years ago, Chief Seattle's letter is rooted in a prehistoric, presocietal morality. Explain how that is true.

Like *Catcher in the Rye,* it suggests a moral view completely contrary to that of *The Lord of the Flies:* not that humans are by their very nature corrupt and must be reigned in by government, but that society as we know it is actually corruptive. Explain.

Chief Seattle seems to have a grasp of the interlocking webs of our environmental and human ecologies better than our government. How do we resolve the legitimate claims of Chief Seattle and the legitimate claims of all those "huddled masses yearning to breathe free"?

How has Chief Seattle's third-last paragraph, which begins "Your destiny . . . ," proven prophetic?

Are we "brothers [and sisters] after all"? It is relatively easy to identify from the daily newspapers the ways in which we are not. Is there any objective evidence to give us hope that we at least might be?

THEME

THE NATION WE SHARE

The community is, ideally, merely an expansion of the web of family relationships; so, the nation—again, ideally—is an expansion of the web of local community relationships. There are services no family nor community nor even megacorporation can provide citizens: bridges, transcontinental highways, defense from invasion, and so on. Like parents of a family, ideally, the national leadership should be: provider, superego, and arbitrator for the people it serves.

But the moral (human) relationship between government and citizens is reciprocal: If government ought to act as a diligent parent, the citizen ought to act as a dutiful family member. If Atticus Finch is right in saying that a jury is only as sound as the individuals who sit on it, then a nation is only as sound as the communities, families, and individuals of which it is made.

But the family is no longer the connection to the larger moral ecology that it used to be, that is, tying the individual through the family into the local community and the nation. Yeats prophesied, "Things fall apart; the centre cannot hold; / Mere anarchy is loosed upon the world." The factors contributing to such a breakdown are numerous: the automobile segments families, media contradict family values, greed and lust became virtues, and thrift and chastity are viewed as vices. We've become accustomed to family-destructive realities that our immediate forebears considered unthinkable: wholesale divorce, abortions, drugs. If the family collapses, so do the community and nation.

What's more, our entire society has grown up (even if it shows little sign of becoming adult). As happens in an individual's adolescence, our very national "bigness" has changed the whole personality of the country and, sadly, has eroded its character—its soul—as well.

Society usually shows up in such phrases as "society's values." Such a "society" is quite external, a web of remote, secondary, impersonal relationships that have nothing to do with the intimacies of family and friendship.

But where is this powerful society located? The name society is used so often to justify modes of behavior, you'd think it would be easy to pin down at least an office. But society is as elusive as Big Brother. It isn't located in the Madison Avenue offices of the media, though they clearly carry out its mandates. It isn't in the halls of government, though they too seem to be its agents. Rather, media and government seem pulled between opinion polls on one side and special interest groups on the other. Both media and government seem to be working under the principle: "Give 'em (or at least: Tell 'em) what they want!" If the daily vote in our democracy is taken by the opinion poll, then, as Pogo said, "We have met the enemy, and they are us." Not "them"; "us."

If a school is only as sound as the individuals who care about and are willing to stand up for the community, so with the nation. But when I question students' care and willingness to stand up for America, about a third of them say, "You're not serious"; another third would give their lives for their country; and the final third answer, "Huh?"

"*I've* never been asked to voice an opinion!" you might retort. Well, in a sense, in a land of free speech, you have. Newspapers—if you read them—are there to let you know what your country is doing for and to you, and what you can do for your country. Every citizen is free to voice an opinion in letters to editors and to address Congress by letter, and, when old enough, to vote and to run for public office. And your silence speaks. Since the Magna Charta, according to the law, silence betokens consent. If you haven't spoken out against something, you're automatically presumed—by law—to be in agreement with it.

AMERICA AS A COMMUNITY

Though this book speaks of the United States, what it says about reversal of national personality and attitude is as true—excepting surface differences of a country's own history—of Canada, Australia, and most of the Western world, since media and transportation have made the world into a Global Village. Change has changed us all, from patriots to skeptics if not to cynics.

People who can remember the time when our country really was a community are all over fifty years old. In fact, America as a coast-to-coast community had probably never existed until 1914. Then, like Camelot, it began to die on November 22, 1963, when, for three days, the whole world stood still.

Before World War I, America, like most countries, was fragmented into small communities: farm towns, neighborhoods, blocks. Everybody knew everybody else; everybody pitched in at a death or a fire or a birth of a new baby. No law; we just did it because it was the right thing to do. Then the two wars and the Depression began to pull the segments together, not always willingly; but we all had a continuing common problem that no small group could solve alone.

Factions didn't disappear, but for a while they became less important. On the battlefield, as in (idealized) old war movies, the baseless antagonisms between redneck and Brooklyn kid and professor yielded to the more pressing problem of staying alive. At home, women were mobilized and worked in factories, and everybody began to realize even the division between sexes wasn't as rigid as people had believed—since the caves. Kids went round the neighborhood collecting papers and cans for recycling. It was an honor to be a Scout or have a religious vocation. We weren't as saintly as the old movies show us, but we were enlivened by a spirit of national unity we never felt before and possibly can never feel again.

However, just as with the unity of a gang or clique, there are problems with nationalism. First, during World War II Americans were not necessarily united *for us* so much as united *against them,* "those dirty Krauts and Japs." After the war, some tried to focus our hatred onto "Commies" for a while, but it didn't work. It was too simple-minded to brand a citizen "subversive" because twenty years before in the Depression or in college, he or she had been to a few Communist rallies. Equally important, Americans weren't uneducated rubes anymore, and we'd become prosperous and thus more confident, not as easily hoaxed. Sophistication was making us less easily led, less vulnerable— but, by that very fact less easily unified, and much less easily fired-up with patriotism.

The assassinations of the 60s, Vietnam, and Watergate all did their part to eclipse those sunny Camelot days and America's sense of cohering into a national community. Like any victim of disillusionment, we seemed as a nation resolved never to be hurt like that again. The media—again giving us only what we seemed to want—began to find warts on anyone who even seemed a hero,

All that is needed for the triumph of evil is that good people be silent.

LORD ACTON

and many citizens pulled back to a kind of wait-and-see attitude, if not to outright cynicism: "Watch; they'll find he has a mistress." (Sure enough, heroes being human, they do.) Our heads began to dominate our hearts; we preferred to be open-minded rather than committed; we began to demand guarantees.

The bicentennial (1976) and rededication of the Statue of Liberty (1986) were superb shows. But one wonders how many Americans were moved to tears of gratitude for being American rather than Ethiopian or Cambodian or Salvadoran or Russian. Life, liberty, the pursuit of happiness—and prosperity, peace and lack of inconvenience—were things many just took for granted. Nobility, honor, and integrity seemed the dreams of idealistic fools like Arthur; and cynical hard-rock lyrics expressed the feelings of a generation.

RELATION OF NATION TO CITIZENS

Democracy is an ideal theory. Yet when you work with real people and try to achieve ideals, the ideals—as Arthur found—become frayed and gradually shatter. The ideals may be unassailable, but if you try to embody them with human beings, each of whom is in varying degrees victim to narcissism and inertia, the process begins to look somewhat naive. But if we never rise for a moment out of skepticism and never consider the ideal seriously, we will never know where we have gone wrong, or how to set about getting to the root of our problems and get down to the business of setting them straight—of growing.

As we've seen, governing—the family, the school, the nation—runs the spectrum from totalitarian to individualist. The totalitarianism society exerts total control; the fundamental rule is conformity. The individualist society imposes no control whatever; the fundamental rule is competition.

In the ideal society, the balancing point of that spectrum that runs from conformity to competition, is cooperation—the point where the rightful demands of the nation are balanced by (flexible) loyalty in the individual, and the rights of the individual are balanced by (reasonable) compromise on the part of the nation.

Ideally, like a good parent, good government should fulfill at least three domestic functions: provider, superego, and arbitrator.

THE NATION AS PROVIDER

Despite windy campaign speeches, the purpose of government is not to provide a car in every garage and a chicken in every pot. The analogy between family and nation does not extend to the point where citizens can expect to be treated as dependent children. The Constitution guarantees our self-evident rights to life, liberty, and the *pursuit* of happiness. In so doing, it also guarantees the right to work for the essentials without which life is impossible: food, clothing, and shelter. But it does not guarantee that the government provide food, clothing, and shelter to healthy capable adults. As the wise Abraham Lincoln advised: Government should provide *only* what citizens are incapable of providing for themselves.

But the family analogy for the nation does extend to citizens who are in fact children or as dependent as children: those unable to work and therefore unable to eat and live. And here is where the thorny topic of **welfare**, or public assistance, programs arises.

Before going further, I beg the reader to let go of everything he or she has ever heard about welfare, unless he or she has reasoned to an objectively evidenced opinion:

◆ gathered data (not from hearsay, but from books),
◆ sifted out the essentials,
◆ put them into logical sequence in order to draw a conclusion,
◆ and put the opinion out to be critiqued.

For twenty-five years I have heard *vehement* denouncements of providing public assistance to "all those deadbeats," the fury of which was fueled by total ignorance. They were opinions based on *no* evidence other than parents' opinions, "everybody knows," and "I know this [one] guy on welfare who caddies for $100 day and drives a Mercedes with a bar in the back."

Not one of those vehement protesters knew what percentage of recipients of public assistance the *experts* believe cheat. Not one knew to whom welfare was limited, how much a family of four received per month, what the official poverty level was that year, or what percentage of Americans were functionally illiterate. And yet every one of those students had an *angrily* uninformed opinion. Here are some facts:

◆ *Fact:* By far the majority of public assistance recipients are children. But while the money is provided primarily for the children, some of their parents may misuse the funds. The greater portion of other welfare recipients are blind people, the elderly, and the disabled. Check an almanac.

◆ *Fact:* The strongest critics of public assistance programs agree that, at most, 10 percent of all recipients cheat. Should payments be cut back across the board for the 90 percent who cannot live without help, in order to catch the ones who cheat?

◆ *Fact:* Check an almanac for the amount of assistance a family of four receives each month in your state. (New York [$550.86], for instance, in 1990 gave nearly five times as much assistance as Alabama [$113.64].) If a family spent one-third of its income on food, how much was that? Now divide that dollar amount by four people. Now divide it by thirty days. How much does one hamburger and fries cost?

◆ *Fact:* The official poverty level (which rises each year) is about $14,000. There are about 33.6 million Americans officially living in poverty, most of whom do *not* receive welfare, work *full*-time, and are still living in poverty. What is

the minimum wage right now—the only wage available to many? How much can someone make per year on the minimum wage? If they spend one third of their income on food, how much is that? Now divide that by four people and then by 365 days.

◆ *Fact:* Although Americans are 99 percent literate, 30 percent are "functionally illiterate"; that is, they are able to read signs, follow simple verbal instructions, and so forth, but they can't read a contract, or directions on a cake-mix box, or make change. They also can't make a budget, read a recipe, or use food stamps prudently. And while the government provides booklets that explain how to get the most nutrition out of the food people on public assistance can afford, many families can't read them.

For your own sake, vow never to express an opinion about welfare until you've read at least one book about it. O'Malley's Law: The less you know, the more certain you can be.

A liar begins making falsehood appear like truth, and ends with making truth itself appear like falsehood.
WILLIAM SHENSTONE

THE NATION AS SUPEREGO

Laws are written for people too dumb to reason for themselves what is right and wrong. In a nation of people who consistently used their heads, there would be no need for laws threatening penalties for zooming through an intersection, littering streets, or exposing oneself to strangers. For that matter, there would be no need for laws against murder, rape, and drug dealing.

We are all in various stages of evolution from the animal id, and today's educational system doesn't seem to be helping things along as well as it might. For people who don't use their heads, government provides what these people don't seem able to provide for themselves: a superego.

Society is a complex of parents, presidents, police, and so forth that acts as an external superego when one's own superego is not strong enough to go it alone—a parent to a child. However, unless checked by a vigilant, enlightened electorate, society becomes a *domineering* parent who keeps adding and subdividing rules, shielding us, trying to do everything for us. To be honest, most times we'd just as soon have it that way, so we can say, "When are *'they'* gonna *do* somethin' about that?" Maybe society does boss us around too much, but it's a fair exchange for not having to reason and decide and forge guidelines for ourselves. When the governed are passive—when society is "them," not "us," society automatically becomes a gentle tyrant, and we become the peaceful slaves of that superego.

IN THIS AGE WHEN THERE CAN BE NO LOSERS IN PEACE AND NO VICTORS IN WAR— WE MUST RECOGNIZE THE OBLIGATION TO MATCH NATIONAL STRENGTH WITH NATIONAL RESTRAINT.
LYNDON JOHNSON

THE NATION AS ARBITRATOR

Every citizen has rights to a fair share of life's necessities (distributive justice). But interaction among people having differing views on what is right (commutative justice) inevitably arises, especially since we are living more and more closely together. Therefore, since each citizen is equal before the law, even though each has a diametrically opposite opinion of what that means, the only agency to step in and arbitrate is the state (social justice). To understand that need, read the story of Solomon and the two women who claimed to be mother of the same baby (1 Kings 3:16-28). The two parties argue vehemently that its side is inescapably right: thus the other side must be inescapably wrong. Who decides? How is the case decided? The only sane solution is arbitration by the wisest, most impartial authority one can find.

No sane or objective person would have a problem about the objective immorality (breach of our shared ecology) of pollution, child abuse, or arson. The agonizing problems arise when both sides in a dispute have solid but conflicting objective evidence to support their cases. The number of these questions is as numerous as the population, so we will consider—far too briefly—only five: racism, sexism, abortion, capital punishment, and obscenity.

Racism

The Declaration of Independence declares that "all men are created equal." But for nearly one hundred years, the nation acted as if that did not include blacks; for one hundred and fifty years, it acted as if it did not include women, even college presidents. Basic fairness (freed of self-serving bias) demands that if someone has been disabled for a long time, some allowances must be made. Blacks and women deserve an "edge" in a choice of candidates for jobs and college placement.

The conflict of rights arises when a better qualified white is passed over in order to rectify past injustice or establish a better mix in the workplace or university. The white may have a genuine grievance, but each complex case has to be judged on its *own* unique evidence. Wholesale condemnation of "reverse discrimination" is as mindless as wholesale condemnation of public assistance programs. Until we have *all* the hard facts about *this* case, we have no right to an opinion. And to condemn a practice of rectifying centuries of injustice says more about the speaker than it says about the practice.

In recent years, there has been a new wave of immigrants, mostly Hispanics and Asians. Many don't speak English. Those who resent such people taking "our jobs" are as unfair as those (often the same) who rail that the Japanese and Germans we defeated in World War II have now begun to defeat us economically. Balderdash. The Japanese and Germans accepted the rules of the capitalist game and played it better than we did. If the members of a Vietnamese family pitch in to make a business succeed, they deserve to succeed. If they get a job and satisfy employers, fine. The counterargument, from ethnic Irish, Italians, and Poles, belies the fact their own grandparents did the same thing.

Unlike mindless bigotry over skin color, the language issue is also considerable. No matter how just employers want to be, they often can't afford to hire a person who can't communicate or understand the requests of others. Those angry about the injustices surrounding the language problem rightly point to the fact that Asian immigrants and their children make a much quicker transition to English and to education. But as with welfare and reverse discrimination, the problem is almost always oversimplified in order to find a too-quick solution.

In the case of Hispanics who have not yet learned English, the "solutions" are often just as simplistic. "When my grandparents came here, they. . . ." But they came to a radically different society: teachers were different, public assistance was different, family life was different. If those who become angriest at people who cannot speak English were to go to Greece or Russia or Puerto Rico for a long period, their anger might lessen. People find it very intimidating when they can't understand what is said even by *children.* What's more, though it's demonstrably possible, it's very difficult for people who do not speak English and who work two jobs to learn English on the side. And I find it almost uncanny how often this latter subject is angrily addressed by a student who himself has an A mind and a C average.

Finally, there is no law against including racist terms in our vocabulary. But if the web of our shared nation depends on the soundness of *each* citizen's character, it behooves each of us to extract such words from our vocabularies—even for our own *self*-interest. Perhaps you don't use racist remarks yourself, but when you hear someone else use them, what do you do?

Sexism

The only objective difference between males and females is their genital difference. A woman can be as analytical, decisive, and tough as a man. In West Germany, 33 percent of the lawyers are women; in Russia, 75 percent of the doctors are women; countries have women presidents, reelected again and again. But in the United States, women account for only 9 percent of full professors, 10 percent of physicians, 7 percent of the lawyers. Education doesn't guarantee a woman equal treatment. A woman college graduate earns, on the average, the same as a male with an eighth-grade education. Ask your working mother.

Again, other than mindless bigotry, there is one objective fact about women that does deserve respectful consideration: women can have babies and men can't. If a woman chooses to remain childless (and there's no law of God or man that says she can't; nuns have done it for centuries), then she deserves scrupulously equal treatment in *any* area of our national life.

But having a baby—which is also not only her right but a life-enriching experience—does present a paradox. Most companies allow a woman some maternity leave, but in the ideal order a child really needs its mother for the first two years of life in order to have a continuous focus of being cared for. Day-care does "cover things," but it often is a changing focus every few weeks and disorienting for a child who can't yet think. If the reason the mother works is sheer survival, as it is with most single-parent mothers or fathers, both child and mother have to adapt and learn what they can from a nonideal situation. But if the reason is merely having a better life style or the satisfaction of a career, the woman might give advance considera-tion to the *consequences* for the *child* in her trying to have it both ways.

Just as inequities are imposed on women and blacks because of differences that are merely accidental, so too with the case of homosexuals. Here again the debate is fueled most often by sheer ignorance.

♦ *Fact:* Reputable psychologists are unanimous in saying homosexuals do not *choose* to be homosexual any more than heterosexuals weigh both options and decide to go with the crowd. Homosexual orientation is no more blamable than left-handedness or asthma. You don't *choose* your dreams and fantasies.

♦ *Fact:* Homosexuality has the highest incidence in macho and competitive societies (Greece, Rome, our own) and doesn't rise much above zero in societies that scorn heroics and thus take the idolatry out of maleness.

♦ *Fact:* Boys whose fathers still routinely touch them in affection well after puberty are the least likely to develop homosexual tendencies.

♦ *Fact:* The percentage of homosexuals who are predatory "recruiters" is about the same as for

heterosexuals. Thus to demand that no homosexual teacher be allowed to teach males is as foolish as saying no heterosexual male should teach girls.

Ignorance of those objective facts gives rise to opinions as harmful to the holders of those opinions as to homosexuals. Psychologists also agree that males who get inordinately angry even at the mere *idea* of homosexuals—even to the point of going out and beating them up—have something seri-ously wrong about their own psychological makeup. Fear of their own softer side (the anima) and a shaky grasp of their own convictions of their masculinity, lead them to project onto the homosexual and then savage a scapegoat.

O'Malley's Law: The less you know, the more certain you can be. Hitler was certain about Jews.

Abortion

Abortion is the most explosively divisive issue in this country since slavery. No one is pro-abortion. Even to those who are pro-choice, abortion is a desperate response that seems the only feasible choice among four bad solutions: abortion, forced marriage, raising the child alone, or adoption. Both pro-choice and pro-life people agree that the sane solution is in personal responsibility, not in the abortion clinic—but long before.

On January 22, 1973, the Supreme Court in *Roe v Wade* left no doubt that abortion during the first six months of pregnancy is *legal*. It made no declaration about whether it is *immoral;* that is not the court's function. The Fourteenth Amendment states: ". . . nor shall any state deprive any person of life, liberty, or property, without due process of law; . . ." *Roe v Wade* was at least based partially on a prior decision denying states any right to interfere with the practice of artificial birth control; what a couple does in their home is outside the law's jurisdiction.

What of the rights of a fetus? It has *legal* rights only if it is, in fact, a legal "person." The Court must use words only in their strictest sense, unless federal laws since the original Constitution expand that sense. By the word *person* the original framers of the Constitution meant white, landholding males. In 1868, the Fourteenth Amendment extended the meaning of *person* to include any male over twenty-one; two years later, the Fifteenth Amendment applied "person" to any adult male, no matter what race. It was not until 1928 that adult women became legal "persons," even though the Court had long held corporations and even ships were legal "persons." In *Roe v Wade,* the Court was stating that the legislative arm of the government had not given it the right to rule on the unborn as "persons."

The abortion issue is severely clouded by such tragic, important but peripheral issues as the much vaunted fear: "If abortion is not legal, women will go back to aborting babies with hangers in backstreet mills." That is a real issue, but not the *focal* issue, which is: What *is* a fetus, and what are you doing when you kill it? (Remember: the tree comes to me; I don't tell it what it is.)

If the fetus in objective *fact* is no more than tissue of the mother, like her appendix, then an aborting a fetus is no more a moral question than an appendectomy. But if the fetus in objective *fact* is a human being, a person, then abortion is premeditated homicide. The question of backstreet abortion mills then becomes a question of whether you want your child assassinated by a medically trained hitman or by a clumsy lout.

The focal issue is the one issue *both* sides at least seem to resolve by assertion rather than by reasoning. Pro-choice advocates say that, since a fetus repeats the stages of evolution (from simple cells to toad to fish to animal to human), it is moral to extract a fetus at least in the first trimester before it becomes a human (moral) entity. Pro-life advocates say that the fetus is a human being from the instant the sperm penetrates the ovum and life begins, since it is the product of two human cells. If you leave it alone, it won't become a banana or a zebra.

If each side didn't have mountains of argumentation to support its position, resolution of the abortion question would be as easy as resolving whether the mother were pregnant or not. The tragic truth is that there is no way to tell certainly when a fetus becomes human—or for that matter what "being human" actually means. It is as perplexing a problem as deciding when a comatose person *ceases* to be human. But one thing is certain: either the fetus is human or it is not. There's no consoling "halfway."

If the fetus is not *human:* No matter how many claim abortion is no more than removing a tumor, it is quite simply and obviously *not* the same. No woman mourns her lost stomach tumor. But women do mourn a lost fetus, even an aborted one. As in all *human* sexual matters, this is not merely a physical matter but also a profoundly psychological one—which many pro-choice advocates pass over too lightly at times.

Simone de Beauvoir, an early and passionate advocate of abortion, had had abortions herself. She says, "The one thing they are sure of is this: this rifled womb, these shreds of crimson life, this child that is not there. For many women the world will never be the same." Psychologist Carol Gilligan, after a prolonged study of women who had abortions, found in almost every case that the women mourned the full nine months until the child would have been delivered. At that point, each either took hold of her own life and said, "This will *never* happen to me again," or sank slowly into despair.

Which part of "no" don't you understand?
Anonymous

If the fetus is *human:* Abortion is homicide, pure and simple. The question is whether this homicide can in any sense, as in war, be called justifiable. If aborting a fetus is only a question of averting six months of shame, it seems difficult at best to justify murder. In the context of having too many children already, one might offer the perhaps too objective question of why the couple took the chance of pregnancy in the first place. In such cases, having another child is a tragic accident, and yet in other tragic accidents like collisions and plane crashes one simply has to accept the fact and begin to realign one's expectations. Harsh, but a reality one can't escape.

In cases of rape or incest, the shame is real, agonizing, tragic; only the heartless could deny that. But does it justify homicide?

I do not *want* an unwanted fetus to be human; I do not *want* a victim of rape or incest to have to pay the penalty of lifelong guilt or bondage to an unwanted child for an act that was unreasoned. But the tree tells me what it is; the fetus tells me what it is—not vice versa, the way I'd prefer.

A fetus is the product of two *human* cells. What's more, it is unarguably *not* merely part of the mother's tissue. It's DNA is utterly unique, a product of both mother's and father's DNAs. A fetus is an individual entity, no matter what *human* means. But the odds are on the side of this being a "human" entity.

Take the analogy, then, of an abortionist who is alone on a hunting trip. He has left his glasses back in the cabin. He sees the bushes move, and he's 80 percent sure it's an animal; he hasn't seen another human being in days. Can he shoot even if there's only a 20 percent chance that the object in the bushes is a human being?

If abortion is, in objective fact, premeditated homicide, no one can justly say that the struggle against abortion is an attempt to force the subjective opinion of one religion against the opinion of the majority of Americans. Objective truth is not established by Harris polls, by subjective opinions; if that is true, the earth would have remained flat until a few hundred years ago. If the fetus is in fact human, killing it is as immoral as killing a child in Auschwitz or Hiroshima.

Other hypothetical—but peripheral—issues are often raised regarding abortion, especially among the poor. For instance you may hear, "Do you want the child to grow up unwanted, hungry, deprived?" Of course not! But the primary question remains: Is the fetus a human being? What's more, focusing on the issue that way completely and self-servingly ignores adoption. Even further, any doctor looking at its family history would have felt quite sure it would be wiser and more humane to abort the Beethoven baby.

It would be naive to believe that, as with prohibition, there will be a constitutional amendment declaring a fetus a "person." When a sizable segment of the citizenry wants liquor or drugs or an abortion, they're going to get it. An uninforceable law is no law. The first realistic achievable goal for opponents of abortion is not total delegalization, but rather limiting the situations in which abortion is legal.

After the fact, any woman who has had an abortion deserves the same compassion as any other victim of a tragic time. But the answer to the abortion tragedy is preventing it *before* the fact.

Almost all our faults are more pardonable than the methods we resort to to hide them.
La Rochefoucauld

Capital Punishment

Capital punishment is, in objective fact, premeditated homicide at the hands of the state. Is the purpose of capital punishment to give the clearly guilty murderers exactly what they gave their victim(s)? Most religions would agree that is its purpose. But at least entertain this question: Is capital punishment, as Camus said, "plain and simple revenge"?

Would life imprisonment be an even worse punishment, but one in which the criminal at least had the *opportunity* of making some contribution—if not perhaps even being rehabilitated? The world would have been impoverished if Cervantes's and Malory's and Dostoevsky's judges had condemned them to death.

The question is whether execution does in fact deter other criminals. Human history, in which capital punishment is taken for granted, doesn't seem to show that capital punishment deters crime. Perhaps more crimes would have been committed without capital punishment, but do stiffer penalties lessen the use of cocaine? How much of a deterrent is school detention? Don't the same people show up for it every day?

Clinton Duffy, who was warden of San Quentin for eleven years, witnessed one hundred and fifty executions, has said: "I have never seen a rich man executed. It has nothing to do with guilt or innocence, but a good lawyer can set a flicker of reasonable doubt and get a hung jury."

Obscenity

The First and Fourteenth Amendments guarantee an American citizen's right to freedom of expression, even of sexual expression, as long it does not infringe on any other citizen's rights. Thus, our government cannot intrude on anyone's sexual habits—so long as they are not enacted on the courthouse lawn. Nor can our government infringe on rights of citizens to view pornographic films, so long as these citizens are in a private place and do not contribute to the delinquency of minors.

However, like any right, freedom of expression is not absolute. I am free to scream "Fire" in my own home; but I am not legitimately free to scream it in a crowded theatre when there is no fire. Nor am I free to poison minds that are incapable of knowing they are being poisoned. Adolf Hitler is sure proof of that.

Many libertarians fudge the pornography issue by saying that obscenity is a matter of taste. Although there is some basis to that argument, unbending puritanism, for example, which sees obscenity even in staid ballroom dancing, the determinant of obscenity is clear: anything that degrades a human being to the level of an animal or lower. There is nothing obscene about the nude human body, but there is something obscene—immoral, inhuman—about nude bodies engaged in sadomasochistic sex. It would take a true naivete to say that the nudes in *Playboy* and *Playgirl* and their even less tasteful imitators are innocent art.

Perhaps one could make a case that, at worst, such pictures are merely stimuli to adolescent curiosity (no matter what age the viewer) and to none-too-serious sexual arousal. They do, however, provoke frustration, which is not good. The serious point is that they degrade human models to mere objects—whether with the models' eager cooperation or not. Someone's willingness to be treated like an animal doesn't justify the treatment.

Mutual respect is the very fiber of the web of the human ecology. The soft-porn magazines market human flesh; they don't respect it, and they keep their audience as permanently adolescent as the people on *Cheers.*

The increase of rape, abuse of children and spouses, and seduction of children in the United States has become stunning, at least to those who think. Defenders of "sexual openness" on television and in ads, and even defenders of brutal sadomasochistic simulations in rock concerts consistently say, "expert opinion is as yet inconclusive to show serious connection between sex, violence, suicide, and drugs in the media and hard-rock lyrics and this increase in sex crimes." Some go so far as to say that, just as rough games are a healthy release for the id, so too are such performances. In a murder case where everyone, even the defense, knows the defendant understands right and wrong, you can always get a panel of experts to say that the defendent did not.

Of itself, music is morally neutral. What brings hard rock into the moral sphere is the *lyrics,* and more than a few songs are, objectively, outrageous. Some of the worst lyrics boast of how the singer is ready to rape and humiliate women. No one evolved who has beyond the sensitivity of a Neanderthal could call such trash morally neutral. The lyrics are, undeniably, degrading to women. And yet, ever so gradually, we become as accustomed to hearing them that we hardly notice the words unless they are blatant—just as we've become hardened to screeching sirens, ugly graffiti, and trash filled highways.

And the web slowly begins to shred. You get the society you're willing to pay for.

We are a confused society, indeed, when we protect lungs from secondary smoke and cancel dams to preserve some species of inedible fish, but balk at protecting minds. "Words," said Aristotle, "are what set human beings, the language-using animals, above lower animals. Not necessarily."

Perhaps, as many young people insist, "We don't listen to the words, just the music"—though the fact they can sing along so readily belies that. But the performances, especially of the hardest hard-rock groups, raise further unnerving questions about their moral—human—significance.

To think that hard-rock groups have made some pact with Satan, or are trying to enjoin young people to suicide, or even actually believe the lyrics they sing is as naive as to claim professional wrestling is a sport. But what is it in the *audience* that craves that kind of stimulus: trashing guitars, shrieking, sweat, blazing lights? There's something more than a circus atmosphere here: body-clutching spandex, leather, studs, bullets, death's heads—all the accoutrements of sadomasochist kinky sex—costumes the audience would run screaming from if they ever met people wearing them in a park. If all that is just "natural, clean fun," then words have no meaning anymore.

RELATION OF CITIZENS TO NATION

Ironically, the principal duty of a citizen to the nation is to forge a unique self: an individual who is curious, honest, able to reason, caring, and willing to stand up and be counted. A healthy, moral, growing nation is not an anthill.

What undermines achievement of an ideal society in reality is Whatever-in-Us-Resists-Civilizing, narcissism and inertia. On one hand, it is too much effort to achieve a self and stand up to be counted; on the other, even if one achieved a self, it is too risky to involve that self in too wide a circle of other people. Large-scale government centralizes programs, makes agencies more efficient, watches over our fate. It doesn't break citizens' wills as a totalitarian state would. Rather large-scale government softens the will, subtly brainwashes, bends, guides. It doesn't call a halt to the personal input of voting, but it does manipulate what voters hear. Trying to please all tastes like fast-food restaurants, the agencies of such a society—media, politics, schools—tend toward standardization and homogenizing: SATs, fashions, political candidates bland enough to offend no segment of the population. As a result, while each citizen still, by nature, wants to be a unique somebody—society urges us to be exactly like everybody else, which is about as tough as trying to be a giant and a midget at the same time.

The root of the problem is an attitude *in the governed* that has not changed since the days of caves or pyramids or sweat shops: the willingness to exchange human values for efficiency, security, and comfort.

The house always wins; the natures of things may wait awhile, but they take their revenge. Unless we bend every effort in this country to lead citizens to take hold of their own humanity and forge personally validated consciences, we can anticipate a gradual erosion of the entire national character to a level of savagery *The Lord of the Flies* could not dare envision. There are 23,000 reported murders in the United States every year—versus 30 in England, 99 in Canada, 68 in Germany, and 37 in Japan. In the richest country in history, 28,000 citizens every year take their own lives. Every day in the United States, two parents kill their children; in fact, infanticide in the United States exceeds the combined total child deaths for tuberculosis, whooping cough, polio, measles, diabetes, rheumatic fever, and appendicitis. Our society has done an admirable job saving bodies; it has done an execrable one making its citizens evolve as human beings.

The final stage of Erik Erikson's evolution of a healthy human personality is the mature individual's achievement of personal integrity: a fusion of independent selfhood with a personal commitment to the whole human family. The alternative, according to Erikson, is despair. The statistics quoted above indicate many of our fellow citizens settle for despair. The focal question for your own personal life is quite simple: How large a self are you willing to settle for?

Your most lethal enemy is shyness: just a self-deceptive synonym for cowardice. You don't put up your hand; you don't see the principal about a teacher gone stale; you don't write your representatives in Congress or the newspaper—never realizing you feel helpless *because* you are silent. If you're fed up with the way you're treated by the media, the government, those who degrade women, and those who deface our cities, and you're looking for the culprit, try looking in the mirror. If you *act* like a nobody, you *are* a nobody.

The first step is the one Jesse Jackson never tires of urging: "I *am . . . some*body!" Who are "they" to limit your choices, your freedom, your ambitions, or your life? Maybe they are right to give you guidelines, but until you make your own guidelines, you will be a slave to other people's expectations, other people's temporary and external approval. You will be a child until you *choose* to be an adult.

You can, indeed, make a difference—if you choose to. Solidarity was just nobodies who took on the most totalitarian society in history. Nobodies—banded together in community—abolished slavery, repealed Prohibition, secured the rights of labor, demanded the dignity of blacks and women, and ended the war in Vietnam. All you've got to do is stand up and shout, "I'm mad as hell! And I'm not going to take it anymore!" If all the nobodies in the world even *whispered* that, all at once, together, how beautiful, how beautiful the noise!

All that's needed for the triumph of evil is that good men and women remain silent.

THE FIRST REQUISITE OF A GOOD CITIZEN IN THIS REPUBLIC OF OURS IS THAT HE SHALL BE ABLE AND WILLING TO PULL HIS WEIGHT.
THEODORE ROOSEVELT

DILEMMA

Pat Ganley looked forward to PTA meetings with as much eagerness as to a root canal from an orangutan. And the woman waiting just outside her classroom door was Mrs. Emma Bloodworth, whose daughter Judith had ardently yearned to be in the choir. But Pat had cut Judith because the girl couldn't carry a tune in a tub—even though her father, Julius, was the school's biggest benefactor and president of its board of trustees.

Pat stood. "Good evening, Mrs. Bloodworth. How nice to see you again." (I'll go to confession.)

"Good evening, Miss Ganley," Mrs. Bloodworth said with a smile that would curdle milk, lowering her well-corseted girth into a chair. "I have *quite* a bone to pick with you."

"Really." (She means *my* backbone.)

"Yes. It is utterly beyond my capacity for suspending disbelief that you are subjecting the boys and girls in your care to this . . . this *Catcher in the Rye.* Judith brought it to me and showed me the words. I was simply *appalled!* These are children!"

"Forgive me, Mrs. Bloodworth, but all of them are well past puberty, capable of producing children themselves."

"And I have no doubt they *will* when they are subjected to such disgusting filth in a *Catholic* school. Have you no conscience?"

"Yes, I do. Have you read the whole book?"

"Surely you're joking."

"How can you pass judgment on a book you've never read?"

"Really, Miss Ganley. One needn't sit through an *entire* pornographic film to know it's obscene. I want you to withdraw this book from your syllabus."

"No, Mrs. Bloodworth. Judith can read some other book if you'd prefer, but the book stays."

Mrs. Bloodworth rose. "Really? Well, I'll have a little chat with your principal about that, shall I?"

"Do." (There goes the job!)

▷ *Questions*

You are the principal. What would you say to Mrs. Bloodworth. To Miss Ganley?

FAITH REFLECTION

Listen, my dear brothers and sisters! God chose the poor people of this world to be rich in faith and to possess the kingdom which God promised to those who love God. But you dishonor the poor! Who are the ones who oppress you and drag you before the judges? The rich! They are the ones who speak evil of that good name which has been given to you.

James 2:5–7 (adapted)

Being poor is not of itself a blessing. Poverty can corrupt and embitter just as well as wealth can. The point is not whether one has money or not, but how one *handles* poverty or wealth. If, God forbid, your parents suddenly lost all their money and the family were forced to live in extreme poverty, how do you think you would handle that? What concrete evidence from your present way of handling obstacles makes you believe that?

Like any suffering, poverty is an opportunity to grow, to forge a stronger ego-soul-self. But too much relentless challenge can demoralize and make one simply want to give up. Have you ever been in a situation like that? Does having gone through it affect the way you can empathize with the third-generation poor?

It is highly unlikely that anyone reading these pages has hauled a poor person into court or foreclosed the mortgage on a family and hurled them out into the cold. But do you find yourself ignoring people who are shabbily dressed, beggars, or street people? Obviously, no one can help all of them; obviously, too, some are going to take the money and buy drugs or liquor. But you don't *know* which those are. Is it worth being "taken" a few times just to know you haven't turned down a truly needy and honest victim—who is, we believe, Jesus in disguise?

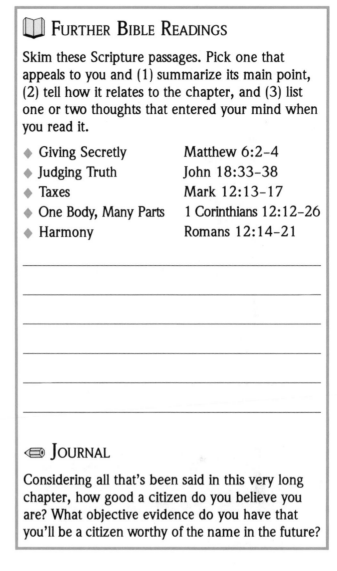

FURTHER BIBLE READINGS

Skim these Scripture passages. Pick one that appeals to you and (1) summarize its main point, (2) tell how it relates to the chapter, and (3) list one or two thoughts that entered your mind when you read it.

◆ Giving Secretly	Matthew 6:2–4
◆ Judging Truth	John 18:33–38
◆ Taxes	Mark 12:13–17
◆ One Body, Many Parts	1 Corinthians 12:12–26
◆ Harmony	Romans 12:14–21

_____

_____

_____

_____

_____

_____

JOURNAL

Considering all that's been said in this very long chapter, how good a citizen do you believe you are? What objective evidence do you have that you'll be a citizen worthy of the name in the future?

Understanding Society

REVIEW

1. What are the three functions the chapter says a nation or society should provide for all citizens? Explain each.

2. What are the factors influencing the disintegration of the family as a community? What effect does that have on society as a whole?

3. What are the drawbacks to even the best-unified nationalisms?

4. What historical realities killed the idealism of the America of the 40s and 50s? What has been the psychological effect on generations since?

5. Who are the people that, by right of their objective humanity, *deserve* public assistance?

6. How much is the AFDC (Aid to Families with Dependent Children) allowance in your state for a family of four? How much does that mean that family can spend on food (one-third their income) per person, per day?

7. What are the effects of citizens letting the media and politicians usurp their Superego?

8. What are the advantages and disadvantages of day-care for working mothers and their babies?

9. What focal question underlies *all* other questions about abortion? What are the arguments for and against the humanity of a fetus?

10. What is the primary obligation of a citizen to the nation? Why is that obligation more important than any other obligation, like paying taxes or serving in the military?

11. Explain O'Malley's Law.

DISCUSS

1. Is it merely a pipe dream that human beings can ever grow into the reasonable, tolerant, wise, and just entities that our cerebral cortexes suggest we were intended to be? What objective evidence at least suggests there might still be hope for us to become fully human?

2. We claim, "Society requires" and "Society demands." Who is "Society"? Who controls "It"? Explain.

3. As with individual adolescence, our very national bigness has changed the whole personality of our country and, sadly, has eroded its character—its soul—as well. Why?

4. Describe the character—the soul—of America now, as you see it. How does it contrast with the character you see in old-time black-white movies?

5. The fury of *vehement* denouncements of welfare for "all those deadbeats" is fueled by total ignorance. Is that opinion true? Give evidence to support your response.

6. Have you ever been to a foreign country whose language you didn't know? What was it like? Describe how you felt? Was it easy to "function" there as an "illiterate"?

7. One objective fact about women does deserve respectful consideration: Women can have babies and men can't. What impact does that have upon a woman who works outside the home in our society?

8. Reputable psychologists are unanimous in saying that homosexuals do not *choose* their homosexual orientation any more than heterosexuals choose their heterosexual orientation. What does ignorance of that fact give rise to?

9. "Expert opinion is as yet inconclusive to show serious connection between sex, violence, suicide, and drugs in the media and hard rock lyrics and increase in sex crimes." Explain why you agree or disagree with those who use that argument to defend "sexual openness" in society.

10. Is capital punishment, as Camus said, "plain and simple revenge"? Explain.

11. The sane solution to the abortion issue is personal responsibility, not the abortion clinic. Why?

12. Your most lethal enemy is shyness: just a self-deceptive synonym for cowardice. Why is that true?

13. If there were a military draft, would you seriously contemplate going to another country if you thought the reasons for the war were objectively unjust?

ACTIVITIES

1. Have you ever become teary-eyed listening to "The Star Spangled Banner"? What does being an American mean to you? Poll the group for responses.

2. Read Emma Lazarus's poem engraved on the Statue of Liberty. What does it say our present society seems to be missing? Why is it missing?

3. If your parents approve, go to your local welfare office and ask a petitioner who is willing to allow you to accompany him or her while he or she applies for AFDC, or tries to get an adjustment in his or her family's assistance. Keep a hawk eye out for every detail while you are there. Then write a report describing what it's like to apply for welfare.

4. If your parents approve, do not shower for a week, put on your grungiest clothes, go to some relatively safe but ugly place in town, and beg money for your lunch. Then write a report describing what it's like to be homeless and fundless.

5. "Most people cheat on their taxes." Research to see whether there is evidence to support the truth of that accusation? Report what you learn.

20. THE HUMAN FAMILY

SURVEY

For a change of pace, let's switch from subjective opinions to objective facts. Circle the correct answer to each item. Then discuss what the answers say about the world we share. Through no fault of your own, you were born in a country where you can live to be seventy, see a doctor without waiting five years, and have more than two homes. It's surely not your fault. But does it suggest that your idea of *enough* is more than most of the human beings who share this planet think is *enough?*

1. If every person in Canada saw a doctor once a year, each doctor would have to see how many patients?
   (A) 570 (B) 2,000 (C) 17,000 (D) 27,000

2. If every person in India saw a doctor once a year, each doctor would have to see how many patients?
   (A) 570 (B) 2,000 (C) 17,000 (D) 27,000

3. Life expectancy for females in the U.S. is about:
   (A) 37. (B) 53. (C) 65. (D) 78.

4. Life expectancy for females in Afghanistan is about:
   (A) 37. (B) 53. (C) 65. (D) 78.

5. The population density in Canada (people per square mile) is:
   (A) 7. (B) 134. (C) 1,100. (D) 1,800.

6. The population density in Bangladesh is:
   (A) 7. (B) 134. (C) 1,100. (D) 1,800.

7. In all the nations of Africa, Latin America, the Near and Far East, how many nations have citizens who, on average, eat diets below daily calorie requirements:
   (A) 17. (B) 28. (C) 143. (D) All

8. What is the most widely spoken language in the world?
   (A) English (B) Spanish (C) Chinese (D) Russian

9. The entire population of China uses as much energy as:
   (A) U.S. air conditioners.
   (B) all heavy industry in the U.S. and Canada.
   (C) all the countries in the Western Hemisphere.
   (D) Russia and Eastern Europe.

10. If all the people in the world lived as well as Americans and Canadians, all of the world's resources would be completely exhausted by the year:
    (A) 2000. (B) 2060. (C) 3000. (D) 3030.

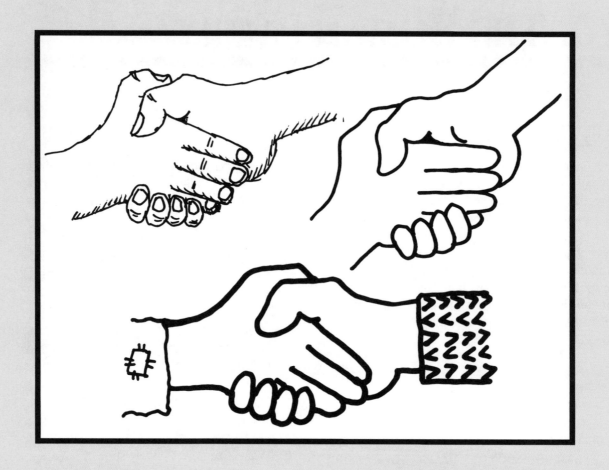

A FABLE

THE LAST GREAT FORGIVING

Once upon a time there were these three brothers, Hick, Hake, and Hock, who lived in a village more boring than the grave. Everyone lived in the same size cottage, with the same size yard, and the same acreage to farm. Every family had good durable clothes and shoes, enough to eat, and enough funds in the village bank to tide them over for a full year if crops failed. If any of the villagers had a longer stretch of bad luck, they borrowed from their neighbors; and if hardship dogged them even further, the villagers met in the square every five years in a solemn ceremony called the Great Forgiving and forgave every debt still outstanding, so that every five years each family had a chance again. Everyone was honorable and secure and peaceful and about as exciting as plain white bread.

So the day after the Great Forgiving, Hick, Hake, and Hock decided they were going to shake the dust of that tomb from their heels and put some zip and pizzazz into their lives. They were gonna ring them bells before they died! So they embraced one another lovingly and promised to meet in the square five years later at the next Great Forgiving.

The weeks and months passed by, and the day of forgiveness of debts arrived. Neighbors embraced one another heartily. "Think nothing of it, friend!" they cried. "You helped me out the same way last time!" And peace settled once again upon the town.

As the villagers drifted from the square toward the Great Hall for the traditional feasting, three young men were left behind, looking shyly from under their brows across the cobbles at one another. One man's face was tattooed with whorls of golden flecks and his body draped in a many-colored gown. "You must be Hick and Hake," he grinned, "because I'm Hock. I've been to a mystic land of gold. I've joined a great tribe." He blushed. "I'm in love with a princess."

One of the other two, dressed in a brocade frock coat and sporting an elegant goatee but a puzzling green pallor to his skin, stepped forward and grasped Hock's hands in both his own. "I'm Hake. I've been to the capital, to the university. I'm becoming a scientist!" He blushed as well. "You're looking at my skin. I apologize. It's from the chemicals."

Finally, the third whooped, "Then I must be Hick!" and embraced his brothers. Hake and Hock winced; their brother smelled like whiskey and unopened cellars; his clothes were shredded, his hair matted and bedraggled, his skin the color of ashes. But Hick stepped back and threw his arms in the air. "I've become a troubadour," he laughed. "I play the pubs and taverns and make a ditch my bed! But if it gladdens people's hearts, it's quite the life for me! Come," he cried. "Let's see if the villagers will forgive us a drink!"

So the brothers joined the villagers, who were taken aback by the changes in the lads, but happy to see them home. The rejoicing went on into the wee hours, and next morning the brothers vowed to meet in five years and regale one another with their adventures.

And so they did. Ten years after they had first left home, Hick, Hake, and Hock returned on the feast of the Great Forgiving. But, ah, what a difference.

Hake had, indeed, become a great scientist and chief supplier of brilliant new explosives for several kingdoms. He arrived at the west gate of the village in a great train of carriages too large for the narrow streets, so he entered the square on foot, dressed in a long ermine cloak and followed by an entourage of footmen and secretaries and liveried leeches.

The astonished villagers curtsied and tugged their forelocks in puzzlement, until a stern personage cleared his throat and shouted, "Make way. . . ," he paused as if wrestling with the crudities of a strange tongue. "Make way for His Plenitude, Hakissimo Ultimo!" Hake smiled and nodded round benignly to the peasants. "Meinke frunderen," he cried, "Oim kim heem fiert dine Greesh Freenge!" The villagers blinked at one another. They couldn't understand a word this stranger said. And they shuddered at his lizard skin and hooded eyes.

Just at that moment, there was a shimmer of trumpets at the east gate of the village, and the astonished townsfolk edged back as a triumphal procession appeared and spread out into the square. Girls in filmy trousers led panthers on diamond leashes; bare-chested hunks in black turbans and pantaloons scowled this way and that at the crowd; and finally, flanked by flamingo plumes, came an ivory chariot with a tall figure in white, his face and shaven head and arms and torso all gleaming gold. He held the reins with one hand and flung his other skyward in reponse to the cheers that did not come from the openmouthed crowd.

The chariot halted, and the golden man scowled to a velvet-gowned scholar. "Hear me!" the scholar cried, puzzling over the strange words. "Behold, base folk, Hoculanus the First and Forever Foremost! Cringe! Look on his works and despair!"

The man who had been Hock flashed a white smile from his golden face. "Poppoloi moi!" he shouted. "Oin gondin economai! Broustaymi Candalino Fruminoin!" The bewildered villagers looked from one to another, then back to the gold figure in the chariot, then to the serpentine man glowering on the other side of the fountain at being upstaged. Gradually, in twos and threes, they began to filter out of the square, too ill at ease and intimidated by these two confounding visitations to feel that this was even their place anymore.

The gold-visaged Hock glared imperiously across the square at the reptilian-visaged Hake. The two snorted once, and each turned his entourage on their respective heels and wheeled out their separate gates.

The only one left in the empty square was a wispy figure in rags huddled at the base of the fountain, his hair and face and hands the color of smoke.

That, they say, was the last time the Great Forgiving was ever celebrated. A few years later, the Emperor Hoculanus the First and Forever Foremost—having seen the inefficiency and backwardness of his birthplace—arrived one day with a great host of soldiers *and liberated the place from its stagnation, sending the people to work in uranium mines. In fact, he liberated the whole kingdom, seizing His Plenitude, Hakissimo Ultimo in the process, allowing him to retain his incomes and titles in exchange for his talents for vaporizing the emperor's enemies.*

Nothing has been heard of Hick in the village—or of music—since that very last Great Forgiving.

▷ Questions

When you graduate from high school and come back for your tenth reunion, you know that even your best friends will not be the same. What will have changed them? Thomas Wolfe said, "You can't go home again." Is that true? How?

Imagine the first encampment of human beings when the tribe has grown too large and too restless. Till then, the community had all held everything in common: a kind of perfect communism. Their customs, language, values were all the same. Then they shook the dust off their heels and headed out into the unknown. What happened to change all they had thought unchangeable? But what remained the same, no matter what the changes were in mere surfaces? What made them still "brothers," even though they found their customs and skin colors weird and their languages unintelligible?

In the world today, what *significant* differences are there between a bone-thin woman in Ethiopia whisking flies from the swimming eyes of her sightless baby, and a portly woman in Australia fanning flies from her face on a broad porch looking out at a seventy-thousand acre sheep ranch in the outback, and a woman fanning herself with *The Daily News* in a New York City welfare office, trying to hush her squalling kids?

If you answer that question, you may be well on your way to understanding "The Human Condition."

A READING

In this selection from The Once and Future King, *by T. H. White, Merlin has transformed Arthur ("the boy") into various animals—a fish, a hawk, an ant, and now a goose—to prepare him to understand people—and therefore how to be a good king.*

He was in a coarse field, in daylight. His companions of the flight were grazing round him. . . . The young female, his neighbour of the mud-flats, was in her first year. She kept an intelligent eye upon him. . . .

Presently the young goose gave him a shove with her bill. She had been acting sentry.

There are too many people and too few human beings.

ROBERT ZEND

"You next," she said.

She lowered her head without waiting for an answer, and began to graze in the same movement. Her feeding took her from his side. . . .

"What are you doing?" she asked, passing him after half an hour.

"I was on guard."

"Go on with you," she said with a giggle. . . . "You are a silly!". . .

"Am I doing it wrong? I don't understand."

"Peck the next one. You have been on for twice your time, at least."

He did as she told him, at which the grazer next to them took over, and then he walked along to feed beside her. They nibbled, noting one another out of beady eyes.

"You think I am stupid," he said shyly, ". . . but it is because I am not a goose. I was born a human. This is my first flight really. . . . I am enjoying it."

"I thought you were. What were you sent for?"

"To learn my education. . . . Are we at war?"

She did not understand the word.

"War?"

"Are we fighting people?"

"Fighting?" she asked doubtfully. "The men fight sometimes, about their wives and that. Of course there is no bloodshed—only scuffling, to find the better man. Is that what you mean?"

"No. I meant fighting against armies—against other geese, for instance."

She was amused.

"How ridiculous! You mean a lot of geese all scuffling at the same time. It would be fun to watch.". . .

"Fun to watch them kill each other?"

"To kill each other? An army of geese to kill each other?"

She began to understand this idea slowly and doubtfully, an expression of distaste coming over her face. . . . She went away to another part of the field in silence. He followed, but she turned her back. Moving round to get a glimpse of her eyes, he was startled by their dislike—a look as if he had made some obscene suggestion.

He said lamely: "I am sorry. I don't understand. . . ."

"Will you stop about it at once! What a horrible mind you must have! . . . There are . . . natural enemies. But what creature could be so low as to . . . to murder others of its own blood?"

"Ants do," he said obstinately. "And I was only trying to learn. . . . But don't they fight each other for the pasture?"

"Dear me, you are a silly," she said. "There are no boundaries among the geese. . . . How can you have boundaries if you fly? Those ants of yours—and the humans too—would have to stop fighting in the end, if they took to the air."

"I like fighting," said the Wart. "It is knightly."

"Because you are a baby."

▷ *Questions*

"She [the goose] lowered her head without waiting for an answer." What does that imply? Why is she amused at his assumption that posting guards must mean they are fighting someone? When she finally understands, why does she turn her back, as if "he had made some obscene suggestion"?

What is the connection between boundaries and fighting? What is the significance of the goose's last comment? What does it say about society?

THOSE IN FAVOR OF THE DEATH PENALTY HAVE MORE AFFINITY WITH ASSASSINS THAN THOSE WHO ARE NOT.
REMY DE GOURMONT

THEME

AN UNDERSTANDING HEART

Since its founding, the United Nations has done the human family some exceptional services: intervened in disputes, retrieved hostages, averted wars. But most people seem to consider the UN, well, irrelevant; that is, it has no bearing on *their* lives. Perhaps most people in the world consider even their own parliaments and congresses irrelevant—unless they happen at the moment to be discussing something of *personal* interest to the particular citizen: taxes, abortion, the drinking age. Most students seem to feel the Congress and the UN are groups of old men (with a handful of women) "doing their thing," shouldering their way in front of TV cameras for some unmemorable speech, wheeler-dealing, playing verbal poker (with cards up their sleeves): a debating society.

Perhaps you've been in a debating society. Often, debate coaches—whose permanent records aren't hurt by a winning streak—lose perspective and, without even realizing it, let their teams "know" that the object of the exercise is not to find the truth, but to *win*—no matter which side of the question they're defending. (I once knew a coach who taught his boys' teams how to make girls' teams cry!)

But we all have been in arguments when we suddenly realized the other side was right, had the truth—and yet we went on arguing. Why? Because we wanted to win—or at least not lose.

What Atticus Finch said of juries is as true of members of any parliament and the delegates to the UN. The soundness of any governing body is only as good as the personal soundness—the integrity of conscience—of each of its members. The health of the world we share depends on at least a significant number of its inhabitants achieving the qualities we've been considering for the length of this book:

◆ a willingness to be guided by the objective truth rather than by subjective and self-serving prejudices;

◆ a personally validated conscience sensitized to the equal humanity of every human being no matter what color or customs;

◆ a sense of the reciprocal obligations we have to one another no matter how many *artificial* boundaries we must cross to get from your home to mine;

◆ a conviction that *people* are more important than political or economic theories.

We must realize that in any relationship—whether a friendship or a marriage or a nation or the world community—if any one of us "wins," we all lose.

One reason organizations like the UN seem so irrelevant to so many ordinary people is that people simply don't want to clutter their minds with what's going on in Bangladesh and Kuwait and Tierra del Fuego: "I've got too many other things on my mind, and they're more important." Perhaps those personal concerns would seem less important—and less anguishing—if we put them in the broader perspective of our shared human family's problems. Nothing gives us a better understanding of the *objective* importance of our own difficulties than a visit to a slum in India or a barrio in El Salvador or a village in Ethiopia—even if it is only a visit through a film.

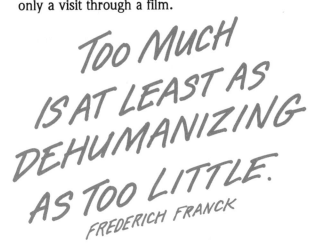

TOO MUCH IS AT LEAST AS DEHUMANIZING AS TOO LITTLE.
FREDERICH FRANCK

The fact that your parents won't let you buy a car or go to Florida on the spring break with your pals assumes its true value—or it ought to—when you genuinely acknowledge that you are already more fortunate than 95 percent of the inhabitants of this planet. No matter what economic bracket you are in, relative to the people in your immediate (and objectively quite constricted) area, as a citizen of America or Canada or Australia, you are on the very top of the pyramid.

For instance, when you simmer because your unfeeling mother has tuna casserole and broccoli again, consider the cause of your distress in the light of this segment from *Time* magazine:

> *The victim of starvation burns up his own body fats, muscles, and tissues for fuel. His body quite literally consumes itself and deteriorates rapidly. The kidneys, liver and endocrine system often cease to function properly. A shortage of carbohydrates, which play a vital role in brain chemistry, affects the mind. Lassitude and confusion set in, so that starvation victims often seem unaware of their plight. The body's defenses drop, disease kills most famine victims before they have time to starve to death. An individual begins to starve when he has lost about a third of his normal body weight. Once this loss exceeds 40%, death is inevitable.*
>
> November 1, 1974

So the first reason for the emergent adult to have an awareness and genuine concern for events outside the narrow radius of the family, the school, or even the nation is precisely that you *are* an emergent adult. You ought to begin seeing things against the background of an objectively broader perspective. You can't begin to be or act like an adult if you still have the narrow, narcissistic, self-confined perspective of a child. Genuine adults are not as upset by lima beans or a missed concert or a spoiled vacation as children are. Genuine adults say, "Oh, well"—which often makes children hopping mad! But adults live in a broader, more realistic landscape.

You can cocoon yourself from that, but to your own peril.

There are no "white" or "colored" signs on the foxholes or graveyards of battle.
John F. Kennedy

A second reason emergent adults ought to be aware of and concerned about their fellow human beings, no matter how far away they live, is sheer self-interest. The future belongs to those prepared for it, and the future will be unimaginably different from what you have gotten used to. Consider, for instance, how many items that you simply take for granted in your home that were not even *invented* forty years ago when I graduated from high school. If you removed those inventions, your home would be bare to the walls.

Sixty years ago we had no television, no VCRs, no PCs, no stereos, no portable cassette players, no quartz batteries, no fax machines. AIDS was also unheard of and didn't loom like a new spectre of the Black Death; abortions and divorce existed but not in epidemic proportions. We also had not accustomed ourselves to thousands of human beings sleeping on subways or in the streets. Rocket ships were fantasies for Saturday cartoons. There were no jets, no Stealth bombers, no nuclear arsenals. Eastern Europe was about to become a Russian suburb; now, sixty years later, it is not. The United States was the richest and most indomitable country in the world; now it is a trillion dollars in debt. Who will deal with that emergent world? You will. Or someone will deal with it for you.

*Every luxury
must be paid for, and
everything is a luxury,
starting with
being in the world.*
CESARE PAVESE

Merely consider a few more facts your generation will have to face: It took 300,000 years for the Earth to contain two billion people; now it adds two billion people every 30 years. By the year 2000, there will be four Asians for every person considered "Western." Most of the developing nations have massive debts to United States' financial institutions that they simply will never be able to pay, and your money will be financing their debt. The world's oil is a finite commodity, and when it's gone, it's gone. In every industrialized country, pollution is already threatening the world's climate.

John Naisbitt has two books about "megatrends" that are well worth perusing if you intend to live on earth for the next forty years. He says, "No longer do we have the luxury of operating within an isolated, self-sufficient, national economic system; we now must acknowledge that we are part of a global economy." Nationalistic short-sightedness and competitiveness simply must give way to a comprehensive worldview and cooperation. In your lifetime, he predicts, Brazil could likely overtake Detroit as the automaker to the world; Japan will take over electronics; and the United States will take over processing of information.

Furthermore, Naisbitt continues, "In an interdependent world, aid is not charity; it is an investment."

You can cocoon yourself from that, but to your own peril.

A third reason for an emergent adult to have a wider worldview is simply to realize how objectively *lucky* you are to be a citizen of this country, which in turn should provoke a sense of gratitude and a need to contribute. On a planet where every single day 150 million children are desperately hungry and 12,000 people die of starvation, Americans spend 3 billion dollars a year on pet food and 6 billion for cosmetics. That isn't cause for a massive guilt trip; it doesn't mean we should toss old Rags off the mountainside, throw out all the cat food, and trash all the mousse and mascara. But it should trigger a response in anyone beyond Neanderthal sensibility: "My God! I'm so *overwhelmingly lucky!*" That would be another sign one is at least beginning to become adult, shedding the delusion that being spoiled is an incurable disease one somehow deserves. At the very least, no one would never again sing "The Star Spangled Banner" cynically.

You can cocoon yourself from that, but to your own peril.

A fourth reason, allied to that, is a sense of *noblesse oblige.* If I have been inordinately gifted—compared to the rest of the human family—the slightest sense of honor would behoove me to share. Now, with the media bringing the world right into our living rooms, we have immediate awareness of who in the Global Village has had a fire or a death in the family or a baby with no food. That provokes two responses: either "Oh, my God! I'm responsible for all that, and I can't do anything," or "Hell, it's impossible; anybody for tennis?" Either wring the hands in despair, or throw them up in frustration. Neither does anyone any good, including the hand-wielder.

You can't crusade for *every*thing, but if you are privileged—as we all are, you by God have to crusade for *some*thing. Even students who can't drive can do something: visit people in nursing homes, pick up litter, watch out for the anonymous kids who eat their lunches alone. That won't change the world much, but it will lessen the pool of heartlessness in the world and it will sensitize the giver. Each anonymous person rescued from anonymity is one more potential recruit for the crusade to lessen our common pain. If every older student became a big brother or big sister, even to someone in the same school, one more human being might be sensitized, given confidence, able to suspect he or she might make a difference.

Your funds are limited, by definition. But there must be *one*—just one—agency serving our desolate brothers and sisters around the world that could use your five bucks a month—which wouldn't kill you, the price of one CD that in a year you'll forget you even have. There are addresses of such groups in any almanac: Bread for the World, CARE, UNICEF. Write them a letter that merely says, "How can I help?"

At the very least, sensitivity to the needs of others around the world might broaden the well of compassion in our human family and make at least a minute encroachment on the reign of evil and insensitivity and thoughtlessness. Lech Walesa began somewhere; Mother Teresa began somewhere. And not on a grand scale.

O'Malley's Law: The less you know, the more certain you can be. The more you know, the more vulnerable you can be. Your genuine sense of compassion for people on the opposite side of this shrinking planet may not do them any good, but it sure would make a difference in *you*, no? It would enrich you, make you a better candidate for parent, for citizen, for human being. An understanding heart.

You can cocoon yourself from that, but to your own peril.

Finally, a sense of the shared planet—the widest extent of the web of our moral ecology—might provoke you to consider the question no one today seems willing to ask: How much is enough? In the fractured folktale that began this chapter, everyone had enough. Enough to live on and enough for a rainy day: when the crops fail, when the unexpected medical bill arises, when the investments lag. What made the brothers restless?

The media and the economy have brainwashed us to believe that no dollar figure is enough. Check me out. If you have a million dollars, would that be enough? Or would you say, "I can get *more*"? And what's wrong with that? Don't walk away from that too quickly. What *is* wrong with that? Have you been better brainwashed than you suspected? Is there anyone who genuinely, objectively *needs* more than a million dollars?

A passage (later rejected) in the original draft of the Constitution stated: "An enormous proportion of property vested in a few individuals is dangerous to the right and destructive to the common happiness of mankind; and therefore, every free state hath the right to discourage the possession of such property." Along with Benjamin Franklin, Thomas Jefferson believed no one ought

A person of humanity is one who, in seeking to establish himself, finds a foothold for others and who, desiring attainment for himself, helps others to attain.
Confucius

to own more property than he or she needed for a living. The rest belonged to the state, that is, to everyone in common. Jefferson surely saw the need for *some* private property as a guarantee of the individual's freedom. But property was also a danger, once it created dramatic inequality. What impelled the Founding Fathers to delete that passage?

Americans and Canadians and Australians and Japanese and Germans surely are "animals more equal than others." We are of the world's *noblesse.* To what does it *oblige?*

How many of the things we in our small-radius cocoons believe to be essential (stereo, color TV, VCR's) are unthinkable luxuries to the rest of the human family? What we spend on an upgraded car, a wider-screen TV, or a compact disc for the old turntable, a family in Peru or Cambodia or Chad could live on for a month. No need to go without the car, the TV, or the turntable. But do we really *need* a better one? Sez who? Do *you* tell you what is truly important, or does your electronically implanted Superego?

You can cocoon yourself from that, but to your own peril.

"Let there be peace on earth. And let it begin with me."

OUR FAMILY'S CHILDREN

The U.S. Bureau of the Census estimates that there will be 58 million American children by the year 2000. For purposes of comparison with other countries:

◆ Each year, 14 million children in the world die from preventable diseases: measles, tetanus, pneumonia, diarrhea; 40 thousand a day could be saved for literally pennies apiece; *all* 14 million children who die each year could be saved for what the world spends on the military in a single *day.*

◆ 30 million world children live in the streets.

◆ 150 million world children are chronically malnourished.

◆ 250 thousand world children die of polio each year, though vaccines are inexpensive.

◆ Each day, 1,000 children go blind because they have no access to twenty cents worth of vitamin A; even if their countries had it, their parents couldn't pay for it.

◆ There are as many refugee children in the world as there are people in New York City.

◆ In 1990, there were 5 billion people on planet Earth; in 2025, there will be 8 billion.

In response to the above statistics, one student said, calmly, "Isn't it better that those 14 million kids die? If they all lived, there'd just be more mouths to feed. And all of them are going to have even *more* kids." What is your response to that? It certainly is a very clear-eyed, left-brain assessment. Is there anything missing from it?

CHILDREN ARE OUR MOST VALUABLE NATURAL RESOURCE.

HERBERT HOOVER

DILEMMA

Since Kathy Beglan, an only child, was a little girl, it had been her parents' fondest dream that she would become a lawyer like themselves, and she never questioned that that was her dream, too. A bright girl, she applied herself in school; and in two weeks she will graduate (probably summa cum laude) from Mt. Holyoke and has been accepted at three law schools.

But tonight at dinner she has a small atomic bomb to present to her parents: "Mom? Dad? I've made a decision."

Her father grinned at her over a forkful of roast beef. "You're running for attorney general *before* you go to law school."

"No," Kathy said softly, "I'm going into the peace corps before I go to law school."

Her parents' forks were suspended before their open mouths. "You're joking."

"Nope. Never more sincere. I even made a retreat to be sure."

"Kathy," her mother said, "think what that will do to your career."

"Improve it, I think. I've spent the last sixteen years toughening my mind. Now I think I need something to toughen my soul."

"Honey," her father said, "just think how out of shape that mind's going to get out there in the middle of nowhere. Hell, you could get malaria or jaundice or . . . or, my God, even get killed!"

"Dad, I've been given so much. I want to give something back."

"Fine. When you finish law school, do *pro bono* work for a few years. You'll help the poor, and you'll get your feet wet. Good experience."

"No. I want to go the whole route."

"Kathy, this Joan of Arc posture is very noble, but we've got to be practical, honey."

"It's eminently practical. Nuts and bolts."

Her father rose and threw down his napkin. "We'll talk about his tomorrow."

▷ *Questions*

It's tomorrow! Role-play Kathy's discussion with her father. Be convincing.

What do you think about Kathy's statement: "Dad, I've been given so much. I want to give something back"? What about her dad's retort: "When you finish law school, do *pro bono* work for a few years."?

FAITH REFLECTION

I am not trying to relieve others by putting a burden on you; but since you have plenty at this time, it is only fair that you should help those who are in need. Then, when you are in need and they have plenty, they will help you. In this way both are treated equally. As the scripture says, "The one who gathered much did not have too much, and the one who gathered little did not have too little."

2 Corinthians 8:13–15

Saint Paul says elsewhere that we needn't impoverish ourselves for the poor. But God expects us to give of our excess. Could you, for instance, go through your dresser and closet and pull out everything you haven't worn in a year? It's undeniable that you don't *need* those items, and that some other person does. What would be the affect on you? Would it be worth the effort?

From the beginning, this book has carefully avoided identifying morality with Christianity. What are the motives that would impel even a good atheist to do whatever he or she could to alleviate— even in some small way—the world's suffering, if only of its children? Those children are only occasionally brought to mind by the media. Is it possible to develop an immunity to others' pain, simply by being so routinely exposed to it? Is there something morally wrong about such an immunity?

What motives does a Christian have for trying to help—even if only in a small way—that go beyond simple human decency?

Kindness in words creates confidence.
Kindness in thinking creates profoundness.
Kindness in giving creates love.
LAO-TZU

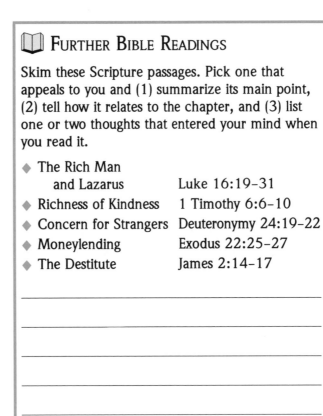

FURTHER BIBLE READINGS

Skim these Scripture passages. Pick one that appeals to you and (1) summarize its main point, (2) tell how it relates to the chapter, and (3) list one or two thoughts that entered your mind when you read it.

- The Rich Man and Lazarus — Luke 16:19–31
- Richness of Kindness — 1 Timothy 6:6–10
- Concern for Strangers — Deuteronymy 24:19–22
- Moneylending — Exodus 22:25–27
- The Destitute — James 2:14–17

_____

_____

_____

_____

_____

_____

JOURNAL

"Let there be peace on earth, and let it begin with me." The sea of inequity and iniquity around the world and at home seems nearly infinite. But it's not. An individual can make a difference, perhaps not a dramatic difference, but a difference nonetheless. We've seen again and again that you simply can't achieve a vague goal. Try to narrow the focus of what you as an emergent adult might do to lessen human suffering, either on a global or a national or a local scale.

Of all the varied forms of anguish the human family shares, what *one* touches your "understanding heart" most? Realistically, how can you begin to do something to relieve that anguish right now?

Understanding the Human Family

REVIEW

1. What are the advantages and disadvantages of the world Hick, Hake, and Hock left to pursue their adventures? What did the improvident Hick discover that Hake and Hock dismissed as valueless? Why was his burpy altruism ungrounded?

2. Explain why our everyday problems would be less important—and less anguishing—if we put them in the broader perspective of our shared human family's problems.

3. What did *noblesse oblige* mean in the Middle Ages and the Renaissance? Historically, what happened in the seventeenth and eighteenth centuries to curdle that ideal in the same way the assassinations of the 1960s, Vietnam, and Watergate curdled the American Ideal? What is the objective connection between privilege and obligation?

4. Define *compassion*. Why is a potential human being impoverished without it?

5. What is objectively essential to a dignified, human life? Be concrete. How many people who are objectively human beings live an objectively human life? Whose fault is it when people do not? It may not be *your* fault; you have no responsibility for the causes. But do you have any responsibility for the results? Explain.

DISCUSS

1. In the world today, what *significant* differences are there between (a) a bone-thin woman in Ethiopia, whisking flies from the swimming eyes of her sightless baby, (b) a portly woman in Australia, fanning flies from her face on a broad porch looking out at a 70,000-acre sheep ranch in the Outback, and (c) a woman fanning herself with the *New York Daily News* in a New York City welfare office, trying to hush her squalling kids?

2. If you are truly an emergent adult, it ought to be evident in the way you see your personal problems within the broader perspective of the whole human family. Until you do that, no matter how old you become, you will still be a child. Why is that true?

3. The future belongs to those preparing for it. The future will also be unimaginably different from what you have gotten used to. Brainstorm all the disconcerting trends in the human family that you are aware of—homelessness, AIDS, rising crime rates, and so on. Who is going to "take care of" those things, or at least stop them from getting worse?

4. What is the result—within an individual—of acknowledging how overwhelmingly lucky one is?

5. Neither wringing your hands in despair nor throwing them up in frustration does anyone any good, including the hand-wielder. What is your opinion? Remember to give the evidence.

6. You can't crusade for *every*thing, but if you are privileged—as we all are—you, by God, have to crusade for *some*thing. Why?

7. Your genuine sense of compassion for people living on the opposite side of this planet may not "do them any good," but it sure would make a difference in *you,* no?

8. How much is "enough" for you? List all the possessions (car, swimming pool, summer home) and all the needs (children's tuition, retirement security, rainy-day funds) that would be "enough" for you so that you could finally say, "Okay. Now everything else goes to the needy."

9. If you had a million dollars, would that be "enough"? Or would you say, "I can get *more*"? What's wrong with that drive?

ACTIVITIES

1. Research the debt that Brazil owes to CitiCorp. Consult a banker or financial expert to find out what would happen if CitiCorp simply *forgave* Brazil's debt—or if it settled for, say, ten cents on the dollar. What would be the effect on Brazil's economy? On CitiCorp stockholders? On the economy of the United States? On the human family we are all members of?

2. In groups, research the (a) per capita income, (b) life expectancy, (c) ratio of doctors to citizens, (d) infant mortality, and (e) ratio of imports to exports for Afghanistan, Australia, Bangladesh, Bulgaria, Canada, Chad, Haiti, Laos, Russia, and the United States of America. (See *The World Almanac and Book of Facts 1992,* pages 734–821.)

3. View the video of one of the many "nostalgia" movies, like *Peggy Sue Gets Married* or the first *Back to the Future.* List all the items that you take for granted in everyday life today that are *not* found in the video.

4. Research the addresses of Bread for the World, CARE, American Leprosy Missions, March of Dimes, Negro College Fund, Save the Children, UNICEF, Hope, Comic Relief, and Catholic Relief Services. Now what?

21. CHRISTIANITY

SURVEY

Circle the number on the rating scale under each statement that best reflects your opinion about that statement. On the scale

+2 = strongly agree,
+1 = agree,
 0 = can't make up my mind,
-1 = disagree,
-2 = strongly disagree.

Then share the reasons for your opinion.

1. The consistent image of God in the Old Testament is a vengeful destroyer.

   +2 +1 0 -1 -2

2. When dealing with sinners, Jesus always demanded restitution before forgiving them.

   +2 +1 0 -1 -2

3. The idea of Christianity is closer to communism than to monopoly capitalism.

   +2 +1 0 -1 -2

4. According to Jesus, the only norm for rejection by God is refusal of baptism.

   +2 +1 0 -1 -2

5. The heroes God chose in the Bible were consistently jerks.

   +2 +1 0 -1 -2

6. The only people Jesus ever bawled out were the clergy.

   +2 +1 0 -1 -2

7. Jesus treated rich people the same way he treated poor people.

   +2 +1 0 -1 -2

8. The basis of Christianity is that we be just and fair to one another.

   +2 +1 0 -1 -2

9. One cannot limit Jesus' command to help the needy only to the *materially* needy.

   +2 +1 0 -1 -2

10. Jesus' principal preoccupation was keeping people from sin and hell.

   +2 +1 0 -1 -2

A FABLE

THE BISHOP'S CANDLESTICKS

Once upon a time there was this young man named Jean Valjean who was very poor. I mean dirt *poor. He lived with his widowed sister and her seven children, supporting them as a pruner, reaper, laborer, even at times as a poacher. Jean had no sweetheart; he had no time to be in love. Then one desolating winter, there simply was no work—no small animals to poach—and no bread for seven children. So one Sunday night, Jean Valjean smashed the window of the shop under the baker's house and grabbed one loaf of bread. But he was caught by the gendarmes and carried off to jail. The hawk-faced judged peered down at the thief and said, "We must make an example of you, young scoundrel. Armed robbery of a private home! What if everyone who was hungry stole from their upright neighbors? Five years in the galleys! Next!"*

So for a pane of glass and a loaf of bread no one would ever eat, Jean Valjean was taken to the seaport at Toulon, an iron collar was riveted to his neck, and he took his place at the great oars in the galleys. His very name was wiped out. Now he was no more than #24601. Stroke! Stroke! to the heavy beat of drum and lash, and every night he was trundled back to the stone prison, the watery soup, and the bare plank bed.

Near the end of his fourth year, Jean Valjean had a chance to escape, and he took it. After thirty-six hours, he was caught; three more years. In the sixth year, he escaped again, and was caught: five more years. In his tenth year, he tried again: three more years. In his thirteenth year, he escaped and received three more years for four hours of freedom. Finally after nineteen years, he was released and given his pay for his life from age twenty-four to forty-three: 119 francs and 15 sous.

The first day Jean Valjean trudged thirty-five miles from Toulon—his hair still shaven short and his beard long and straggly—to the town of Digne. Wearily, he pushed into the inn. "I need food," he said. "And a bed for the night. I have money."

The innkeeper beamed, "Of course, monsieur. And your papers?"

Jean Valjean brought out the yellow passport of the released convict, and the innkeeper's face fell. "I'm sorry, monsieur," he said. "There is a fair in town. Every room is taken by the muleteers."

Jean scowled at him. "Then put me in the stable." The innkeeper shook his head, "It is filled with mules."

Jean held his temper. "But where can I go?"

The innkeeper slammed the door, "Anywhere but here."

Jean Valjean trudged past the empty stable and tried all the other inns, but as soon as the innkeepers saw the yellow passport, they showed him to the door. He even tried the jail, but they had heard he was in town and drove him away too. Finally, he stopped an old woman and asked if there was a place for poor travelers. She nodded at a house next to the church and said, "Knock there."

So Jean Valjean knocked on the door, and in a moment it was opened by a squat little man in a cassock. His cherub face beamed. "Yes?" he said.

"Father, I've tried everywhere. No one will take me in. I was a convict. For nineteen years. But I can pay. I have 119 francs and 15 sous. . . ."

"But of course," Bishop Bienvenu smiled and called over his shoulder, "Madame Magloire, set another place, would you? And put clean sheets on the alcove bed. And use the real silverware, Madame Magloire. We have a guest! Come in, monsieur."

"But I am Jean Valjean. A convict. A shed . . ."

"Hush," the bishop said. "I knew your name before you told me."

"But how. . . ?"

"Because your name is my brother. Now come." And he led Jean Valjean into the parlor and sat him by the fire till supper was ready, chatting about the bitter weather and the shortage of fuel. When the meal was ready, the bishop led Jean into the dining room where the silver gleamed at the side of each plate.

Jean Valjean ate like a wolf: thick soup and thick bread, wine, the shimmering tableware and the silver candlesticks. When supper was over, the housekeeper rose to wash the dishes and then joined Jean Valjean and the bishop for evening prayers in the parlor.

When the prayers were done, the bishop said, "Let me show you to your room," and he took one of the silver candlesticks and led Jean Valjean through the dining room, through his own room, to the bed in the alcove. As they passed through the dining room, Madame Magloire was putting the guest silver into the cabinet. "Sleep well, my brother," the bishop said, and pulled the curtain on the alcove where Jean Valjean fell to sleep almost immediately.

The cathedral clock struck two, and Jean Valjean sprang full awake, unused to even four hours' sleep. For an hour he lay there, pawing through the nineteen years the state had robbed from him—the squalor, the indignities, the pain, and the screaming madness. When the clock tolled three, he rose in the darkness and padded in his stocking feet past the sleeping bishop, looking only for a moment at the outstretched arms of the crucifix over the bishop's softly snoring head. Jean Valjean quietly opened the cupboard, lifted out the basket of silver, and escaped into the night.

Next morning, as Madame Magloire implored heaven at the loss of the silverware, Bishop Bienvenu sat absently stirring his coffee. Suddenly, there was a harsh rap on the door, and the bishop rose to answer it. There in the doorway stood two gendarmes holding Jean Valjean and the officer standing at attention.

"Bishop," the officer began, holding out the basket of silverware.

"But he's only a priest," Jean Valjean moaned.

"Silence!" barked the officer.

"Ah, my friend," Bishop Bienvenu said, "I'm so glad you returned. You forgot that I gave you the silver candlesticks too. Madame Magloire? Would you fetch the candlesticks for Monsieur Valjean?"

"Bishop," the officer said dubiously, "do you mean that what this man said is . . ."

"True?" the bishop smiled, "But of course. He told you a priest had given him that silverware, no?"

"Yes, but . . ."

"Well, that is absolutely true. I give it to him with all my heart. Ah, and here. The candlesticks as well. There, my brother," he said and handed the two silver candlesticks to the bewildered Jean Valjean. "And whenever you are in Digne, you have a home here. Go with God, my son. In peace." And he touched Jean Valjean's stubbly cheek, smiled, and closed the door.

The officer shrugged at the two gendarmes and led them out through the gate and left Jean Valjean standing speechless with a basket of silverware in one hand and two silver candlesticks in the other.

▷ Questions

Put yourself in the bishop's place. If the real silver comes out only when there are guests, he is not rich. Honestly, what would you have done in the bishop's place? *Why* is his reception of Jean Valjean different from those of the other, presumably Christian, citizens of the town? What does he see in Jean Valjean that they do not, and why don't they see it?

In French, what does *bienvenu* mean? What does it have to do with the core of the Christian gospel?

A READING

Saint Luke's gospel tells us that Jesus told this parable to tax collectors and other outcasts, as the Pharisees and the teachers of the Law listened.

"There was once a man who had two sons. The younger one said to him, 'Father, give me my share of the property now.' So the man divided his property between his two sons. After a few days the younger son sold his part of the property and left home with the money. He went to a country far away, where he wasted his money in reckless living. He spent everything he had. Then a severe famine spread over that country, and he was left without a thing. So he went to work for one of the citizens of that country, who sent him out to his farm to take care of the pigs. He wished he could fill himself with the bean pods the pigs ate, but no one gave him anything to eat. At last he came to his senses and said, 'All my father's hired workers have more than they can eat, and here I am about to starve! I will get up and go to my father and say, "Father, I have sinned against God and against you. I am no longer fit to be called your son; treat me as one of your hired workers."' So he got up and started back to his father.

"He was still a long way from home when his father saw him; his heart was filled with pity, and he ran, threw his arms around his son, and kissed him. 'Father,' the son said, 'I have sinned against God and against you. I am no longer fit to be called your son.' But the father called to his servants, 'Hurry!' he said. 'Bring the best robe and put it on him. Put a ring on his finger and shoes on his feet. Then go and get the prize calf and kill it, and let us celebrate with a feast! For this son of mine was dead, but now he is alive; he was lost, but now he has been found.' And so the feasting began.

"In the meantime, the older son was out in the field. On his way back, when he came close to the house, he heard the music and dancing. So he called one of the servants and asked him, 'What's going on?' 'Your brother has come back home,' the servant answered, 'and your father has killed the prize calf, because he got him back safe and sound.' The older brother was so angry that he would not go into the house; so his father came out and begged him to come in. But he spoke back to his father, 'Look, all these years I have worked for you like a slave, and I have never disobeyed your orders. What have you given me? Not even a goat for me to have a feast with my friends! But this son of yours wasted all your property on prostitutes, and when he comes back home you kill the prize calf for him!' 'My son,' the father answered, 'you are always here with me, and everything I have is yours. But we had to celebrate and be happy, because your brother was dead, but now he is alive; he was lost, but now he has been found.'"

Luke 15:11–32

▷ Questions

This story is often called the parable of the Prodigal Son. *Prodigal* means "excessively generous." But the runaway son appears in only one half of the story. Who appears in both halves? Who is really excessively generous in both stories?

Count the ways in which the father in the story shows "an understanding heart." When the son asks for "his" half of the property his father has worked for all his life, what does the father's reaction say about the father's character? What does it say about God?

When the son finally comes to his senses, he returns home, but "he was still a long way off when his father saw him." What does that imply? Who runs to whom? What does that show, not only about the father but about God?

Before he returns, the boy memorizes a speech, but he isn't able to finish it. Why? What does it say about God? Is there any evidence the father demanded to know how the boy had spent each shekel of his hard-earned money? Does he ask what sins the boy has committed? What penance does he give the boy to atone for his sins?

What is the *only* thing important to the father—and to God? What is Jesus saying about our relationships with our parents, siblings, teachers, friends, and strangers?

In the second half of the story, again who comes to whom? Look very carefully at what the second son says: How does he distort the evidence? What does he accuse his brother of—for which he has no evidence at all? This second son has never strayed; he has been dutiful all his life, and yet he has been farther away from his father's real intentions than the runaway ever was. Explain that. What is the difference between the two boys' attitudes toward their father? How is it reflected in the difference between the reactions of Peter and Judas to their own sins?

If this is a story about how God deals with sinners and how God expects us to deal with sinners, what does it tell you about your grudges?

According to Jesus—not according to what you've been taught, but according to Jesus—what is the *only* thing a sinner *must* do in order to be forgiven?

What is the third-last petition in the Our Father? How many times have you said that petition? From now on, are you really going to mean it?

It is easy enough to be friendly to one's friends. But to befriend the one who regards himself as your enemy is the quintessence of true religion.
Mohandas Gandhi

THEME

BEYOND JUSTICE AND FAIRNESS

So far in this book, although there have been concluding sections throughout paralleling the text with quotations from scripture and Catholic tradition, there has been hardly a word in the text itself about Catholicism, Christianity, or even God. The reason for that is that morality is *not* restricted to religion or to religious people. A particular religion may give a unique slant to objective morality: Muslims are more strict about alcohol but rather generous about polygamy; Catholics may have strict ideas about eating meat on Friday during Lent but no quarrel at all with bingo. But objective morality is in the *natures of things,* which antedated Catholicism and Islam and even atheism. It was wicked of Cain to slay Abel, even though the Ten Commandments weren't even published yet, because of the nature of Abel as a fellow human being and, worse, he was a blood brother of Cain.

But despite what some might call twelve years of Christian "brainwashing," many Christians (perhaps the majority) persist in believing that Christianity is limited to being moral—not hurting anybody, and being nice (at least to one's family and friends). That is not true at all. Christians have no monopoly on morality. Good Jews and Muslims and even atheists want to be moral; otherwise, you couldn't call them "good." But they're quite definitely not Christians.

Whenever I'm asked to preside at a marriage, I always ask the engaged couple if they practice their faith. It needn't be an unbroken series of Sundays, or active participation in some form of service, or prayer every day. But why do they want a priest at their wedding—not me as their friend, but any priest, even a stranger? The Mass is the core of my life, and I'm not going to prostitute it as an excuse for the dress up and the flowers and the Purcell "Trumpet Voluntary." I refuse to be a justice of the peace in drag.

One prospective groom wrote that no one could live in any big city without being aware of Christ in agony—the homeless, the disenfranchised, the dead-ended. A moving letter. But I asked him—though he didn't attend Mass and, in fact, deferred to his future wife to bring up the children as Jews ("more for ethnic and family reasons than religious ones")—did he himself at least pray occasionally, try to sustain a connection to God? He said, "Not really." Yet he still sincerely maintained he was in a very real sense a "practicing Christian" and at least radically Catholic. He was using those words in the same contentedly self-deceptive way characters on "soaps" use the words "making love," that is, when self-giving hasn't the slightest thing to do with the relationship.

I can't blame the man's former teachers for the groom's attitude, since *I* was one of his former teachers. Somehow, I hadn't beaten the opposition and convinced him being Catholic—or even Christian—means more than being just a good human being.

Morality is not a burden laid only on Christians. To be moral is merely to treat human beings better than animals, or self-serving means, or suckers. "Do[ing] unto others as you would have others do unto you" is not a Christian monopoly. It is the underpinning of every religion ever begun on earth and the core of every altruistic philosophy ever expounded. And it is a matter of human survival.

That confusion of morality and religion also results in a conviction that the central issue of our religion is "being good"—not in the sense of *doing* good for others, but in the sense of *not* being bad. When Mommy sends us off to school, she says, "Now, you be good!" By that she means, "Don't show off, don't make waves, and don't embarrass me in front of your teacher." Hardly an exhortation to stand up and be counted, to make a difference, to be a healer and an apostle—which is precisely what the Christian gospel is all about.

There is a real distinction between the moral evil we have been considering through this book and sin. Moral evil rends the "horizontal" web of human relationships that binds us to all other people on this planet. Sin adds a new "vertical" dimension; it rends a relationship between oneself and the One who creates and sustains us. So, too, with good actions. When atheists show kindness to someone in need, they are reaching out to a fellow human being; when Christians do the same action, they have a *double* motive: reaching not only to a fellow human being but also to Jesus Christ, who we truly believe is embodied in that person. We are not just fellow human beings who share the same planet; we are sons and daughters of God and brothers and sisters of Jesus Christ. We are not just members of the human family; we are also members of the Trinity Family. That new dimension to our relationships further ennobles our kindnesses and further degrades our cruelties.

To be fair to Jesus' executioners, they didn't kill him because he was a nice moral teacher trying to get people to be nice to one another. You don't execute a mild irrelevance. They killed him for only *one* reason: Jesus claimed to be the Son of God, and he refused to back down about it. The populace of Jerusalem cheered Jesus as he walked through the streets on Palm Sunday; but that very same populace cried, "Crucify him!" the following Friday. Why? Because he blasphemed. When the High Priest asked him, "Are you the Messiah, the Son of the Blessed God?" Jesus answered, "I am" (Mark 14: 61–62). What further need had they of testimony? Jesus claimed to be God.

Either Jesus was who he claimed to be, or he was a madman claiming to be God, or he was a con artist, like many of the old-time tent preachers, out to make a buck. Yet everything he said and did made eminent good sense. When Mahatma Gandhi was asked what he thought of Christianity, he said, "It's perfectly marvelous; I just wish someone would try it." Jesus gave every indication of being stark raving sane.

Nor did Jesus ever profit from his preaching. He had no home or salary; he died penniless. And if he had been a con artist out to become king, surely he would have cut out all those unnerving statements about taking the last place, washing one another's feet, taking up a cross, giving preference to the detested, yielding—as he did—to the unbending will of his Father. Surely he would have chosen a more seemly death. Not much concern for audience ratings in anything he said or did.

Neither mad nor a con artist. The only other option? He was precisely who he claimed to be.

What, then, does "Christian" add to "human"? Well, Jesus said that finding the Kingdom of God is like finding a treasure in a field. Nice; what's next? Unless you decompact his metaphor, you don't understand what he's saying. Picture yourself bopping through a field. Your toe hits something and you bend to check it out. "La!" you say, "it looks like a box." And you scrabble away the dirt and, lo, it *is* a box. You crack open the rusty lock with a rock, creak open the lid, and it's *filled* with rubies and gold and emeralds! And it's all *yours!* I don't know about you, but the first thing out of my mouth would be, "Yee-*OOW!!*" So if you haven't said, "Yee-*OOW!!*" about being a Christian, you haven't found the Kingdom of God yet.

Two false taken-for-granteds get in the way of your saying "Ye-*OOW!!*" about your Christianity: First, the fact that most of us are doing rather well on our own just now; second, the belief that our own death is so far away as to be practically negligible.

The first taken-for-granted is that most people, most of the time, are doing OK. Only when unexpected tragedy comes along do we remember God. The problem is that God doesn't just exist when we need a handout. And God is the one who opened the door to existence; without that gift, no other gift would be possible.

302

Granted, if you never existed, you wouldn't know the difference. But you *do* exist, and my God it's wonderful! Try to list all the things and people you love. Without that first gift—existence—none of it would have been possible. And you did *nothing* to deserve it; you didn't exist, how could you deserve anything?

Say a zillionaire gave you a million bucks, no strings attached; but said, "I'd enjoy it if you'd drop around once in a while to talk about how things are going." If you took a gift that huge and didn't even try to find out who that person was, if you didn't stop around, if you didn't ask that person's advice, you'd be a pretty mean-spirited "swine," no? Then how about God?

The second taken-for-granted is time. There are three unarguable facts about death: One, it's inevitable; two, it's unpredictable; and three, it's final, at least as far as your life here on earth is concerned. You're not going to avoid death; no one does. But we can't waste our lives thinking about it all the time—too morbid. But not thinking about it at all is just as damaging: You live an illusion that you're going to go on practically forever. No, you're not: unless Jesus was right.

Life expectancy statistics say that two thirds of American males will live to be seventy-one, females to seventy-eight. Reassuring. Provided you're in that two thirds. Every day in the papers you read about teenagers and even children dying from accidents, shootings, or disease. They were in the other third. Where's your guarantee? Sobering, but the objective truth.

Until you acknowledge the objective facts that everything you have is an undeserved gift and that you have only a finite number of days to enjoy it, you'll never say "Yee-*OOW!!*" about being a Christian. Jesus Christ is our great invitation into forever.

There is, surely, a content to the Christian faith, doctrines that are nonnegotiable and that anyone may not believe and still be a good person—

perhaps even a saint like Gandhi—but not a Christian. These are the elements of the faith that *any* Christian holds, no matter what denomination, and it's better to grasp first what unites us rather than cluttering the issue with what divides us. At the risk of presumption, I will give four. Just four.

First, Jesus is the embodiment of God. Somehow, from beyond time and space, God became the man, Jesus Christ. Don't ask how—any more than you'd ask how gravity keeps us glued to the earth; leave that to the experts.

Second, Jesus, the Son of God, died and rose from the dead *in order* to remove the curse from death and to share with us the eternal aliveness of God. From the day we personally accept our baptism, we acknowledge that we are immortal—not at death; but here and now.

Third, to be one with Jesus/God, we give up the values of what Saint Paul called "The World" (*me* first) and take on the values of what Jesus called "The Kingdom" (*them* first)—God and neighbor. Christians are subversives against all the World holds dear: domination, monopoly, conspicuous consumption. And we hold most precious all the world sneers at: vulnerability, service without charge, healing the unpleasant people Jesus healed, forgiveness of debts.

Fourth, we celebrate our oneness with Jesus/God in a community of service and in a weekly meal.

There they are, the four nonnegotiables: the divinity of Jesus, the resurrection, the antimaterialism of the Kingdom, and the serving and worshipping community. All the rest is, in varying degrees, negotiable.

The true Christian is in all countries a pilgrim and a stranger.
George Santayana

If you want to understand God's personality—what God likes and dislikes—you have only to look at Jesus. Both the Hebrew and the Christian scriptures show that God has an inordinate protectiveness for the needy, the widow, the orphan, and the stranger. The list of scripture passages at the end of this chapter should be enough to establish that.

The reason many Christians wrongly believe God's fundamental personality is the vengeful destroyer is that, unlike Jews, most Christians begin to read the Bible at the beginning, with the "angry" God of Genesis rather than with the "liberating" God of Exodus—who was and is the essence of Yahweh for Jews. Nor did either Yahweh or Jesus limit themselves to liberating only the *materially* needy, though many very spiritual people read the Bible with only materialist eyes and believe only those who serve the literally poor are Christian. No, David and Solomon were rich; so were Nicodemus and the Lazarus family. And Yahweh and Jesus had time for them too. If the good Samaritan hadn't been "at least comfortable," he would only have had soothing words to offer the man in the ditch.

Who can say the pain in the belly of a Cambodian child is greater than the anguish in the soul of a suburban American child? If we are missioned, as Yahweh and Jesus Christ are, to the needy, there are plenty of people in need of healing and they're right at our elbows.

You can tell the personality of Jesus/Yahweh, too, from the sorts of heroes they chose, most of them embarrassing klutzes: Noah (a drunk with an eccentric family), Abraham and Sarah (barren as a pair of bricks), Moses (a stammerer), Gideon (a coward), David (a spindly shepherd). Surely if you were looking for the mother of the Messiah, you'd look in Rome or Athens or Alexandria. Nope, an up-country girl from a no-name village in a no-name province—*and* God humbly begs her to accept his offer. Surely if you were choosing the first leader of a new world crusade, the last person you'd consider is your best friend who'd deserted you and then denied you three times—and not to a soldier with a knife at his throat but to a *waitress.* If you wanted a logo for that worldwide crusade, surely a crucifix would be an inadvisable choice.

The God of both testaments shows an outrageous favoritism for Cinderellas.

There must be some virtue in imperfection, because God made us imperfect, and God supposedly knows everything. God loves us fumblers as unconditionally as a mother loves her baby nine months before she's even seen it. God created us out of sheer love without any need for us, invited us to the Ball when we didn't even exist and thus could do nothing to deserve an invitation, loves us even when we sin, as helplessly as a mother still loves her son on death row.

"Well, if God loves me even when I sin, then why not go ahead and sin?" Hearing that God loves us, even when we sin, some people get the idea God will forgive them—even if they don't have the time or inclination to apologize. But these people forget the crucial element in the story of the prodigal son: The father's hands were tied; he *couldn't* forgive until his son came home.

Because we ourselves are reluctant to be as vulnerable as God, because we see forgiveness of debts without penalties (the Great Forgiving) as, at best, lousy business practice, we might begin to look on God as a patsy.

But God *is* a patsy! "God gives rain to those who are good and to those who do evil" (Matthew 5:45). When the prodigal asks for his half of the inheritance, the father gives it to him cheerfully! God gave us the freedom *not* to love him, *not* to act humanly. And God forgives without strings, without penances, without our groveling. The *only* condition is that we come home. Thus, the main consideration about sin is to acknowledge and accept not what our sins do to God but what they do to *us.* (Read *Picture of Dorian Gray,* by Oscar Wilde.)

Moral evil and sin make us mean-spirited, as contemptible as the soldier who spat in Jesus' face. And the fact Jesus forgives us even as the spittle is running down his cheek makes us even more contemptible. But there is one unnerving aspect of God that Jesus refuses to let us forget: God may be a patsy about forgiveness, but God is not answerable to us.

Death, suffering, and sin—the problem of physical and moral evil—are the most profound arguments against the existence of a good, provident, forgiving God. The problem of evil is the substance of most great literature from the Book of Job through *Candide* to *Brothers Karamazov* to *Waiting for Godot.* Why would a good God allow the innocent to suffer? Why would a good God give freedom to an as yet imperfectly evolved tribe of apes—so that we could be cruel to one another?

When God finally showed up to answer Job's woeful pleas for an answer to the question about physical suffering, God seemed to evade it: "Where were you when I made the world? If you know so much, tell me about it" (Job 38:4). Or to put it another way, "Do I have to check out my plans with you?" God didn't give an answer; God *was* the answer—not to Job's mind, but to his heart.

I am a creature and God is God, and God must have a wider perspective than a child can have. Jesus, too, was demonstrably good and yet he suffered unspeakably: "Father, my Father! All things are possible for you. Take this cup of suffering away from me. Yet not what I want, but what you want" (Mark 14:36). And God did not take the cup away. Why? To show us how it's done; that the only road to rebirth into a wider dimension of existence lies up the hill to Calvary. As every prophet has discovered, the only place to discover and grasp one's soul is in the barren wilderness, in hell.

What about the second question about more evil and the human capacity for wickedness? In giving us freedom—without the certitude so eagerly sought by Adam and Eve (equality with God)—

an all-knowing God opened the possibility that we would use that freedom unwisely, that we would act not as the human beings God had intended but as the animals God had separated us from. Why? Because God thought love worth the risk. And there can't be love without freedom. To compel love is a contradiction. So, too, is to compel humanity and goodness.

We are the only creatures whose nature is an invitation. The only way we can attain our full dignity is to use our freedom wisely. When people ask why God doesn't step in and do something about human wickedness, the answer is obvious: God did step in; God invented you.

> Second: Jesus, the Son of God, died and rose from the dead in order to remove the curse from death and to share with us the eternal aliveness of God.

Jesus is the last stage of evolution. Over the millenia, God patiently nursed us from the inanimate soup that covered the earth, to vegetative life, to animal sensitivity, to human intelligence. Jesus came to show us what God had intended us to evolve into all along: God's "divinized" sons and daughters.

Adam and Eve's wish was "to become like God." Jesus fulfilled that wish—which God had intended all along, but in the way God had intended it to happen, not the way Adam and Eve intended it. Besides removing our lives and deaths from meaninglessness, there is the Good News: We are divinized—right *now.* Just as humanity is an invitation to a quantum leap above animality, Christianity is an invitation to a quantum leap beyond humanity. Yee-*OOW!!*

What's more, Jesus makes us his adopted brothers and sisters. We acknowledge, humbly, that we are not equal to God, something many of us all the way back to Adam and Eve have tried to be. But we also acknowledge, proudly, that no matter what we think of ourselves, God thinks enough of us to make us peers of the realm! Then if we are peers in nobility with Jesus (!), noblesse oblige. We have been gifted with adoption, then we are obliged by that very gift to share it with others, just as Jesus shared it with us. We share the office of Jesus: healing.

> Third: To be one with Jesus/God, we give up the values of "The World" (me first) and take on the values of "The Kingdom" (them first)— God and neighbor.

Here is where we see the clear distinction between what we have seen all the way through this book—moral relationships between equally human beings and the further commitment we take on when we personally accept our own baptisms as Christians. Morality is about justice and fairness, what our fellow human beings *deserve* simply because they *are* objectively human. Christianity goes much further; it asks us to love them; and, as we saw before, love is not a feeling, but love is an act of the will that takes over when the feelings fail, when the object of our love is no longer even likable. Human fairness demands that when perpetrators make restitution, the debt must be forgiven. Christian love demands that perpetrators must be forgiven *before* they deserve it.

THE GLORY OF CHRISTIANITY IS TO CONQUER BY FORGIVENESS.
WILLIAM BLAKE

At the last supper, Jesus said, "As I have loved you, so you must love one another" (John 13:34). But note carefully: we must love one another *as* Jesus loved others. And how did Jesus love? Not with hugs and kisses, surely. How did Jesus love the rich young man, even as the man walked away when he couldn't accept Jesus' invitation to become a full-fledged disciple? How did Jesus love Peter, even after Peter deserted him and denied him? How did Jesus love even his own torturers when he cried, "Forgive them, Father! They don't know what they are doing" (Luke 23:34)? Jesus loved (and loves) with an understanding heart. Jesus was *not judgmental.* As Saint Paul described love:

> *Love is patient and kind; love is not jealous or conceited or proud; love is not ill-mannered or selfish or irritable; love does not keep a record of wrongs; love is not happy with evil, but is happy with the truth. Love never gives up; and its faith, hope, and patience never fail.*
> 1 Corinthians 13:4–7

It is stunning to see how Jesus—who was without sin himself—was so unfailingly compassionate toward sinners. That is the kind of love he asks of us. And for whom? The parable of the Good Samaritan answers that. (Luke 10:25–37)

Like Jesus' parable about finding a treasure in a field, his saying about taking the last place (Matthew 20:20–28) needs to be decompacted too. Jesus says to the disciples who were always jockeying to be Number One, "If you want the first place, take the last place." But how could that be, unless of course you're the only person in the race? There are *two* races! And they're heading in opposite directions from each other: One is The World race, and people like James Bond are pretty much at the head of it; the other is The Kingdom race, and Mother Teresa is pretty close to the head of that one.

Christians are subversives against all the World holds dear: domination, monopoly, conspicuous consumption. And we hold most precious all the world sneers at: vulnerability, service without charge, healing the unpleasant people Jesus healed, forgiveness of debts.

There is a good touchstone of whether one is a genuine Christian or merely a pagan with the Christian label misapplied: Which direction are you heading, toward James Bond values, or toward Mother Teresa values? Will your being Christian, for instance, have any effect at all on your choice of career or calling? Or are your motives no different from those of the Muslim or Jew or atheist down the block?

On the very first day of his public ministry, Jesus went to the synagogue and read a passage from the Book of the Prophet Isaiah to his fellow villagers that would be the platform of his campaign, his inaugural address:

The Spirit of the Lord is upon me,
because God has chosen me to bring good
news to the poor.
God has sent me to proclaim liberty to the
captives and recovery of sight to the blind,
to set free the oppressed and announce that
the time has come
when the Lord will save God's people."
Luke 4:18–19 (adapted)

Others translate that final clause as "to proclaim the Lord's year of favor. . . ." a custom in the Jewish Year of Jubilee of forgiving all outstanding debts. What Jesus came to proclaim was the amnesty of God! The Great Forgiving! Jesus came to shout to all sinners: "Ally-ally-in-come-*free!*" Hard to believe, isn't it? That's Good News, indeed, if you admit you're a sinner.

Frequently in these pages, we have asked what *success* means, what will bring us fulfillment. Jesus answered that question; he *was* the answer of God to that question: "Be like Jesus." But Jesus also answers the meaning of success more specifically. At the Last Judgment, there will be only *one* question asked of you to determine whether, in the eyes of God, your life was worth living. On the one hand, you will not be asked your SATs, or your salary, or how many times you had your name in the paper. On the other, you will not be asked how many times you missed Mass, or cheated on exams, or ate meat on Friday in Lent. We have it on an authority higher than all the popes put together that there will be only *one* question: I was hungry . . . I was thirsty . . . I was in prison . . . I was the one they called "nerd," "moron," "loser." What did you do about that?

Noblesse oblige.

Fourth: We celebrate our oneness with Jesus/God in a community of service and in a weekly meal.

The idea of a "solitary Christian" is a contradiction in terms. The entire texture of the gospel constantly asserts that to be with Jesus is to serve others. Even cloistered monks and nuns are praying for the rest of us.

What's more, as Saint Paul never tires of pointing out, we can serve far better as an organic body: your strengths make up for my shortcomings, and mine make up for yours. Each of us has different talents: some can preach, some can teach, some can work soup kitchens, some can go to the missions, some can raise funds, some can play the clown and keep the rest of us from taking ourselves too seriously.

A frequent objection to communal worship is: "Why can't I just go out in the woods and worship alone?" Three answers to that. First, the solitary Christian is a contradiction. Second, it's a perfectly wonderful idea; when was the last time you actually *did* it—or do you just like using it as a dodge? And third, why does it have to be either/or? Why not do both? Dare ya. You might be very surprised. And to go through the entire week without once dealing personally with God alone and then come into church on Sunday expecting to be zapped in an hour is as ridiculous as thinking you can be zapped by any other friend when you give him or her only one hour or less a week.

Mass is boring. I'd be the last one on earth to deny that. But it's not quite that simple. First, it's boring because of our expectations. It's not a rock concert where you sit to be entertained; you've got to put something into it, something from your gut. What's more, no matter what kind of show the church put on every Sunday, even Michael Jackson couldn't make it work if the members of the audience (congregation) are all zipped up in their insulated cocoons, worrying that everybody else is looking at them. Jesus said we've got to believe so strongly that we're unafraid to climb up and shout it from the housetops; most Sunday congregations belie a genuine belief in that. As Eldridge Cleaver said, "If you're not part of the solution, you're part of the problem."

In the end, we come back to the zillionaire, to God who invited us to the Ball when we had no way to deserve an invitation. We can never repay that gift; everything we could give back would be part of the gift! But how do we at least show our gratitude? The Giver said, "Do *this* in memory of me."

We're free not to, of course. But what does ingratitude on that scale make of us? Not what does it do to God; what does it do to *you?* I, personally, don't go to Mass every week because the Third Commandment "commands" it, any more than I went to see my mother in a nursing home every Sunday for eight years (and I rarely "got anything out of it") because the Fourth Commandment "commanded" it. I go and I went because without God and my mother, I wouldn't have *existed.* No commandment commands me; *I* command me. If I didn't, I couldn't live with myself.

You can be a very good person without being a Christian—perhaps even a saint. But is it possible— just possible—you might be missing something? If your parents bequeath you what looks like a crumby old trunk, it's in your own self-interest at least to open it and honestly appraise it before you toss it away. It could be full of diamonds and rubies and gold.

And if the challenge of Jesus to stand up and be counted, to make a difference, to be a healer, is boring and not unnerving, it might be a wise idea to check that treasure chest again.

Many promising reconciliations have broken down because, while both parties came prepared to forgive, neither party came to be forgiven.

Charles Williams

DILEMMA

School had always come easy to Jim Wilde. But this year he is first-string tight end, practices are brutal, and at night all he has the energy to do is to wolf down dinner and fall into bed. He failed to hand in four of the eight papers for his advanced-placement English class, but he figured he would make it up next quarter when football was over. But when he got his report card, there it was: a big fat F in English.

"Hey, Father," he said to his English teacher, "you knew I was playing football. You're at all the games."

"Yep," said Father Corcoran, "and I knew Eddie Dowling and Charlie Banks play football too. They got everything in. The only way you can fail this course is not to hand things in. You didn't. I was just going along with your choice."

"You're benching me."

"No, Jim! You benched you!"

Jim turned and ran away, hiding in the locker room so that no one would see him crying. Then he bashed in a locker door with his fist and went home.

For two weeks, Jim sat in the back of the English class like an impending storm, till one afternoon Father Corcoran snagged him at the end of class. "Let's talk."

Jim slumped into a chair, his head sagging and his eyes averted.

"Jim, when do you forgive the two of us?" Silence. "Are you gonna drag this anchor around with you for the rest of the year?" Silence. "Jim, you're only hurting yourself. You're making me uncomfortable, but you don't make me regret what I did. Football's great, but you're here to learn—not just English, responsibility."

Jim stood. "Is that all?"

"If that's all you want. But I need to be forgiven. So do you."

Jim slammed out of the room.

▷ *Questions*

Responsibility. Forgiveness. How did Jim Wilde live them? How did Father Corcoran live them? How are responsibility and forgiveness at the core of Christianity?

Father Corcoran said to Jim, "No, Jim! You benched you!" What did he mean? How does Father Corcoran's response serve as a measure of our successes and failures?

FAITH REFLECTION

Jesus rose from the table, took off his outer garment, and tied a towel around his waist. Then he poured some water into a washbasin and began to wash the disciples' feet and dry them with the towel around his waist. He came to Simon Peter, who said to him, "Are you going to wash my feet, Lord?"

Jesus answered him, "You do not understand now what I am doing, but you will understand later."

Peter declared, "Never at any time will you wash my feet!"

"If I do not wash your feet," Jesus answered, "you will no longer be my disciple."

Simon Peter answered, "Lord, do not wash only my feet, then! Wash my hands and head, too!"

"I, your Lord and teacher, have just washed your feet. You, then, should wash one another's feet."

John 13: 4–9, 14

Washing feet was a slave's job. Yet Jesus, Lord and Teacher, does that job for his disciples and tells them they should do the same for one another. What is Jesus trying to tell us about a Christian's relationship with other Christians through this symbolic act? Does it unnerve you? If it does, you're beginning to discover what Christianity really entails.

Nor did Jesus restrict our service to one another only to literally washing people's feet. Symbols are not that restrictive. Who are the people you know or know of who spend their lives "washing people's feet" working in nursing homes for low pay, running soup kitchens, teaching people who don't want to expend the effort to learn, running camps for impaired children. Nor are all the "foot washers" in organized groups. Good parents spend a great part of their lives "washing feet." In what ways? Do they expect anything back?

Now the hard part: What about you? Whom do you already serve? Whom *could* you serve without too much imposition on your time and efforts? The world would be a better place, if only by a bit. And the more often you do it, the better place it will be.

📖 FURTHER BIBLE READINGS

Skim these Scripture passages. Pick one that appeals to you and (1) summarize its main point, (2) tell how it relates to the chapter, and (3) list one or two thoughts that entered your mind when you read it.

- ◆ Different Service   Romans 12:1–13
- ◆ Divinizing Humans   Ephesians 3:14–19
- ◆ Common Life   Acts 2:43–47
- ◆ Judging Success   Matthew 25:31–46
- ◆ The Magnificat   Luke 1:46–55

_____

_____

_____

_____

_____

_____

✎ JOURNAL

Compose a prayer that is just between you and God and the journal in which you try to say, in no matter how confused a manner, what being a Christian means to you. No problem with confusion, as long as it's honestly put out in the open to be healed.

Understanding Christianity

REVIEW

1. What reasons does this book give for delaying the consideration of Christianity until this final chapter?

2. What is the difference between moral wickedness and sin?

3. Explain why a Christian who does a kind action has a *double* motive.

4. Jesus suffered terribly. Why? Explain why the only road to rebirth into a wider dimension of existence lies up the hill to Calvary.

5. Explain these statements:

   a. Either Jesus was who he claimed to be or he was a madman claiming to be God or he was a con artist.

   b. If you haven't said, "Yee-OOW!!" about being a Christian, you haven't found the Kingdom yet.

   c. Jesus is the last stage of evolution.

   d. "If you want the first place, take the last place."

6. What two false taken-for-granteds get in the way of even Christians seeing the importance of Christianity? Explain.

7. What are the four nonnegotiables of Christianity without which you can be a saint but not a Christian? Explain why each is essential.

8. The God of both the Old and New Testaments shows an outrageous favoritism for Cinderellas. Give evidence for that.

9. None of us did anything to *deserve* existence. What effect should that objective fact have on our way of living our lives?

10. How could a good God allow physical and moral evil?

11. How ought the fact of the resurrection affect one's view of life and one's priorities?

12. When Jesus set out on his public life of preaching and healing, what was the essence of his "platform"?

13. Explain the significance to a Christian that there will be only *one* question to determine the value of one's life: "I was hungry . . . I was thirsty . . . I was in prison . . ." In other words, I was the one they called "nerd," "slut," "loser" and what did you do about that?

DISCUSS

1. Objective morality is in the *nature of things.* That fact antedates Catholicism and Judaism and even atheism. Explain.

2. "Do unto others as you would have others do unto you" is not a Christian monopoly. It is the underpinning of every religion ever begun on earth and the core of every altruistic philosophy ever expounded. And it is a matter of human survival. Why is this true?

3. Is it unfair—or at least unfeeling—for a priest to preside at a wedding of a couple whose idea of "Christianity" is no more than a sense of basic human sensitivity and morality?

4. Consider the question of the zillionaire giving you a million bucks. Is there any excuse you could offer for not paying him or her some significant attention for the rest of your life?

5. Many very spiritual Christians read the Bible with only materialist eyes, believing only those who serve the literally poor are Christian. Why does that happen?

6. God is not answerable to us. What does the story of Job say about that?

7. Since Jesus had a loving, understanding relationship with so many rich people, how does one explain his statement: "It is much harder for a rich person to enter the Kingdom than for a camel to go through the eye of a needle"?

8. "Why can't I just go out in the woods and worship alone?" How would you respond to that question?

ACTIVITIES

1. Research what elements in the celebration of the Mass are nonnegotiable. Then plan a Mass—keeping those essentials. Use other elements that would make the celebration of Mass more meaningful for people your age—not more interesting, but more meaningful. Present your plan to the person or committee in charge of planning liturgies in your school or parish and have them review it. Then with one or two others (*not* on your own) present the plan as tactfully as you can to your pastor. Write a paper on what the reasons those people offered for and against your proposal.

2. There is surely someone in the group who can write music. As a group write a hymn that will present the real message of Jesus, not the message that says "lie-down-and-roll-over-and-Jesus-will-take-care-of-everything," but the message that shows Jesus challenging us to stand up and be counted.

3. Interview someone you believe really projects the freedom and joy that being a Christian ought to mean. Someone you suspect has said, "Yee-OOW!!" about being a Christian. How does that person's life seem "different" from the lives of other people you know? Ask him or her: What are the important things in life? What gives you joy? How often do you pray? What does worship mean to you?